T0307482

Alarmstart East

Alarmstart East

The German Fighter Pilot's Experience on the Eastern Front 1941–1945

PATRICK G. ERIKSSON

AMBERLEY

First published 2018

Amberley Publishing
The Hill, Stroud
Gloucestershire, GL5 4EP

www.amberley-books.com

British Library Cataloguing in Publication Data.
A catalogue record for this book is available from the British Library.

ISBN 978 1 4456 7566 4 (hardback)
ISBN 978 1 4456 7567 1 (ebook)

Map on page 18 by Thomas Bohm, User Design.

Typesetting and Origination by Amberley Publishing.
Printed in the UK.

Contents

Preface

This volume follows *Alarmstart*[1] and complements that book's focus on the air war over western Europe with its examination of aerial warfare and the German fighter pilot experience over the Eastern Front, against the Russians. In direct contrast to the western conflict, where fair battle practices largely prevailed, and to the war fought in the Mediterranean theatre (see *Alarmstart South to North*, the third volume in this planned trilogy), the ground war in the East was one of extreme brutality and even genocidal in character. While this incontrovertible savagery prevailed on *terra firma*, the aerial battle remained largely fair and mostly avoided practices like those of American fighter pilots over Germany, some of whom shot at helpless enemies on their parachutes or in force-landed aircraft on the ground. However, it is also a characteristic of aerial combat that its speed largely removes the participants from the realities of war and their often horrific effects on the human frame – though not always, as detailed below by *Leutnant* Hans Strelow, *5/JG 51* as he confided in his diary[2] on 5 October 1941. He claimed three Russian DB-3 bombers shot down on this day and wrote of the last one: 'Two men bailed out, but one's parachute became entangled on the tail plane or the gunner's position of the burning machine. I clearly saw him wriggling frantically. Actually dreadful to witness! I also felt sorry for him for a moment.' His last sentence says much of German attitudes towards their Russian foes, whom many considered to be their racial inferiors. Despite prevailing attitudes, especially at that stage of the air war in Russian territory, this very driven young man felt some sympathy, albeit briefly, for one of his opponents.

While for the German fighter pilots the air war was mostly far removed from the horrors of what was happening on the ground, they nevertheless were often influenced by Nazi perceptions of the Russians as *Untermenschen*, who were not seen as the equals of the Germans fighting them. A good example of this attitude is provided by an interview conducted long after the war with *General* Johannes Steinhoff, who had begun the war as a *Staffelkapitän* and ended it as a highly successful *Oberst* who commanded the first jet *Geschwader*, the Me 262-equipped *Jagdgeschwader 7*, until terribly burned in a crash in one of these revolutionary aircraft in 1945.[3] No doubt his long-remembered negative views on the Russians were also coloured by his having served through much of the Cold War in senior positions in Germany and NATO. In the interview, Steinhoff described the Russian pilots as poorly trained, lacking intelligence, having limited ability and being uninspired fighters in the air.

Other veterans went much further in their criticism, as the quote from *Unteroffizier* Heinz Ludwig, Me 110 rear-gunner in *I/ZG 1* with whom he flew over the Russian front from May 1942 to July 1943, makes abundantly clear: 'The Russian fighter pilots up till 1943 were very cowardly and only very few were met. In most contacts, they always cleared off, I could never quite work out why they were there at all. From the end of 1943 through the aircraft deliveries of the Americans they had become a feared opponent by the end of the war.' A bias against Russian aircraft quality and an overstated expression of the importance of Allied aid to Russia is also obvious in this viewpoint (an uncommonly negative one, though). Some pilots expressed their assumed superiority right at the end of the war, by which time Russian aircraft, tactics and training, never mind accumulated experience, had made them very dangerous opponents. One such was *Obergefreiter* Pay Kleber, *EJG 1* who only flew against the Russians from January to the end of March 1945, and it is unclear if he scored any successes against them. He rather arrogantly stated: 'I did not experience a superiority of the Russian fighter pilots. Everything that was seen, we shot down.'

A far more realistic and balanced appraisal of the Russians is provided by *Oberstleutnant* Günther Scholz (25 eastern victories out of 34 claimed altogether), who flew as *Staffelkapitän 7/JG 54* from June 1941 to February 1942 before leading *III/JG 5* in the far north on the Ice Sea front from March 1942 till May 1943; after this he commanded *Jagdgeschwader 5* before becoming *Jagdfliegerführer* (*Jafü*, fighter leader) for Norway in May 1944.[4] His more senior rank, much larger responsibility and much greater experience equate with the sober impression he retained of his former enemies: 'The Russians fought just as bravely as we or the English did, but in the beginning had much inferior aircraft with the I-15, Mig-3 or Lagg-3; only from about the end of 1943 with the Jak-9 and the new

Lavochkin (La-5) did they achieve parity and even superiority over the Me and the Fw.' A similar view is given by *Feldwebel* Alfred Rauch, who flew on the central part of the Eastern Front from August 1941 till late 1942 in *5/JG 51*: 'On the Russian side at the beginning of the war only obsolete aircraft were encountered; large numbers of them but no quality. From later in 1941 already, partly from English and American deliveries, partly from their own manufacture, fighters like the Laggs, Jaks and Airacobras began to operate against us. Those of us flying the Me 109 had to be hellishly careful, to avoid being surprised. The Russians also copied our flying tactics; they flew in fighting formations comprised of pairs, fours etc.'

Stalin's irrational and massive purges of the armed forces' top structures, which began in June 1937, remain relevant also; in the end over 41,000 officers were affected but most were dismissed from their posts rather than being executed.[5] By 1940 almost a third had been reappointed; the purges also mainly affected ranks from colonel and above.[6] By 1941 over 100,000 new officers were being trained and joining the forces annually as massive expansion took place.[7] While lower ranks were relatively unaffected by the purges, the main result was to stifle initiative and independent military thinking at higher levels, but also at operational levels where caution became the watchword;[8] this must also have filtered down. In concert with this, the reintroduction of political officers or commissars of minor or no military background further diluted professionalism and reaction speeds under duress.[9]

While it is true, as Alfred Rauch stated above, that the VVS (*Voyenno-Vozdushnye Sily* or Military Air Forces) were largely equipped with obsolete fighters like the Polikarpov I-15, I-153 and I-16, by the onset of *Barbarossa* on 22 June 1941, a total of 1,946 more modern fighters (Mig-3, Lagg-3 and Yak-1) had been supplied, which made up about one-fifth of Russian fighters.[10] While many German sources make much of the impact of American and British aid to Russia, much of this encompassed aircraft such as the P-40 and later on P-39 fighters, as well as ex-RAF Hurricanes (many rather clapped out, slower than I-16s!); the first such aircraft started to trickle through by August 1941.[11] It is to the Russians' credit that they were able to make a success out of the P-39 Airacobra from early 1943, in distinct contrast to both the USAAF and RAF, which could not. In addition, new fighters such as the Yak-9 and La-5 began to come in by late 1942, along with improved tactics and better strategic leadership at the same time, and this began to turn the *Jagdwaffe* tide.

However, fighter pilots of all nations are almost by definition aggressive and driven, showing initiative within the fighting units; they also make the best use they can of their equipment. That this applied equally to Russian opponents is borne out by another diary entry[12] from *Leutnant* Hans Strelow, *5/JG 51* made in autumn 1941 for a combat against a lone J-61 – otherwise known as a Mig-3:

> An old *Feldwebel* and I had an air combat with two Russian fighters near Jelnja. The one disappeared fast, while the other one exhibited an amazing aggressiveness. He kept on attacking the two of us, no sooner had he escaped from the attention of one of us then he took on the other one again. After I had had a tight-turning dogfight with him, he suddenly dived down to ground level. I went after him, but did not get properly in range as I had briefly hesitated to follow. As our fuel was running short, the *Feldwebel* who was nearer attacked the J-61 once more. After the fourth burst of fire, the Russian suddenly pulled up vertically to about 400 m, turned onto his back, so that we thought he was going to bail out, but then he went vertically into the ground where he exploded – a pity! – he had done so well, that I would not have begrudged him getting away with it.

Once the pervasive German attitude of racial superiority is stripped away, their Russian enemies emerge as respectable opponents no different to any others, as correctly stated above by *Oberstleutnant* Günther Scholz of *JG 54* and *5*.

After all, the Russians were not idiots and did not want to die if they could avoid it. Russian fighter pilots had also benefitted, like the *Luftwaffe*, from fighting in the Spanish Civil War, on the Republican side where they pitted their Polikarpov biplanes and the more modern I-16 monoplanes against German Heinkel 51 biplanes and early models of the Me 109. This war (July 1936–January 1939) served as an opportunity for the Italians and Germans to expose their armed forces to active combat conditions and to test weapons, particularly aircraft. The *Legion Kondor* which was sent to Spain comprised a *Gruppe* each of bombers, Stukas (dive bombers), fighters, reconnaissance aircraft and marine aircraft.[13] Aircrew received ranks one grade higher than their *Luftwaffe* designations, were very well paid (including a danger allowance) and officers normally served one year in action in Spain before relief exposed another pilot to active combat operations.[14]

Jagdgruppe J 88 was equipped initially with the He 51 fighter, replaced in 1937 by the Bf 109 B (and later, by the C-model) in the first two *Staffeln*, with the third and fourth retaining their He 51s, which were used in the ground attack role.[15] The He 51 showed itself to be inferior to the Russian I-15 and I-16 fighters supplied to the Republican side, hence their reversion to a ground attack assignment. *3/J 88* was the unit to which all new pilots were assigned, and was led by the famous Adolf Galland from May 1937 till May 1938, when he was replaced by the equally famous Werner Mölders.[16] The latter was able to get this *Staffel* re-equipped with the Me 109 B as well, and thereafter became the top German ace of this conflict with 14 victories.[17] The Soviets also saw the conflict in Spain as an opportunity to test equipment, tactics and give their airmen experience; they managed to expose 160 'volunteer' fighter pilots to this war.[18]

The combat experience which *Luftwaffe* fighter pilots obtained in Spain was extremely valuable and improved tactics and formations – particularly the 'finger-four' formation of two pairs (still used today) evolved by Günther Lützow[19] and perfected in action by Mölders – put them at the forefront of fighter pilots internationally not long before the outbreak of the Second World War. The *Luftwaffe* made certain that experienced pilots from Spain passed their knowledge on throughout the fighter arm. Necessary improvements to the Me 109 shown up by sustained operations in Spain ensured that most teething troubles of this aircraft were dealt with well before the Second World War.[20] *Jagdgruppe 88* was accredited with 314 confirmed aerial victories in the Spanish Civil War; these victories were shared among 118 individual pilots, and losses were 26 fighter pilots in action and a further eight due to accidents or disease.[21] Among *Jagdgruppe J 88*'s veterans was Günther Scholz, who flew with *3/J 88* and scored one success there:[22]

> In 1938 I volunteered for service in Spain (as a member of what was called *RLM – Reichsluftfahrtministerium* or Air Ministry – *Sonderstab* [special staff] *10*), in search of adventure and not from political convictions, and flew in the *Staffel* of Galland and Mölders. The Spanish Civil War certainly contributed a lot to war experience on land, at sea and in the air. As bad as it may sound, Spain was one large troop training area, also for the Soviet forces. The soviet I-15 of that time, called the "Chato" was inferior to the Me 109 C but was superior to the He 51. It was thus forbidden to initiate air combat with a He 51. This aircraft was used only for low level ground attacks (*Staffel* Galland). One learnt to recognise enemy positions from the air, to see the enemy early in the air, and to creep up on him if at all possible without being seen, and much more.

From 1937 to 1940 Russian fighter pilots also fought against the Japanese over China, and intense aerial battles erupted in the so-called 'Nomonhan Incident' over the area of the Khalkh River along the disputed Mongolia–Manchuria border between 11 May and 14 September 1939.[23] The VVS committed 515 aircraft to this conflict, the fighter component being made up of 311 I-153 and I-16 'Rata' fighters; Russian losses totalled 207 machines in all, including 160 of their fighters, which in turn claimed

589 victories.[24] The Japanese fighters for their part claimed 1,093 aircraft destroyed and another 209 probably so, while admitting 63 pilots lost.[25] The final conflict before Operation *Barbarossa* (the invasion of the Soviet Union) where Russian fighter pilots were able to pick up experience was the Finnish Winter War, from November 1939 to March 1940.[26] The much smaller Finnish air force fought valiantly and effectively, claiming 521 Soviet machines through aircraft and flak branches for the loss of only 68 of their own aircraft, which included 36 fighters.[27] VVS claims were much inflated at 362 aircraft, and their losses of 261 machines reflect a much more reasonable Finnish over-claim rate of about two to one.[28]

Training of new fighter pilots appears to have been a significant differential factor for the *Luftwaffe* and the VVS. There are a lot of claims considering the extremely limited flying hours (eight to ten hours solo) of these newly minted Soviet fighter pilots arriving at their frontline units,[29] and some exaggeration would appear to be inherent in many of these. The Soviets also laid special emphasis on training within fighter units themselves before dispatch to the front, as tired units which had suffered heavy casualties were often withdrawn to a rear area to re-equip and absorb new pilots for several months at a time. Rapid expansion of the VVS preceding the German invasion, as well as conversion from old on to new fighter types, would have exacerbated training shortcomings, and these two factors would have continued during the war itself. However, as Russian efforts to improve the combat readiness of their fighter units bore fruit as the conflict continued, so too did German fighter pilot training begin to suffer. By late 1942–early 1943 Soviet fighter units had begun a resurgence, first over Stalingrad and then in spring 1943 over the Kuban peninsula. By 1943 German training schools faced distinct problems themselves, as detailed in the next chapter, which examines *Luftwaffe* fighter pilot training. While this short examination of the topic is generic to all fronts where *Jagdflieger* trainees were posted, training may have been a more important differential on the Eastern Front, at least in the initial 18–24 months of battle.

Studies of the air war over the Eastern Front are hindered by a lack of preserved or available wartime records for the *Jagdwaffe*. Their detailed study could go a long way towards a better understanding of the enormous victory claims of the top German aces in the East and would help get a handle on the always controversial topic of over-claiming. In this respect the value of the *Startkladde* for 7/JG 51 in the East for the time period 13 September 1943–18 April 1944 cannot be overstated. This record has resurfaced and is available to all researchers courtesy of Andreas Zapf.[30] This is basically a daily log of all flights made by the *Staffel* and equates well with the so-called RAF Form 541; however it goes further in that it also provides relatively detailed claims data for all combats, from damaged through to destroyed aircraft. The *Startkladde* is a very long document, handwritten and in *Sütterlinschrift*, an archaic script deliberately applied for security reasons; mastering this script is well worthwhile in terms of the valuable data in the *Kladde*. The entire topic of German fighter claims – their submission in frontline units, their processing higher up the various command chains and then the final recognition (or not) of accredited victories – is dealt with in detail in the final chapter. What is at issue is not the rather strict and cumbersome system of *Luftwaffe* claim submissions, but the definitions of an aerial victory which were applied, and how their recognition came about; even more relevant is how these aspects changed during the war, much more on the Eastern Front than on those in the West or Mediterranean, and how probable victories almost became the norm in the East. It is also in this framework that having a detailed primary document from *7/JG 51* becomes important as it greatly facilitates understanding of high claims made in the East, and how they were handled by the relevant bureaucracy.

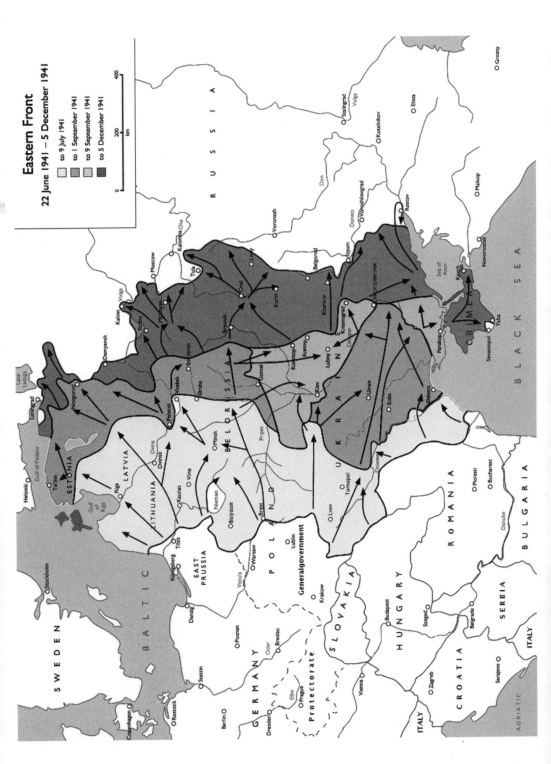

Eastern Front
22 June 1941 – 5 December 1941

to 9 July 1941
to 1 September 1941
to 9 September 1941
to 5 December 1941

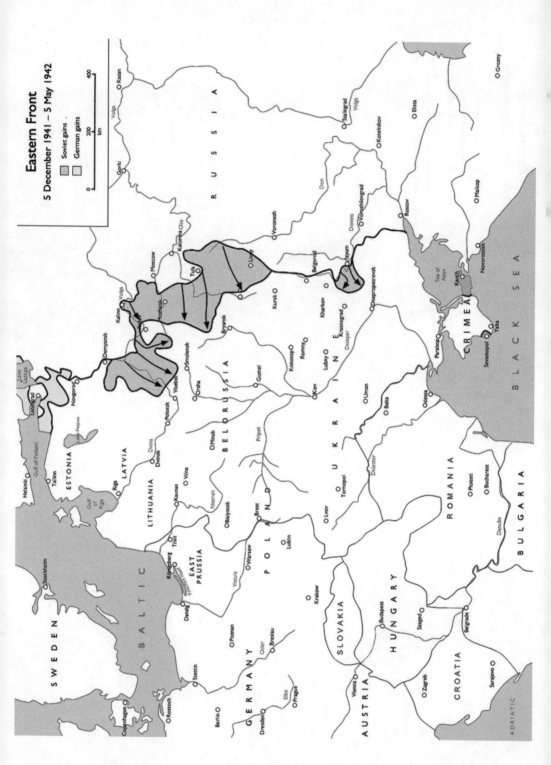

Eastern Front
5 December 1941 – 5 May 1942

Soviet gains
German gains

400
200
0
km

RUSSIA

Kazan
Volga
Gorki
Volga

Stalingrad
Kotelnikov
Bira
Grozny

Don

Voronezh
Belgorod
Voroshilovgrad
Rostov
Maikop

Moscow
Kalinin Oka
Tula
Izyum
Donets
Sea of Azov
Kerch
Novorossisk

Kaluga
Kalinin
Volga
Mozhaisk
Kursk
Kharkov
Dnepropetrovsk
Dnieper
Krasnograd
Parakopo
CRIMEA
Sevastopol
Yalta

Demyansk
Bryansk
Smolensk
Konotop
Romny
Lubny
Kiev
Uman
Balta
Odessa
BLACK SEA

Orsha
Gomel
Pripet

Polotsk
Minsk
BELORUSSIA

Novgorod
Vitebsk

Leningrad
Lake Ladoga
Lake Peipus
Gulf of Finland

Helsinki
Tallinn
ESTONIA
Riga
Drina
Dvinsk
LATVIA
Kaunas
Vilna
LITHUANIA

Lvov
Tornopol
Dniester
ROMANIA
Ploesti
Bucharest
BULGARIA
Danube

Stockholm
Gulf of Riga

SWEDEN

BALTIC SEA

Tilsit
Königsberg
EAST PRUSSIA
Frisches Haff
Danzig
Bialystok
Brest
Lublin
POLAND
Niemen
Warsaw
Vistula
Bug

Rostock
Stettin
Poznan
Breslau
Oder
GERMANY
Berlin
Dresden
Elbe
Prague

Copenhagen

Krakow
SLOVAKIA
HUNGARY
Budapest
Szeged
Belgrade
Vienna
Zagreb
Sarajevo
AUSTRIA
CROATIA
ADRIATIC

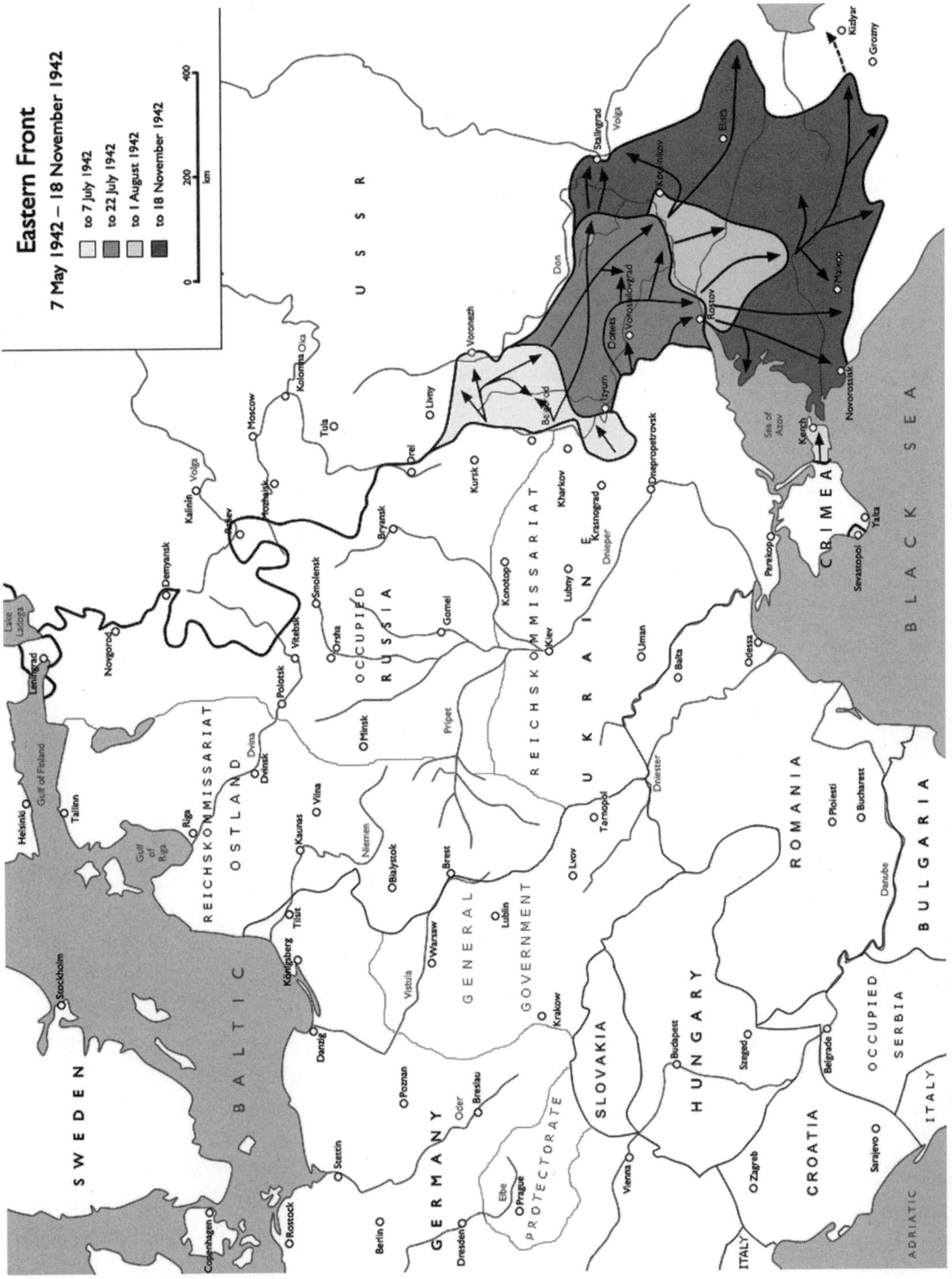

Eastern Front
7 May 1942 – 18 November 1942
to 7 July 1942
to 22 July 1942
to 1 August 1942
to 18 November 1942
0
200
400
km
SWEDEN
BALTIC
GERMANY
PROTECTORATE
SLOVAKIA
HUNGARY
CROATIA
OCCUPIED SERBIA
ITALY
ADRIATIC
BULGARIA
ROMANIA
GENERAL GOVERNMENT
REICHSKOMMISSARIAT OSTLAND
OCCUPIED RUSSIA
REICHSKOMMISSARIAT UKRAINE
CRIMEA
BLACK SEA
Sea of Azov
USSR
Gulf of Finland
Gulf of Riga
Lake Ladoga
Copenhagen
Rostock
Berlin
Stettin
Dresden
Prague
Elbe
Oder
Breslau
Poznan
Danzig
Stockholm
Königsberg
Tilsit
Vistula
Warsaw
Lublin
Krakow
Vienna
Budapest
Szeged
Zagreb
Sarajevo
Belgrade
Danube
Ploiesti
Bucharest
Lvov
Tarnopol
Dniester
Brest
Bialystok
Niemen
Kaunas
Vilna
Riga
Tallinn
Helsinki
Dvinsk
Dvina
Minsk
Pripet
Polotsk
Leningrad
Novgorod
Demyansk
Vitebsk
Orsha
Smolensk
Gomel
Kiev
Konotop
Bryansk
Rzhev
Kalinin
Volga
Mozhaisk
Moscow
Kolomna
Oka
Tula
Orel
Livny
Kursk
Voronezh
Belgorod
Kharkov
Izyum
Krasnograd
Lubny
Uman
Balta
Odessa
Dnieper
Dnepropetrovsk
Perekop
Sevastopol
Yalta
Kerch
Novorossisk
Maikop
Rostov
Voroshilovgrad
Donets
Don
Stalingrad
Elista
Kizlyar
Grozny

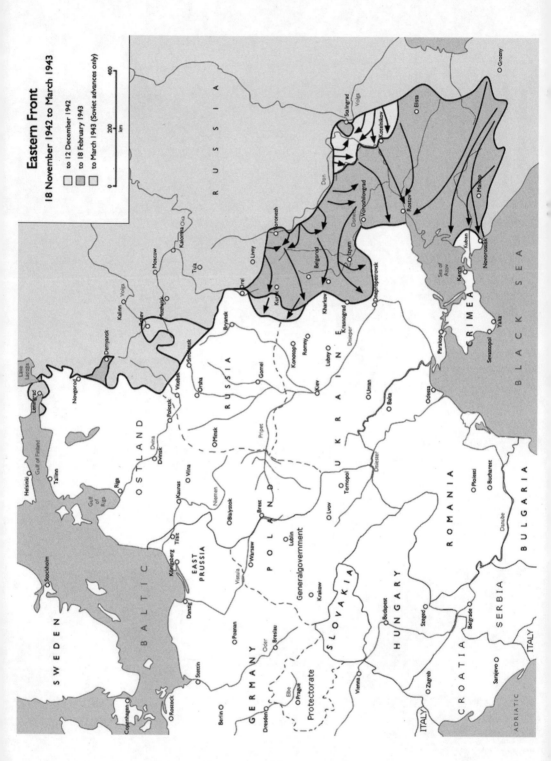

Eastern Front
18 November 1942 to March 1943

- to 12 December 1942
- to 18 February 1943
- to March 1943 (Soviet advances only)

0   200   400
km

SWEDEN

Stockholm

Helsinki

Gulf of Finland

Tallinn

Gulf of Riga

BALTIC

Copenhagen

Rostock

Stettin

Danzig

Königsberg

EAST PRUSSIA

Berlin O

Oder

Dresden

Elbe

Prague

Protectorate

GERMANY

Breslau

Kraków

POLAND

Poznan

Warsaw

Lublin

Generalgovernment

Vistula

Brest

Bialystok

Vilna

Kaunas

Tilsit

Riga

Dvinsk

Dvina

OSTLAND

Polotsk

Minsk

Pripet

Niemen

SLOVAKIA

Vienna

Budapest

HUNGARY

Szeged

CROATIA

Zagreb

Sarajevo O

SERBIA

Belgrade

Danube

ROMANIA

Ploesti

Bucharest

BULGARIA

ITALY

ADRIATIC

Lwow

Tarnopol

UKRAINE

Dniester

Uman

Balta

Odessa

Dnieper

Kiev

Luby O

Konotop O

Romny O

Gomel

Orsha

Smolensk

Bryansk

RUSSIA

Vitebsk

Novgorod

Leningrad

Lake Ladoga

Demyansk

Kalinin

Volga

Moscow

Kaluga

Oka

Tula

Orel

Kursk

Livny

Voronezh

Don

Belgorod

Kharkov

Krasnograd

Dnepropetrovsk

Donets

Izyum

Voroshilovgrad

Rostov

Sea of Azov

CRIMEA

Parlakop

Sevastopol

Yalta

Kerch

Kuban

Novorossisk

Maikop

BLACK SEA

Stalingrad

Volga

Kotelnikov

Elista

Grozny

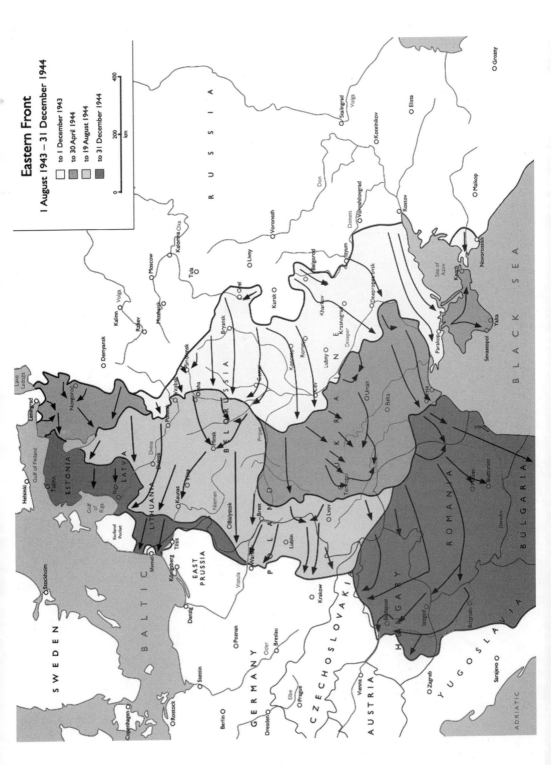

Eastern Front
1 August 1943 – 31 December 1944

- to 1 December 1943
- to 30 April 1944
- to 19 August 1944
- to 31 December 1944

400

200

km

0

RUSSIA

Lake Ladoga

Leningrad

Helsinki

Gulf of Finland

ESTONIA

Tallinn

SWEDEN

Stockholm

BALTIC

Gulf of Riga

LATVIA

Riga

Kurland Pocket

Memel

Tilsit

LITHUANIA

Kaunas

Dvina

Polotsk

Niemen

EAST PRUSSIA

Königsberg

Danzig

Copenhagen

Rostock

Stettin

Poznan

Breslau

Oder

Berlin

Dresden

Elbe

Prague

GERMANY

CZECHOSLOVAKIA

AUSTRIA

Vienna

Zagreb

YUGOSLAVIA

Sarajevo

ADRIATIC

BULGARIA

ROMANIA

Belgrade

Sofia

Bucharest

Ploesti

Danube

HUNGARY

Budapest

Szeged

Krakow

Lublin

Warsaw

Vistula

POLAND

Brest

Bialystok

Lvov

UKRAINE

Ternopol

BELORUSSIA

Minsk

Pinsk

Pripet

Dnieper

Bug

Kiev

Rovno

Balta

Uman

Odessa

Dniepropetrovsk

Krasnograd

Kharkov

Krivoi Rog

Lubny

Romny

Kagoovets

BLACK SEA

Sevastopol

Parakop

Yalta

Kerch

Novorossisk

Sea of Azov

Rostov

Voroshilovgrad

Donets

Izyum

Belgorad

Kursk

Bryansk

Orel

Voronezh

Livny

Don

Stalingrad

Volga

Kotelnikov

Elista

Maikop

Grozny

Oka

Kolomna

Kaluga

Tula

Moscow

Mozhajsk

Rzhev

Kalin

Volga

Demyansk

Novgorod

Vitebsk

Smolensk

17

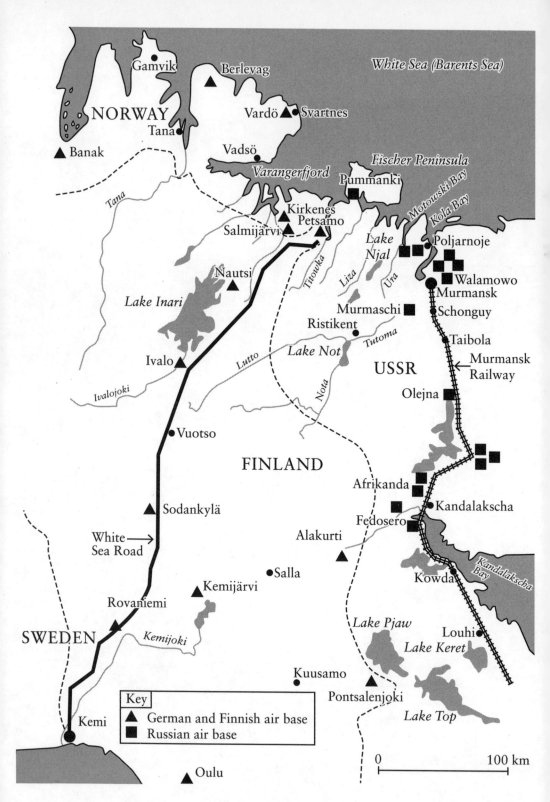

White Sea (Barents Sea)

NORWAY

Gamvik

Berlevag

Vardö Svartnes

Tana

Banak

Vadsö

Varangerfjord

Fischer Peninsula

Pummanki

Motowski Bay

Kola Bay

Kirkenes
Petsamo

Salmijärvi

Lake
Njal

Poljarnoje

Walamowo

Murmansk

Nautsi

Titowka

Liza

Ura

Murmaschi

Schonguy

Lake Inari

Murmaschi

Ristikent

Lake Not

Tutoma

Taibola

Murmansk
Railway

Ivalo

Lutto

Nota

USSR

Olejna

Ivalojoki

Vuotso

FINLAND

Afrikanda

Kandalakscha

Sodankylä

Fedosero

White
Sea Road

Alakurti

Kowda

Kandalakscha Bay

Salla

Lake Pjaw

Kemijärvi

Lake Keret

Louhi

Rovaniemi

Kemijoki

SWEDEN

Kuusamo

Pontsalenjoki

Lake Top

Key
▲ German and Finnish air base
■ Russian air base

Kemi

0   100 km

Oulu

18

1

Training to Be a Fighter Pilot

Pilot training generally, and specifically for fighter pilots in the *Luftwaffe*, was exceptionally thorough. It emphasized exposure of student pilots to a great variety of different aircraft, and also made generous allowances for anybody who required longer time periods for any specific part of the training. Many young Germans were able to train as glider pilots before the war, this sport being widely popular and supported by the state for many years before hostilities broke out. Those interested in flying were generally able to obtain a lot of experience flying gliders, with a distinct advantage in feel of flying. The *DLV* (*Deutschen Luftsportverband* or German Aerial Sport Association) was set up by the Nazi Party in 1932 and was the predecessor to the *NSFK*.[1] The *NSFK* (National Socialist Flying Corps) also ran a number of fairly large gliding schools,[2] and the Hitler Youth organisation had many branches including a flying one, again emphasizing gliding but also including powered flight.

Günther Scholz, who later flew in the East with *JG 54* and *5*, learned to fly with the *DLV* through private funding:

As a reward for completing the matric (*Abitur*) my father gave me the funds for the pilot's A2 licence. As a result I became a member of the *DLV*; the President was Bruno Loerzer, fighter pilot from the First World War, later my commander in *Jagdfliegerverband Bernburg* (Fighter Unit Bernburg); the first units did not yet have numbers. The *DLV* organised flying days with aerobatic displays etc, in which I took part. It was here that my delight and despair in flying arose. I gave up my studies at the *Technische Hochschule* (University) Hannover due to the poor prospect for academic careers – the great unemployment in 1932–1933 – and joined the Navy in 1934, who then handled the military training of future air force officers.

Pre-war training was generally in small groups of about half a dozen pupils to an instructor. Flight training throughout the war generally comprised a number of phases, with basic military training followed by basic flight training known as *AB Schule* (sometimes with an introductory theoretical school, sometimes not), which gave the students the A2 and B2 licences and also qualified them as military pilots (equivalent to obtaining the wings in the RAF or USAAF). Thereafter, they would attend a *Jagdfliegerschule* (fighter training school), sometimes with a preliminary pre-fighter school (*Jagdfliegervorschule*), and then finally round things off with operational training in a *Jagdergänzungsgruppe* (operational training unit, OTU). Early in the war these were specific to each *Geschwader* in the form of an *Ergänzungsstaffel* or -*gruppe*, but later were more centralised in *Jagdergänzungsgruppen* West, Ost and *Süd*, reflecting the western European theatre, the Eastern Front and the southern or Mediterranean theatre respectively.

In the *AB Schule* only light and mostly relatively forgiving training aircraft were flown, but more advanced types, including obsolete fighters and earlier marks of operational aircraft such as the Me 109 and Fw 190, were mastered at the *Jagdfliegerschule*. In the operational training units (*Jagdergänzungsgruppen*), flying fully operational aircraft, the emphasis was on actual combat training, including some operational sorties under less strenuous conditions, and if need for interceptions arose in their training area – for example, unescorted bomber formations flying close to training airfields – some of the operational training units of Eastern Front *Geschwadern* also stationed *Staffeln* on operational airfields for limited combat exposure. Horst Petzschler, who served mainly in *JG 51* in the East, with a few months in *JG 3* in the West also, was one of those who met his first enemy aircraft while with a training unit:

> After successfully completing the *AB Schule*, I was supposed to go to C-school to be trained as a bomber pilot. That was a 'no' for me, and via the testing school at Prenzlau, the next stop was *Jagdfliegerschule* at Paris-Villacoublay! We flew the Me 109 E, Dewoitine 520 and then eventually the Fw 190 A-4. Here in Paris in April 1943, with seven other young pilots and one experienced instructor, I met for the first time 200 B-17 Flying Fortresses, bombing the radar centre in Guyancourt; we finished one only, because we were too excited!! The *Kommandeur* (*Gruppe* C/O) wanted to lock us all up, for having been so stupid! 'Soon they will come with escorts,' he said, 'then the good time for shooting them down is gone!' And he was right!

Pilots training towards multi-engined aircraft (such as the twin-engined Me 110 long-range fighter known as the *Zerstörer* [destroyer], and intending night fighters) would also have to do the C-licence (which included instrument training), attend *Zerstörerschule*, followed by the normal rounding off in both *Jagdfliegerschule* and *Ergänzungsgruppe*. Jochen Schröder, pilot in *ZG 1* and *76* in 1939–1940, commented very positively on his training:

> I still consider today that the flying training we received was pedagogically and psychologically outstanding. We were introduced gradually to all difficulties in flying, in small groups of six cadets (*Fähnrichen*). Our instructors (mine was *Feldwebel* Niemann) ensured a very thorough grounding and training with demonstration of finger-tip flying, using both praise and censure, and with comradeship and very hard work. Hermann Göring before the war, wanted his pilots to have a thorough, many-faceted flying training. In November 1938 we joined active units for practical training.

Pre-war operational training was thus normally handled within the fighter *Geschwader* themselves, without any specialised *Ergänzungs*-units attached to their parent bodies. Georg Pavenzinger recalled: 'After my fighter pilot training I joined *2/JG 51* at Bad Aibling on 1 June 1939. Here, apart from flying sorties, we also received operational-type training such as shooting at drogues. We also practiced aerial combat with a bomber formation with cameras recording the action.' Privately trained pre-war pilots could progress rapidly through training and to a frontline unit, as experienced by Dr Felix Sauer, *JG 53*: 'At the beginning of the war, on 1 September 1939, I was teaching biology at a *Gymnasium* (high school). With *c.* 700 other former private pilots, I was drafted at once and – in a series of rapid courses – trained as a fighter pilot. As early as September 1940 I was sent to fly sorties at the Channel Coast, over England.'

The table below provides some figures for the duration of the various training phases, for pilots completing their training and joining operational units within a specific year; these figures are from individuals who managed to retain their service records, and the number of such individuals per category in the table is shown in brackets (small sample numbers affect the value of statistics). The average total training time, from pre-war to 1944, was about two years. There is a significant increase in time spent within basic flight training schools for 1943; this possibly reflects experienced instructors joining operational units, to be replaced by injured and wounded veteran pilots no longer able to fly operationally, and who were not necessarily the best and most supportive instructors.

Average durations (in months) for training phases, per year(s) in which pilot joined an operational unit

	1939–40	1941–42	1943	Pre-1939 to 1944 (overall averages)
Basic military training	6.1 (4)	3.33 (6)	5.8 (6)	5.5 (17)
AB Schule	8.6 (7)	9.0 (15)	14.75 (8)	10.0 (31)
Jagdfliegerschule	3.25 (6)	7.9 (8)	3.9 (6)	5.6 (26)
Jagdergänzungsgruppe	1.6 (2)	3.65 (10)	1.4 (6)	2.6 (19)

Another explanation for the much extended AB school training time in 1943 could lie in fuel shortages, which already played a role in 1942, as described next by Werner Killer, who later served in *JG 77* in North Africa. His detailed account provides an excellent example of how thorough *Luftwaffe* fighter pilot training was.

Soon after joining the air force on 1 October 1940 I was given a flying medical; I was luckily one of the seven assessed as suitable for pilot selection, from seventy applicants. After a hard infantry training, on 1 April 1941 I began my flying training in the Fw 44 Stieglitz. In the initial period there was already severe sieving and one third of the students had to pack their bags. Apart from theory of navigation, meteorology, airframes, instruments and engines we had to also master radio transmitting/receiving and swot up our Q-groups. When the weather was good we flew: safety instruction, spinning, steep turns, pinpoint landings from various heights, landings off the airfield, navigational flights with preparation of maps and course calculations. The conversion to other aircraft types such as the Bü 131, Klemm 35, E 39, Arado 66, Focke Wulf 56, NAA 64, Heinkel 45, Junkers W 34, followed one after the other, as well as exposure to the obsolete fighters Heinkel He 51 and Arado 65. Aerobatics were performed on the Fw 44 with Udet-carburettor, night flights on the Ar 66 and the W 34, blind flying in the W 34. Long distance flights were undertaken with the twin-engined Fw 58 Weihe, the French Caudron and the W 34 with a radio operator. With the AB and aerobatics certificates I had earned the military pilot's licence. Following *Jagdfliegervorschule*, from 1 April 1942 I was at *Jagdfliegerschule 5* in Villacoublay. Due to fuel shortages the training was often interrupted. Training proceeded largely on the Arado 96 and the Me 109. After a test, which consisted of several take-offs and landings with the Me 109 E, I was transferred to the *Jagdergänzungsgruppe (Süd)* in St. Jean d'Angely. Here, realistic training was undertaken with operational types Me 109 F and G, also the so-called 'finger-*Schwarm*' (finger four formation) introduced by Mölders. I was now 20 years old, an *Unteroffizier* and fighter pilot.

What is surprising in the table above is the variation in time spent in the flying training phases. *AB Schule* took between four and 16 months for various recorded individuals, and there is one case of just over 30 months. Of the 31 pilots who provided information on their basic flight training, two were sent for seven months to a communications flight for flying experience before returning to *AB Schule* for a final polish. The *Luftwaffe* thus made every effort to afford their pilots a solid grounding in basic flying ability. The same flexibility was accorded to individuals in both *Jagdfliegerschule* and *Jagdergänzungsgruppe* phases of their training: between one and 11 months in the former (and one case of 16 months), with between one and 10 months in the latter. Of course, in most courses and schools, time would have been wasted with that well-known military pursuit of doing pretty much nothing (*gammeln* in fighter pilot parlance). This suggests that once a candidate was accepted for pilot training, bearing in mind very strict admission criteria, and once he showed some promise, every effort was made to accommodate the different learning paces of individuals; a surprisingly non-Germanic and non-regimented approach.

In 1941–1943, training was still very thorough, averaging roughly two years, as witnessed by Ernst Richter, who served in 1943 over Russia in *JG 54* as wingman to the famous ace Nowotny, before flying over the Normandy Invasion area in 1944:

After *Vorschule* with *Unteroffizier* (NCO) training, I had my first introductory flight on 28 March 1941, at the *AB Schule 82*. There I was able to fly my first solo on 7 May 1941. After exactly 629 take-offs I received the military pilot's licence, class B2. The training had comprised a round figure of 242 hours in the air and was completed on 3 March 1942. The training included forced landings, precision landings, aerobatics in both A-class and B-class licences; also formation flights, long distance flights, night landings, high altitude flights, sideslip practice and blind flying. The latter was done on the W 34. During the AB training I flew seventeen different aircraft, amongst others the W 33 and the He 70 (Heinkel Blitz) and the C 445, a French machine. Via the *Jagdvorschule* I came to the *Jagdschule* at Bad-Aibling. Here I experienced a total of 131 take-offs on Ar 96, Na 64,

Me 109 and Fw 190. The school moved to Chateauroux in France in March 1943. On 3 April 1943 I had my first flight in the *Jagdergänzungsgruppe Ost*, also in France, and finally I ended up in Blagnac (Toulouse) and from there was transferred to *JG 54* in the East.

However, by 1944, fighter pilots tended to have shorter and less thorough training, due to high casualty rates in operational units and the ever-worsening fuel supply situation, which reached crisis proportions in the second half of the year. Gerd Hauter, who flew on the Eastern Front in the second half of 1944 with *JG 52*, recalled his training period.

I was transferred in April 1943 as *Obergefreiter* to the pilot's *AB Schule* in Klagenfurt, after basic military training. Here, after a short stint of glider training, we began flying powered aircraft on the following types: Bücker 181, Bücker 131, Klemm 35, Arado 66, Arado 96 and Saimann 202 (Italian). After successful final tests we were sent to the *Jagdfliegerschule* Zerbst near Magdeburg and then at Roth near Nürnberg, and there trained further on the Bücker 133, Heinkel 51, Focke Wulf 56 and finally Me 109 G. In parallel we practised aerial combat and target shooting, and especially made ourselves familiar with the Me 109 that was very hard to take off in and especially to land. Towards the middle of 1944 I arrived at *Jagdergänzungsgruppe Ost* at an airfield in Upper Silesia, as an *Unteroffizier*, where we were given the final polish for operational capability.

Several hours spent with Karl-Heinz Hirsch, ex-*Gefreiter* in *III/JG 27*, revealed an unusually complex and very lengthy training in the *Luftwaffe*, also culminating in a posting to *Jagdergänzungsgruppe Ost* for intending Eastern Front pilots. He also emphasized the dangers of green pilots converting onto Me 109s. After almost three years and around 2,000 hours' flying time he eventually reached a fighter school. Finally, the day came to fly the Me 109 F and there were no two-seater versions to acquaint one with its highly dangerous take-off characteristics: until a speed of about 100 km/h was reached there were no problems with the torque effect (due to propeller rotation), but as the tail was lifted, without any warning, the full impact of a very strong torque movement to the left became immediately effective. The solution was to apply full right rudder just before lifting the tail. Hirsch saw ten of his fellow trainees die in burning Me 109 Fs due to this characteristic. This training was succeeded by two months at the *Luftwaffe* test centre in Rechlin where he was able to fly captured and repaired Spitfire 9 and Mustang fighters and the latest marks of Me 109 in mock combats against each other. A final three months of realistic frontline training in *Jagdergänzungsgruppe Ost* included harsh advice from one of the instructors, *Leutnant* Gerhard Hoffmann, a *Ritterkreuzträger* (Knights Cross holder) from *JG 52* on the Eastern Front; experienced by the trainees as a brutal pilot and personality, he taught them to choose between being brutal themselves or being dead, and to fly their aircraft to their limits, as well as showing them some dirty combat tricks. Despite his being prepared for service in the East, Hirsch ended up flying over Germany late in the war.

Otto Schmid, an experienced pilot from *II/JG 1*, was given a break from operational flying to teach students the tricks of the trade at *Jagdergänzungsgruppe West* in Cazaux, France in 1943–1944. As these student pilots were intended for service in the Home Defence or over the Channel, emphasis was laid on methods for attacking the four-engined bomber formations so prevalent in the western theatres.

This was the final training of the pilots when they came to us from the fighter schools. As they had only flown the Me 109 B or C models at the latter schools, they were converted to the Me 109 F-4. Until the end of August 1943 every incoming pupil was given a test flight in the Arado 96 B to provide a picture of their flying abilities. This procedure was stopped after August 1943, why I cannot remember, but it was not due to fuel shortages. The whole time I was in Cazaux, we always had enough fuel. Thereafter the real training could begin, with '*Rotten*' flights (a pair) within formations and the same for '*Schwarms*' (2 pairs). Then, high-altitude flights up to 8,000 m, low-level flying over land and water, air combat exercises, shooting practice at ground targets. Shooting practice at airborne drogues was not possible as we did not have the requisite materiel. Practical exercises probably helped little, as in reality in combat, overwhelming escort fighters were present also. Furthermore, pupils were taught the correct procedures during sea emergencies, seeing as most operations at the Channel front took place over water. A very strong emphasis was placed on informing the pupils about the tactic for attacking four-engined bombers; this was done with model aircraft. The most effective attack method against four-engined bombers, particularly with the Fw 190, was from head-on and slightly above, so that one had enough speed coming in. Training groups were mostly 12 to 14 men strong. The training lasted *c.* 14 to 16 days. In the summer months we could fly from 08h00 to 12h00 and then again from16h00 hours; from 12h00-16h00 hours it was too hot. On other days there was additional theoretical training, mainly in the late morning. On two to three days of the week daily flying time was at least eight hours for the instructors, which worked them to the bone, as apart from watching the sky generally, one had to keep all the pupils constantly within vision. In the course of the summer of 1943 we received also the Fw 190 and Me 109 G as training aircraft.

Tackling the large four-engined bomber formations remained a thorny problem for the *Luftwaffe* throughout the war, and tended to be emphasized in the final stages of training in 1943 and 1944. Richard Raupach, *JG 54* veteran and instructor at *Jagdergänzungsgruppe Ost* from June 1944 to January 1945, notes that this also applied to intending fighter pilots for the Eastern Front. 'At *Jagdergänzungsgruppe Ost* in Liegnitz and Sagan we practised with fellow pupils attack techniques against the American B-17 bombers. To this end we were allocated, every now and then, a German twin-engined Do 17 bomber with crew. We would overtake the bomber and fly far ahead, until the Dornier was only visible as a small object in the sky. Then we turned and flew at the bomber from head-on. We flew these attacks in a column, one behind the other. The head-on attack was successful, because the B-17 formations had a very strong defensive fire power to the rear.'

In contrast, pilot training before the war and in its early stages was much more relaxed. Rudolf Miese, *4/JG 2* reached the front during the Battle of Britain in 1940, and experienced a combination of peacetime and early wartime training.

At age fifteen and sixteen, we built models of gliders and took part in competitions, at age seventeen we built the SG 9 under instruction, a glider for initial training. At seventeen also, I flew the gliding A licence, at eighteen on the Isle of Sylt, the B licence on the wind, and at the 'red cliff' the C licence (leading to award of the *NSFK* gliding wings). With this prior knowledge, after labour service duty (*Arbeitsdienst*) in the winter of 1938/1939 I had the opportunity to take part in the pilot training at the *DLV* School in Windelsbleiche near Bielefeld, from 1 April 1939 to 30 September 1939. It was a wonderful time: twenty three pupil fliers with five instructors, just flying, theoretical learning in the relevant subjects and with bad weather ('*qbi*') practical training in the workshop. Later, during long distance flights, only civilian airfields with accompanying service, were used. After five months I had completed the A2, B1 and aerobatics K1 licences. The initial training was on the Klemm KL 25, for beginners a really hard machine to fly, but this was an advantage for later training. Then everything changed. On 28 August 1939, three days before the outbreak of war on 1 September, the pupils were transferred to barracks in Detmold. Now we were soldiers and basic training followed. Eventually on 10 January 1940, a transfer to the *AB Schule* in Prague-Gbell. Here we trained on the W 34 (Junkers) and later on the most variable types. The last test for the B2 licence was on 10 May 1940. Thus we were military pilots and received the pilot's badge of the *Luftwaffe*. On 13 May transfer to *Jagdfliegerschule 1* at Werneuchen near Berlin followed. Initially a start to fighter pilot training was made on the Arado Ar 68, very difficult and exhausting to fly. The beautiful touring aircraft, the Messerschmitt Me 108 served as preparation for the Me 109, it had a retractable undercarriage, landing flaps and wing slots. Then came the first flights in the single seater, fast and heavy machine, the Me 109 B. After eight weeks fighter pilot training, transfer to the *Jagdergänzungsgruppe* in Merseburg followed in mid-July 1940 where we converted onto the front line Me 109 E.

In distinct contrast to the account of Rudolf Miese, Ernst Schröder, who joined *5/JG 300* in July 1944, paints a much more sombre picture of the inadequately trained pilots he served with in the final period of the war flying against both eastern and western enemies.

I differentiated myself from the majority of pilots in my group in that I had still received an at least partially adequate training as a day fighter pilot. My subsequent adherence to the really few and simple rules of day fighter tactics was responsible for my survival – along with a great deal of luck! The overwhelming majority of my comrades unfortunately did not receive such training – perhaps it was felt that *Sturmgruppen* (massed, heavily armoured fighter units focussed on attacking four-engined bomber formations, of which *II/JG 300* was one) with their narrow aim of shooting down such bombers at all costs, didn't need thorough training. At least one had this impression – as mostly we had ex-instructors or hastily and inadequately trained young pilots in the *JG 300 Staffeln*. In 1945 we got people who had only flown a few circuits in the Fw 190 fighter!! Pilot training suffered chronically from about the beginning of 1944 from the fuel shortage – the result was that the already shortened programme was reduced even more. As an example, I needed ninety one flying hours in 1943 before I was a trained 'pilot', and I had 96 hours at fighter school and *Jagdergänzungsgruppe* combined, compared to about 122 hours flying in JG 300 for a total aviation career of 310 hours!! Besides, at fighter school and *Jagdergänzungsgruppe West* in Orange, I was fully trained on the Me 109 G-6. Through a lucky chance that pilots were required to ferry about 20 Fw 190s from Avignon/France to Märkisch-Friedland on 12 June 1944, I was able to convert onto this type – I thank this circumstance for my survival! With the normal short training times I would never have been able to master the Fw 190 in action! I am of the opinion that the insane losses of the fighter arm in 1944 and 1945 in the first place can be ascribed to the fact that no suitable and adequate training of pilots was possible anymore after 1943. The technical differences between German and Allied fighter aircraft were not great enough to explain the rapid downfall of the German aerial defence.

And thus towards the end of the aerial war along the Eastern Front, the training differential had become reversed; now it was the Germans who had been too rapidly trained and were inadequately prepared to battle their better-prepared young Russian opponents.

2

Character of the Russian War

Hauptmann Günther Schack, a major ace with *I* and *III/JG 51* in the East where he claimed 174 victories and was awarded the *Eichenlaub* to the *Ritterkreuz* (Oak Leaves to the Knights Cross), was lucky to be accepted as a pilot at all:

Due to a skiing accident and a botched operation, I was not eligible for service in the *Wehrmacht*, as I had been left with the one leg 3 cm shorter than the other. I was a technology student at Aachen when war broke out; the university was closed, and I was then at home in Elbing (my father was Superintendent of Elbing). I volunteered myself for the *Luftwaffe* as I did not want to study further, while others had to pay the ultimate sacrifice. After the war I found out that I had saved my father from being sent to prison or a concentration camp, as at exactly this time I had appeared before Hitler to receive the *Eichenlaub*. [Günther's father held a position akin to dean in Elbing's Protestant Church, and was part of the Confessing Church movement that resisted Nazi infiltration.[1]] It has nothing to do with National Socialism when one wants to defend one's fatherland, but this is, thank God, very difficult to explain to the next generation.

I was one of the very few pilots who fought through the entire Russian campaign in the *Geschwader*. Actually, as a *Gefreiter* (the second-lowest rank in the *Luftwaffe* overall and the lowest given to newly qualified aircrew) and in place of the courier pilot of the *Geschwader*, I was in the *Geschwaderstab* for a short while, and I had to fetch the movement order that transferred the *Geschwader* to the East from the division staff

(*General* Osterkamp) on the Channel front in 1941, with the Fieseler Storch. At that time almost all units were already in Poland. In the beginning in *JG 51* I really battled as I had two take-off crashes from the concrete runway. Never before during training had we practised taking off from a concrete runway with a cross-wind. I pulled back on the throttle as the machine turned sharply, that was completely the wrong thing to do and nobody told me what I had done wrong. As a result I had to wait then in St Omer for a machine to be repaired. In addition, no one else in the *Geschwader* made it from *Gefreiter* to *Gruppenkommandeur*. Living conditions on the ground in the East were highly variable, in the beginning very primitive in winter, in summer in tents. In the first winter (1941–1942) there were sometimes problems with supplies of special rations for flying crews. Our quarters were shared, in animal stalls and barns. However, this is now more than enough about me!

Alfred Grislawski, a tough NCO in *9/JG 52* flying on the southern front in the East, was a much more reticent witness and very succinctly summed up his duties during 1941–1942: 'Flying free chases, escort missions and low-level attacks.' The iconic Il-2 ground attack aircraft, in many ways the definitive Russian aerial weapon, was always a tough nut for its *Luftwaffe* foes to shoot down. If you were a good shot and could ambush them, then the best solution, according to *Feldwebel* Grislawski, was 'a surprise attack from below and behind aiming for the oil cooler'. He ended the war in the West as a *Hauptmann*.

It is always important to bear in mind that the fighting pilots were supported by a large team of ground staff, who enjoyed far fewer perks and performed immense labours under often very challenging conditions. It is thus fitting to provide a recollection from just such a man, *Waffenmeister* (chief armourer) Ernst Brunns of *I/JG 54*.

Living conditions on the ground in the Leningrad sector in the winter of 1941–1942 we experienced generally being accommodated in solidly built quarters, and we also had some hangars available, and that enabled jobs to be carried out with initiative. Big problems occurred with servicing the machines, the engines had to be warmed up hourly. The weapons were treated with frost-proof grease, and rifle oil mixed with offal was a good way of combating freezing. Until Christmas 1941 the front was relatively quiet, but at the beginning of 1942 it really became active. Personally I often had to transfer to a different field base, and either a Ju 52, a Weihe (Fw 58), a W 34 or a Me 108 were available; indirectly thus I was also part of the 'flying personnel' – I enjoyed the Me 108 a lot. Thus I got to know Russia very well. As a dendrologist (botanist) I found Russia particularly interesting, the large forests were especially stimulating. On a flight in 1942 I was able to glimpse the Kremlin in Moscow from an aircraft, for a short moment. Forty five years later, I was invited there as a guest, which was a special experience. I personally do not hate any previous enemy, and so it must stay.

However, sentiments during the war in the East were very different.

The Eastern Front was really a war within a war, a theatre unto itself, marked by an unmitigated savagery on both sides and where the established rules of war went unheeded. The Hague (1907) and Geneva (1929) Conventions were effectively ignored in this war zone; while Imperial Russia had strongly supported the former convention, its communist successor government repudiated it, and the Soviet Union was not a signatory to the latter convention.[2] The Germans were, but saw no reason to apply it to an enemy who had not signed,[3] and also had some additional plans of their own which had not the faintest connections to trying to control the worst excesses of war. The *Einsatzgruppen* (abetted by German police battalions and local militias, particularly in the Baltic states and Ukraine), which were the formalised murder squads sent in behind the German frontline troops for the express purpose of killing all Jews found in the conquered territory, plus also killing Communist functionaries, partisans (real and imagined) and any figures about whom subject peoples might rally,[4] were a new martial dimension not seen before the Second World War (and used already in Poland). This was to be a war of annihilation with no (or very little) quarter asked or given. This soon applied to both sides as extreme violence from the invaders engendered a comparable reply from defenders, egged on from the Soviet side by widespread use of terror by Stalin and his functionaries, mainly through the offices of the NKVD (essentially the state elite troops and security forces) and applied as much to their own side as to the enemy.[5] On the German side, a deliberate and cold-blooded plan to starve at least 10–20 million and likely even more, up to 30 million Russians, mainly within conquered cities, formed part of military planning for the campaign.[6] One can imagine the trepidation that a forced-landing or parachute jump into enemy territory must have held for the German fighter pilots, who found themselves caught up in a genocidal conflict.

The Germans began this new war with the greatest confidence, despite their recent defeat (mostly denied in the vast majority of *Jagdflieger* quarters) in the Battle of Britain. Once again the *Blitzkrieg* technique of rapid and powerful armoured thrusts accompanied by well-practised and effective *Luftwaffe* ground support operations would succeed, and it was thought that the Russians would only last a few months. The German army (unlike the *Luftwaffe*, who were prepared) made no efforts to provide the men with winter clothing and equipment as they were sure it would all be over before the Russian winter struck. This was a return to a good war on land, with no English Channel to impede the progress of the German army. This savage conflict in the East was to be fought as a racial war and one where the German intent was quite clearly to win *Lebensraum* (living space, never mind the vast agricultural, mineral and industrial resources of the Soviet Union) and depopulate it except for a pool of necessary slave labour. Hitler's infamous 'Commissar order', which made it both compulsory and legal to eliminate anyone identified or even suspected of being such a person,[7] eroded any remaining threads of the rules of engagement in this theatre right from the beginning. It did not take long for a broad and blurred vision to develop where unwelcome elements to be exterminated encompassed commissars, Jews, partisans (and 'partisans'), inferred spies and agents, and anyone seen as undesirable in the newly conquered living space.[8]

The scene was thus set right from the outset for a war of unparalleled savagery and extermination. And the killings were not restricted only to the organised murdering forces dedicated to ethnic cleansing behind the frontline troops, but the German army and even personnel from the *Luftwaffe* also became complicit in the extermination and wholesale slaughter, on a scale by no means insignificant.[9] *Oberstleutnant* Günther Lützow, *Kommodore* of *JG 3*, demurred when a small *Einsatzgruppe* detachment asked for assistance from his men (as many as possible) to help in liquidating 'undesirables'; to his great credit, and also at the risk of his position if not also his life, Lützow formally paraded his entire unit and lectured them passionately on the evil inherent in these murderous activities and swore to discard his own uniform if even one of them volunteered to help in such actions.[10] *Major* Hanns Trübenbach, *Kommodore* of *JG 52* and at the same time *Jagdfliegerführer* of the German *Luftwaffe* Mission in Romania, was directly responsible for the defence of the Ploiesti oilfields there. He landed with his wingman at Tiraspol airfield, about 60 km north-west of besieged Odessa, on 16 September 1941; here he was an even earlier witness than Lützow to the massacres of Jews in this recently conquered area:

The field base at Tiraspol was enormous and the fighting front had moved on further to the east when we landed. An army *Feldwebel* reported to me after we landed, to show us to our quarters. Before taking us there, this *Feldwebel* drove us along the edge of the field, to let us see the mass graves, in which the Jewish men, women and children lay, who had been shot by the Romanians and allegedly also by German SS-commandos. The graves were only very superficially filled in and for Wiese (my Adjutant and wingman) and I this was the most horrible experience, certainly that I ever had to go through in the entire war.

This first-person account stands in direct contrast to the memoirs of Günther Rall, also a member of *JG 52* and famous as the third-highest-claiming German ace (275 victories) and a NATO general later on, where he records only having heard of the Holocaust at the end of the war,[11] a by no means uncommon memory expressed by veterans.

Hans Strelow, a very young pilot who flew in *5/JG 51* in the East, was a serious young man driven to fight for his country above all else; this rather unfortunate youngster had a father who (in person and by letters to the front) zealously urged him on to strive for greatness, filling him with a feeling akin to almost seeking a holy grail.[12] He joined *JG 51* in February 1941, when still only 18 years old, celebrating his 19th birthday the next month, and struggled for a long time to achieve success in the air, not at all helped by the excessive, unhealthy obsession and ambition of his father.[13] Transferred to the East for Operation *Barbarossa*, Strelow's anxiety became heightened as his colleagues' scores really took off, but on 25 June he also finally got his first victory.[14]

Despite a further two victory claims in the following weeks, the freshly promoted *Leutnant* took his lack of successes compared to those of his friends so seriously that he requested his *Staffelkapitän* (*Oberleutnant* Hartmann Grasser, who had earlier flown as wingman to *Kommodore* Mölders of *JG 51*) to relieve him for being ineffective; however Grasser took him under his wing, and slowly Strelow learned his trade and in time became very successful.[15] In January 1942, despite being only 19, he replaced Grasser as *Staffelkapitän*, the youngest then in the entire *Luftwaffe*.[16] He was awarded the *Ritterkreuz* on 18 March 1942 for 52 victories, and six days later the *Eichenlaub*.[17] And then, almost inevitably, it happened: on 22 May 1942, while on a weather reconnaissance mission with an inexperienced wingman, he shot down a bomber in flames (68th victory), but the Russian rear-gunner, gallant to the last, put a bullet in his radiator, and Strelow had to force-land behind the lines; German POWs later heard that when surprised by Russian troops while trying to camouflage his belly-landed Me 109, he sprang into the cockpit and shot himself.[18] Many *Luftwaffe* pilots feared being taken prisoner by the Russians the most, and this was certainly not the only such suicide; once more it underlines the nature of this Eastern Front conflict and the attitudes on both sides. Hans Strelow's final comment to his wingman, who rather stupidly congratulated him on his 68th victory as his Me 109 went down, was a game quip that he himself was now the 69th.[19]

The Russians have always referred to the war on the Eastern Front as the *Great Patriotic War*, a name that attests to the great patriotism involved, brought on also by Stalin's invocation of Russian history and partially divorcing this war from the Communist regime.[20] To most Russians this was an almost sacred war, and their patriotism and love of Mother Russia ran very deep.[21] Despite Stalin to some extent pushing a broader and more ancient patriotism to the fore, and letting Communism take something of a backseat, the draconian measures necessary to turn the German tide, to fight back from seemingly hopeless positions, to move huge industries from threatened areas to the east, to drum up new armies in short time periods, to produce the sinews of war and to simply keep going, would not have been possible under any other state system.[22] It was the Stalin regime's brutal control, and its will and ability to sacrifice people, wellbeing, quality of life and almost anything else to win the war that made the winning of it possible at all.[23]

3

Air War on an Epic Scale; Statistics

The cost of the Great Patriotic War was enormous. Total Soviet losses are estimated at 26–27 million people (nearly half of all Second World War casualties), of which 11.4 million were military battlefield losses (i.e. killed in action or died of wounds, died of illness or frostbite, missing, shot by their own side, or POWs).[1] Not far short of 3 million of the military losses did in fact return (from encircled forces which had been written off, from being cut off and joining partisan units, and over 1.86 million liberated prisoners who were placed back into battle almost immediately after their camps were overrun); many of these returnees ultimately faced nothing better than the Gulags.[2] German military dead on the Eastern Front were about 4.3 million.[3] Civilians were used by both sides for extreme labour tasks, and their safety during active operations was of little concern to the Russians themselves, and even less so to the Germans and their allies.[4] Their losses were no less mind-boggling than the military casualties. To provide some perspective on Russian military losses, the famous Battle of Alamein (often called the turn of the tide)[5] cost 55,000 Axis casualties out of fewer than 100,000 engaged. The sizes of the armies employed in the East, and the cost, greatly exceeded such statistics.

The scale of everything in the East dwarfed anything on any other front: the armies engaged were huge, as were their losses as seen above; there was almost constant battle somewhere on the long front (up to 3,200 km at its maximum in late 1942) throughout.[6] And as the Germans moved ever further eastwards during 1941, and then after recovering from their defeat and recoil before Moscow that first winter, during 1942's advance to Stalingrad and into the Caucasus, so the front extended itself due to the geography of Russia, which broadens in that region towards the east.[7] Logistics also became a worsening nightmare in concert with these advances and the limited Russian railway network (of different gauge to that of Europe) and poor roads both subject to the vagaries of Russian weather (a terrible winter, and the spring and late autumn/early winter mud periods). To an extent, German armies were forced to live off the country despite the Russian scorched-earth policy in their retreats.[8]

Gerd Schindler, an Austrian from Graz who joined *JG 52* in July 1942 as a *Fahnenjunker* (officer cadet), in the Caucasus had an experience relatively typical of the Russian theatre, and its vast spaces and its emptiness (this description is based on a copy of a published account he sent me in 1989). At the time he had just joined *Stab III/ JG 52* where he gained his first experiences under the sympathetic guiding hand of *Oberleutnant* Adolf Dickfeld, a leading ace who later became the inspector of the *Fliegender Hitlerjugend*. On 26 August 1942 Schindler was sent, with a non-flying staff officer, on a courier flight from his base at Gonstakowka to Mineralnye Vody, but on the return flight in the evening he became disoriented among the endless forests and fields, and as it got dark he landed in one of the many large fields. There he and his comrade spent an anxious night under the wing of their Klemm 35 light aircraft, with nothing else for company except some distant cattle and a starry sky, alternately standing guard with pistol and jack knife. As the dawn broke, and having seen not a soul, they took off again with ease, flew westwards for a few minutes and found their home base.

The claims made by the German fighter pilots over the Eastern Front also formed part of the set of extreme values related to this enormous war. Total German fighter claims (in the air) against the Soviets given by Ernst Obermaier were about 45,000 aircraft out of a total estimated destroyed (by fighters, flak and on the ground) of 77,000 machines.[9] Of the estimated total of Eastern (*c.* 45,000) and Western (*c.* 25,000) victories claimed (thus *c.* 70,000 in total for the entire war) by German fighter aircraft, it is calculated that about 51,400 of these victories fell to only around 965 *Experten* claiming 20 or more victories each.[10] This means that fewer than 1,000 leading fighter pilots (day and night fighters, *Zerstörer* pilots and those flying the *Jabos* or fighter-bombers) were responsible for over 73 per cent of all claimed successes; this is similar in all air forces, in all conflicts – the aces were always relatively few in number and the vast majority of fighter pilots scored only a few victories or none at all. These proportions and achievements appear to have been much higher in the *Luftwaffe*, however, with 105 fighter pilots each claiming more than 100 successes.[11] As the claims totals demonstrate, so also were the highest *Luftwaffe* scorers greatly skewed towards those with predominantly Russian aircraft claims.[12]

Top-scoring German fighter aces in the war; Eastern Front claims *versus* total claims

Pilot	Total claims	Eastern claims
Major Erich Hartmann (*JG 52, JG 53*)	352	350
Major Gerhard Barkhorn (*JG 52, JG 6, JV 44*)	301	301
Major Günther Rall (*JG 52, JG 11*)	275	272
Oberleutnant Otto Kittel (*JG 54*)	267	267
Major Walter Nowotny (*JG 54, Kdo. Nowotny*)	258	255
Major Wilhelm Batz (*JG 52*)	237	232
Major Erich Rudorffer (*JG 2, JG 54, JG 7*)	222	136
Oberstleutnant Heinz Bär (*JG 51, JG 77, JG 1, JG 3, JV 44*)	220	96
Oberst Hermann Graf (*JG 52, JG 50, JG 11*)	212	202
Major Theodor Weissenberger (*JG 5, JG 7*)	208	175
Oberstleutnant Hans Philipp (*JG 54, JG 1*)	206	177
Oberleutnant Walter Schuck (*JG 5, JG 7*)	206	198
Major Heinrich Ehrler (*JG 5, JG 7*)	205	200
Oberleutnant Anton Hafner (*JG 51*)	204	184
Hauptmann Helmut Lipfert (*JG 52, JG 53*)	203	201

Most of these top aces were also leaders of *Gruppen* or even entire *Geschwadern*; while not all major aces made good leaders, many were held in high regard. *Leutnant* Gerd Schindler, who served in *Stab III* and *9/JG 52*, recalls: 'One can only report good things on [Günther] Rall, he had an excellent character, and he is today practically the only one from *JG 52* who attends all get-togethers apart from Hrabak and Krupinsky. Rall is a warm and receptive person; we enjoy it every time we meet again. His late wife was a Viennese.'

In contrast, the *Luftwaffe*'s top ace, in the East and for the entire war altogether, Erich Hartmann, has an image among some veterans that is less than flattering. An anonymous colleague had the following to say about Hartmann: 'In the first volume of the *JG 52* series (*Das Jagdgeschwader 52* by Niko Fast)[13] the same findings on Hartmann are given twice, one can even go so far as to say self-congratulationary findings. He was always odd/strange, even though for a long time (!) he shot nothing down and one spoke already of dismissal; he comes to no get-togethers and left the new *Bundesluftwaffe* on early pension and with resentment.' Another colleague who flew with Hartmann was much more balanced in his appraisal, written in 1989: 'Hartmann was very impersonal. He was, as I can see from today's perspective, very young at 24 and an absolute superstar, admired by everyone but rather moody, bad-tempered even and thus not so popular, and difficult to get to know. This is my honest personal opinion, and no criticism is intended and especially not to diminish the enormous achievements of *Hauptmann* Hartmann. He was a real loner, which also showed after the war, when he rejoined the *Bundesluftwaffe*. It is obviously not my place to criticise *Herr* Hartmann but I have been honest.'

The von Rohden document collection[14] provides summary data for all inferred Russian aircraft combat losses (and, concomitantly, German claims), as estimated from all German sources (including intelligence assets), for the first three years of the Russian war (66,000 aircraft in total), up until June 1944, summarised in the table below.

Russian aircraft losses at the front[15]	Year of war in the East: First (22 June 1941-22 June 1942)	Second year	Third year
Bombers	7,500	2,600	2,600
Ground attack	800	5,000	7,300
Fighters	15,900	12,000	8,200
Other aircraft	1,900	800	900
Total	26,100	20,900	19,000

This should be considered against the 77,000 total combat losses of Russian aircraft estimated by Obermaier,[16] and in that context does appear reasonable, leaving *c.* 11,000 aircraft destroyed in the period June 1944 to May 1945. The relevant von Rohden document goes further, noting the steady decline in German successes, which continued into the first half of the fourth year of war in the East (i.e. into the second half of 1944), and suggested several reasons why this had occurred: (1) increasing combat experience of Russian aircrews; (2) improved training of Russian aircrew; (3) steadily increasing numerical superiority of the Soviet air forces; (4) significant increase in the quality of Russian aircraft employed at the front, particularly of the fighters, and achievement of equality between German and the latest Soviet fighter aircraft; (5) decreasing strength of *Luftwaffe* air forces employed on the Eastern Front.[17] This relatively realistic intelligence appreciation of the improvement in the Soviet air force, and especially of its fighter effectiveness, supports the equally sober judgement given in the preface by *Kommodore* Günther Scholz of *JG 54* and *JG 5* on their Russian opponents.

A comparison of German claims in the East with data for Russian aircraft losses is now necessary. Among the most up-to-date and authoritative figures are those provided by Krivosheev in 1997: total Russian aircraft losses due directly to combat-related causes during the war was 46,100; of these, *c.* 20,000 were lost to air combat, with the balance of *c.* 26,100 being lost to other causes related to combat[18] (i.e. to flak, destroyed on the ground in airfield attacks, etc.). A different source, also using summaries derived from official statistics, gives 43,100 total combat losses for the war, including 10,000 bombers, 12,400 ground attack aircraft (i.e. Il-2s) and 20,700 fighters.[19] This total figure of 43,100 is also cited by a couple of other sources.[20] Two other total combat loss figures are given by another source: 37,165 and 38,409.[21]

These four figures are not that dissimilar, and some other confirmatory calibrations can be made. The original Soviet air war official history, translated into English in 1973,[22] gave little away but did provide figures for total sorties flown in the war, annual sortie rates, as well as sorties per (combat) loss for the years 1941, 1943 and 1945. These enable rough calculations for annual losses for those specified three years, and by graphing these, values for the two intervening years of 1942 and 1944 could be interpolated; the result is 42,625 total combat losses for the war. While this relies on coarse averages and very few data points, the result is surprisingly close to the figures quoted above from official sources. Total Soviet combat-related aircraft losses for the war in the East thus total somewhere between 46,100 and 37,165 – the total German fighter claims of *c.* 45,000 aircraft fit perfectly into this bracket, but of course leave no room for combat losses due to any other cause (flak, bombing on the ground, claims by bombers, ground attack aircraft, etc.). Krivosheev's total of *c.* 20,000 aerial combat losses of Soviet aircraft[23] against the 45,000 German fighter claims suggests an over-claim factor of approximately two and a quarter for the German fighter pilots. However, this would be a minimum over-claim estimation as no claims by other German aircraft types are included.

As in all aerial wars, and as in all theatres of the Second World War, the Germans (and obviously the Russians too) flying on the Eastern Front claimed more successes than they shot down, apparently something in excess of two claims for every victory. This implies that all the main aces listed in the table above almost certainly did not reach any of those enormous scores in reality. But even applying a *c.* 2.25 over-claim factor still leaves the Germans with the highest-scoring aces of the war and of all time. Of course, this was a 'reality' pushed very hard by the Nazi propaganda system, and one of obvious useful application on a front (and in the entire war in its later stages) where they were mostly outnumbered and where this fact, allied to increasing Russian quality, made their lives more and more difficult.

The claim was then – and in many ways has remained so ever since – that the German fighter pilots, the *Experten* to use the German term for their aces, really were superior, or just made better fighter pilots. There is even something almost obscene in the numbers of deaths inherent in these enormous scores; success for one side always implies death and injury to the other. Of course, the implied superiority of the German fighter pilots has to be seen for the Nazi racial prejudice and superman principle (to balance against the multitudinous *Untermenschen* who were beating them on the Eastern Front) which it most indubitably was. As will be seen from the graphs given in the illustrations (illustrations 7 and 8) and the discussion thereof below, air superiority was lost to the Germans in the East some time in about mid-1943, and the very survival thereafter of the limited fighter *Gruppen* necessitated special tactics, rigidly applied, which also could deliver high scorers when used correctly and with discipline. This fact becomes apparent in a real sense based on the surviving *Startkladde* (comprehensive flight log) records of 7/JG 51 for the September 1943–April 1944 period in the central part of the Eastern Front. The detail preserved in this remarkable record enables a daily log of combat to be reconstructed, and the tactics stand out clearly, as do the few successful major aces (full discussion of the *Kladde* in chapter 9).

The creation of small numbers of major aces in the later war years in the East was thus a product of a survival tactic applied by the German fighter arm, allied to common encounters with small Soviet formations and the use of the bounce from on high almost to perfection. While this tactic produced the aces, kept the German fighter *Gruppen* in existence and made them look good against a backdrop of increasingly large Soviet numbers, from a strategic point of view it was really a waste of time as air superiority had passed into the hands of the Soviet air forces in mid-1943 and was never in any danger of being lost.

Tactical success at the cost of strategic failure – a repeat of the German fighter operations over North Africa. This reflects poor leadership at the top or otherwise deliberate maintenance of a façade of success within a larger context of known total failure at the strategic scale. In any case, the Germans were not supermen, and their top aces were not the greatest airmen of all time, as witnessed in their abject failure when placed in the Western theatres, as happened to many in 1943–1944, when they fell in droves alongside their inexperienced colleagues during an intense strategic air war which was all about gaining and keeping air superiority over Germany.

It is also noticeable that the increasing scores of the German fighter pilots during the course of the war in the East steadily pushed the envelope used for awarding the top decorations. Successively, once 100 victories was no longer such a rare achievement, the first to 150

(Gordon Gollob as acting *Kommodore* of *JG 52*, on 29 August 1942), to 200 (Hermann Graf, *Staffelkapitän* of 9/*JG 52*, on 2 October 1942), to 250 (Walter Nowotny, *Gruppenkommandeur I/JG 54*, on 14 October 1943) and finally to 300 (Erich Hartmann, *Staffelkapitän* of Graf's old 9/*JG 52*, on 24 August 1944; he raised that to just over 350 by the end of the war[24]) were all awarded the *Brillanten* (Diamonds) to the *Ritterkreuz*,[25] the highest possible distinction (the Golden *Eichenlaub* given to Stuka ace Rudel alone excluded). Success and rewards were thus keyed intimately and almost exclusively to numbers of victory claims, a strategic detour of a motivating factor, as is now obvious. Noticeably, each of these four major propaganda figures was also a staunch Nazi: Gollob ordained by Himmler in the last few months of the war, on the basis of his political reliability, as the successor to Galland as *General der Jagdflieger*;[26] Graf, a leading light in the *NSFK* and thus by definition a Party member also;[27] Nowotny, already a Party member in Austria before the war; Hartmann, who attended a special political school (*Napoli*) for some time.[28]

Luftwaffe Assets Stationed on the Eastern Front
Despite a steady increase in the size of the *Luftwaffe* fighter arm during the war, this never really helped to strengthen forces stationed on the Eastern Front. In fact, the latter soon decreased, never to grow significantly again until close to the end of the war (illustration 7). Rather than reinforcing the Eastern Front, the increasing numbers of German fighter *Gruppen* from June 1941 onwards were mainly preoccupied with vastly increased commitments to the Battle of Germany from early 1943 and prior to that, and to a much lesser extent, by reinforcement of the Mediterranean theatre from late 1941, after which time this commitment basically maintained its scale. Units stationed in south-eastern Europe from 1944 onwards faced both the Russians flying in support of their advancing armies, and Western escorted bomber incursions. *Luftwaffe* fighter commitments in France remained basically the same, with a major spike during the June 1944 invasion and the following few months.

Gruppen assigned to the Eastern Front slowly decreased during the war, despite the increase in total fighters available, reaching a lowest point in late 1944, before a big reinforcement in 1945 which was too late to be effective (illustration 7). If commitments of available *Jagdgruppen* are expressed as percentages of total fighter *Gruppen* assigned to each major front, it can be seen clearly that the major part of the available fighter force was only assigned to the Russian front during its opening few months (illustration 8). During the Soviet counter-offensive over the 1941/42 winter, the Mediterranean conflict swallowed up significant assets previously assigned in the East, and once the German summer offensive in Russia (*Fall Blau*) began in 1942 some of the *Jagdgruppen* returned to the East but never in the numbers seen during 1941. In fact, during the summer and early autumn of 1942, commitments of German fighters to Eastern and Western spheres of conflict were almost exactly equal at 50 per cent each; thereafter, from October 1942 onwards, a relatively rapid reduction of fighters available in the East took place fuelled largely by German home defence requirements.

Even in July 1943 for the last throw in the East, the massive Kursk salient offensive, German commitments of fighters showed no significant reversal of this trend of reduction (illustration 8). Within a few months after Kursk, only about 25 per cent of available fighters were stationed on the Russian front and even this small number gradually shrunk until the end of 1944. Clearly the Germans began to lose broad-based air superiority in the East from early 1943 (coincident with the hard Kuban aerial battle) and by the time of Kursk could only achieve it locally and over a short time period; once that battle was lost any vestige of air superiority had been replaced by what was essentially a holding action. Fighter units kept their tactics such that their own casualties were minimised and those of their enemies maximised (by overemphasis of scores and reliance on the bounce from height), but in the process surrendered any strategic control of the airspace in the East.

The overall pattern of a steady decline in *Jagdgruppen* posted on the Eastern Front is obvious in illustration 9. In this plot, the high numbers of fighters assigned for the two summer offensives in 1941 and 1942 are very apparent. Interestingly, for four of what can be considered major battles (1941 Soviet Winter offensive; November 1942 Stalingrad encirclement; July 1943 Kursk offensive; June 1944 Russian Bagration offensive) each one was preceded by a reduction of German fighters on the front (illustration 9). Such consistency of poor strategic vision and planning must have been at least something of an embarrassment for the *Luftwaffe*'s upper echelons! The plateau of 11 fighter *Gruppen* assigned in the East from October 1943 till April 1944 (illustration 9) seems to have been considered the minimum number to provide a modicum of cover and to act as a fire brigade for the overstretched German army. From this it is again clear that after August 1943 only a holding action was considered for the Eastern theatre. The weight of the *Luftwaffe*'s defensive capability was solidly in the centre of the *Reich*, fighting (and losing) the Battle of Germany, the necessary prerequisite for a successful invasion of France by the Western Allies in June 1944.

German fighter losses on the Eastern Front can be taken as a reflection of resource allocation and fighting intensity. These losses when compared to analogous losses for the other fronts (data derived from the US Strategic Bombing Survey)[29] show very clearly that *Luftwaffe* fighter resources were concentrated on the Russian Front in 1941 and early 1942, but already in the second and third quarters of 1942 such resources were equally divided between Eastern and Western theatres (illustration 10). By the fourth quarter of 1942 Western fighter allocations had become predominant, and from the second quarter of 1943 *Luftwaffe* fighter presence in the East remained almost static and vastly inferior to that allocated to the Western fronts. There was thus, already partly from late 1942 and definitely from second quarter 1943, no more intention of achieving air superiority over the Eastern Front. Merely a holding action was intended, with the minimum German fighter presence and the preservation thereof, the minimisation of pilot casualties and the maximisation of claims against the Russians.

All of this underpinned the *Experten* of the Eastern Front – the tactics favoured the bounce from altitude, with minimum risk and predominance of fighter victims rather than Il-2s or bombers – the experienced pilots, those with the talent, thus became single-minded and dedicated experts in this method and enormous scores resulted. However, the impact on Russian air force (VVS) strategy was minimal. The image of the German 'superman' pilot nevertheless grew, underpinning propaganda and surviving until the present. Nazi racial theories were thus felt to have been brought to life. However, when such units were transferred to the West, as for several *Staffeln* in June 1944, they were slaughtered, almost to a man, high-scoring Eastern experts included, within a few weeks – their abilities, experience and tactics from the East were of almost no use in the West, where a war of attrition and definite strategic intent to hold on to air superiority by the USAAF and RAF was paramount. At the end of the day this is a total failure of the *Luftwaffe* leadership. High-scoring *Experten* aside, if *Luftwaffe* single-engined fighter loss data are related to numbers of *Jagdgruppen* stationed on the Eastern Front, then it becomes clear that the German fighter loss rate was climbing steadily from year to year,[30] as decreasing German numbers allied to increasing Russian quantity and quality inexorably increased casualties among the sparingly applied *Luftwaffe* fighter assets (illustration 11).

However, what choice did they have but to concentrate limited resources in 'the centre', for the Battle of Germany? Their ongoing fuel crisis limited what could be done and their analogous crisis in pilot training (all data below on average training hours from US Strategic Bombing Survey),[31] 'fuelled' by the lack of aviation gas, greatly restricted the strategic choices that could be made by the German air force. Over the fourth quarter of 1941 already, with the 1939–September 1942 average training hours of 240 still intact for the novice pilot, time on operational fighter types was reduced from close to 85 hours to about 45 hours, this time now replaced by experience on light training aircraft, using much less fuel. In the fourth quarter of 1942, total training hours shrank by about 35 hours, and in the first quarter of 1943 were reduced to about 170 hours (with operational type time reduced to under 30 hours). Further reductions in total training hours from the beginning of 1944 reduced this overall figure, on average, to only *c.* 112 hours, less than half of what it had been.

The fuel crisis in tandem with a neglect of pilot training overall, had affected not only pilot supply, but even worse, greatly reduced pilot quality. The maintenance of total fighter casualties in the East (illustration 10) at almost static levels through 1943 and 1944 thus reflects a careful policy of combat tactics allied to very gradual introduction of novice pilots to combat and the reduction of casualties to an affordable minimum. In the simplest terms, much lower numbers of German fighters, fed by new pilots to replace casualties whose quality was deteriorating, had to contend on the Eastern Front with rapidly increasing Russian numbers and quality (yet the German losses remained almost constant). This was only achieved by restricted use of available German resources and the most careful of tactics, which in themselves were ruinous to strategy. The Germans had only prepared for, and only had the air force resources for, a quick war (a *Blitzkrieg*) and were in no way prepared for or resourced for a war of attrition. Yet that is what they faced in the East and the West – in the West this had started already by the deliberate attrition policy adopted by the RAF for fighting the Battle of Britain.

The much higher-scoring aces (in terms of victory claims submitted, not verifiable successes which are anyway almost impossible to quantify for any nation in any aerial struggle) of the *Luftwaffe* thus, especially in the East, reflect a number of factors, which worked in concert to produce high scores, as detailed below.

(1) Greater German fighter experience from the Spanish Civil War and the advantageous *Rotten* and *Schwarm* fighting formations that evolved there.

(2) The *Richthofen* tradition from the First World War – victories at all costs, emphasis on the score, trophies, rewards, etc.

(3) In the Second World War, a similar emphasis, even obsession, with a fighter pilot's score, and a graduated reward system of decorations based almost entirely on scored victories ('neck pain' or *Halsschmerz*, desire for the *Ritterkreuz*); promotions to leadership positions also based largely on achieved combat victories.

(4) In the East a thinly veiled (and in many cases totally unveiled!) contempt existed for the Russian opponents as stupid, *stur* (stubborn),

unimaginative, over-obedient to a strict political system at unit level, etc.; this was reinforced by the early fighting dominated by obsolescent Russian aircraft and huge casualties inflicted through the initial surprise of Operation *Barbarossa*.

(5) Nazi racial attitudes and policies, with the wholesale slaughter of Jews, Communists, 'partisans' (real and imagined/assumed) and Slavs in general often enough, widely known among the fighting soldiers and airmen (despite a post-war blanket of denial until fairly recent exposure of this long-upheld deceit), and reinforcing the perceived superiority of the better-trained German pilots in the early time on the Eastern Front.

(6) From *c*. 9 August 1942 onwards, in the East, the definition of the *Abschuss* (final destruction not observed) replaced the *Luftsieg* (total destruction seen) as the basis of almost all victory claims – the *Abschüsse* still had to be witnessed (normally in the air and often from afar when a smoke trail was seen by someone not flying in the immediate combat in question). Victory confirmation certificates, however, for claims made after early August 1942 credited units with *Luftsiege*, the resultant obfuscation of definition and terminology hiding widespread probable victories being acknowledged by the system.

(7) From late 1942 and definitely from mid-1943 onwards, the Germans lacked the fighters to adequately fight an attrition battle in the East, and replacement pilots became fewer and of poorer quality; the only way to maintain the fighter's existence was to change to a deliberate and carefully practised bounce tactic as the basis of fighter combat – this allowed talented and experienced aces to achieve very high scores at little risk, with no lack of Russian opponents, and the aces enjoyed the full support of the *Luftwaffe* leadership at all levels, and idolisation of very successful individuals with concomitant awards and misuse by the propaganda machine became common if not almost endemic.

Unfortunately, all of this has resulted in the myth of the German superman pilot (from the war years when it was a useful tool for boosting morale of outnumbered and strategically helpless air forces) being maintained even today – somehow the Germans were better pilots and fighters than anyone else, particularly the Russians. Of course this racially skewed perception is not true, but misunderstanding of the full context of the growth and development of the *Experten* (particularly on the Eastern Front), the role of propaganda, over-claiming and in a few cases pure dishonesty and overriding ambition, have ensured its adherents still exist. Chapter 10 in this volume will examine these issues in some detail.

However, not all was doom and gloom in terms of *Luftwaffe* allocations of resources to the Eastern Front. There was huge growth in

Schlachtgruppen (ground attack units) in the *Luftwaffe* from mid-1943 onwards and this was greatly enhanced from mid-1944; at the same time the vast majority of these units were allocated to the Eastern Front.[32] Just like the Russian air force, ground attack (*Jabo*) operations in direct support of the army had become critical to the Germans also; while their fighter units shrank steadily in the East, the fighter-bomber units expanded enormously (illustration 12). Even within established *Luftwaffe* Eastern fighter *Geschwader*, some ground attack units were created. In *JG 51*, in August 1942, a *Panzerjägerstaffel/JG 51* was added to the *Geschwader*.[33] On 26 November 1942, *6/JG 51* was renamed as *Stabstaffel/JG 51* (a full-strength *Staffel*, not the normal four-aircraft staff flight) which largely concentrated on *Jabo* operations.[34]

Similar was the deployment of the *Nachtschlachtgruppen* (night ground attack *Gruppen*), which were phased in from October 1942, starting with parts of two *Gruppen* which reached four and two-thirds *Gruppen* by February 1943, five by June 1943, six by October 1943, and seven by November 1943.[35] Up till then they were all employed against the Soviets. In January 1944 their use over Italy began with half a *Gruppe*, expanded to a whole *Gruppe* by March 1944, and from July 1944 till the end of the war one *Gruppe* remained operational over Italy.[36] In September 1944 they also began operations against the Western Allies over France with half a *Gruppe*, expanded to one and a third *Gruppen* by October 1944, and two and two-thirds *Gruppen* by December 1944, which continued to the end of the war.[37] Over Norway, a single *Gruppe* served from August 1944 till the end of that year. Deployments of *Nachtschlachtgruppen* against the Soviets continued from December 1943 (seven *Gruppen*), increasing to seven and a half by January 1944 and eight and a half *Gruppen* by March 1944 but decreasing from then till the end of the war, when five and a half *Gruppen* were still operating against the Russians.[38]

4

Operation *Barbarossa* and the Russian Winter Offensive (22 June 1941–February 1942)

On the eve of Operation *Barbarossa*, the invasion of Russia, launched in the early hours of 22 June 1941, the *Luftwaffe* fighter forces were disposed across the huge front, supporting Army Groups (AG) North, Centre and South:[1]

AG North: *Luftflotte 1*'s *Fliegerkorps 1* deployed *Stab, I, II* and *III/JG 54*, as well as *4* and *5/JG 53*;

AG Centre: *Luftflotte 2* directly controlled *Stab, I* and *III/JG 53*, while its *Fliegerkorps 8* deployed *Stab, II* and *III/JG 27, II/JG 52*, and *Stab, I* and *II/ZG 26; Fliegerkorps 2* deployed *Stab, I, II, III* and *IV/JG 51*;

AG South: *Luftflotte 4* had *Fliegerkorps 5* with *Stab, I, II* and *III/JG 3* in the north of its area and *Fliegerkorps 4* in its southern area with *I/ LG 2, Stab, II* and *III/JG 77* (in addition, to the rear, *Stab* and *III/JG 52* defended the Romanian airspace and particularly the Ploiesti oilfields);[2]

In the far North, on the Murmansk front (and further south in northern Finland), *Jagdgruppe Petsamo* was deployed which in 1942 became *II/JG 5*;[3] a *Zerstörerstaffel, 1(Z)/JG 77*, also operated there.[4]

This assembly of fighter forces ranged against the Russians reflected the majority of available *Gruppen*, with only *JG 2* and *JG 26* defending France and Belgium, one *Gruppe* of the nascent *JG 1* in Germany, *I/JG 27* in North Africa, *I/JG 52* and *6/JG 53* in Holland.[5] Most of the fighter *Gruppen* ranged against the Russians were equipped with the new Me 109 F, except for the two *Gruppen* of *JG 27* and parts of *JG 77*, while *ZG 26* flew the Me 110.[6]

Several witnesses recall very clearly the events as this great conflict opened before dawn on 22 June 1941, a fateful day for the Germans and Russians alike, one that would see Germany eventually collapse in utter defeat, invaded from east and west. The dreaded two-front war had arrived, yet few of the pilots seem to have had any foreboding of what lay ahead. The opening round, as was the wont of the *Wehrmacht* in its previous invasions, began with massed air attacks on air bases, the Russians being totally surprised tactically although their very well-stocked airfields indicated a strategic fear of imminent attack. German claims this first day amounted to an incredible 1,489 Russian aircraft destroyed on the ground (where they were mostly neatly parked in rows, making their demise much easier) and 322 shot down in the air, against total Russian losses of 1,200 machines, 336 of them shot down and the balance destroyed on their airfields.[7] While Russian losses were catastrophic, *Luftwaffe* casualties were by no means insignificant at 78 aircraft written off (61 directly related to enemy action) and 89 more damaged (50 in action).[8] Among the German fighter *Geschwader* it was *JG 53* that led the scoring this day with 74 claims,[9] despite having a *Staffel* left behind in Holland; one of their successful pilots was *Oberfeldwebel* Josef Kronschnabel, flying with the *9/JG 53* with Army Group Centre, whose Me 109 was also among the German aircraft lost in these first encounters, as related below.

I can still remember the day the war against Russia began on 22 June 1941. Our airfield (Suwalki) lay close to the border. On the evening of 21 June 1941 *Hauptmann* Wilcke called the pilots of his *III Gruppe* together and explained to us that the *Führer* had ordered the commencement of the war against Russia, to forestall an attack by the Russians on us. We were surprised. At the time I had no thoughts on the outcome at all. Wilcke showed us photos of the Russian aircraft types and told us the approximate numbers of them that were available. At the same time he showed us an aerial photograph of a Russian airfield that we were to attack the next morning at low level. On 22 June 1941 towards dawn our 9th *Staffel* took off. The front was already marked by fires. We then attacked the Russian airbase with our guns (the enemy machines were standing in neat rows). There was no reaction from the enemy flak. During the flight we also saw no sign of an enemy aircraft in the air. While in Volume 1 of the unit history of *JG 53* on page 238 it is said that the 9th *Staffel* flew attacks on enemy tanks, this is not true (he is referring here to Jochen Prien's first volume on the history of *JG 53*).[10]

On our second sortie still early in the day, on the Russian side of the lines we met several I-15 Ratas[11] and there was a combat. In the dogfight a Rata came straight at me, head-on, and fired at me. I could do nothing else except shoot back, after which we flashed past each other. As I turned sharply I saw that the Rata was diving down, burning, towards the ground. On the third mission of this day (at about midday) I flew a free chase sortie over Russian territory with my wingman (*Rottenflieger*). As we were flying at about 2,000 m and about 20 km into enemy territory, my engine suddenly stopped without any warning. As I glided towards the west, I passed over a marshy area. Once I was past this and not very high any more I saw an open flat space with a farm on it within a forested area. I made a belly-landing in this open space. I did not know whether I was in enemy territory or not; I just heard artillery fire and rifle salvoes, and therefore I hid myself in the forest. Soon afterwards a German soldier on a motorbike with sidecar appeared (my landing had been observed) and it was as if a stone had fallen from my heart that I was in German-held territory. A lorry carrying wounded brought me back to my airfield.

The massed Russian ground and air forces close to their western border areas and their concomitant enormous casualties in the immediate aftermath of the surprise German attack are often taken as evidence to support the notion of a planned Russian attack in the opposite direction. A Russian plan did in fact exist, though not yet a detailed *operational* plan nor one intended for use as yet, but the idea was widely believed within the German forces and homeland then, and still is even today.[12] One of those convinced of the veracity of this possibility was the *Luftwaffe*'s leading ace, Werner Mölders, soon to be first pilot in history to achieve 100 victories. His brother, *Oberleutnant* Victor Mölders, *Staffelkapitän 2/JG 51* in the Battle of Britain, where he was shot down and became a prisoner, heard after the war from his mother in this regard:

Something else: when my brother (Werner Mölders, *Kommodore of JG 51*) came home on leave shortly after the start of the Russian campaign, he told our mother: 'You must be thankful that we attacked Russia. Fourteen days later and they would have attacked us and would have been in Berlin.' The fact that the Russians were ready to attack Germany explains the huge successes that the German armed forces achieved in the first few weeks in the East. Today (writing in 1989) even the Russians acknowledge that Stalin wanted to attack Germany to support the Allies. Churchill would much preferred to have seen a Russian attack on Germany much earlier.

The idea of a Russian attack at some future opportunity occurred also to another witness, *Oberleutnant* Günther Scholz, *Staffelkapitän 7/JG 54* flying in support of Army Group North:

> After the end of the brief Balkan campaign against Yugoslavia the *Staffel* (*7/JG 54*) was transferred to Stolp in Pommerania to convert to the Me 109 F. The old Me 109 Es were flown to Bucharest and handed over to the Romanians. The *Staffelkapitäns* were allowed to travel by car from Belgrad, via Budapest, Prague to Stolp. I was thus able to visit my wife in Chemnitz also. After converting to the new model 109 F the *Staffel* moved to Schlossberg/Insterburg in East Prussia under strictest secrecy. We were not allowed to fly at our field base at all. The aircraft dispersal points were fully camouflaged in forests and bushes. On 22 June 1941 in the early morning at 03h00 the first intrusion over the Soviet border took place; our target was the airbases near Kowno. I will never forget flying over the border. As far as one could see from our height of approximately 2,000 m in the emerging dawn, to the north and to the south, white and red Very lights were ascending high into the sky and army units on the ground and fliers in the air crossed the border punctually at 03h00. The Soviet Union appeared to have expected an attack, as all airfields close to the border were full of bombers and fighters. We destroyed the majority of them using bombs and low-level strafing, especially as these aircraft were not camouflaged, but arranged close to each other in orderly rows. Perhaps they had not expected to be attacked quite yet.

Operations against Murmansk on the White Sea, and over
Army Group North
Far to the north of these massive unfolding events involving Army Groups North, Centre and South, a much smaller German army and allied Finnish units in northernmost Norway attacked towards Petsamo on the Arctic coast, to the west of the critical ice-free port of Murmansk, through which Allied aid began to arrive as early as 12 October 1941; further south in north-central Finland, German and Finnish troops tried to cut the railway leading south from Murmansk.[13] Initial Finnish and German advances were held within the first few months and static warfare dominated thereafter in this inhospitable terrain and climate.[14] German fighters in these far northern areas were limited to the *Jagdgruppe Petsamo* and a *Zerstörerstaffel*; *Oberleutnant* Karl-Friedrich Schlossstein flew with the latter (*1(Z)/JG 77*) and describes their operations up to the winter of 1941/42.

I am certainly one of the last witnesses who can report on the beginning of the eastern campaign in the Far North, as none of my then-comrades survived the war. At the beginning of the Russian campaign, we moved to Kirkenes, and from there flew missions against Murmansk – airfields, harbour, ships – and supported the mountain army in the Far North – low-level attacks against troop concentrations, artillery etc. In the winter of 1941/1942 we operated from Finland (Rovannieme/Kemijervi) against troop movements, supporting the Finns, and especially attacks on the train traffic on the Murmansk railway, that transported war materiel that had been delivered by the English and American convoys to Murmansk harbour.

To the south of this Arctic theatre, Army Group North rapidly conquered Lithuania and Latvia, and by 9 July 1941 had already penetrated into southern Estonia and reached the outskirts of Pskov, south-west of Leningrad; the latter city was under siege by 1 September 1941.[15] These movements were supported by the fighters of *JG 54* and two *Staffeln* of *II/JG 53*. *Oberleutnant* Günther Scholz, *Staffelkapitän 7/JG 54* was with them all the way, being shot down and wounded in August before returning to the Leningrad area by the onset of winter, where the city's only link to outside help was now via the famous ice road across frozen Lake Ladoga.

The rapid advance of the army resulted in our continuously moving to new field bases, via Kowno/Kauna, Dünaburg (Daugarpils)/Latvia. Until *c.* September 1941, the *Staffel* lived in tents. One thing remains stuck in my memory about Dünaburg: the city and the airfield were next to the River Düna. Due to days of heavy rain the river flooded over its banks and when I woke up one morning I found the water about 5 cm deep inside my tent, my shoes were floating in the water; fortunately I had an iron field bed with feet. We moved the tents to a higher-lying area. Each pilot also possessed a hammock and we could thus sleep between missions, as up to six operations were flown on some days. Further bases we advanced to included Pskow (Pleskau) and Ostrow. We bartered bread, chocolate and cigarettes with the local farmers for pigs.

At the beginning of the war against the Soviet Union the *Staffel* had accumulated a score of 120 *Luftsiege* (aerial victories) in Belgium, France, England and Yugoslavia. By the end of 1941 it had risen to 270. Near Luga, south of Leningrad, I was shot down (on 1 August 1941, Me 109 was 40 per cent damaged)[16] by the rear gunner of a plunging Soviet bomber that I had already shot into flames; he destroyed my oil tank, oil covered the cockpit canopy, and I was too low to bail out, so I had to jettison the canopy and try a belly landing in a forest glade. The impact was very hard so that I broke one of my vertebrae. I could only lie flat, and was sent to a hospital in Königsberg and later to Magdeburg (where my parents lived); six weeks of recuperation and delay.

In the meantime the *Geschwader* was now stationed in Siverskaja, the *Staffel* (7/JG 54) was quartered in a workers' housing estate in a factory complex. A very bleak place and winter was approaching. On the airfield the men of the ground crews and the pilots built themselves bunkers in the earth that were heated with cast iron stoves or self-made stoves built from petrol tins, to ward off the extreme cold. The main tasks of the *Geschwader*: escort of bomber *Gruppen* to Leningrad, strafing at low level of the supply vehicles on the frozen Lake Ladoga (*Ladosekoe ozero*) and protection of our ground forces and supply columns in the areas of Nowgorod, Staraja Russa on Lake Ilmen. Everywhere we experienced heavy flak as well as soviet fighters particularly over Leningrad. The most 'fun', when one can use such a term, were the attacks on the lorries on the ice road over Lake Ladoga, the only supply route available to the besieged city. After the war I visited Leningrad twice (a wonderful city on the Newa River, Hermitage, Peter-Paul Cathedral, Admiralty, canals and bridges, Isaak Cathedral) and visited the memorials; the population suffered terribly during the more than 900 days of the siege.

Flying with the second *Gruppe* of *JG 54* on the Northern/Leningrad front, *Oberleutnant* Wolfgang Späte, promoted to lead the 5th *Staffel* in the autumn,[17] made a somewhat tongue-in-cheek comment on the effect of *Luftwaffe* successes on Russian aircraft quality: 'During the advance in summer 1941 the Russians used aircraft in the first few weeks that were distinctly inferior to our own (SB-2, DB-3, I-16). Already in the winter of 1941/1942 the quality of the enemy bombers and fighters improved (probably because we had shot down all the bad ones).' Despite tough conditions on the ground, *Leutnant* Erwin Leykauf of Günther Scholz's *Staffel* and later with *Stab III/ JG 54* managed to preserve his sense of humour as well: 'The living conditions 1941–1942 in Russia varied from accommodation in houses to tent living, and to so-called quarters in ex-Russian barracks. Food supplies were almost always problem-free. Lice and flees often took care of night-time entertainment!'

Flying over Army Group Centre
The weight of German ground forces and fighter cover, however, was concentrated under Army Group Centre. After smashing Russian forces near the frontiers in the first two weeks of Operation *Barbarossa*, the Battle of Smolensk (10 July–10 September 1941) stopped the central advance on Moscow, at least for the moment, albeit at heavy cost to

both sides.[18] As a result, Hitler diverted the valuable armoured forces north to Leningrad, and south to encircle Kiev in cooperation with Army Group South, where an enormous battle of encirclement smashed Russian forces.[19] *JG 51*, led by *Oberstleutnant* Werner Mölders, was at the core of the German fighters supporting Army Group Centre; from an early stage in the new theatre, missions flown in *Schwarm* or even only *Rotten* strength became the norm.[20] On 30 June they brought their victory total to 1,000, with 1,200 already by 12 July, which included the 500th Russian claim, and on 15 July 1941 Mölders broke the magic 100-victory mark; however, the operational tempo also took its toll, with 89 Me 109s being written off in *I, II* and *III/JG 51* by the same day as Mölders made history.[21]

While his *Kommodore* was achieving these laurels, one of his youngest pilots, *Leutnant* Hans Strelow of *5/JG 51*, had finally managed to down his very first opponent, as he noted in his diary for 25 June 1941.[22]

Today I finally got the hang of it. In a six-machine formation we flew along the southern highway. Suddenly, north of Lake Wygonowski, we saw the dust clouds from exploding bombs and soon after that, already below us, 15 Russian bombers. I was flying with *Feldwebel* Helber in the cover *Rotte* and saw these boys exactly below us. I straight away went into a steep spiral downwards, but overshot due to excessive speed. To have pulled up and away would have achieved nothing so I flew a 360-degree turn behind them. Then I shot at a DB-3 from behind at a range of *c.* 80 m, so that pieces flew off the fuselage and the left engine showed a white smoke trail. Then I had to pull up and to the left to avoid overshooting. Just as I wanted to attack him again, suddenly another Messerschmitt shot at my victim that immediately caught fire. At that I found myself another machine that I shot at from directly astern. After some hits the left engine caught fire. The flames, at first small, grew rapidly until the DB-3 rolled to the left and plunged vertically into the forest and burned. That was my first *Abschuss*.

The inexperience of this serious-minded young pilot (only 19 at the time) is obvious in this account, and just over a week later, on 3 July 1941 he was unable to achieve a repeat performance, as he wrote in his dairy for that day once again.[23]

Today I flew with Jochen (*Leutnant* Steffens) over Rogatschew. East of it we saw a DB-3 bomber, that I attacked first, but without any result. Jochen then shot it down, so that it belly-landed. Then he shot it up on the ground until it burned. Soon after that we happened upon two more DB-3s. I took the front one, Jochen the back one. I attacked several times and soon could only fire with the machine guns as the cannon had jammed. However I was missing by a wide margin, as Jochen told me later. Jochen had already shot his down and now guided my next attack. I hit him many times, but also missed with many shots. The right engine was smoking, the undercarriage fell out, but the plane flew on. Suddenly several Ratas crossed our path about 600 m ahead, but appeared not to have seen us yet. We approached ever closer. Jochen said 'Attack the DB-3 again, I will watch out!' However, I let myself be distracted by the Ratas and fired from too far away. Then we turned away and flew home at top speed.

No claim was entered by Strelow for this combat.

Also flying in support of Army Group Centre were *Stab*, *I* and *III/JG 53*. Among the members of the latter *Gruppe* was *Unteroffizier* Alfred Seidl, who summed up their duties in this theatre:

In June 1941 we flew from Mannheim to East Prussia (Suwalki) where we took part in the Russian campaign until the beginning of October 1941. Initially I only flew as a *Rottenflieger* (*Katschmareck* – wingman), and then later as a *Rottenführer*. In Russia we flew low-level attacks, protected the panzers of Army Group Centre (area of Wilna-Smolensk-Jarzewo), and escorted our bombers, Stukas and reconnaissance aircraft. We had aerial combats with Russian fighters, low-level ground attack aircraft, reconnaissance aircraft and bomber formations. For the last few weeks in Russia we were deployed in the south: Kiev pocket battle and then to the Dniepr River. After this we left our aircraft with *JG 51* and flew back to Warsaw with Ju 52s. After that we converted to the Bf 109 F-4, and *III/JG 53* moved to Husum, on the German Bight.

The main *Luftwaffe* fighter presence over Kiev was *JG 3*, flying in support of Army Group South. *Feldwebel* Alfred Heckmann was an experienced pilot with *4/JG 3* who had already shot down his first three victories over France and England in 1940, claiming a further 24 by October 1941 over Russia:[24] 'During 1941–1942, the Russians did not use good formations, and these tended to scatter with the first attack on them. Their aircraft were also inferior to our machines.'

The wide open spaces of Russia and a frontline that was often porous as a result, where intense battle was not being fought, allowed many a German fighter pilot to return from forced landings far behind the lines. One such lucky flier was the veteran *Oberfeldwebel* Josef Ederer of *3/JG 53*:

In 1941 in Russia, I had to force-land after being hit by flak, *c.* 100 km into Russian territory. After crashing against a railway embankment the canopy was stuck. It took a lot of trouble for me to be able to get out of the machine, after which I fled frantically from approaching Russians, through a wheat field. After walking for seven hours through enemy territory, I reached German positions. A motorbike dispatch rider from the infantry brought me back to my field base. I had been shot down in the early morning, at about 04h30, and on the same day, by 23h00 I had reached my base again. During the campaign I destroyed or shot up several aircraft on the ground at Russian airbases, and attacked forces on the ground repeatedly. The spirit amongst the fighter pilots was excellent.

I/JG 53 was pulled out of the Russian campaign in early August 1941 already (they would return for a few months during the advance on Stalingrad in 1942), as was the *Stab/JG 53* as well; the *II Gruppe* of *JG 53* flying over Leningrad remained till early October before they too were withdrawn.[25]

The *Stab*, *II* and *III Gruppen* of *JG 27* were also relatively short-lived participants in the Russian theatre, *II Gruppe* departing in late July already and the other two units in mid-October; none of them returned to the theatre.[26] Pilots from *III/JG 27* particularly recall the early onset of the night nuisance raiders, light Po-2 biplanes that circled German lines and airfields for most of the night hours, dropping desultory small bombs to disturb soldiers and airmen alike from much-needed sleep and rest, and the manoeuvrability of the Russian Ratas. *Feldwebel* Heinrich Rosenberg, *9/JG 27* reported:

> In Russia in 1941 the German fighters were superior, technically and tactically. The Russians flew obstinately on in formation and we were able to attack them and shoot them down from one side of the (bomber) formation to the other. This was obviously not the rule but it did happen. The manoeuvrable 'Rata' (I-16) very rapidly flew at one from head-on, when attacked. On the ground we lived rather primitively in tents, mostly in swampy ground next to our airfields, and at night were often disturbed by quietly flying biplanes, known as 'sewing machines', that threw small bombs overboard by hand.

His colleague *Oberleutnant* Erhard Braune, *Staffelkapitän* *7/JG 27* provided a brief but insightful comment on the main German and Russian fighters in 1941. 'On aerial combat with the "Rata" one can only say that due to its extraordinary manoeuvrability, a Messerschmitt (*"Grossraumvogel"*; i.e. needed large airspace to manoeuvre) could only be successful when surprise was achieved. The Russian pilots themselves were not very "manoeuvrable", particularly in the case of the bombers that flew without effective escort, which led to serious losses.'

JG 52 was spread across half of Europe, with the *Stab* and *III Gruppe* in Romania under the direct command of the *Kommodore, Major* Hanns Trübenbach (of whom more below), and *I/JG 52* was in Holland until late September 1941, when they joined *II Gruppe* in the renewed advance on Moscow.[27] A surviving pilot's logbook from *Unteroffizier* Adolf Glunz, flying with *4/JG 52* on the Central Front, gives a picture of operational tasks for an individual pilot in Russia during the first few weeks of the campaign (see the table below). What is rather surprising is that few days show more than one operation, reflecting a rather relaxed campaign, at least for this pilot. Note also the frequent changes of air bases due to the rapid advance eastwards of the German armies in the first few weeks before the Russian stand at Smolensk, and the large number of free chase missions that he was able to fly.

Example of a fighter pilot's operational life, Eastern Front 1941, based on flying logbook, 22 June 1941–16 July 1941: *Unteroffizier* Adolf Glunz, *4/JG 52*. (Adolf Glunz via Lothair Vanoverbeke)

JUNE

9–13:   *II/JG 52* moves from **Ostende**, via Münster, Lüneburg, Stargard, Elbing to **Suwalki**.

22:     Stuka escort, 02h50–03h46 (24th operational flight, or *Feindflug*)
        Low-level attacks on airfields, 15h50–17h00 (25th *Feindflug*)

23:     Free chase, 16h45–17h54 (26th *Feindflug*)

24:     Low-level attacks on tanks at Grodno, 17h46–18h43 (27th *Feindflug*)

25:     *II/JG 52* moves to **Varena**

26:     Scramble, 09h30–09h57 (28th *Feindflug*); DB 3 shot down (3rd *Abschuss*)

28:     *II/JG 52* moves to **Maladzyechna**

30:     Scramble, 13h45–13h58 (29th *Feindflug*)

JULY

1:      Free chase, 09h25–10h25 (30th *Feindflug*)

3:      Free chase, 17h28–18h56 (31st *Feindflug*); 2 DB-3s shot down near Borisew (4th and 5th *Abschüsse*)

6:      15h20–15h45; *II/JG 52* moves to **Sloboda**, and from 16h35–16h50, moves to **Lepel**
        Scramble, 18h05–18h30 (32nd *Feindflug*); combat with DB-3

7:      Free chase, 19h05–20h14 (33rd *Feindflug*)

8:      Free chase, 18h15–18h55 (34th *Feindflug*); early return due to engine trouble

9:      Free chase, 13h12–13h54 (35th *Feindflug*)

10:     Free chase and escort, 19h22–20h43 (36th *Feindflug*); Gerodet–Witebsk area

11:     Free chase, 04h44–06h05 (37th *Feindflug*)
12:     Free chase, 18h16–19h04 (38th *Feindflug*); combat with DB-3, broken
        off due to weapons being jammed
13:     *II/JG 52* moves to **Vitebsk**
14:     Free chase, 03h32–04h40 (39th *Feindflug*)
        Patrol base, 16h13–17h30 (40th *Feindflug*)
16:     Free chase, 04h50–05h42 (41st *Feindflug*); landed early due to engine trouble

Adolf Glunz himself had this to say of his short service on the Russian front:

> I was only there for three weeks at the beginning of the Russian campaign and shot down three twin-engined bombers (DB-3s). After that I was transferred to the Channel coast again and achieved all my other victories there. It is true to say that at least the Russian bombers flew very stubbornly through our area to reach their targets. I have seen how entire formations of 20 to 30 machines were shot down by us with no survivors. It was different with the fighters. While they were significantly slower than our Me 109s, they were in contrast enormously manoeuvrable, such that we could not enter into dogfights with them. Our strength lay, due to our high speed, rather in surprise attacks. The Russians mostly reacted too late. Allied to this was most likely a not very good training received by them, which could explain their stubbornness.

Stubbornly pushing through to their targets could also mark the Russian bomber pilots as being very brave, but this seldom seems to have occurred to the German fighter pilots, who often assumed poor piloting skills and insufficient training of their opponents, almost as a matter of course.

By the end of August 1941, *Leutnant* Hans Strelow in *5/JG 51* had become more experienced, and his growing confidence as a result of this began to pay off. In a diary entry[28] for 30 August he describes several encounters with small formations of Russian bombers and fighters typical of much of the fighting in the East, and the sad end of a courageous Russian rear-gunner. In an exhibition of slight *Schadenfreude* Strelow even felt sorry for the Russian – briefly. Also of note in this diary extract is the description of attacking a Mig-1 fighter from very close range, and seeing an explosion and the aircraft then descending smoking heavily, only to recover and fly on – this illustrates the ever-present difficulty for a pilot flying a high-speed aircraft in violent manoeuvres to observe fully the fate of one of his possible victims in order to confirm his victory claim.

Today *Feldwebel* Mink and I each shot down three Russians. It happened as follows: we were sitting in our aircraft at immediate readiness – which we recently did more often, as otherwise the scramble took too long – when suddenly the heavy flak opened up. That meant for us to take off immediately. We leapt into the air and immediately received the direction that the retreating Russians were taking, the two of us in hot pursuit. Suddenly I saw in the far distance two machines crossing our path in a north-easterly direction. I reported this, and we pressed on after them. However it took quite a while until we closed with them. Then we could see that they consisted of three bombers (Pe-2) and one fighter (J-18) (Mig-1).

When the bombers saw us – we closed on them at about 1,500 m altitude – they dived to pick up speed and to reach ground level before us, because they were vulnerable in their bellies. Mink said, 'I will take the J-18, you go for the bombers.' I got within range (*c.* 100 m) of the left-hand bomber at about 400 m altitude, gave a first few short bursts of fire at the rear gunner and then from 70-30 m range shot the right engine into flames. As the gunner was no longer firing, I flew about 30 m away from the burning aircraft and saw how the gunner pulled himself up in his position and then stood there looking around. When he saw me, he shook his fist at me. Then he looked forwards towards his pilot, completely helplessly and desperately, then at the earth, and then at me again. He was now flying at only about 15 m above the ground and could thus not bail out. The strange thing was that his helplessness affected me also for a moment. I thought to myself, 'How will he get out of this?' Then the machine was already hitting the tree tops and then taking half trees with him and – bang – it was lying in the forest, now just a sea of flames.

In the meantime, *Feldwebel* Mink had already shot down the J-18. I went for the second bomber, and then saw at once that about 800 m ahead of us there was another formation of exactly the same make-up – three Pe-2s, one J-18. For the second bomber I needed two attacks. On the first the rear gunner ceased fire, on the second the right-hand engine caught fire. The machine flew straight into the ground at a shallow angle just like the first one. As the third Pe-2 had unobtrusively vanished in the meantime, we pulled after the formation in front of us, which took quite some time. We were already 120 km past the frontline. The area where we were flying had long ago left my map behind.

This time I took the fighter and Mink went for the bombers; a good honest division of labour. None of these boys noticed anything, not even the fighter, even though Mink was hanging close behind him at the same height. As the bunch of aircraft were flying at a height of 1,000 m, I wanted to attack the fighter in a classic manoeuvre from below, but I pulled up too fast and found myself behind him instead. When I was 50 m away from him, Mink said, 'Shoot now!' But I waited till there was only 30 m between us. I had closed slowly, aimed carefully and now – rrrrt. There in front of me I could see only the smoke of an explosion, oil and petrol vapour and small flying fragments. As I saw no more of the J-18, I pulled away and saw then that it was disappearing downwards trailing a thick smoke trail. In the meantime Mink had got a bomber. The J-18 flew on below me for a short way, but it must have crashed; but I said to myself that could still take a while. Craftily he now placed himself exactly beneath the one Pe-2, so that he was well covered by the bombers' ventral gunner. However I attacked him again and from 30 m hit him again, as Mink started to yell at me, 'Pull up, pull up!' I had actually expected this because of the Pe-2 and then pulled away. I watched as the J-18 burned lightly from his exhausts and from underneath the engine covers. Then Mink reported he had crashed into the forest. Together we shot down a second Pe-2. Then we turned about, flying straight for home and arrived – more by chance than design – exactly over our base. There was much joy on the ground as we both waggled our wings three times over the field. The *Staffelkapitän* – *Oberleutnant* Grasser – was especially glad at my three *Abschüsse*.

However, it was not just Russians being lost, and on the very next day one of the leading aces of *JG 53*, *Oberleutnant* Erich Schmidt of the *III Gruppe*, was shot down. Like many another German fighter pilot he is known to have survived being shot down, but never returned and became one of the many missing servicemen of the Eastern Front. *Oberfeldwebel* Josef Kronschnabel, 9/*JG 53* describes his demise: '*Leutnant* Erich Schmidt was a brave and spirited fighter pilot and an example to us. He was respected as a person, friendly, and being always in a good mood was generally held in great affection by all. He was shot down attacking a Russian airfield (bailed out near Dubno).[29] Some weeks later the Russians dropped leaflets over the German lines, on which a photograph of a column of German prisoners was shown with Schmidt at the front and he thus obviously entered captivity unwounded. As I never heard anything of him ever again, he must have died in captivity.'

Horst Geyer, whom I met in September 1990 while he was on a holiday in South Africa, had a very interesting career. He had originally trained as a fighter pilot in 1936, after which he was a test pilot at the *Luftwaffe*'s Rechlin Test Centre. He began the war as a *Leutnant* with *KG 2* flying fuel into frontline airfields during the Polish campaign. After his return to Rechlin, he was appointed as Udet's adjutant. *General* Udet, a famous ace of the First World War (62 victories) and an extremely gifted pilot, was head of the *Luftwaffe*'s technical section and also in charge of aircraft production. Geyer remembered him as a wonderful person, very popular and loved by the troops, but no soldier. In his new job Geyer got to visit many frontline units with his chief during the invasion of France and the Battle of Britain.

One of these visits was to Werner Mölders, then *Kommodore* of *JG 51* on the Channel coast, and as a result Horst got himself a temporary posting to this *Geschwader* from January to May 1941. But after that it was back to his adjutant's job. In July he wangled himself another short attachment to Mölders' *Geschwader*, joining *5/JG 51* on the Russian front where he was able to claim 11 victories up till early September 1941. Then on 14 September, while flying home from a sortie just below a cloud bank, some Mig fighters suddenly flashed past overhead from head-on. Unseen by *Oberleutnant* Geyer and his wingman, the Migs turned around and came back, and Horst was suddenly shocked to hear and feel hits on his aircraft – the windshield on his left was shattered and his instrument panel hit. The offending Mig didn't take the chance to finish him off, but turned back and headed for home. Geyer in the meantime started feeling a bit faint, then saw blood coming out of his left glove; a bullet had gone through his left hand near the thumb, travelled further through his instrument panel, his boot and foot, and then out – the floor of his aircraft was covered in blood which explained his feeling faint. With the moral support of his wingman he made it back to his airfield and was sent to hospital in Königsberg, where his wife and daughter were living. After recovering he rejoined his boss Udet once again.

Also in September 1941, Hans Strelow was much more successful in an encounter with a Mig-1 fighter, being able to redress the harm inflicted on his *5/JG 51 Staffelkamerad* Geyer by dispatching one with only seven rounds of cannon ammunition. The combat was described in his diary entry[30] for 6 September:

At the moment we are stationed in Nowgorod, ... I have just been flying again with Mink and – boom – we have again found something to shoot at. We were just out flying a free chase mission when *Feldwebel* Mink reported flak bursts to the north of us. We roared off in that direction, throttles wide open. I saw the two machines first; the flak was aimed at two Russian fighters, who were flying off to the east, and they were soon recognisable as J-18s (Mig-1s). I stayed a bit behind my *Rottenführer* and couldn't quite keep up despite his having throttled back. The J-18s were flying in *c.* 200 m altitude, and we were at only 20 m, so that they would not see us. The right hand Russian also flew a bit behind his leader, as we noticed as we got closer. Mink attacked the front one. I stayed behind him so that my sudden appearance would not scare our prey. As he shot, the leading J-18 immediately showed a smoke trail; however the left-hand one noticed something and pulled sharp right across in front of the other one and seemed to want to get behind Mink. He had not noticed me at all. Mink let him briefly fly through his fire, then I turned in right behind him, cutting across the Russian's curve, and as long as I could hold my turn gave him three short bursts from my cannon. When he was turning too tightly for me to follow, I pulled up, so as to attack him again from above. While still pulling up I saw him make a roll and then spin down to the right from only 200 m to crash and explode on the ground. Then I flew towards my *Rottenführer*, and saw how his J-18 made a belly-landing on a marshy meadow, skidding for the last 30-40 m sideways along the ground. We shot the machine up on the ground, without it catching fire, and then flew home again. There it turned out that only ten rounds from the 2-cm cannon and 45 rounds from each of the machine guns had been fired. According to this usage I had only required 7 cannon shells for my *Abschuss*. Mink told me he had seen fragments flying off the tail of the machine. This was my nicest *Abschuss* to date: a fighter in a turn with seven rounds of ammunition.

Of interest here is the fact that *Leutnant* Strelow flew as wingman to his more experienced NCO comrade and obeyed his orders in the air; once on the ground again their relative seniority would be reversed. This was a general practice in *Luftwaffe* fighter circles, that the most experienced pilot led a *Rotte* or *Schwarm* irrespective of rank. The very next day, Strelow had a frightening experience of the vast spaces of Russia, getting himself horribly lost after a combat, as detailed in his diary entry of 8 September 1941:

Yesterday I experienced one of the most unpleasant missions up till now, although I did manage to shoot down an SB-2 on it. I had taken off with *Oberleutnant* Grasser as part of the indirect escort for Stukas to Konotop. There were lots of cumulus clouds and strong glare from the sun. Suddenly bombers were reported amongst the clouds. I saw straight away two lone bombers, of which *Oberleutnant* Grasser wanted to take the right-hand one, but it was shot away from in front of his nose. I took the left-hand bomber. He flew through every available cloud. But I waylaid him and on the first attack from behind shot up his right engine so that it smoked heavily. Then I had to turn away as the rear gunners stubbornly defended the aircraft from dorsal and ventral positions, and on my second attack I came in from directly behind and took a bead on him.

First I shot only with the two machine guns and then in the shortest bursts with the cannon directly into the fuselage. The gunners thereupon soon stopped shooting. I then shot up the left-hand engine, which only showed a thin smoke trail. The left-hand undercarriage leg fell out. I then pulled past him at my leisure to the right as the bomber was now flying damn slowly, to get myself away from him again. Then I saw that the elevator was entirely missing up to the wingtip except for a few ribs still visible. In the fuselage there were holes the size of dinner plates from my cannon shells. I then had to fly a 360 degree circle ... and saw how another Me 109 then attacked the bomber and shouted at me over the radio, 'Don't shoot! This herring belongs to both of us!' My colleague then turned away, but told me after the landing that almost half the rudder had also been missing. I then approached him slowly once more and shot into the left hand wing tank that immediately went up in flames. The aircraft descended at a shallow angle from 50 m height, hit the ground and burned there.

That was my eighth *Abschuss*. Subsequently I shot up an R-3 also, flying very low, but had to turn away as firstly another R-3 was sitting behind me and shooting at me, secondly because my windscreen became completely covered in oil, and thirdly as I was quite alone. *Oberleutnant* Grasser had told me after my *Abschuss* that he was ahead of me and to the right; I also saw him in the distance. When I got closer, however, it turned out to be the R-3. After that I had no more radio contact with him and wanted to fly home. I assumed that I was near Konotop (my *Abschuss* had been at Krolewetz) and flew to the north. Now came the grand tour. I flew and flew. Actually, I should have soon reached Nowgorod. However it did not appear. I must have passed it already, but did not know if I had done so to the east or west of it. I still had 200 litres of fuel. I flew even further to the north, then somewhat to the west, then to the north again. Now I only had 130 litres of fuel left. I saw no reference point to orientate myself. Gradually I began to sweat, I did not even know if I was above Russian territory or over my own troops.

Suddenly I saw a city in the far distance, and flew towards it. I could not find it on the map, and my red fuel warning light was already burning. I flew over the city at 10 m height, to see whether it was occupied by the Germans or the Russians. They were Russians. I noticed straight roads that ran parallel to the railway line. I looked for it again on the map and found it exactly on the top edge. 'To Briansk' was printed next to it. My city was Karatschew, east of Briansk. I was overjoyed once I had worked this out. My red light was burning brightly as I flew in the direction of

Tjecktschinskaja, which was the safest for me. After exactly two hours in the air, I landed there with an already lightly coughing engine. The flight had eaten away at my nerves like only one other, on the first day of the war, to Radom.

Some less fortunate fighter pilots had to fly the Me 110 rather than the sleek Me 109 F; they also had to carry out far more of the dangerous ground attack missions to which this aircraft was ideally suited, although losses to the ever-effective Russian flak were always to be reckoned with. *Unteroffizier* Josef Neuhaus, 6/ZG 26 was one of these *Zerstörer* pilots. 'In 1941 we moved to Suwalki in East Prussia for the Russian campaign. From June 1941 until summer 1942 I flew *Zerstörer* operations on the Northern, Central and Southern fronts: low-level attacks strafing troops, vehicles, railways, also using 50 kg bombs. My personal successes included thirteen aerial victories claimed, eighteen locomotives destroyed as well as *c.* 450 vehicles on the ground. I was wounded quite seriously twice, but was able to return to my base each time. In autumn 1942 the entire unit moved to Germany for conversion to night fighters.'

The German Luftwaffe Mission to Romania

Far to the south of all the activities of Army Group Centre, and removed even from those of Army Group South, *Major* Hanns Trübenbach, *Kommodore* of *JG 52*, found himself transferred to the relative backwater of Romania just before *Barbarossa* began, as he describes below. Despite his senior appointment in Romania he was determined to still fly active operations whenever possible, and was also the first to use a centrally mounted 30 cm MK 108 cannon on the Me 109 F.

On 20 June 1941 came the transfer order for Bucharest. I flew via Vienna–Aspern, where we exchanged our aircraft for the very latest version of the Me 109 F. This machine had the legendary centrally placed cannon, calibre 3 cm, Type MK 108, as well as two extra-heavy machine guns, that shot between the propeller blades while the cannon shot through the propeller hub; that means that all weapons were aligned with the long axis of the aircraft's fuselage.

Because I came originally from the *Lehrgeschwader* (*Kommandeur I/LG 2*) I always got to use the latest models with the newest improvements. While in Vienna I was invited to supper by my old chief from the Seaplane School List at Sylt, 1927-1928, *General* Scheurlen. He was a long-time friend of our then-ambassador in Moscow, Count von Schulenburg. After the partition of Poland by Russia and Germany, one day the Japanese Ambassador was seen off by Stalin at the railway station. As Stalin waved to the departing Japanese

Ambassador he shortly thereafter put his arm around the Count and said, 'My dear Schulenburg, now nothing more can go wrong with us two.' This event was described by our German Ambassador to Moscow, Graf von Schulenburg, to his friend the *Luftwaffe General* Heinz Scheurlen on his subsequent visit to Germany. This memorable supper in the well-known Viennese restaurant 'Drei Hussaren' was no meeting under four eyes only, but took place in the presence of my own Ia, *Hauptmann* Kirschstein and an *Oberleutnant* Leo from the staff of *General* Scheurlen. It was thus witnessed and the truth thereof soon confirmed.

Up until 22 June 1941 Stalin let the unending trainloads of grain, ore etc. from the Ukraine roll to Germany, as had been agreed in the treaty with Russia. When Hitler gave the order to invade Russia and after the first shots had already been fired, the trains loaded with ore were still being processed at the border by the customs services. One whispered behind your hand that the German foreign minister von Ribbentrop had long been informed that Hitler's war must be accepted as inevitable. This also, in those weeks thus, when Stalin and Count von Schulenberg together with the Japanese Ambassador still lived with the certainty that the axis Moscow-Berlin-Tokyo would preserve the peace. And so I flew with my adjutant *Oberleutnant* Wiese and our brand new aircraft to Bucharest–Pipera and on 5 July 1941 took over the air control of Romania as *Jagdfliegerführer* (*Jafü* – fighter leader) of the German *Luftwaffe* Mission, to protect the oil fields of Ploiesti. My *Geschwaderstab* was stationed complete at the large airfield of Pipera, the flying units on airfields such as Mamaia near Constanza, Mizil and Otopeni. Some Romanian fighter units were also placed under me tactically.

Building up and overseeing such a difficult protective task kept me for a long time in Bucharest and on the inner Romanian fields. On the northern edge of Bucharest, at the airbase of Otopeni, the Rumanian *VI Jagdgruppe* was stationed, that was tactically subordinated to me, equipped with Polish PZL fighter aircraft. Before my time in Romania, probably in the area around Ploiesti, within two days they had apparently scored thirty-seven *Abschüsse* under the leadership of their *Kommandeur Hauptmann* Bascilla, while *III/JG 52* whose Staffeln were stationed in Mizil and Mamaia, knew nothing about Russian incursions and as a result were severely criticised by Göring. On 11 July 1941 the Romanian commander was then summoned for an explanation, on whose authority and on what grounds remained unknown to me, as basically I wanted nothing to do with the Romanian air force leadership. The tactical subordination of Romanian fighters to me was in any case only sporadic and was never utilised by me either. On 13 July the 9th *Staffel* of *III/JG 52* was in Mizil, the 7th and 8th *Staffeln* were already with the *Gruppenstab* in Mamaia. And my complete *Geschwader* staff was safely at Bucharest–Pipera and enjoyed its life there, as it had almost no work to perform. Apart from Wiese and me the other staff gentlemen included no pilots. This entire, somewhat strange-seeming military situation around Bucharest and Ploiesti, which I encountered already when I took over, was related of course to the rapid advance of the front to the east.

Seeing as my adjutant had not yet scored any victories, I asked for permission to be able to carry out some active missions again at last. As my *I* and *II Jagdgruppen* were stationed, respectively, in Holland and the central front in Russia, there remained only the *III Gruppe* (of *JG 52*) as well as the flying *Geschwaderstabs-Rotte* consisting of Wiese and yours truly. Until the end of October 1941 I had no enemy contact over Romania! With the permission of my commanding general in Bucharest I decided to move my *Stabsrotte* with the minimum necessary ground staff to Tiraspol, a freed-up field base, about 300 km north-eastwards of Bucharest.

Before the small team was in place in Tiraspol, I had the opportunity on 13 July to carry out an extended reconnaissance together with *Oberleutnant* Wiese. As was our practice we flew far apart in about 4,000 m altitude, in order to have a wide view. Over the Black Sea we climbed to 6,000 m but without seeing anything at all. Having turned northwards we approached the enormous Danube delta that formed a huge swampy area east of Tulcea. It had an extent of about 50–60 square kilometres and was bordered in both north and south by tributaries of the Danube. Anyone who had to force-land here would be lost. When we began running out of time and I was just going to turn southwards again, I saw a small formation of Russian Martin bombers about 35 km north-eastwards of Tulcea, flying eastwards. And as luck would have it flying at only 300 m above this dreadful jungle area. I thought to myself that such a fat twin-engined buzzard would make a fitting prey for my central cannon, and dived down at full throttle to their height. Then I was able to hit the cockpit and the right-hand engine after only a few tracer rounds of the MK 108, the engine burning immediately. Then the bomber dived straight down into the water. As already noted above, this cannon and the aircraft's axis were the same. One could see the individual rounds leaving the cannon and even when flying inverted one could easily aim with the entire machine and send the rounds wherever you wanted them to go. Unfortunately we could not attack again, as we had urgently to head back for Mamaia. Force-landings due to running out of fuel were severely punished!

This victory of *Major* Trübenbach has been related to a raid on the Ploiesti oilfields, which is also described as having caused heavy damage in a published source.[31] As the person responsible for the aerial defence of

Ploiesti at the time, Hanns Trübenbach was able to clarify the situation in Romania:

> If on this day (13 July 1941) even one bomb had fallen on my area of protective responsibility, Ploiesti/Bucharest/Snagowsee, then I would immediately have been placed before a court martial. My *Abschuss* north of Tulcea over the outer reaches of the Danube delta anyway had nothing to do with any attack on Ploiesti. Also, in the entire time of my command of the fighter forces protecting Ploiesti, no aircraft of *JG 77* were operating over Romania, as I had nothing whatsoever to do with this *Geschwader*. In Romania during my official command there, the units of *Jagdgeschwader 77* fell under totally different command structures and were already moving to the front in Russia. That these units were stationed up in the Jassy area, that is in the north of Romania and were also being rapidly regrouped by *Luftflotte 4*, had nothing to do with my command responsibility of the German *Luftwaffe* Mission in Bucharest. When I am thus talking about Romania then this implies always 'my Romania' where during my entire time there not a single bomb fell, even when other commands assumed this to have happened, such as the so-called *Luftwaffe* Southeast Command had done and which I was never aware of, up to today (1994). This command was most likely an army unit or some other higher command of the army group, with whom I had nothing to do. I also never heard anything about such an organisation from my commanding *General* Speidel, as we fell *directly* under the authority of the *Reichsminister* of the *Luftwaffe* and Supreme Commander Göring.

Hanns Trübenbach had a long wait with diverse duties in Romania, a trip to Hitler's headquarters in East Prussia and a lunch with various dignitaries and the *Führer* in Odessa before he was able to get back to flying active operations again, based with his two-man *Geschwaderstab JG 52* in Tiraspol. Once there he was able to make up for lost time.

> During my entire time in Romania I never saw a single German infantryman, as the army was already long past Odessa, and similarly Tiraspol airbase had also already been left behind by the *Luftwaffe*. For my specially approved frontal flights from Tiraspol I thus had to bring my own *Geschwaderstab* people from Bucharest–Pipera with me to Tiraspol, such as mechanics and armourers and radio mechanics. And during this entire period, the deepest peace reigned around all of the Bucharest area.
>
> While situated at the field base Tiraspol, about 60 km northwest of Odessa, my plan to fly active missions (*Frontflüge*) so that my young adjutant *Oberleutnant* Wiese could also get to make closer contact with air combat,

was suddenly interrupted. I received the order to report at the *Führer's* Headquarters in East Prussia at the *Wolfsschanze* as soon as possible. On 21 August 1941, Wiese and I flew in the Me 108 via Winniza to East Prussia. The advanced headquarters of *Luftflotte* Southeast lay in Winniza. Once there I reported as was customary to the chief of staff, General Korten, whose mother was a long-time friend of my mother-in-law in Essen. He told me in a very serious tone that if we did not conquer the oil area of Maikop by late autumn, then our flying would be limited to exhibitions only. Now, as the war's history would show, we did conquer Maikop (in 1942), but most of the oil installations were completely destroyed.

In 1944 in the attempt on Hitler's life the completely innocent Chief of the *Luftwaffe's* General Staff, Korten, was seriously wounded by the bomb. He died as a result. Once we had landed in East Prussia, I was informed it was high time that I stopped flying at the front. Due to my wide and long experience I was to take over the *Jagdgeschwader 104* in Nurmberg–Fürth (a training *Jagdgeschwader*), that comprised two *Gruppen*. And subsequently I was to become a fighter leader or senior controller (*Jagdfliegerführer*) in the Home Defence. I thereupon asked the Inspector for permission to maintain my command in Romania until 1 November, so that I could at least get in some frontal flights with the new weapon (3 cm cannon). This was granted. Then we flew together again, to visit our families for a few hours, and on 28 August 1941, landed back in Bucharest, having come from Prague.

In Romania there was still much for me to do, especially with the individual defensive fighter units. Then after the fall of Odessa Hitler made a rapid decision to visit the front there, and I was invited to lunch there. At lunch in the city, where I was a guest, as well as one of my *Jagdgruppenkommandeurs* directly from the advancing front line, Hitler wanted to know exactly how accurate the Russian flak was. Field Marshall Keitel immediately cut in and said the Russian flak was not worth mentioning at all. At this, Hitler, quite annoyed, asked my young *Kommandeur* if he could substantiate this. 'No,' this young pilot said, 'I can only confirm the opposite, as there are significant losses to flak at the front.' Now, the effectiveness of flak was always based on personal experience, and I had to admit in concert with Wiese to never having been hit by Russian flak at all. At the end of the meal we were able to go and see the old German tram coaches that had been running in Odessa since 1914!

Due to these and other internal reasons I could only get round to re-joining Wiese and our machines in Tiraspol on 16 September 1941 where we occupied our old quarters. Here in the region of Tiraspol/Odessa there were many contacts with the well-known Ratas that had already flown on the Republican side in the Spanish Civil War. On 18 September we were flying in a cloudy sky and quite suddenly found ourselves in the middle of a bunch of about 25 of these buzzards. These extremely manoeuvrable fighters attacked us immediately from all sides, so that we had to first of all save ourselves by climbing steeply away and then at our leisure watch what these boys would do. Then we watched as two Ratas detached themselves from the formation and took us on from below, shooting almost vertically up at us, and with this stupid move lost their comrades who flew off to the east. Then this pair dived steeply to within a few hundred metres of the ground. We were in close pursuit and I had to open fire from far away while the two were still flying on a fixed course to join up with their comrades. With our fast Me 109 Fs we quickly caught up with the now wildly manoeuvring Russians. I followed all the twists and turns of the Rata and could thus watch the trajectories of my 3 cm tracer rounds very easily. Eventually we were both flying inverted! I aimed now only with the aircraft itself and my rounds drilled into the fuselage of the Rata. It flew apart and crashed in flames.

In this region the Russians tended to fly only in medium altitudes; we were told that they only had limited oxygen facilities and always had to try and save them. In these aerial combats we both had to be hellishly careful as we were only two. On 19 September Wiese and I flew four missions without meeting any enemy aircraft, but wondered why everywhere we went we received strong flak fire. When Wiese eventually got his first victory, we found ourselves in a complete muddle of these nimble Ratas. Because I had to obviously confirm this victory and perforce for a few seconds had my eyes on this, a Rata was able to attack me from head-on, hitting some of my instruments and on pulling rapidly up I could only hope to be able to reach Tiraspol with my hide in one piece. There the mechanics established that only a single round (a machine gun armour-piercing bullet) had passed obliquely through the left-hand engine bearer, thereby losing its armoured casing and with the armour-piercing core then passing un-deformed through the upper left carriage plate of the MG 151, penetrating through to the base of the breach. Seeing as Wiese had also received some hits we had to quickly fly our aircraft to the workshops in Mamaia to get our birds serviceable again. The mechanics had to use a blowtorch three times before they could get the bullet core out for me as a souvenir. Today (1990) it stands on my desk, even if only the bullet core (a very interesting fabrication). If the Rata had aimed only 5 mm higher or lower, I would have been finished.

On 22 September we were back at the front and under strong flak fire had an air combat with four Ratas – but without result. On 23 September we made a low-level attack on a Russian auxiliary field base and destroyed some trucks under strong flak fire. On the same day I was able to surprise a Rata and hit it with a single 3 cm explosive round in the belly, upon which it exploded into a thousand pieces and I had to quickly warn Wiese to pull away upwards, so that he did not fly into the middle of this floating mass of fragments. On the 24 September we flew another three missions, with a combat with six Pe-2 bombers and seven Ratas without any visible definite result (one bomber and one Rata possibly shot down – but probables did not count). On 25 September, another three missions each of something more than an hour followed. Before midday we landed unexpectedly in a swirling mass of 15 Ratas, who attacked us from all sides so that we were unable to get into position to shoot. It was a wild dogfight that had to end without result. Thereafter I had to go with Wiese to Bucharest for some days for receipt of further orders and also to visit the troops.

On 1 October 1941 we were back in Tiraspol and flew four missions with heavy flak fire, without seeing anything in the air. Then on the next day we had a completely unique experience which achieved some publicity. 'Radio and Press Release of 4 and 5 October. A Soviet tank advance forced back by low-level attack: Two aircraft of a German *Jagdgeschwader*, flown by the *Kommodore* and an *Oberleutnant* turned back an advance of Soviet tanks against an artillery position on 2 October 1941 in a heroic operation. In ten successive low-level attacks the two fighter pilots destroyed four enemy tanks and forced the rest to flee. The attack was carried out against the fiercest defensive flak fire, from which one of the aircraft received two serious hits. Despite this serious damage the aircraft remained in action and landed safely at its field base after defeating the tank attack.'

Kommodore Major Hanns Trübenbach and Adjutant *Oberleutnant* Johannes Wiese took off from Tiraspol airfield at 09h30 and in lovely weather climbed, as usual, to 4,000 m. As was known this was the height that the Russians generally operated at, and apart from that one could see the airspace as well as the ground below well.

It was pure coincidence that below and to the left we saw a number of red flares being fired, that usually indicated an emergency situation. We descended rapidly and then I recognised in front the tank attack that was developing westwards against the small town of Dalnik. There where red flares continued to be fired I saw that the first tanks had already penetrated into the German position and were attacking an artillery battery that did not possess an adequate anti-tank defence. As we continued to approach closer I reminded myself that these rolling monsters could only be damaged if one aimed at their large exhausts. The air was crystal clear and there wasn't a trace of cloud or mist as we went in. Our Messerschmitts were held very steady as we carefully aimed ahead of the targets with the correct deflection to be able to hit them effectively. And I knew also, that a single 30 cm round from our MK 108 central cannons would suffice to create a disastrous effect in the tanks' interiors. Although we were not hit ourselves, I had to escort Wiese back to the field at low speed as his aircraft was seriously damaged, but he was unwounded as was I – also there had been no Ratas – lucky!

On 5 October I again flew four missions, at about 10h00 there was a brief fight with three Ratas, of which I was able to shoot one down in flames and with that my time at the front came to an end, at least as a flying unit leader. On this day I flew three of the missions with Wiese and then between 13h00 and 14h00 I flew a so-called test flight, to check on my aircraft's condition, while Wiese's machine was still unserviceable. Over the front it appeared to be lunchtime too and so I drifted slowly up to 6,000 m in wonderful visibility. Far to the east I saw a shining object far below that soon showed itself to be a single aircraft and which naturally attracted my interest. I flew further to the east and was able to observe it easily.

When the machine had reached an altitude of about 4,000 m I recognised it as the latest new Mig-3. A marvellous aircraft, painted grass green and polished and shiny like bacon rind, with a red star. I placed myself behind him and then below him; it was a shiny beast as we called such new models in flying jargon. Visible weapons were not to be seen, such as for example our 20 cm Oerlikon cannons in the Me 109 E-4 that stuck out noticeably from the front of the wing. The Russian was still climbing on the same course and flew at a very constant throttle setting to avoid taxing his machine.

As it slowly became time for me to return to Tiraspol, I pulled my Me very close to him so as to see into his cabin from the right-hand side. The sun was on our left and thus illuminated the steadily west-flying pilot, who had still not noticed my long nose. Now I was able to observe at my leisure that this pilot was also performing either a serviceability or a test flight. He had big headphones in his flying helmet and a large paper-covered writing pad on his knees and while constantly watching his instruments, recorded their performance data. And now at last he saw me, pulled his left hand from below the pad and raised both arms from pure astonishment. So we grinned at each other, raised our hands to our caps and greeted each other, while I indicated to him that I would dive away to the starboard. As indicated, so done, each one made his turn away and flew homewards.

If the Russian aircraft was armed or carried any ammunition in case of trouble, I could not determine. In any case I had been in the advantageous position of having been able to easily have got him from all possible angles. It would have been an *Abschuss* without any witness, and apart from that an extremely unfair and cowardly thing to have done. He would have been an easy prey; however in those days one had been raised with too much of a knightly attitude to have shot down a defenceless opponent from behind, that would go totally against the fighter pilot spirit.

On 6 October we had to return to Mamaia on the Black Sea where we arrived at 14h30. As we came in to land I saw a Ju 52 with red crosses standing near the headquarters. To the side were three sisters, of whom one (it was Sister Oberin) was explaining something to an army officer that she could see in his hand. He was an elderly *Major* of the old *Landwehr*, a Herr von Colditz, and we both came from Saxony. I had a vivid memory of a military cavalry exhibition in Dresden where one of his relations jumped with his horse over two adjacent tables, without touching the champagne bottles on them. Sister Oberin let the old man's hand go and told him that his future didn't look so good and that he would also soon lose a relation (his son, *Leutnant* von Colditz, was killed as a tank commander exactly eight days after Sister Oberin had read the lines on his hand). I naturally also wanted my future read and stretched out my hand to her. 'Aah,' she said, 'You cannot die, never!' With a further three operations on 8 October 1941 over the front in the Nikolajew area, Wiese and I flew to Pipera/Bucharest, where our paths finally separated.

Major Hanns Trübenbach, *Kommodore JG 52* belonged to an earlier generation than most Second World War fighter pilots, having already begun his active flying career in 1927; his personal code was thus both honourable and rather rare. Interestingly, his descriptions of dogfighting the I-16 Ratas shows that, at least in his experience, Russian opponents could be highly aggressive and even effective opponents in machines which were so inferior to the Me 109 F.

Advance on Moscow and the Russian Counterattack

While *Kommodore* Trübenbach had been ensuring a bomb-proof southern Romania and leading his single *Rotte* of Messerschmitts into action over the Black Sea area when he got the chance, things further north were heating up considerably. On 30 September 1941, the German armies had regrouped and the armoured units had rejoined Army Group Centre for resumption of the much-delayed advance on Moscow.[32] Despite an initial massive pocket battle at Vyazma–Yelnya that was completed by 23 October 1941 and even more successful than that at Kiev earlier in the campaign, the advance slowly became bogged down under increasingly difficult logistical conditions, the late autumn/early winter mud period and then the onset of a freezing winter, never mind continued Russian resistance.[33]

By mid-October, *Luftwaffe* fighter support for the Moscow battle was reduced to *I/JG 52* (newly arrived from Holland), *II/JG 52*, two *Gruppen* of ZG 26 (one of which left on 18 October) and three of the four *Gruppen* comprising *JG 51* (one of these went to the Leningrad front at the end of October), plus *II* and *III/JG 3* transferred from the southern fronts at the beginning of October, only to depart again after four to six weeks; the *JG 27* and *JG 53* components had departed for Germany and Africa by mid-October.[34] Still operating with *5/JG 51*, *Leutnant* Hans Strelow reported in his diary[35] on a mission flown on 13 October 1941 to Mzensk, between Orel and Tula along the path that *General* Heinz Guderian's panzers were taking towards Moscow; by now he was an experienced fighter pilot trying to teach a comrade how to avoid the same mistakes he had made as a novice.

> This afternoon I flew a free chase mission to Mzensk as *Rottenführer* with *Oberfeldwebel* X. After we had already had a combat with three I-16s, at Mzensk I sighted a R-3 that was flying patrol lines on its own at 1,500 m. We flew towards it and I gave X, who was already an old soldier, the order to attack. He went in and I said, 'Now, throttle back! Slowly!' But he missed, having fired only for a short while, like me in my early fights. Then his guns jammed. I then went in behind the R-3 to 40 m range and fired a couple of bursts, which caused fragments to fly off and after the last burst the oil cooler gave off a strong smoke trail. The undercarriage had also half fallen out. The crate then made a belly-landing on a railway embankment northeast of Mzensk. I shot it up on the ground, but without it catching fire. I gave the *Abschuss* to X, but he would not take credit for it. I then gave him the order to waggle his wings over our base, with which the matter was decided.

By November 1941 the German advance had struggled to within sight of the Kremlin on a clear day in some areas, and even to the outermost outskirts of the vast city in places. Little did the Germans suspect that a stunning surprise and counter-offensive was soon to be launched that would change everything and make it clear that the dream of a *Blitzkrieg* conquest of the Soviet Union was beyond their capabilities in 1941. In fact, Army Group Centre itself would come within an ace of destruction. Another diarist[36] from *JG 51*, Günther Schack, flying in the *III Gruppe*, recorded some of the events and combats of this tense period before the storm broke over Army Group Centre and he kept up the practice till almost the end of the war, summarising also his views on the advantages of flying the Fw 190 later in this theatre and comparing this to the new Russian opponents that he encountered.

> For almost the entire war in the East I kept a diary and shortly after the war I took these four handwritten volumes and typed up a highly summarised version of them (in 800 *Feindflüge* there were by definition many repetitive

activities). Sadly I flew mostly the Me 109, of my 800 operational flights (*Feindflüge* – defined as a flight with enemy contact or an escort mission over enemy territory) I at least got 100 in on the Fw 190, a machine that suited me much better; on these 100 missions I was able to score ninety two victories. The armament of the Fw 190 was much better for me. However, Jak-9s were faster and climbed better.

Hauptmann Günther Schack who flew with *I* and *III/JG 51*, as part of our correspondence in August and September 1989, was kind enough to send me some excerpts from this typed volume of his experiences, and these will be presented at various points in this chapter. Then still a lowly *Gefreiter*, Günther Schack, *7/JG 51* recorded a sad event for 22 November 1941:

In the evening we were sitting with our non-flying general purpose officer, *Oberleutnant* Hamberger, enjoying a pleasant drink, when the *Unteroffizier* on duty entered and reported that *Oberst* Mölders had been killed in an air crash. It was as if St Peter had grieved with us when it rained without a break for the next three days. Then the *Gruppe* was paraded, to remember our beloved *Kommodore* (by then Mölders had already been serving as General of Fighters). From now on we were no longer *JG 51* but *JG 51* Mölders. After the parade I had to report at headquarters: the *Kommandeur* pinned the *Frontflugspange* (missions clasp) in Gold on my chest.

Mölders had been killed as a passenger in the crash of a He 111 bomber in very bad weather, on a flight to Berlin for the state funeral of *General* Udet. As Udet's adjutant, Horst Geyer, who had served in *5/JG 51* with Hans Strelow, was able to report the tragic events personally when I met him in 1990. On 17 November 1941 there was a party at Udet's house in Berlin, and his staff were also in attendance plus a few friends and his girlfriend. Udet was in an apparently very cheerful mood and over lunch asked a doctor friend how best to shoot yourself, and was told that best practice was from the base of the skull, pointing upwards. Geyer left the party early as he was to fly out on duty, but just after take-off for Vienna the undercarriage of his aircraft would not retract and so they landed once more. The airfield was very close to Udet's house and they received the news there that something had happened at the general's house. Geyer rushed back and found that Udet had shot himself on his bed; on the headboard was written in lipstick that Göring had betrayed him (he had removed some of Udet's responsibilities and given them to Göring's deputy, Field Marshall Milch).

Horst Geyer was the *Ordensträger* (bearer of his decorations) at Udet's state funeral later in November and had to hold his decorations for two hours, including the 1 kg Chinese star Udet had been awarded, making his arms very tired. After this shattering experience it was back to the Russian front for him again, as *Staffelkapitän 5/JG 51* till around January 1942. Geyer expressed the opinion that the very high scores the *Luftwaffe* attained in the East in 1941 were due to Russian aircraft and combat tactics being very poor, and that it was much easier to score there than in the West. He himself flew the Rata at the *Luftwaffe's* Rechlin test centre and found it incredibly manoeuvrable but very slow. He also emphasized that the early Russian aircraft had no self-sealing fuel tanks and thus burnt more easily when attacked than German aircraft. They also tended to fly in large and unsystematic formations and often circled aimlessly. Their formations were confused.

Günther Schack was also one of those flying protective sorties over Guderian's tank forces near Tula, which were still trying desperately hard to reach Moscow; his diary for 28 November 1941 recorded a rather unsuccessful mission.

Today we are flying again, a free chase in the area of Kaschira. This is as far as Guderian's advanced panzers have reached, but to get there we have to fly for a long distance over Russian territory, as the route via Tula is too long. However, we had to fly a mission due to bad weather, over Tula itself. The city has been surrounded. From above it has a modern appearance, as the streets are laid out completely symmetrically. A Pe-2 gets away from us in the clouds. In the meantime the real winter has begun. In clear cold weather we are able to fly lots of missions, but unfortunately there are few *Abschüsse*. One has to be lucky to meet a Russian at all. With Brücher (Heinz Brücher) I had the uncommon good luck to meet an enemy right over our airfield, however I was too happy too soon in being able to go through the motions of an *Abschuss*. When I had this machine – as big as a barn door – in front of me and pressed my triggers, the weapons remained silent. Brücher shot at it and it caught fire, however the burning Russian was able to fly on and we could no longer follow him due to being short of fuel.

Just over a week later, at dawn on 6 December 1941, the Russian counteroffensive erupted and German forces were thrown into immediate confusion and for the first time the German army was to suffer a large scale defeat, and near-catastrophic retreat to the west.[37] By then fighter pilots like Günther Schack were experiencing a very changed frontal situation, and although they were largely spared the carnage on the ground the *Jagdgruppen* were also subjected to precipitate retreats. Schack and his colleagues in *7/JG 51* enjoyed a rather depressing Christmas, as he recorded in his diary for 15 December 1941.

> One day we flew from Rusa, to protect ground forces who had to abandon the airfield due to advancing Russians. This was a situation we had not previously experienced. Only the *Kommandeur* was able to shoot down an aircraft; little enough from a fighter combat of six against six. Something is wrong with our leadership in the air. After two days we also move to the west. How things have changed. The advance has petered out, as one says, in the mud and due to insufficient supplies. Once again we are flying from Juchnow. Dietrich, who had visited me in Malojaroslawez, is in Juchnow once more. We spent a few hours together. Our operational area is Kaluga, where our *II Gruppe* had to evacuate the airfield in a hurry. With the re-conquest by the Russians the city went up in flames. On one of the days before Christmas I learned that I could go on leave. As I did not want to be travelling on Christmas Eve, I decided to leave on the next day. In addition it did not appear totally hopeless that there might be an aircraft to be flown to the repair shops in the rear areas. On 24 December while the rest were happily flying operations, I did not climb into another crate. But one remains somewhat superstitious. From someone returning from leave I received a parcel from home, containing the ordered Christmas tree decorations. In the pilots' quarters I was able to set up a beautiful tree.

Like *II/JG 51*, *II/JG 52* also had to evacuate their airfield in a hurry. Stationed at Klin, they lost seven Messerschmitts to Russian bombing on 13 December 1941, and were thus rendered effectively no longer operational, and pilots and ground staff had to get out fast, leaving unserviceable aircraft and all equipment behind, as the advancing Russians took Klin on 15 December.[38] In the emergency situation created by the surprise Russian winter offensive, as the German armies retreated in great disorder, some centres of resistance managed to hold on, and in one of these west of Dugino airfield to where *II/JG 52* had retreated precipitately, pilots and ground staff were involved in ground combat, losing six men (including two pilots, one an 18-victory ace and the *Gruppe* Adjutant) with 14 wounded.[39] As a result *II/JG 52* had to be withdrawn to Germany to recover from their ordeal and their losses by mid-January 1942; *I/JG 52* had already left at the end of December.[40]

At the beginning of January 1942 fighter units available over the chaotic Army Group Centre area were limited to *Stab, II, III* and *IV/JG 51, II/ZG1* as well as *I* and *II/ZG 26*.[41] In addition to their other troubles, temperatures really dropped seriously in the new year, leaving much of the *Luftwaffe* unable to operate in the extreme cold, especially from poorly equipped field bases, while their Russian opponents were fully operational, mainly from good bases around Moscow, and dominated the skies in January 1942.[42] By late January the *Luftwaffe* started to recover and by the end of February 1942 the Russian winter offensive had effectively come to a halt, leaving a complicated front marked by the Rzhev salient west of Moscow and large isolated bodies of German troops, particularly at Demyansk and at Kholm where a smaller body of Germans was trapped.[43]

Günther Schack, now promoted to *Unteroffizier* but still flying with *7/JG 51 Mölders*, had retreated westwards with the rest of the *Wehrmacht* before Moscow, and now found himself operating over Rzhev, as he noted in his diary for 11 February 1942.

To introduce myself to the (new) operational area, I joined the next mission. *Oberleutnant* Lohoff (*Staffelkapitän 7/JG 51*) and I – the other *Rotte* was led by *Eichenlaubträger* (holder of the Knights Cross with Oak Leaves) *Hauptmann* Bär, who was flying briefly as part of the *Geschwaderstab*, as our *Kommodore* (*Oberstleutnant* Friedrich Beckh, wounded on 16 September 1941 in combat) was still not flying again, his injuries are not yet properly healed. At present he is leading the *Geschwader* from the ground. Gassen (Gottfried Gassen) was flying with Bär. Our operational area is around Rzhev. Right at the beginning of this mission we saw seven Pe-2s below us, speeding off to the east. We were right behind, *Oberleutnant* Lohoff attacked the last one but he immediately pulled away and as this bird showed no signs of having been hit, I went for it. I could not believe my eyes, as shortly after my burst, the bomber struck the ground at a shallow angle and disintegrated in flames.

I was ecstatic, but did I have any witness? I thought not, as the boss answered my question with his own, asking if I had shot one down. 'I am flying southwards,' he added. I circled twice more over the site of my victory and saw a man hiding himself in the wreckage, and then saw two Messerschmitts haring past me in an eastwards direction. I joined in behind them and saw how *Hauptmann* Bär sent a small biplane down in bright flames into the everlasting hunting grounds. As I assumed that I had no witness for my own victory, I did not waggle my wings over our airfield upon our return. I was thus overjoyed when *Hauptmann* Bär congratulated me on my *Abschuss*. He and Gassen had seen it clearly. Bär gave both Gassen and me five Marks, as we had been witnesses of his 90th *Abschuss*; most probably he would have to go and collect his Swords (to the *Ritterkreuz*) now. The five Marks was in place of anything to drink that at the moment was nowhere to be found. Bär, like me, came up from the ranks to be an officer.

That same day (it is unclear if it was on this same mission), *Oberleutnant* Lohoff was shot down by the gunner of a Pe-2 he had just dispatched, and force-landed behind the lines, becoming a POW; his successor as *Staffelkapitän 7/JG 51, Leutnant* Niess, lasted exactly 11 days before he was killed strafing a Russian airfield.[44]

Not only did the German army suffer grievously in the Russian winter counter-offensive, but the *Luftwaffe* also endured significant losses in this disaster. The German forces in Russia were greatly weakened by the defeat and morale also suffered a major shock. In the new campaigning season of 1942, there were no longer enough military resources available on the Eastern Front to advance everywhere as had been the case at the onset of Operation *Barbarossa* less than a year before.

5

1942: New Offensives by the *Wehrmacht*; Stalingrad

After the shock of the winter battles which left Army Groups Centre and North exhausted, and incapable of major offensive operations, it fell to Army Group South to launch the major operations in 1942, known as *Fall Blau* (Case Blue). This would encompass an advance to Voronezh on the Don, an advance down this river on its western bank and then a two-part attack: (1) towards the East to take Stalingrad, cut off river traffic on the Volga and destroy a major industrial centre; (2) advance further to the south and south-east to conquer the Caucasus with its major oil supplies.[1] Prior to this the Russians suffered a large-scale reverse in an ill-judged attack on Kharkov, and twin disasters occurred at Kerch and Sevastopol in the Crimea. On the White Sea front in the far north, Allied aid to Russia began to make its presence felt in aerial operations, while combat over the Northern Front concentrated over the Demyansk and Kholm pockets. Over Army Group Centre costly battles in the area of the Rzhev salient dominated, in the air and on the ground.[2]

On the White Sea Front: First Contact with British
and American Aircraft Types
The primary tasks set for the fighter pilots in the far north, on the *Eismeerfront*, remained as they had been in 1941: escorting bombers and Stukas to attack Murmansk, the ice-free port (in winter) where vital Anglo-American supplies were landed, and the railway line leading south from this port to the rest of Russia, which transported the supplies to the interior of the country. The experiences of *Oberleutnant* Karl-Friedrich Schlossstein who flew Me 110s in *10* and *13/(Z)/JG 5* were fairly typical:

In 1941–1942 I flew *c.* 250 *Feindflüge* against Murmansk and the railway line to the south. I was shot down by Russian flak over Murmansk (26 October 1942)[3] and force-landed my Me 110 in the Tundra. I was discovered by my own unit's search party and saved from no-man's land by Fieseler Storch. The pilot was *Oberstleutnant* Handrick (Olympic champion in 1936 in the pentathlon), my *Geschwader Kommkodore*, who personally rescued me. In 1942 I became *Staffelkapitän* (summer 1942–June 1943)[4] of the *10 (Zerstörer)/JG 5*, later renamed *13(Z)/JG 5*, and in 1943 was transferred to the *Zerstörer* School at Memmingen as *Kommandeur* of the training *Gruppe*.

During 1942 the supply of Anglo-American aircraft had an impact on the opponents encountered by the German fighters in this far northern theatre. *Leutnant* Friedrich Lüdecke, who flew in *6/JG 5*, recalls the difficulties imposed on them by the fighting being concentrated far across the Russian lines, over Murmansk, and the harsh conditions endured on the ground, especially by the ground crews.

In 1942/1943 we fought, as long as we were in action, against Russian, American and English fighter aircraft: Lagg-3, Lagg-5, Yak-1 and -7, Mig-1 and -3, Curtiss P-40 Kittyhawk, P-39 Airacobra and Hurricane. The ratio was approximately 50:50 Russian versus Anglo-American aircraft. The Russian aircraft were more manoeuvrable than our Me 109 E, F and G, but about 70–100 km slower in top speed. The American and English machines were about equal to the Me 109, actually just as good. We mostly fought against superior numbers: about a *Schwarm* (four aircraft) against 15–20 Russians. These battles took place 100–150 km over enemy territory, and as a result many of our pilots were taken prisoner or perished trying to walk back to our lines.

Often the Russians would form a defensive circle when we attacked. They were brave and fought well, but attacked only rarely. Their training was not as good as that of our pilots. When we wanted to shoot them down, we mostly had to enter dogfights, despite our Messerschmitts not being so manoeuvrable. As a result we were often hit in combat and thereby lost both aircraft and pilots. Conditions on the ground were poor; rations, quarters and distractions between missions – these were boringly monotonous, insufficient or even almost non-existent. We talked of 'Polar syndrome' and tried to guard against this psychologically: we went for long skiing trips, fished or hunted for polar rabbits and wild birds. We used the sauna a lot to calm us down – and enjoyed drinking in the evenings, when we did not have to fly any more until the next day. Life was particularly hard for our ground crews, who at minus ten to minus thirty degrees of frost had to change engines, load ammunition belts and generally perform hard labour.

In 1941 there had only been one Me 109-equipped *Gruppe* in this area, the *Jagdgruppe Petsamo*, later renamed as *II/JG 5*, and in the course of 1942 a second *Gruppe* was formed.[5] *Hauptmann* Günther Scholz, who had previously led *7/JG 54* on the Leningrad front, was appointed to lead this new *Gruppe* (*III/JG 5*) and describes an additional mission set before his pilots apart from attacking Murmansk and its rail link southwards, namely escorting bombers and torpedo carriers far out over the Arctic Ocean to attack the Anglo-American supply convoys.

> In February 1942 I was named *Kommandeur* of the newly formed *III/JG 5*, stationed first in Jever, then in Trondheim in Norway and finally (from the end of April 1942)[6] based at Petsamo, northern Finland. The tasks of *JG 5* in northern Finland included escorting the attacks on the Anglo-American convoys in the Arctic Ocean and raids on the harbour of Murmansk. We also flew low-level attacks on goods trains moving southwards from Murmansk on the famous and notorious railway line (thousands of Soviet convicts are thought to have died during its construction). The missions against the convoys were very unpleasant: flights of several hundred kilometres over the sea, aerial combat against Anglo-American carrier aircraft (one carrier was always present). If a ditching occurred neither life vest nor a dinghy helped in the least, as super-cooling and death soon ensued. Search and rescue flights were not undertaken as these areas were too far over potentially enemy-controlled sea areas. As far as I remember, we escorted bombers and torpedo planes three times, far out into the Arctic Ocean to attack the Anglo-American convoys; very unpleasant flying so far over water under ice-cold temperatures.

One of Scholz's pilots in his *III Gruppe*, *Leutnant* Bodo Helms, found it rather irksome that they were equipped with the old E model of the Me 109, which tended to limit their operations to bomber escorts much of the time.

> I was only on the *Eismeerfront* flying from Petsamo for three months, from 5 May to 5 August 1942, and following that endured years of Soviet captivity. During this time my *Staffel* (*7/JG 5*) flew almost only direct escort for Ju 88 bombers on their missions in the Murmansk area. We were flying the old Me 109 E in contrast to the other *Staffels* that were already flying the Me 109 F and later the G model and thus were used for the free chase missions. I only had a few aerial combats. In my time we were superior to the Russians in ability and especially in tactics; I had got to know the English on the Channel in 1941 and experienced them as equal opponents. The Russians often flew behind their 'Commissars', used the defensive circle

as a protective manoeuvre and it was relatively easy to dive into those. Admittedly in prison camps I heard from comrades that as the war went on they had learnt a lot and then often were equal as opponents. Our tactics were always, whenever possible, to attack from above, but where one always had to remember that the turning circle of the Hurricane was much smaller than that of the Me 109. On the ground we lived in barracks, and one could describe the living conditions as good. We always had enough to eat, even though in the far north it was often dried vegetables and potatoes. Additional rations could easily be obtained in the form of salmon from the small streams.

Friedrich Lüdecke knew two of the three leading aces of *JG 5* on the *Eismeerfront* very well, Heinrich Ehrler and Theo Weissenberger (number three was Walter Schuck, who arrived with the newly created *III Gruppe* in Petsamo in April 1942).[7] Ehrler rose from the ranks to command of *JG 5* as a *Major* and was made one of the main scapegoats in the loss of the battleship *Tirpitz* to RAF bombers on 12 November 1944; Weissenberger, also promoted to officer's rank in the field, ended up also a *Major* and commanding the famous jet fighter *Geschwader*, *JG 7*.[8] Both scored most of their successes in *JG 5* on the *Eismeerfront*: 204 in all for Ehrler and 175 for Weissenberger.[9] Friedrich Lüdecke commented on these two tyros:

Heinrich Ehrler, my *Staffelführer*, was a *Leutnant* like myself, and the third officer in the 6th *Staffel* was *Leutnant* Theo Weissenberger, with whom I shared a room and who had just departed on his *Ritterkreuz* leave, when I was shot down on 25 January 1943 and became a prisoner. Ehrler had been promoted from the NCO's corps, had not attended any high school and no war academy like most of the officers had enjoyed. The same applied to Theo Weissenberger. Both became officers due to their bravery and successes (*Abschüsse*). Ehrler had been an *Unteroffizier* in the flak arm in the *Legion Condor* during the Spanish Civil War. He began flight training which he completed in 1939 and in 1940 finished his fighter training. He was a soldier through and through, meaning that he was a very conscientious person. He was tough and expected the same from others that he himself did. He strove to fly missions when they were free chases over Russian airbases. Certainly, he was ambitious but in a healthy way without causing danger to others. He did not talk a lot, confining himself to the minimum necessary conversation. It was thus not easy to get to know him. I relate that to his lacking a matric (*Abitur*) and he thus avoided talking on subjects that he knew little about. He measured people, especially his pilots, on the basis of their achievements. Those who proved that they had learned something in combat, received his recognition.

In the North: Aerial Operations over German
and Russian Pockets; Demyansk, Volkhov

While relatively static conditions characterised the ground fighting in the far north, the same did not at all pertain further southwards. In the area of Army Group North, the turn of the new year found *I* and *III/JG 54* stationed close to Leningrad, the former *Gruppe* staying there the entire year and the latter only moving away from Leningrad (to Smolensk) in December 1942; *II/JG 54* had been in Germany and returned to the Leningrad area on 2 February 1942 before being sent south to Rjelbitzy (west of Lake Ilmen) on 20 March where they were to remain most of the time, till December 1942.[10] *I/JG 51* had been surrounded at Staraya Russa, north-west of the Demyansk pocket, at Christmas 1941 and stayed there and at Szolzy and Rjelbitzy in the same area till 24 May 1942 (with some missions also flown from Orel over Army Group Centre).[11] *III/JG 3* also operated from Szolzy (10 February–14 April 1942).[12]

Essentially, *I* and *III/JG 54* were thus stationed close to Leningrad, and flew missions against that city from the south, and also against waterborne traffic supplying Leningrad across Lake Ladoga in the summer and against the equivalent ice road in the winter parts of the year; they also supported the German troops along the Volkhov River, flowing north from Lake Ilmen into Lake Ladoga.[13] *Oberleutnant* Heinz Lange, *Staffelkapitän 1/JG 54* was one of those flying over the Leningrad area: 'On the Leningrad front 1941/1942: the Russians had learned much since the beginning of the fighting in the East and were opponents to be taken seriously. Also, their aircraft were now largely more modern and more efficient than the earlier-utilised I-15 and I-16, for example.' Heinz Lange's 1st *Staffel* plus the 2nd (both from July to August 1942) and 7/*JG 54* (June–July 1942) had brief assignments to the Karelian isthmus on the western side of Lake Ladoga to combat Russian supply shipping to Leningrad.[14]

To the east of Leningrad, as part of the great Soviet winter offensive, the 2nd Shock Army had pushed a deep salient into the German lines in the Volkhov offensive (7 January–28 June 1942); however, this advance became bogged down and was eventually cut off and destroyed by the Germans.[15] It was particularly *II* and *III/JG 54* (and to a lesser extent *I/JG 54*) that operated over the Volkhov front from January to June 1942.[16] *Oberleutnant* Pichon-Kalau von Hofe was the *Geschwader* Technical Officer (T/O), and during a free chase operation over the Russian fighter airfields in the Volkhov region he flew back over the Volkhov encirclement (where the Russian 2nd Shock Army was now trapped after its unsuccessful attempt to relieve the siege of Leningrad)[17] during the afternoon of 26 April 1942 and was shot down over a small field in the *Kessel* (cf., pocket) used by Russian light aircraft at night.

Pichon-Kalau von Hofe had circled the field a couple of times to ensure it was empty, and the Russian flak cleverly kept quiet until he had unsuspectingly turned homewards and then hit him with their first round, forcing him to glide down, his windscreen covered in oil; he was very lucky and managed to put down in a small swamp in the widespread forests without injury. He managed to get away from the vicinity of the aircraft and then for two nights and days walked approximately north-westwards, mainly at night, and towards the end of day two made it to the German lines. Although he heard sounds of rifles and artillery being fired at times, he met nobody until almost at the German lines; another lucky escape from Russian territory. This account was sent to me by Werner Pichon-Kalau von Hofe in 1992, and was later published in 2006.[18] While he had been shot down during daylight operations over the Volkhov pocket, JG 54 also flew quite a number of night-time missions over this area, scoring 56 victories with Me 109s after dark.[19] Werner recalled further: 'I was not personally involved in the night missions over the *Wolchowkessel* January–July 1942. Erwin Leykauf (*III/JG 54*) is the most competent to report on this. As far as I remember he was the most successful pilot here.' Leykauf actually scored eight night victories there, including six on 22 June 1942, as the third most successful *JG 54* nocturnal pilot in this battle.[20]

To the south-east of Lake Ilmen, a large pocket of German troops (an entire army corps of *c.* 100,000 men) had been surrounded at Demyansk in the Valday Hills, with a much smaller pocket at Kholm (*c.* 5,000 men) roughly 90 km further south-west; Demyansk was cut off from 8 February and Kholm from 28 January 1942.[21] The mass of men at Demyansk was supplied by *c.* 500 *Luftwaffe* transport aircraft and was relieved by 21 April, with Kholm being relieved on 5 May 1942.[22] While transport aircraft could land at Demyansk, at Kholm supplies were mainly through air drops and freight gliders (80 used and many lost; 27 Ju 52s lost as well).[23] Escort for these massive airlift operations was provided by the three fighter *Gruppen* stationed in the Lake Ilmen area at Szolzy, Rjelbitzy and Staraya Russa: *II/JG 54*, *I/JG 51* and *III/JG 3*, with *9/JG 54* also involved (from 20 January to 16 February 1942).[24]

Even after the relief of Demyansk, which only established a narrow corridor to the main German forces to the west, strong air support had to be maintained along the very extensive frontal area created by the long, narrow salient, with *II/JG 54* remaining in this area till almost the end of the year – *III/JG 3* and *I/JG 51* had departed in April and May respectively. Total losses of transport aircraft (20 February–18 May 1942) in the Demyansk–Kholm airlifts amounted to 265 aircraft (60 per cent and higher states of damage – all write-offs) and 387 crewmen.[25]

Despite the narrow corridor linking what was now the Demyansk salient with the German lines, airlift operations had to be continued to October, with a reduced transport force, escorted by *II/JG 54*, supported by *II/JG 3* from 27 September to 25 November 1942[26] and briefly also by *III/JG 77* (from 7 to 16 October 1942).[27] One of the pilots flying out of Rjelbitzy during this later period was *Oberleutnant* Hans Beisswenger, who took over as *Staffelkapitän 6/JG 54* on 11 August after the death of his predecessor, *Hauptmann* Sattig.[28] A page from his logbook[29] lists 18 missions flown in September 1942, comprising nine free chases, five escorts for Ju 52s, two bomber escorts, and two weather reconnaissance missions; there was no contact with enemy aircraft during this time. The operating base of Rjelbitzy given in the logbook page implies that these sorties would have been mainly over the Demyansk salient.

Another pilot to fly over Demyansk from late September till end November 1942 was Helmut Notemann of *II/JG 3*, following a few weeks' action over the Rzhev salient (see below). On 23 August 1942, *II/JG 3* had been pulled out of the line from operating over the Don bend west of Stalingrad, and transferred briefly (for three weeks) to Königsberg–Neuhausen to re-equip with new aircraft, Me 109 G-2s.[30] It was here also that a number of fresh pilots joined them, including newly qualified fighter pilot *Feldwebel* Notemann, who was assigned to *5/JG 3*.

I was born on 16 April 1918 in Krefeld and joined the *Luftwaffe* voluntarily in 1937, starting at Handorf–Hornheide near Munster in Westphalia. At the end of 1939 I joined candidate (pilot) battalion 'Monte Rosa' at Stettin. From there I went to flying school in Kaufbeuren (from middle 1940 to July 1941). Following that it was fighter pilot preparatory school at Lachen–Speyerdorf near Neustadt on the wine route, and thereafter to fighter pilot school at Fürth (Herzogenaurach) for about half a year. In the *Ergänzungsgruppe Mannheim-Darmstadt* I got my final polish from the instructors there, *Ritterkreuz* winners Schentke, Schleef and von Boremski, all from *JG 3 Udet*. In September 1942 the *II Gruppe* of *JG 3* was re-equipped with the Me 109 G-2 in Königsberg–Neuhausen. *Kommandeur* of *II/JG 3* was *Hauptmann* Brändle, *Staffelkapitän* of 5th *Staffel* was *Oberleutnant* Kirschner and the other pilots included: *Leutnant* Myhre, *Oberfeldwebel* Heckmann, *Feldwebels* Grünberg, Schütte, Notemann, Trapan, *Unteroffiziers* Mohn, Bringmann, Scheibe, and *Leutnant* Bohatsch.

After this re-equipment, *II/JG 3* were sent back to the front (9–11 September 1942), first to Smolensk, and from there straightaway to their field base at Dedjurewo within the Rzhev salient.[31] After a few weeks there, they moved again, this time to Szolzy to fly missions over the Demyansk salient and around Lake Ilmen, which they continued to do until transferred to the Stalingrad area on 8 December 1942, where the crisis had broken.[32] Helmut Notemann recalled the operations over Rzhev and Demyansk: 'After some days of getting used to our new aircraft we flew to the front. Our first base was Dedjurewo near Rshew. There we flew, as conditions required, escort missions, free chases, strafing attacks in support of our infantry, attacks on trains (carrying weapons and munitions) and protection flights for our tanks. Mostly we flew in *Rotten* and *Schwärme*, but also on escort missions in *Staffel* and even *Gruppe* strength. These operations were flown from Dedjurewo and after a few weeks from Szolzy (Demyansk salient near Lake Ilmen).'

Fighting between reinforced and effective Russian fighter forces and the *Luftwaffe* airlift and fighter units over Demyansk was intense with heavy losses to both sides in March 1942, before a change in tactics by using large formations of transport aircraft and strong Me 109 escorts in April brought losses down.[33] The biggest damage done to the *Luftwaffe* by the success of supplying the cut-off troops at Demyansk and Kholm lay in the future, when assumption of similar success for the significantly larger German Sixth Army surrounded at Stalingrad at the end of the year led to tragic failure.

During these first few months of 1942, the *Luftwaffe* fighter arm fought hard above Army Group North, scoring many successes but also suffering losses which included several *Experten* such as *Leutnant* Eckhardt Hübner of 7/*JG* 3, who had 47 victories to his name, and *Feldwebel* Gerhard Lautenschläger of 3/*JG* 54, with a score of 31.[34] *Hauptmann* Hans Philipp, *Kommandeur* of I/*JG* 54, operating largely over Leningrad, had been awarded with the Swords to the *Ritterkreuz* on 12 April as the first recipient in his *Geschwader* and achieved his 100th victory claim on the last day of March 1942.[35] Ernst Brunns, *Waffenmeister* (chief armourer) of I/*JG54*, still retained fond memories of Philipp long after the war:

Hans Philipp was a very quiet person, quiet and modest. He was also an officer of the old guard. He couldn't take the reporters from the large newspapers and would have far preferred being in the trenches to having to face them. I often had to chase the people from the press, Philipp would then give me his pistol and then I had to get rid of these curious people, right off the airfield. He told me once, that it was really hard to shoot down another person, perhaps the poor man had a family, a beloved wife, children, or a professional qualification.

JG 54's second Swords winner, *Oberleutnant* Max-Hellmuth Ostermann (102 victory claims), *Staffelkapitän* of the 7th *Staffel*, was killed in combat with a Russian fighter far behind the Russian lines east of the

Lake Ilmen area on 9 August, and the leader of *6/JG 54*, *Hauptmann* Karl Sattig (53 victory claims), went missing over the Rzhev salient the next day.[36] *Kommodore* Hannes Trautloft was deeply shocked by Ostermann's loss; he had been an uncommon genius in combat,[37] almost in the Marseille mode as described by Professor Paul Skawran, the *Luftwaffe* psychologist.[38] Skawran also identified Hans Strelow (*5/JG 51*) as belonging to the same psychologically defined group of fighter pilots as Marseille (top *Luftwaffe* scorer against Western opponents, mostly in North Africa) and Ostermann, the '*Kindlich-Naiven Jagdflieger*' – the childlike-naïve fighter pilots, who were all uncommon air combat geniuses.[39] *Waffenmeister* Ernst Brunns remembers Ostermann as having 'preferred dogfighting, an outstanding fighter pilot and a quiet and modest person; only shot when very close to his opponent using very little ammunition'. Indeed, an artist like Marseille.

The services of specialist armourers like *Unteroffizier* Brunns were an essential element in the success of a *Jagdgeschwader*, as was the support of the entire ground staff. Ernst Brunns summarised his main duties in *I/JG 54*.

Our ammunition encompassed: armour-piercing rounds, explosive rounds, tracer rounds, all 2 cm calibre, and then there were incendiary rounds of 7.9 mm calibre for the machine guns. Good fighter pilots used very little ammunition, often only a few rounds. The ammunition supply functioned very well, and we armourers were careful to always ensure there were adequate supplies available. When we changed bases I had to load a motor bike and eight crates (200 rounds per crate) of 2 cm into a Ju 52. The captain of the aircraft gave me a friendly look around once airborne. It was not always so easy on field bases to try and cadge ammunition from other units, one often had to listen to "nice language" when this was necessary; best that one talked with a silver tongue. Gun harmonisation: all weapons were harmonised at 200 m, and from conversations with other weapons specialists, it was clear there were no exceptions to this rule. We worked at this job until everything was working perfectly, normally for several hours, and the motor mechanics had also to be on hand for this job.

Following *General* Erich von Manstein's conquest of Sevastopol, the great fortress in the Crimea, at the beginning of July 1942, the newly promoted field marshal moved north with his 11th Army, planning to put paid to another fortress city, Leningrad, by linking up with the Finns in the Karelian isthmus.[40] In order to forestall this and to use up the fighting power of these added troops, the Russians launched an offensive (19 August–1 October 1942) to the east of Leningrad in the Sinyavino area, which achieved this purpose but didn't break the blockade.[41] Apart from units of *JG 54* (*I* and *III Gruppen*), *III/JG 77* (6 September–7 October 1942) also provided fighter cover over this successful German defence south of Lake Ladoga.[42] The iron ring around Leningrad was finally broken, albeit only with a narrow corridor into the city immediately south of Lake Ladoga, when the Russians smashed the Sinyavino–Schlüsselburg salient in a battle that raged from 12 to 18 January 1943, enabling the establishment of a tenuous rail link with the besieged city.[43]

On the Central Front; the Rzhev Salient Battles

In the area of Army Group Centre, the two sides had fought each other to exhaustion by early 1941 and the German troops were in serious disarray; following the Moscow offensive which saved the capital, the Russians followed on with the Rzhev–Vyazma offensive (8 January–20 October 1942) which left the large (German) Rzhev salient, running roughly north to south, with a parallel Russian salient to its west.[44] While the April rains and mud decreased operations significantly, May to early June saw local attacks and elimination of small Russian pockets behind the German lines, and the lines gradually stabilised around the large salient; it was also in May 1942 that the career of *Leutnant* Hans Strelow of *II/JG 51* came to an end, as already recounted.[45]

In the general area of the Rzhev salient there were four main battles during 1942. First came the German operations (Operation *Seydlitz*) to eliminate a Russian force along the western margin of the first-formed Rzhev salient in the Bely (Bjeloj) area from 2 to 23 July 1942). Next came the first Rzhev battle (Rzhev–Sychevka battle), with Russian attacks from the east along the eastern face of the north–south salient from 30 July to 23 August 1942 (some sources have it continuing till the end of September), with three main attacks at Rzhev, to the east of Vyazma and in the Belev area east of Bryansk. After this was the second Rzhev battle in same area (25 November–20 December 1942), and finally there was the battle of Velikiye Luki, lying to the west of Rzhev on the main German line, just south of the boundary between Army Groups North and Centre. This occurred between 24 November 1942 and 20 January 1943.[46]

The Rzhev battles were supported by all four *Gruppen* of *JG 51*, reinforced for limited periods by *II/JG 3* (flew from Dedjurewo, between Rzhev and Vyazma; 9–27 September 1942), *II/JG 54* (at Vyazma 5–16 August 1942 when they moved to Orel, staying there till 29 August) and *I/JG 52* (Orel 15–24 August 1942; Dedjurewo 24 August–22 September 1942).[47]

I/JG 51 was briefly in the Smolensk area (west-south-west of the Rzhev salient) in early August before deploying to Germany to re-equip with the Fw 190, followed by a spell near Leningrad, and was finally stationed at Vyazma (in the south of the salient) from 18 October 1942 to early January 1943.[48] *II/JG 51* flew out of Bryansk (southern part of Army Group Centre) from the beginning of the year till 17 July when they moved to Orel to the south-east, leaving the Eastern Front for good on 7 October 1942 for Germany and then the Mediterranean.[49] *III/JG 51* spent the entire year around Smolensk apart from the interval of 12 November–17 December 1942 when they were in Germany converting to the Fw 190.[50] After using various bases in the southern part of Army Group Centre's area, *IV/JG 51* returned from a brief posting to East Prussia on 6 July to the Smolensk–Roslavl area (till 27 September 1942); they flew from Staraya Russa near Demyansk till 6 October and then till the end of the year from Vitebsk, north-west of Smolensk.[51] The Spanish *Staffel 15/JG 51* was stationed in Orel from June 1942 for the next year.[52] The main fighter concentration was thus at the first Rzhev battle (*II, III* and *IV/JG 51, II/JG 54, I/JG 52, II/JG 3*), with Operation *Seydlitz* being protected only by *III/JG 51*, the second Rzhev battle by *I/JG 51*, and the Velikiye Luki battle by *IV/JG 51*. *Unteroffizier* Günther Schack, *7/JG 51* was caught up in the thick of the most intense fighting above the Rzhev salient in August 1942, during the first Rzhev battle there, as recorded in a number of his diary[53] entries:

4 August: At 05h00 we were sent into the old stamping grounds, this time I was flying with *Leutnant* Weber. East of Subzow the Russians had broken through in the night. After having escorted He 111s till they had dropped their bombs, we encountered ten *Zementbomber* (literally 'concrete bombers' – the heavily armoured Il-2s), Gantz and Stoltmann were already going at them, each of them having singled one out, but neither of them could get theirs to fall. My chosen Il-2 was losing big chunks to my cannon shots, but the beast flew happily on, and I exhausted all my ammunition with no further result, nor did the others fare any better. We landed in a bad mood. Our *Gruppe* had been very unlucky recently. After our *Kommandeur* had fallen out (wounded two days previously), today *Oberleutnant* Schlitzer, the boss of the 9th *Staffel*, suffered two bullets through his lungs (and died two days later).[54] A young *Leutnant* of the 9th *Staffel* died of wounds received, and an *Unteroffizier* of the same *Staffel* was seriously wounded. Several forced-landings had also strongly reduced our aircraft complement. During a low level attack on our airfield, several workers building the new concrete runway lost their lives.

6 August: *Leutnant* Gantz, who in the last few days was always able to waggle his wings two or three times over the field, after scoring his 17th *Abschuss*, was shot down and killed at low level over Russian territory. His aircraft literally exploded into myriads of fragments. Groundcrew as well as pilots honoured the memory of this much loved officer. But the war goes on, as if nothing has changed. Once again I shot big fragments out of *Zementbombers* and yet they would not fall, and the same with the other pilots. Hunting luck especially eludes the boss (*Hauptmann* Herbert Wehnelt) and I. Weber (*Leutnant* Karl-Heinz Weber, known as 'Benjamin', who figures prominently later in this volume when the *7/JG 51 Startkladde* is discussed in chapter 9) today achieved his 20th victory. In the evening I receive a telegram from Erna that Werner has died of his wounds. She asks that I come to Lublin for the funeral, but this already took place on 31 July, the telegram took over a week to get here.

10 August: Early in the day already there were wild dogfights, there were so many Russians that one became bathed in sweat. But with these manoeuvrable boys everything I shot at went past their tails, they know only too well that tight turns are their survival. At 10h00 I fly the second mission with Gassen, in a formation of eight aircraft from the *Staffel*, what a proud number. We had to escort Ju 88s which was made very difficult by a mob of Russian fighters. All types were present, even original-Ratas. Finally *Zementbombers* also turned up, possibly the fighters were meant to clear the airspace ahead of them. Eventually after a lot of effort I managed to down one of them – number seven. Seeing as Gassen stuck to my wing like glue, we carried on dogfighting, as the air was full of Russians. It was a great mission, as despite the many German and Russian birds and all the twisting and turning we did not get lost.

It was still not dark when we had visitors at our airfield. The first bombs dropped were so effective that immediately several aircraft caught fire and this made finding the target very easy for the further bombers that followed them. The whole night it continued to thunder at the field. We spent several hours in the slit trenches and got slightly the wind-up. Especially the bomb sticks, where every bomb is nearer than its predecessors to where we are, are really horrible. Our aircraft losses are not inconsiderable, fortunately the human losses are minor. And we are able to fly again the next day. Though the airfield is a real mass of craters, we are able to take off and land along a narrow strip. In order to avoid exposing the remaining machines to such an attack again, after the last mission we land at another nearby small field. Naturally, on this night, no bombs fall.

On **12 August** I am able to score my 8th *Abschuss*. After completing an escort mission, a lone Pe-2 turns up. Before it can save itself in the clouds, large flames come out of the right wing after my burst. She falls into the Volga with a big splash. One man was able to save himself with his parachute. On the next day I was able to shoot down another Pe-2, this time from a bomber formation. Just after that I was sitting behind a fighter, he was turning wildly for all he was worth, but he could not get me off his tail. This went on for several minutes between 500 and 2,000 m height. The sweat was running down me. All the time I was missing him with my bursts of fire, he did not fall, eventually getting away from me at low level trailing smoke, over the front. My nicest aerial combat to date, even if it did not lead to success, I had never got so much out of my old Messerschmitt before. If only I would use more deflection. The seed planted by *Leutnant* Gantz seems to have germinated. With Friedel Gassen (his wingman, unfortunately killed 3 September 1942), who sticks on my tail even through the wildest dogfights, flying is especially enjoyable. Almost every day we meet enemy aircraft, mostly fighter combats, and always the same picture, I miss again. Still to shoot someone down, when one has already been seen by him, one must first out-manoeuvre him, and that we have almost always been able to achieve in the last few days.

18 August: I was lucky as even though *c.* 15 Mes were flying free chases over Rzhev, I got the only Pe-2. I caught up with him right over the middle of the town, now just not to miss, as at least 10 other comrades behind me were just waiting for their chance for a shot. However, I was not giving up my favourable shooting position until the bomber went down in flames, still dropping leaflets. He crashed in flames onto the airfield on the town's outskirts – number 10. This was the only success of the *Gruppe* on this day. The situation on the ground had worsened. The Russians have taken Subzow and are close to the railway line between Rzhev and Wjasma. Our airfield lies approximately midway between these two places, close to the railway on the western side.

24 August: After completing an escort assignment we met nine bombers, to whom we attached ourselves, but before I could get into position to open fire, I saw two fighters behind and above me. A wild dogfight ensued. These machines I could not recognise at all. They were certainly not slower than us, and climbed just as well also. Probably they are American aircraft, one had seen them somewhere before, once. As I tried to get behind these two, there was a sudden loud bang in my machine. There must thus have been more of these strange birds around, and so I quickly sought open space with Gassen, as we each had one behind us. After landing, and following my description of these aircraft, it was confirmed to me that they were 'Airacobras', American fighter aircraft. These birds stand out by their long noses. The engine in this type sits behind the pilot. A machine gun round had flattened itself against my back-armour which saved me from further damage. Two hours later my aircraft was serviceable again.

What is noticeable in these diary entries of Günther Schack, who had already been serving on the Eastern Front for over a year, is that it was not easy to shoot down an enemy aircraft. He also makes obvious his joy in exhilarating yet obviously always risky dogfights, and displays no contempt for his enemies or their fighting and flying abilities.

In the South; Russian Disasters at Kerch, Sevastopol and Kharkov

It was in the south that the Germans were to make their major strategic effort during 1942; they no longer had the troops and materiel to advance everywhere, and a more static style of warfare had already become dominant for Army Groups North and Centre, as described briefly above. Russian counterattacks in the winter of 1941/42 in the south had driven the Germans out of Rostov and left them on the defensive along the Mius River, and also driven in the Izyum salient into the German lines southeast of Kharkov.[55] Many fighter *Gruppen* of the units providing cover for Army Group South had been withdrawn to Germany over the winter (or at least part of it): *I* and *II/JG 3* (*III/JG 3* had a short break and then flew on the northern parts of the front), *I* and *II/JG 52*, and *II/JG 77*.[56] It was only *III/JG 52*, *I/LG 2* (on 6 January 1942 became *I/JG 77*) and *III/JG 77* that had to endure a full winter at the southern front: in the beginning of 1942, *III/JG 52* were stationed in the Kharkov area (1 January–29 April 1942), *I/JG 77* in the Taganrog–Stalino area covering the Mius front (1 January–5 May 1942), and *III/JG 77* in the Crimea (1 January–20 March 1942).[57]

The Me 110s of *I/ZG 1* were also flying over the Mius area, and as for all crews flying in a Russian winter, a forced-landing was almost always an ordeal, as related by *Unteroffizier* Heinz Ludwig, *3/ZG 1*:

The duties and functions of a radio-operator/gunner were many; I underwent training for almost two years before joining my unit. Navigating and avoiding getting lost were a major duty, and that was not always that simple in a new operational area, particularly over Russia for which only poor maps were available. During training I spent six weeks at an instrument flying school in Norway with eight hours daily in a Ju 52, attended a sea rescue course in Denmark and at *Zerstörerschule* (Me-110 school) I was amongst the best radio operators. This saved our lives in Russia during a winter mission in early 1942 north of Rostov.

After having been hit by flak and by now flying alone, I managed to get two radio fixes, but everywhere we were refused permission to land (Taganrog and Millerovo), due to a cloud ceiling of 50 m and horizontal visibility of only 50 m as well. We thus flew in circles above the clouds trending westwards, and eventually had to make a belly-landing behind Russian lines. Now the question arose: where are we? For a day and a half we marched westwards at -42 degrees of frost, following our compass, eating Pervetin tablets and Schoka-Cola to avoid falling asleep, and managed to penetrate the thinly manned Russian frontline by listening carefully and to reach German troops; we had landed 25 km behind the lines, and always had our pistols in our hands. Thank God that our comrades in the infantry immediately recognised us as German fliers; they must have had previous experience of this sort of thing. A halftrack from our engineering section (sited only 25 km behind our lines) picked us up from the infantry. Once again, we celebrated our birthdays!!![58]

In the Crimea, the great fortress of Sevastopol had been isolated since November 1941 and bombarded ever since December 1941, and to relieve pressure on this city and major Russian naval base the Russians had successfully retaken the Kerch peninsula in eastern Crimea in late December 1941–early January 1942.[59] In the spring and after the muddy period, the Germans retook the Kerch peninsula in a major battle (8–21 May 1942), and at almost the same time the Russians launched a spoiling attack from the Izyum salient (11–29 May 1942) to reconquer Kharkov and prevent an expected major German offensive towards Moscow from the south-south-west, but this, like Kerch, was a costly failure.[60] The third major operation in the south before Operation *Blau* was the battle to take Sevastopol and its eventual fall to the Germans (2 June–9 July 1942).[61]

The reconquest of the Kerch peninsula in the Crimea was a short-lived battle, supported by three fighter *Gruppen* who were each posted to this region for only a short period: *II/JG 52* (7–14 May 1942), *III/JG 52* (29 April–12 May 1942) and *I/JG 3* (6–14 May 1942).[62] Devastating attacks on overcrowded Russian airbases in the peninsula on 8 May went hand in hand with large and successful air battles for the *Luftwaffe*, and 57 aerial successes were claimed (47 of them by *III/JG 52*), but as always happens in combat others were less successful; their sister *Gruppe II/JG 52* lost five of their own aircraft for three claims.[63]

It was here also that one of the leading *Jagdflieger* in not just *JG 52* but also in the entire air force began to stand out: *Leutnant* Hermann Graf, *Staffelkapitän 9/JG 52*, who claimed 28 victories in the two weeks' fighting over Kerch, raising his score to 107 and being awarded the *Eichenlaub* and *Schwerten* (Oak Leaves and Swords to the Knights Cross) soon after.[64] In addition to the fighters, ground attack units were also in action there as *Feldwebel* Hermann Buchner remembered: 'On 26 April 1942 I moved with *III/SG 1*, 8th *Staffel*, to the Eastern Front from Germany, for the reconquest of the Kertsch peninsula in the Crimea. Until 1943 we flew exclusively in the Me 109 E. This was a good aircraft and we could keep up with the Russian fighters (Lagg-3, Lagg-5) well, I never had any problems in this regard.' Russian army casualties amounted to 177,000 at Kerch.[65]

The Russian offensive launched from the Izyum bend towards Kharkov was a massive attack, and considerable *Luftwaffe* reinforcements were brought in to cover the army units which successfully staved it off and finally cut off and destroyed a large part of the Soviet forces, causing 277,000 casualties.[66] When this offensive began only *III/JG 77* was stationed in the area (from 8 to 31 May 1942), but within days seven more fighter *Gruppen* were added, many of them remaining within this area for quite some time after the Izyum battle was over: *I/JG 52* (20 May–3 July 1942), *II/JG 52* (14 May–3 July 1942), *III/JG 52* (12 May–8 July 1942), *I/JG 3* (14 May–23 June 1942), *II/JG 3* (19 May–24 June 1942), *III/JG 3* (20–31 May 1942) and part of *I/JG 77* (15 May–late May 1942).[67] Total *Luftwaffe* claims in the Kharkov battle (12–28 May) amounted to 596 aerial victories and another 19 destroyed in ground attacks, with actual total Russian aircraft losses of 542 recorded; the Germans lost 49 aircraft.[68] One of these losses is described by a pilot who joined *II/JG 3* in 1943, *Leutnant* Walter Bohatsch, *5/JG 3*:

> In general my memories are of flying with the *II Gruppe* of *JG 3* and partly with the *I Gruppe*, but particularly of experiences with the 5th *Staffel*. The history of *JG 3 Udet* is strongly bound with the Bohatsch family as my brother was *Staffelkapitän* of *1/JG 3* and went missing in the Kharkov area in 1942. My brother Heinz was three years older than me. He was already a pilot in the Austrian forces and became a *Leutnant* in the German *Luftwaffe* after the 1938 annexation. In April 1942 he became *Staffelkapitän* of the 1st *Staffel* of *Jagdgeschwader 3* (*Udet*). He was shot down by Russian fighters on 21 May 1942, when operating out of Tschugujeff.

The eight-month-long siege of Sevastopol was a heroic Russian defence which cost German and Romanian ground troops dear; in the air 118 victories were claimed by *Luftwaffe* fighters between 2 June and 3 July 1942, balanced against 69 Russian aircraft lost (from 25 May to 1 July 1942).[69] Four German fighter *Gruppen* took part in these operations, *III/JG 3* and all three from *JG 77*, with *II/JG 77* having been in the Crimea already since early March 1942 and the other three being transferred in for the final stages of the siege.[70] Before Sevastopol had finally fallen (4 July 1942), the main German operation, *Blau*, was launched on 28 June 1942.

Originally *Blau* was foreseen to have encompassed four *successive* parts. *Blau 1* was an advance from the Kursk area eastwards to take Voronezh on a tributary of the Don; *Blau 2* would turn the main force south-south-eastwards towards the Millerovo area, building a flank along the Don as they went; *Blau 3* was to advance to Stalingrad and at least neutralise that city; and *Blau 4* would then advance into the Caucasus to seize the oil centres of Grozny and Maikop, Hitler's real target and of critical importance in supplying the German war economy with oil.[71] The new Russian tactic of making planned retreats before encirclements could be effective led the Germans to be overconfident, and Hitler thus launched *simultaneous* major attacks towards Stalingrad and into the Caucasus – a classic military error of splitting forces.[72] In the event the German forces would take Maikop but find its oilfields destroyed, and the offensive towards Grozny was brought up short along the Terek River area and the great battle of Stalingrad put an end to any further Caucasian adventures.[73]

The German Offensive against Stalingrad and the Caucasus; Fall Blau

German fighter units were concentrated in the Kursk region to support the attack on Voronezh – including all three *Gruppen* of *JG 3* and two of *JG 52* (*III/JG 52* was further south in the Kharkov area) – while *I/JG 53*, newly arrived on the southern front in late May, was at Taganrog on the Sea of Azov; *II/JG 77* was also at Kursk, but would remain behind in the Voronezh area until 7 November when they left Russia for transfer to Africa, and *I* and *III/JG 77* were still in the Crimea when *Fall Blau* (Case Blue) was launched.[74] Neither unit would play any part in the Stalingrad or Caucasus battles to come, the former going to the Mediterranean theatre in late June and the latter later serving on the northern part of the Eastern Front.[75] *JG 52* and *JG 3* both took part in the rapid advance to the south-south-east, while *I/JG 53* advanced from the Taganrog region north-eastwards; their destinations were variously Rostov, Taganrog and the Morozovskaya areas.[76] One of the pilots with *III/JG 52*, *Unteroffizier* Hermann Wolf, serving with Hermann Graf's famous 9th *Staffel*, has described this rapid advance from one ill-prepared field base to the next, in the case of this *Gruppe* also involving a much further-removed set of transfers eventually all the way to the Terek front in the Caucasus:

> After *Jagdergänzungsgruppe* training, I went to the front in May 1942. My initial frontal experience in *9/JG 52* was in the *Staffel* of the later *Oberst* Hermann Graf, and I flew with well-known fighter pilots such as Hartmann, Steinbatz, Zwernemann, Krupinski, Füllgrabe, Süss etc. Our units were seldom accommodated on developed airfields during the advances in 1942. Mostly we occupied poorly prepared meadows or even fallow land for field

bases, often directly behind the advancing panzer columns and in front of the infantry, to protect the tanks. In the first few days only the most necessary ground crewmen were with us. By the time the main body of support personnel caught up with us we were often already on the next advanced field base. Our quarters were then in tents or if a village was nearby, in a farmer's hut. We slept on air mattresses in sleeping bags. We only very seldom came near any populated towns or cities. As in the beginning we had the better aircraft in aerial combats we could mostly attack enemy fighters from above in surprise attacks.

By 23 July 1942, Rostov had fallen and the gateway to the Caucasus and its precious oil was open; Hitler's new directive sent Army Group A (17th Army, 1st and 4th Panzer Armies) into the Caucasus, while Army Group B (2nd Hungarian Army, 8th Italian Army, 6th German Army; 3rd Romanian Army joined later, in September, from the Caucasus)[77] was to take Stalingrad and cut off the Volga transport route (including Russia's main remaining oil supplies, from Grozny).[78] The 4th Panzer Army was sent back to Stalingrad from the Caucasus on 31 July 1942 and had the 4th Romanian Army under command; both armies took part in the advance to Stalingrad from the south-west.[79] Once Stalingrad was invested and the vicious battle within the largely destroyed city began, protection for the flanks of the two German assaulting armies (6th Army and 4th Panzer) was provided by the 4th Romanian Army to the south of the city while to the west and north-west, strung out along the Don down which the Germans had advanced at the beginning of Operation *Blau*, were the 3rd Romanian, 8th Italian and furthest upstream, 2nd Hungarian armies.[80]

By now, German fighters were concentrated close to Stalingrad in the Frolow–Tusow area, and comprised all three Gruppen of *JG 3* (*I/JG 3* there from 28 July to 13 September 1942; *II/JG 3* from 27 July before leaving for the Central Eastern Front on 23 August; *III/JG 3* 27 July–10 September 1942), *II/JG 52* (20 August–1 September 1942) and *I/JG 53* (12 August–10 September 1942).[81] Following this, as Pitomnik airfield, immediately west of the stricken city, was taken by the Germans, *I/JG 3*, *III/JG 3* and *I/JG 53* were moved there; the latter *Gruppe* remained there only till 27 September when they were withdrawn to the Mediterranean theatre.[82] Also involved in the advance towards Stalingrad and the intense aerial fighting over the city was *I/ZG1*, and *Unteroffizier* Heinz Ludwig of the 3rd *Staffel* describes an exciting mission at the time:

The main jobs of the Me 110 in Russia were quite simply everything: pin-point bombing on all sorts of targets: tanks, trains, supply columns, airfields, plus also strafing runs in support of our ground troops, and naturally also aerial combat with enemy fighters and Il-2 ground attack aircraft. In November 1942 during the advance on Stalingrad we attacked enemy tank columns with bombs near Werbovka, and in pulling up to rejoin our comrades after the attack we all found ourselves in the middle of a number of Mig-5s (*sic*, most likely Lag-5s). My *Kutscher* (literally, coachman; i.e. his pilot) had one (Mig-5) about 100 m in front of him in our defensive circle, flying behind the wingman of our *Schwarmführer*, and I had another Mig 30–50 m behind the tail and flying somewhat lower than the tail, so that I could not fire at him without hitting our own tail. I kept seeing the face of this Russian pilot appearing in my view, but could not shoot. I called to my *Kaczmarek* (buddy, wingman) who was somewhere, who knows exactly where, that he should catch up, as I had an 'Indian' behind me. The latter must have had jammed guns otherwise he would have shot me down.

And so for several minutes we flew together in our circle and my backside was twitching. Then my wingman's aircraft appeared, but the circling continued, and he could also not shoot at the Mig without facing the danger of hitting us also. I suggested to my pilot that he should take some avoiding action so that I could get at the Ivan with the 'Hitler saw' (*Hitlersäge*; rear-facing double machine-gun mounting). But it did not come to this, as the Mig in front of us tried to leave the circle with a right turn, and Bruno (pilot *Unteroffizier* Bruno Baumeister) opened up with all his guns, hit the Mig fully and all I could see was a fireball, the aircraft having exploded in mid-air. When I turned around again, the Mig behind me had disappeared. After this we did not make any strafing runs, as we had to turn back to base, as the fuel was getting too low. It was a lovely feeling of being able to waggle our wings when we returned before landing, signifying our victory.

The Stalingrad Airlift

Before dawn on 19 November 1942, the great Russian counterattack at Stalingrad began. First Russian forces smashed the 3rd Romanian Army to the north-west of the city, along the Don; the next day it was the turn of the 4th Romanian Army, south of Stalingrad, and by 23 November the two wings of the Soviet attack had linked up and Stalingrad was surrounded, trapping 330,000 troops comprising the entire 6th German Army, parts of 4th Panzer Army and lesser numbers of Romanians and Italians.[83] It was now that the success story of the Demyansk airlift played its part in a growing tragedy. Now three times as many men had to be supplied, the distance to be flown was longer and the opposition from Russian air force and flak would be much tougher.

Against the advice of *General* Wolfram von Richthofen, the *Luftwaffe* commander of *Luftflotte* 4 on the spot, *Luftwaffe* Chief of Staff *General*

Hans Jeschonnek, let Hitler know that a temporary air supply might be possible; Göring's staff also stressed to him that a maximum daily supply of 350 tons could be possible, again for a short period, but in a fateful move Göring assured Hitler that the Stalingrad forces could be adequately supplied.[84] As a result, by 24 November Hitler took a decision that the 6th Army would remain in 'fortress Stalingrad' until relieved.[85] In the event, the average daily delivery was only slightly above 100 tons.[86] The weather was the dominant negative factor reducing supply flights, allied to low serviceability rates of the already overworked Ju 52 transport units available in southern Russia.[87] Extra transport aircraft and crews were desperately needed, and the only available source was the *Luftwaffe*'s training establishment, mainly from the highly trained instrument and multi-engine flying instructor units.[88] A more short-sighted solution is hard to imagine and this alone and the inevitable losses in the airlift, paid a blow to these training units and the entire transport fleet from which it never fully recovered; this should not have been a surprise to any of the responsible commanders and once again the *Luftwaffe* suffered from very poor leadership at the top.

One of the instructors affected by this rash decision was *Oberfeldwebel* Rudolf Hener, later a fighter pilot with *2/JG 3* in the West and the East, who had initially qualified as a fully trained instructor and more specifically an instrument-flying instructor, and who found himself caught up in the Stalingrad airlift.

When in the winter of 1942/1943 the destruction of the trapped German 6th Army in Stalingrad loomed, an additional transport *Geschwader* was set up in great haste, to aid in supplying this army, comprising 180 Junkers transport aircraft. The pilots were all instrument flying instructors. I was also commandeered into this unit and for four months I flew at the front under the harshest conditions, laden to the gills with ammunition on the way in and with wounded on the way out. When only forty of the 180 Ju 52 aircraft and crews were left, the *Geschwader* was terminated again. After that, from May 1943 I was again an instructor and instrument flying instructor at the training school in Stettin. I was especially involved in training young pilots who were intended to join the single-engined night fighters (*Wilde Sau*), flying the Me 109.

Platzschutzstaffel Pitomnik in the Stalingrad Pocket

When the Russian counterattack opened on 19 November, *I* and *III/JG 3* were still stationed at Pitomnik airfield just west of the city. The former were pulled out of Pitomnik on 20 November and the latter two days later.[89] However, parts of *I/JG 3* kept operating from this field, served also

97

by the most essential ground crew men, and from about 12 December 1942 a special unit called *Platzschutzstaffel Pitomnik* (literally airfield protection *Staffel* Pitomnik) was informally established.[90] It comprised pilots mainly from *I* and *II/JG 3* (but also from *III Gruppe*)[91] with an intention to rotate tired pilots and ground crew out of the pocket,[92] but as will be seen below, this did not always happen.

Feldwebel Kurt Ebener, its leading ace, has detailed the extremely hard conditions under which it operated, and also the efforts and sacrifices of the fliers of the transport planes, of the few Stukas still stationed at Pitomnik, as well as the ground crew, radiomen and flak soldiers.[93] Ebener also recorded the names of 20 pilots of *JG 3* who served in Pitomnik under siege, led for a long time by *Hauptmann* Germeroth, plus two other pilots who flew in on 15 January 1943 with orders that all aircrew were to leave the pocket when Pitomnik looked like falling.[94] Some did not get out (as described below by *Feldwebel* Hans Grünberg) and 66 ground crewmen from *I/JG 3* remained missing after the fall of the pocket.[95] The *Platzschutzstaffel* lost only three pilots while claiming 130 victories from the beginning of December 1942 till 15 January 1943 (this includes some also by elements of *I/JG 3* flying from Pitomnik before formation of this special *Staffel*).[96] Kurt Ebener (*4/JG 3*) scored 33 victories over Pitomnik under the hardest possible conditions, with primitive accommodation, dreadful cold and very poor rations, and was awarded the *Ritterkreuz* in April 1943.[97] Another pilot from *JG 3* who also flew in this *Staffel* was *Feldwebel* Helmut Notemann of the 5th *Staffel*: 'In Pitomnik we flew almost exclusively airfield protection and free chase missions.'

An astounding eyewitness account of flying with *Platzschutzstaffel Pitomnik* is provided by *Feldwebel* Hans Grünberg, *5/JG 3* who survived by the very skin of his teeth, as described below.

At the beginning of November 1942 (*sic*; it was actually from 23 November) Stalingrad was surrounded by the Russians. At the time, *II/JG 3* lay at Solzi near Lake Ilmen and was supposed to transfer quite suddenly to the Don area (Oblivskaya). In the Middle Eastern Front winter had already begun quite some time earlier; as a result there were only a few airfields that could be utilised by the Me 109s. It was not wise to hurry as daylight at this time of year was very short.

With the transfer a fiasco soon became apparent. With the landings in deep snow aircraft nosed over, turned right over and there were forced-landings also. Only a limited number of the *Gruppe* reached the new base with great difficulty. The *II Gruppe* now had to continuously provide pilots for the *Staffel* (known as *Platzschutzstaffel Pitomnik*) of *Hauptmann* Germeroth in Stalingrad. In the beginning the pilots had great successes in the pocket.

One day – it was at the beginning of December – I was ordered to lead four machines to Stalingrad (Pitomnik) for a week's flying. What I found there was bad. My bed was a medical stretcher. We slept and ate in a smoky earth bunker. Thank God I had taken a sleeping bag with me. I knew of course that no luxury hotel awaited me in Pitomnik, but I had never spent the night in such quarters. I obtained two old blankets from my comrades, to avoid freezing. The initially planned one week of operations in Pitomnik then became extended until this airfield was abandoned, as our relief never took place. We thus had to stay to the bitter end in the pocket.

In Pitomnik we were 12 fighter pilots, from different *Staffels* of *JG Udet*. Our duties there were to protect the ground troops and the few German aircraft from enemy air attack, and to protect the landings and take-offs of the transport planes. Often it was not possible with only one or two Me 109s to protect the airfield as well as transport machines unloading supplies and loading in the wounded. We had to watch as Ju 52s, Ju 88s and He 111s were shot down as they collected in the air for the return flights, and fell burning with the wounded on board, to their deaths on the ground. In January 1943 the cold was almost unbearable. There were days when our ground crewmen, at 25 to 30 degrees (Celsius) below freezing, were not able to start the available serviceable Me 109s. The reason was that the heating devices were almost all defective and ripe for the scrapheap. On 17 January 1943 on the field and in our bunker we could quite clearly hear the impacts of the enemy artillery shells. We knew then, that the Russians had broken through the western front of the pocket and could thus be expected to advance on the most important place in the pocket, Pitomnik.

Of the succeeding sequence of events I can still remember everything with crystal clarity. I was supposed to fly airfield protection the next morning. On the previous evening *Oberleutnant* Lukas, who had flown escort for supply aircraft and become involved in an aerial combat on the way, landed at Pitomnik. His Me 109 was no longer serviceable and there was thus no question of taking off again straightaway. *Oberleutnant* Lukas thus had to spend the night with us. His Me 109 was supposed to be the first Me 109 to be warmed up the next morning and made ready for take-off. For this one needed a lot of time, as the temperatures hovered around minus 25 degrees.

Finally his Me 109 was started and Lukas took off. He wanted to fly protection over the field until my Me 109 was also ready to lift off. After a while Lukas flew off to the west. At almost the same time the last Ju 87s (Stukas) took off, climbed to 300 m, and dived on the southern boundary of the field, dropping their bombs. We pilots and ground crew looked at each other and suddenly one of the mechanics said that the Russians were coming. I saw only soldiers in white camouflage suits, but these were already Russian infantrymen. My Me 109 would not start and on the second attempt to get the engine to fire one of the mechanics got hit by a bullet in the hand and shouted to me, 'Quick, out of the aircraft, the Russians are here.' The airfield had been overrun. Chaos followed.

What happened next defies description. German vehicles and tanks drove over German wounded soldiers. In their hundreds our emaciated infantrymen threw away their rifles, fell exhausted into the snow after a few metres, and died. For a long time there had been nothing substantial to eat. We pilots received daily a loaf of bread between seven men and a tin of sardines in oil between each three to four men. We could still take off and land on this, but it was no longer possible to turn tightly in the air or to become involved in an aerial combat. When turning we became dizzy and then could no longer see properly. The panic was now complete. All those who could still walk departed for the field at Gumerak that was about 25 km away. We marched through the freezing cold through deep snow, with nothing to eat and the journey was broken by attacks of enemy ground attack aircraft (Il-2s). A forced march like this is a real challenge for members of the *Luftwaffe*, but the will to survive made us strong and able to overcome these obstacles.

On 18 January shortly before it got dark we reached Gumerak (6 km outside Stalingrad). On the night of 18/19 January some supply aircraft still managed to land at Pitomnik. On the Eastern Front outside of Stalingrad it was not known yet that the Russians had taken this airfield. The Russians did not shoot at the landing aircraft. The aircraft and the supplies they carried were gratefully received by them. When it became known that Pitomnik had fallen, the supply planes were rerouted to Gumerak. The aircraft had orders not to land but to throw the supplies from the aircraft over Gumerak.

On 19 January in the early morning darkness a Ju 52 landed in Gumerak between the bomb craters. The crew was made up of four *Unteroffizieren*. According to their orders they were to take off immediately. I joined them and now had a small hope, to escape the hell of Stalingrad. I was able to be of great assistance to my fellow fliers from the Ju 52. I was able to explain to them that we would only be saved if we turned to the south and then flew at low level across the steppes. Several times we shuddered with fright as we could see Russian aircraft higher up. In the Caucasus (Krasnodar) we had to land to refuel. I then had to pursue my further journey to II *Gruppe* JG 3 on foot and by pick-up truck. After five days I reached the II *Gruppe* in the Donets area.

While Hans Grünberg had been very lucky to escape the pocket and almost certain death there, the price of the Stalingrad airlift (24 November 1942–2 February 1943) to the *Luftwaffe* was excessively high: 488 aircraft lost (destroyed, missing, written off) encompassing 266 Ju 52s, 165 He 111s, 42 Ju 86s, nine Fw 200s, five He 177s and one Ju 290, plus roughly 1,000 aircrew.[98] While the blow to the *Luftwaffe* transport arm was very serious, it was the loss of so many highly experienced aviators and of many instructional personnel that was even worse,[99] as emphasized above by Rudolf Hener. *Luftwaffe* training during the war went steadily down in terms of overall hours flown and also hours flown on operational aircraft, and the loss of instructors was thus almost catastrophic to future output.

Flying over the Caucasus

While the struggle for Stalingrad was continuing, *III/JG 52* was largely employed flying cover for the German armies pushing forward in the Caucasus area, aiming for the Maikop and Grozny oilfields (they reached the first, found them destroyed, but never got to the second, with the front stabilising along the Terek River) and the Black Sea ports remaining with the Soviet navy south of the Caucasus mountains.[100] Gerd Schindler joined the *Stab* of this *Gruppe* in August 1942 as a *Fahnenjunker-Unteroffizier* (*Unteroffizier*-officer cadet), and provides some interesting accounts of that particular theatre: 'In the Caucasus in 1942–earliest part of 1943 we met I-153 biplanes with retractable undercarriages, I-16 Ratas (apparently without gun sights, aimed using the entire aircraft), Lagg-3s, Mig-1s, Jak-1s, Il-2s without rear gunners, Pe-2s, Su-2s (met only once) and American Douglas Boston bombers. The newer types soon grew in numbers but only the I-153 and I-16 disappeared completely.'

II/JG 52 also flew over the Caucasus battlefields from 6 September till 26 November, and were then involved in supporting the Stalingrad airlift and the failed attempt to relieve the pocket from the south-west, before returning to the northern Caucasus at Salsk on 30 December 1942.[101] *I/JG 52*, on leave from early November apart from a ten-man team (*Kommando Wiese*) flying in the Woronesch area (9 November–6 December 1942) and thereafter from Rossosch (6 December 1942–15 January 1943), had been spared the Stalingrad debacle directly.[102]

Gerd Schindler in the *III Gruppe* was able to use his *Leistungsbuch* (an operational performance record), as well as diary entries and letters to his parents to reconstruct his experiences on the Eastern Front in some detail. In 1989 he sent me a copy of a published (in the *Jägerblatt?*) article he wrote on these experiences, used as the basis for the account here, embellished in a few places from the *III/JG 52* history[103] and letters he wrote to me. In July 1942 he and six fellow newly graduated fighter pilots took the train to Mariupol on the Sea of Azov in the Ukraine, to join *JG 52*. Here they met some members of *II/JG 52* who advised that the *Stab/*

JG 52 was in Rostov, but once they got there it had advanced once more, destination unknown. Finally in Armavir in the Caucasus they caught up with the *Geschwaderstab*. Schindler was then assigned to *III/JG 52*, joining the *Staff* flight of that *Gruppe* thanks to his friend Bert Korts who was already flying with them. His well-respected *Gruppenkommandeur* was *Major* von Bonin from Berlin, who when he reported to him asked Gerd where he came from and upon learning it was from Graz/Steiermark in Austria replied with some astonishment that there were reportedly still bears there in the wild.

Gerd soon became acclimatised to front conditions, by practising flying, shooting and also hitting a target, tutored by *Eichenlaub* winner and famous ace *Oberleutnant* Adolf Dickfeld, who already had over 100 of his eventual total of 136 victory claims. 'Dickfeld was an outstanding mentor and teacher at the front, helped one learn how to get into the right position behind an opponent and then shoot him down, he was no egotist. He gave me an exceptionally positive recommendation when he left *III/JG 52*. He came originally from the *Reichsjugendführung* (*Reichs* Youth Leadership, cf. Hitler Youth) and stayed with *Stab III/JG 52* only for a relatively short time. After the war there were rumours about him, I can only report good things of him. He is still alive (writing in 1990) but no one has heard or seen anything of him, he has not attended any get-togethers.' After *III/JG 52* converted to the Me 109 G-6 in Armavir, they moved on to Mineralnye Vody where Schindler flew his first operations (August 1942) and saw his first Russians.

After only three days it was forward again, to Gonstkowka, where Schindler soon had an interesting experience with his Me 109, a G-2 model equipped with two under-wing cannons which when fired in long bursts shook the plane so that the undercarriage fell out, without him necessarily always noticing this at first. This had advantages sometimes, as on 17 September 1942[104] when he had to force-land on the steppe during a mission and was pleasantly surprised by a smooth wheels-down landing instead of the expected belly-landing! As a result he was temporarily posted missing.

On this occasion he had flown a last mission with his *Rottenführer Oberleutnant* Dickfeld (with whom he got on splendidly), who had just been informed of his immediate transfer to the English Channel theatre and departed that afternoon with 130 victories under his belt (actually 129 claims according to the unit history of *III/JG 52*).[105] He and Dickfeld had taken off at 05h45 on 17 September 1942 as they knew the Russian fighters normally flew over their lines at 06h15. They experienced a beautiful day for flying, with almost the entire Caucasus visible from 4,000 m including the high mountains and glaciers glistening in the early sun. A few Russian flak bursts close by put an end to this sightseeing and as they turned away towards the interior of the Caucasus they discovered 12 enemy fighters, punctually at 06h20, resulting in a bitter dogfight and after an exciting time Schindler was able to shoot one down as his sixth victory claim.

Pulling up to escape the attentions of two more Russian fighters, he lost sight of Dickfeld and to get rid of the pursuing fighters had to dive away vertically, knowing no Russian could follow and keep up with such a manoeuvre. As he decided to fly home alone he discovered an approaching Il-2 formation and attacked one slightly separated aircraft, leaving it flying off to the east trailing smoke after he had shot some bits out of it. Schindler was convinced this Il-2 would have been forced down far into its own territory, so no victory to be claimed as his fuel did not allow a pursuit. Now he found that he had also been hit, and his engine stuttered as the fuel gauge showed zero, and he force-landed near some German vehicles. Due to the vibration stemming from his combats the undercarriage was in fact out and his expected belly-landing became a smooth one, the terrain allowing him to get away with it also.

Soon the *Gruppe*'s Fieseler Storch appeared, flown by Dickfeld, and he was among friends once again. Later he was able to return and fly the Messerschmitt out. By 19 October 1942 he had brought his score to 11 (he and his friend and *Rottenführer* Bert Korts each got an Il-2 over the Terek area that day) and had received the *Frontflugspange Gold* (Missions Clasp in Gold) for fighter pilots, for 110 missions flown. At the end of October he got jaundice and after a stay in hospital went home on leave, only returning to the front on 19 January 1943. While away he had been promoted to *Leutnant* on 1 December 1942. Schindler still recalled many details of his time flying in the Caucasus, and some of these are provided by him below.

During the heavy battles in Stalingrad the greater part of the *III Gruppe JG 52* (mine) lay in the Caucasus area, with only a *Schwarm* from each *Staffel* flying over the Stalingrad area, operating from Kalatsch and Pitomnik; I believe they were led by Knights Cross with Diamonds winner Graf (first great ace to reach 200 victory claims, on 2 October 1942).[106] In the Caucasus the fighter activity had its own character. We flew in well-defined *Rotte* and *Schwarm* formations, the Russian fighters we could see already from far away. They typically flew in large beehive formations of 20–30 aircraft, one can say in bullet-shaped masses. We tried to burst through them or to pick one off flying on the edge of their formations.

Formations of ground attack aircraft, Il-2s, in those days still flying without gunners – rear gunner cockpits were added later and were manned partly by women (!), and the aircraft also flown by women sometimes; when attacked they formed a defensive circle and protected each other's tails, or flew on stubbornly towards their targets. They relied on their strong armour, our rounds bouncing right off these cumbersome aircraft. We soon found out that successful hits could be obtained in their bellies if you could hit the oil coolers, or during dogfights if you could fire directly into the cockpits. Ratas and I-153 biplanes with retractable undercarriages initially had no gun sights apparently and aimed their fire with the entire aircraft.

Noticeable at this time and also later were the Russian night disturbance aircraft, known colloquially as 'sewing machines' due to their tinny engines. These were small single biplanes that dropped small, un-aimed high explosive bombs; it was said that they dropped them by hand. They came after darkness had set in almost every night, for hours, hit very little, but they robbed us of sleep and rest and that was also their purpose! Douglas Boston bombers flew stubbornly on for their targets, alone or in formations up to 10 aircraft. Parachute jumps from shot-up Russian aircraft were as far as I remember, seldom observed, it being rumoured they were either not allowed to or did not have any chutes.

Living conditions on the ground, as I experienced them, were never primitive! That means we always made the best of a situation. The personal equipment ensured an endurable life in all circumstances: every pilot from *Gefreiter* to *Kommodore* possessed a clothes bag, air mattress and down sleeping bag. On the field bases there were one- or two-man tents, or use was made of private quarters, Russian huts (in one of which I was treated very kindly by an old Russian women after crashing onto my back while landing), in schools, other buildings or even in brick-built quarters on some established air bases; according to frontal region we even sometimes lived in beautiful villas!

For the flying personnel we lived an essentially mess-based lifestyle, in which the *Gefreiter* up to the *Oberst* sat at a set table with tablecloths, and we always had our chairs and tables along with us, even if they were only made from crates. We celebrated often, at any excuse, the kitchen was excellent, except in emergency situations such as when we had to evacuate a base. In the Caucasus for example we also built comfortable earth bunkers lined with wood, which were very popular with the mice. However, sadly nothing came of our planned winter quarters, as we had to evacuate. In large centres, soldier's clubs, cinemas and *Wehrmacht* support services improved front life.

Tactics used against Russian aircraft varied according to type and their use. For fighters we tried to surprise them from altitude, from out of the sun and behind, or in dogfights we shot at them with the relevant deflection using MGs or 2 cm cannons. Il-2s we tried to attack from behind at the same height or from slightly below with the aim of hitting the oil cooler beneath the machine. Later we had to beware of the rear-gunners, including women! It was best to hit this type of aircraft in the oil cooler as that was their one vulnerable spot. Otherwise the strong armour led to all rounds bouncing off. Alternatively, one could try and hit the cockpits in turning dogfights. Bombers we attacked from behind trying first to eliminate the rear gunners, and then to hit either wing tanks or engines to set the aircraft on fire. Our MG belts were loaded with different types of ammunition such as explosive rounds, armour-piercing, incendiary rounds and tracer bullets etc.

There is a minor element of contempt in some of the remarks made above by Gerd Schindler, such as Russian Ratas and I-153 fighters lacking gunsights and aiming with the entire axis of the aircraft. In this regard, one needs to recall *JG 52 Kommodore* Hanns Trübenbach's remarks when he first used the MK 108 3 cm cannon installed in his brand new Me 109 F in 1941 in dogfights over the Black Sea area, described in chapter 4. He had found that the centrally placed nose cannon enabled aiming with the entire aircraft and that this was a distinct benefit! Schindler's claims that parachutes were lacking or banned from use in the Russian air force must also be considered somewhat equivocal.

6

1943: Year of Decision, the Tide Turns; Kuban and Kursk

Oberfeldwebel Richard Raupach was a senior NCO who flew in *JG 54* for almost two years, and he spent almost the entire year of 1943 over the northern part of the front, in Army Group North's area, first with *I/JG 54* and then with the *IV/JG 54* from about August 1943. Below is his recollection of the relatively static nature of ground operations in the north, where the main aerial opponents were the tough Il-2s. While this is a nice example of the 1943 experience for a fighter pilot flying over Army Group North, the fighting in this theatre contrasts strongly with what occurred in the south and centre of the Eastern Front during this fateful year, as will be discussed in this chapter.

Personally I was only stationed on the Eastern Front from June 1942 (when I joined *1/JG 54* at Gatschina outside Leningrad) till May 1944. I achieved 16 *Abschüsse*: 14 Il-2s, one J-154 (a biplane fighter aircraft with retractable undercarriage) and one Pe-2. In addition I also flew 144 missions as fighter-bomber; with the Fw 190 we dropped 500 kg bombs, with the Me 109 250 kg bombs, but also smaller bombs and munitions containers. In about April 1943 we flew bombing attacks with the Fw 190 on Russian positions. A comrade, *Feldwebel* Paul Rätz, did not return from one of these operations. I never heard anything of him again, as was often the case.

Recently (writing in 1992) at the last get-together of the fighter pilots in the previous year at Geisenheim, I was approached about this event. A British illustrated publication had published a report with photos, that English researchers had discovered this belly-landed aircraft in Russia. They had bought the wreck and shipped it to England. *Feldwebel* Rätz had survived the belly-landing in good shape, but had died in Russian captivity. Contact had also been made with his family in Hamburg. I belly-landed the Fw 190 three times, and survived two more as a passenger in a Fw 58 (Weihe) and another as passenger in a Me 108. I also made a successful one-wheel landing with a W 34.

After the war only did I hear that I had apparently been in *JG 7* (in some publication) and could not believe this. In June 1944 I had left *IV/JG 54* and transferred to the *E-Gruppe (Jagdergänzungsgruppe) East* in Lignitz as an instructor. I remained there until the capitulation to the English in Schleswig-Holstein in May 1945 (we had moved there in January 1945). The *IV Gruppe* was totally destroyed in the Home Defence. It was disbanded and the remnants transferred to *JG 7*. If I had not joined the *E-Gruppe* as an instructor in June 1944, I would not have been able to write this reminiscence.

I can add my experience of the Il-2. Apart from a very short time, I was always stationed in the northern sector of the Eastern Front. There it was mainly a static war. The main war events always played themselves out on the Southern Front. In that area was also where the vast majority of the Russian fighters were stationed. In our northern area the Il-2s actually always came without escort. They attacked our frontline positions, but also the hinterland. They normally came only in pairs but also in formations up to nine machines. The Il-2 was very strongly armoured and also had a rear-gunner, who served a machine gun in a cabin that was open at the top. The Il-2 could not be shot down by machine gun fire. Even with our 2 cm explosive ammunition (Oerlikon cannons) it was often difficult to get one to fall down. One had success when firing at the Il-2 at the same altitude from obliquely to the side and behind. The pilot often had the side panel of his cabin open due to the heat. The 2 cm shells from our two MG 151s in the Fw 190 already caused considerable damage. Sometimes the Fw 190 was armed with four MG 151s. We also always had in addition the two MG 131s of *c.* 12.7 mm calibre; they shot between the rotating propeller blades.

As fliers, the Russians were not so flexible nor as resourceful as the Germans. In contrast the Anglo-Saxons were much harder for us to combat and were often superior fliers. During the course of the war the Russians caught up more and more tactically. Their fighter the Jak-9 with a 3 cm cannon at the end was the equal of our Me 109. The Russians were very tough and steadfast soldiers. Their strengths were the infantry, artillery and tank arms. In my eyes the Russians were second only to the Spanish and the Turks as soldiers. In the northern part of the front we had the Spanish 'Blue Division'. This the Russians never dared to attack.

1943 saw the final surrender at Stalingrad at the beginning of the year, and the critical air battle over the Kuban bridgehead in April and May, where for the first time Soviet tactics were determined by experience and the strong input of Russian combat veterans. The *Luftwaffe* fighter pilots were finally up against an equal opponent in many ways. Preceded by two months of intense aerial fighting, the massive battle of the Kursk salient followed in July, with immediate Soviet counterattacks in later July and in August 1943 making major inroads into the German lines. After that the virtually unending German retreat in the East began, with Kiev, the capital of Ukraine, falling by 6 November. As the defence of the Homeland absorbed more and more of the German fighter arm, forces available on the Eastern Front shrunk and an almost nomadic lifestyle became common for many *Jagdgruppen*, shifted from one critical point to the next, always retreating in the face of the Russian advances.

Operations in the Far North

In the far north, on the *Eismeer* Front, the war on the ground also remained essentially static; II and III/JG 5 were the two single-engined fighter units in action there, mostly operating from Petsamo, Kirkenes and sometimes further south, along the Finnish–Russian front to the west of the famous Murmansk railway line. The main tasks of these two *JG 5 Gruppen* lay, as before during 1942, in escorting German bombers to Murmansk, defending their own bases and attacking the Murmansk railway line. *Hauptmann* Günther Scholz, *Kommandeur* of III/JG 5, recounts one of the many tasks set for them in the far north, encompassed in a set of missions flown sometime between February and June 1943:

Theatre: Karelia, target the Murmansk railway. As *Kommandeur* of III/JG 5 I received the instruction to use a fighter-bomber *Staffel* (Fw 190s) and a *Stukastaffel* (Ju 87s) for a persistent attack to either destroy or interrupt the Murmansk railway line (the line leading south from the Murmansk harbour, ice-free in winter). Where and how I did this was up to me. We flew from Petsamo (now Petschenga) to Alakurti. Alakurti was a Finnish airfield and lay closest of any to the railway line. From there we discovered a small station, by taking a *Schwarm* and flying along a long section of the tracks; at the same time we found Russian airfields in the same area, including some occupied by 'real' aircraft. The Russians were masters in equipping decoy airfields that were occupied by dummy aircraft in wooden protective boxes. During the winter the snow behind the dispersed 'aircraft' and on the runway was blown away or swept, so that it looked authentic. With the help of our radar, however, we could establish from where the Russians were really taking off.

With my *Schwarm* I flew at low level over the decoy airfields to be sure and saw unoccupied wooden buildings. From altitude the airfield looked completely genuine. When the ceiling was reasonably high we attacked a small station with several sets of tracks and some huts as well as parked locomotives, and used bombs to destroy the tracks and our guns to destroy the locomotives. We repeated this for four days, as the tracks were repaired at night. We flew many sorties, there were aerial combats, we lost two Ju 87s and as far as I remember six Russian fighters were shot down (one by myself). On the fifth day the weather turned bad, the clouds hung low, and it rained and there was no visibility, so that we had to stop the attacks. But for a good five days no train carrying American war material was able to transport it from Murmansk harbour southwards.

During 1943, in the far north, *II* and *III/JG 5* claimed 474 victories over Russian aircraft with seven more added by *13(Z)/JG 5*'s *Zerstörers* and two by the fighter-bombers of *14(Jabo)/JG 5*.[1] A late arrival to this theatre in 1943 was *Leutnant* Ernst Scheufele of *5/JG 5*: 'I only managed to get transferred to *II/JG 5* on the *Eismeerfront* in October 1943 (prior to this he had flown with *IV/JG 5* in Norway since June 1942). There I was able to get my first *Abschuss* on 3 November 1943.' Also on 3 November 1943, *II/JG 5* moved to northern Russia (Pleskau) where it remained until March 1944.[2]

Operations from Leningrad to Orel, First Half of 1943
In early 1943, despite the major actions related to the Russian winter offensives in the south, there was also a Russian advance westwards by the Bryansk and Central Fronts against German Army Group Centre positions in the Orel–Bryansk area, which was unsuccessful (12 February–21 March 1943).[3] The Germans, however, very short of troops after the large-scale winter battles across Russia and especially the preceding Stalingrad debacle, evacuated the Rhzev salient (Army Group Centre) between 27 February and 22 March 1943, as well as the Demyansk salient (Army Group North; between 15 and 28 February 1943).[4] While Velikiye Luki on the Central Front was liberated in January 1943, a Soviet assault westwards towards Staraya Russa (Army Group North) was beaten off by the Germans (4–17 March 1943).[5]

JG 54 had always been the main *Luftwaffe* fighter unit supporting Army Group North, but at the beginning of 1943 it was planned to swap *JG 26* along the Channel front with *JG 54* in the East, and initially *I/JG 26* and *7/JG 26* went east, while *III/JG 54* and *4/JG 54* went west.[6] *III/JG 54* had been at Smolensk until 12 February 1943 when they were posted to northern France and Belgium. *I/JG 26* flew in the East from 15 February 1943 till early in June, initially from Rielbitzi and Dno (both in February 1943) and then operated in the Staraya Russa area south of Lake Ilmen;

then they moved to Schatalovka (just south of Smolensk; March–April 1943) and in May flew out of Smolensk, Ossinovka (southeast of Smolensk), and Orel.[7] The intended swap of the entire *JG 26* from West to East, and of *JG 54* in the opposite direction, never went further than *I/JG 26*'s brief sojourn on the Russian front (plus 7/*JG 26*, which flew in the Leningrad area from mid-February till end of June 1943); while *I/JG 26* returned to the West, *III/JG 54* remained in their new western home.[8] *II/JG 54* had lost the 4th *Staffel* during February 1943, swapped for 7/*JG 26*, but the former *Staffel* did not return to *JG 54* when 7/*JG 26* was transferred back to the West.[9]

Feldwebel Georg Füreder had almost the opposite experience in the *JG 26–JG 54* swaps, coming east with *1/JG 26*, and soon after it had left again, being sent to *IV/JG 54* in Russia; here he describes his experiences in *JG 54* in the East.

> My times in Russia (*I/JG 26*, 15 February–6 June 1943; *IV/JG 54*, July 1943–March 1944) were rather short and as a young beginner at first not very successful either. During the period of preparation for the Kursk–Orel battle, I belonged to *I Gruppe* (1st *Staffel*) of *JG 26* – in the Bryansk sector. Our area of operations then lay to the north-east and north of Orel (on the southern part of the Central Front – later adjacent to the northern part of the Kursk salient) and our secondary task was the protection of our own airbase that was packed with bombers (Ju 88s) and reconnaissance aircraft. This Gruppe of *JG 26* was exchanged from the West (Northern France–Belgium), replacing *III Gruppe* of *JG 54* which went to the Channel. Even though both *Gruppen* were successful in their new operational areas, the exchange was cancelled, in the light of the fact that differing conditions between East and West were in fact bigger than first envisaged. Thus the exchanged *Gruppe* of *JG 26* returned to Northern France (Poix) in May 1943 (however, *III/JG 54* did not return to the East).[10] I also transferred back to France with the *I/JG 26* and enjoyed two months of fun as a result – in the air and on the ground.

Oberfeldwebel Alfred Heckmann, who had flown in the East in 1941–1942 with *JG 3*, returned there in 1943 as part of *I/JG 26*, and commented that 'by now the Russians had better aircraft, but still used poor formations'. The fighting that was taking place over the Kuban while *I/JG 26* was still operating over Soviet territory would soon change such generalised perceptions of Russian fighter opposition.

The balance of *II/JG 54* (excluding 4th *Staffel*) began the year at Kalinin, about 80 km north-west of Bryansk, moving to Orel in May and flying there till August 1943.[11] One of those flying in *II/JG 54* from Kalinin was *Leutnant* Wolfgang Kretschmer of 6th *Staffel*, for whom a page of what appears to be a handwritten and shortened copy of his *Leistungsbuch* has appeared on the web.[12] This records a total of 21 missions over 18 days (4–21 March 1943), flown on 11 of the 18 days; Kretschmer flew eight of the 21 missions as part of a *Schwarm*, the other 13 as part of a *Rotte*. The 21 missions can be broken down into 13 free chase operations, seven bomber escorts (four times of Ju 88s, twice of He 111s, once of Ju 87s) and one scramble. Operations flown per active flying day varied between one and three in number. Enemy aircraft were met on 11 of the 21 missions and three victories were claimed by Kretschmer.

Single Russian aircraft were met on four of the missions (Pe-2, Il-2, Yak-4), three Il-2's on another, with larger formations of fighters being encountered four times, respectively ten Lagg-3s and P-40s, six P-40s, six Lagg-3s, eight Lagg-3s, and on one operation he met a total of four Il-2s escorted by six Lagg-3s and eight of the old I-16s. Enemy aircraft met on one mission were not recorded.[13] What is interesting is that only small formations or single aircraft were met on most occasions from this sample from March 1943, with only one operation out of 11 with enemy contact, meeting a large formation of 18 Soviet aircraft; this is typical of the Russian front after the first month or two in June 1941 up till late 1943, and also typical of much of the time on the Northern Front of the German forces, as also recorded by *Oberfeldwebel* Richard Raupach of *I* and *IV/JG 54* above. Promoted later to *Oberleutnant*, Wolfgang Kretschmer survived the war with a total of 19 claimed victories, and the *Ehrenpokal* (Honour Goblet); at the time of the March 1943 operational sample detailed above he was still one month short of his 21st birthday.[14]

I/JG 54 operated in the Leningrad area till February 1943 when a return to Germany ensued for conversion onto the Fw 190, and in March they were back, flying from Staraya Russa till May, and then protecting German supply convoys in the Gulf of Finland while based at Nikolskoye (on Esel Island off the coast of Estonia – today known as Saaremaa Island; May–June 1943).[15] *Unteroffizier* Ernst Richter was a newly joined member of the *Gruppe* who began his operational career there in May: 'On the Narva Front we also flew cover for shipping in the Gulf of Finland; a really unpleasant duty, especially when the cloud ceiling was only at about 300 m. Then it could also happen that the ships we were protecting would open fire on us when we approached too close to them, even though we had fired the colours of the day. When flying over the water with only one engine one imaged all sorts of unpleasant sounds from the engine.'

I/JG 51 began the year in Vyazma, and then (6 January 1943) moved to Izocha (*c.* 45 km south-west of Velikiye Luki) till 27 January, followed by a move to Orel, and in March to Bryansk where they stayed till May.[16] *III/JG 51* saw in the New Year in the Rhzev salient at Dugino and on

27 January moved to Orel, before returning to Dugino again later in February; in March they were back at Gatchina, south of Leningrad, where they stayed until May.[17] The *IV Gruppe* of the *Mölders Geschwader* began the year in Vitebsk, moving to Izocha, south-west of Velikiye Luki on 9 January, before returning to Germany on 3 February due to their conversion to the Fw 190.[18] Following their return to the East, they were stationed at Orel from late February till 2 August 1943.[19]

There were still a couple of *Zerstörergruppen* stationed in Russia in the first part of 1943. *II/ZG 1* operated north-east of Rostov at the beginning of the year, then moved to Dnepropetrovsk until March 1943 when they returned to Germany; *I/ZG 1* flew over the Russian front from the beginning of the year until July when they also returned to Germany.[20] Their bases included Krasnodar in the Kuban (1– 21 January 1943), Poltava? (uncertain; January–March 1943), Kharkov (March to April), Kramatorskaya (about 80 km north of Stalino; April–May 1943) and then finally in the Orel area (May–July 1943).[21] By this stage in the Eastern Front operations the Me 110s were used mainly for ground attack missions, as reported below for 2 May 1943 by *Unteroffizier* Heinz Ludwig who flew as an air gunner/radio operator in *3/ZG 1*.

Based at the airfield at Orel-Ledna we had two Me 109 photo-reconnaissance machines of *NAG 4*. For weeks they brought back photographs of a large terrain with wider than normal wheel tracks that could not have been made by any known vehicle. But from 4,000 m everything looked like a covered-over network with distinct grid-forms (like the English airfields in the Battle of Britain). With the latest photographs from the end of April 1943, we knew that this was an airfield. The east–west running stripes on the photographs were hedges as high as a man in which the tails of the machines were pushed. Everything was made ready for an operation. I flew as radio-operator with *Staffelkapitän Hauptmann* Herrmann because he wanted to complete his 200th mission together with his own radio-man. With five aircraft we taxied to the take-off point in the dark, with *Leutnant* Stratmann in the middle, the later *Staffelkapitän* in the Home Defence with ZG 26. And this Stratmann had not closed his cockpit roof correctly, so that shortly before lifting off it detached and hit the radio-operator hard on his skull and broke the antennae mast off. He had to break off the take-off with great difficulty, the aircraft was seriously damaged – but he was lucky!

As the Russians were masters in camouflage we could hardly make out the airfield from 4,000 m when we reached it as the sun came up. We circled once and flew a bit further to the east into the rising sun. *Simba 1* ordered the others to circle and told them that he was going to make a run alone first to 'examine' the field. We prepared ourselves for a sudden attack coming in at 70° out of the sun. Once he had dropped his bombs he shot the field up with all his guns, and I also shot as we pulled up. And then we saw them standing in the bushes, by the sun's rays which reflected off the cabin glass. Two rows of machines in the bushes! He called: 'Hallo, there they are' and gave the order that the other three aircraft should drop their bombs close to where ours had made clouds of smoke, and this was done with excellent results. Still no flak opposition.

He then ordered us to formate again away from the field, and we flew about 15 km to the east, turned round, now at about 1,000 m and next came: 'Get ready to *Rolle, Rolle* (=low level attack)!' Now the sun was blood red in the east, and we came right out of it. At a height of only 10 m we roared one behind the other across the field and shot with everything we had, also myself as we pulled up. Then a left turn, still at 10 m height and away to the east. I saw some machines on the ground burning and exploding. Then turn again, second attack, still no flak, and we shot up the right-hand row of bushes, and again several aircraft caught fire. Over the field there were black smoke clouds from oil and fuel, and the smoke drifted to the east which was great for us as Ivan could not see us coming, as we now came in out of the smoke, for the third attack and still no flak!

The third aircraft now reported that its guns had jammed and it could no longer shoot. *Hauptmann* Herrmann ordered him to fly in the attack despite this. And then he got it. I saw to the left how the flak burst exploded in the machine, *Feldwebel* Menard pulled the aircraft up high, the right engine was on fire, the radio-operator *Unteroffizier* Walter bailed out with his parachute, and is missing; the Me 110 hung in the air like a ripe plum and then dropped its right wing, crashing into the ground in flames with the pilot. My heart almost stopped, I reported this to my pilot; he said 'we must make another attack, all the aircraft must be destroyed'. And this we did. He ordered the other two to close up for the last attack. And then the three of us roared over the field once more, 50 m apart. My heart was in my mouth, some more aircraft exploded on the ground, the flak was now silent; we circled once more, now at 1,500 m and the field was just an inferno, with nothing left alive down there. As the flak had stood really close to the machines it must have been taken out by the explosions. And then we flew home, my pilot reporting the destruction of the airfield.

We all waggled our wings in overflying our base, but we had lost a comrade. If the cockpit roof of *Leutnant* Stratmann had not come off, he would have been flying in the number three position instead of *Feldwebel* Menard – Kismet! After doing the combat reports, the report was sent to the headquarters of the *Luftflotte*, to *General* von Richthofen. On the next morning in the *Wehrmacht* communique: 'Special report: Under the leadership of *Hauptmann* Herrmann at dawn on 2 May 1943 a *Schwarm* of *Zerstörer* attacked an enemy airfield and destroyed 32 American aircraft on the ground.' From pictures taken by *NAG 4* afterwards the field was seen to be totally destroyed. So, it was done. Also, after we landed from this *Feindflug* we had not a single round of ammunition left, neither in front nor at the back where I sat. Up till now I have only told very little about this event, as our youth have very negative attitudes, as they are taught in the schools that we had all been war criminals. We had only remained faithful to our flag and only fought for Germany, and absolutely fairly at that!

This sortie would have formed part of the increasingly fierce air battle fought over the Kursk salient well before the ground struggle began, from May to June 1943; as usual Russian camouflage was excellent and there were many dummy airfields within the salient.[22] It is also possible that this attack by the Me 110 pilots of *3/ZG 1* was on just such an establishment.

Battles in the South in the First Half of 1943
In late January 1943, just as the last resistance in Stalingrad was crumbling, the greater Soviet winter offensive was launched in several areas. Advances launched westwards along the Voronezh and Southwestern Fronts took Belgorod, Kursk (fell on 8 February 1943) and Kharkov (fell 16 February), opening up a huge gap between German Army Group Centre and the southern German armies.[23] Rapid withdrawal of German forces from the Caucasus was achieved, and Rostov fell to the Russians on 14 February 1943, leaving the German 17th Army isolated in the Taman peninsula where a significant air battle was to take place in April–May 1943 over the Kuban front there.[24] The Russian advances continued towards Poltava and Dnepropetrovsk in the Ukraine, threatening to cut off the southern German armies from their major supply lines, but were caught off their guard by a strong armoured German counterattack, launched on 20 February; this drove back the Russian advances towards the Dnieper River, and rapidly retook Kharkov (15 March 1943), Belgorod soon after, and re-established a stable frontline along the Mius and Donets rivers.[25]

JG 52 spent much of the early part of 1943 retreating: *I/JG 52* moved essentially westwards back from Rossosh to Kursk and then Kharkov (1 January–4 February 1943); *II/JG 52* moved north-westwards out of the Caucasus, through Rostov and then Koteinikovo, and thence transferred to the Kuban front (1 January–10 February); *III/JG 52* followed a similar path from the Caucasus, and then through Taganrog and Nikolayev, also to the Kuban front (1 January–15 March).[26] *II/JG 52* remained in the Kuban the longest, until 1 September, while *III Gruppe* stayed there until just before the Kursk offensive broke (till 2 July 1943).[27] *I/JG 52* meanwhile enjoyed much more of the nomadic lifestyle, with four moves between the Kharkov and Poltava areas up till 5 April 1943, before joining their comrades in the Kuban; on 29 April they were sent back to Kharkov till 15 May after which it was back to the Kuban once more until 3 July, again just before the Kursk battle began.[28]

In correspondence with the author, *Leutnant* Gerd Schindler described his return to the front after sick leave over Christmas 1942/43. He returned on 19 January and, luckily for him, when the train stopped at Armavir in the Caucasus (beyond which the train no longer ran) he found the *Stab III/JG 52* in that town as well. There followed some pleasant days in Armavir without any missions to be flown, only the *Gruppenstab* of *III/JG 52* being stationed there. But then, one day, with the town burning, they had to leave with the Storch and Klemm light aircraft, following low-level attacks on the railway station and with a sandstorm up to 100 m height through which a milky sun was visible. Due to mist their Me 109s had to be blown up, and Schindler and his friend Bertl Korts flew off in the tightly packed Klemm, another pilot in the Storch, and *Gruppenkommandeur* von Bonin and the ground staff by road.

After some confusion of moves and transfers, they ended up at Nikolayev (8 February–14 March 1943),[29] where *Hauptmann* Rall was acting *Gruppenkommandeur* while von Bonin was on leave. On 19 February Schindler and some others were flown to Mariupol in haste in a Ju 52 to evacuate aircraft there threatened by the Russian advance, and he flew a Hs 126 to safety at Nikolayev. Four days later the entire *Gruppe* was taken to Krakow in Poland to receive new aircraft, but after some days were sent to Vienna by train, as the new Me 109s were to be collected from the factory at Wiener Neustadt. Schindler even got to spend a few hours at home during a 24-hour leave in the Austrian capital.

In their brand-new aircraft the *Gruppe* took off again to return to the front, first stop at Krakow again, but bad weather led to several pilots parachuting from their machines and most others got lost and landed all over the place; Gerd Schindler and two others (out of 23 in total!) made it through safely. After 10 days to collect the *Gruppe* together again, it was back to Nikolayev. On 11 March Gerd Schindler and *Feldwebel* Klaus Dadd were sent back once more to Krakow to pick up two more new aircraft; poor Klaus Dadd was to be wounded in the throat on 6 June 1943 in combat, and managed to land at his base but died 13 days later.[30] On 15 March 1943 the *III/JG 52* left Nikolayev for the Crimea.[31]

The exhausted *I/JG 3* pulled out of supporting the Stalingrad airlift (from Morozovskaya) in the first few days of January 1943 and moved to a base north-east of Rostov from where they were transferred to Germany on 20 January (apart from some pilots still flying in *Platzschutzstaffel Pitomnik*), not to see the Eastern Front again till 1945.[32] *II/JG 3* was similarly moved to north-east of Rostov in early January (but with significant participation in the *Pitomnik Staffel*), after which they were stationed at various points along the Mius front until 5 April.[33]

The *II Gruppe* took part in the intense air battle of the Kuban (5 April–1 May 1943 and 7–16 May 1943).[34] *III/JG 3* followed the same path from Morozovskaya to north-east of Rostov (till 25 January), then flew over the Mius front (Stalino area) till 20 February, when they transferred to the area around and north of Zaporozhye (20 February–5 April 1943); flying from Kerch they fought on the Kuban front (5–26 April) before moving to the north of Stalino till 4 July.[35] *Feldwebel* Hans Grünberg of *5/JG 3* recalled flying briefly with their Hungarian allies during their stay on the Mius front:

In early 1943 the German troops occupied Kharkov once again after having lost it previously for a short time. The *II Gruppe* of *JG 3* then lay in Rogan, near Kharkov (his memory is at fault here as actually they were at Rowenky and Makeyevka on the Mius front, further south, from January 1943 till 5 April, after which they went to the Kuban front and only after that to the Kharkov region).[36] One day our *Kommandeur* let us know that a Hungarian fighter *Staffel* was stationed close by and that we should be careful not to mistakenly shoot one of their aircraft down. We soon met the Hungarian fliers and found them to be first-class comrades. They complained that they had poorly trained mechanics and that their Me 109s were not well serviced. As a result they had too few serviceable aircraft. Our *Kommandeur*, *Major* Brändle, immediately ordered some of our key mechanics over to the Hungarians to bring their old Me 109s up to scratch. During this time we had the Hungarian pilots with us. Each *Staffel* and the *Stab* got two or three Hungarian pilots allotted to it. In the 5th *Staffel* from now on *Leutnant* Bohatsch and I flew in a vic of three and soon established that the Hungarians were very good pilots, and that they could also shoot a lot but seldom hit their targets.

I can still clearly recall exactly my first *Feindflug* with a Hungarian pilot. We were flying in a vic of three on a free chase mission. It did not take long before I saw some enemy aircraft. I told my two wingmen that things were now going to happen and that we should go and take a look at the Russians. I wondered whether my Hungarian pilot was to be exposed to such a combat, but then thought they were supposed to learn something from us. Not long after, I got an *Abschuss*. The combat lasted for about 10 more minutes. But for us there was no second success as the number of the enemy aircraft was too large. To my horror I now found out that my Hungarian had disappeared in the sky. It was also not possible to establish via the radio whether he was still flying or already on the ground. I thus landed at our base with my *Rottenflieger*. I waited for a while, then went to our headquarters and had to admit that I did not know where my Hungarian comrade was. It was painful always, to lose someone on their first flight with you.

After about two hours a Me 109 with Hungarian markings suddenly appeared over our field and landed. I did not believe my eyes when my lost Hungarian pilot climbed out of the aircraft and came directly to me. He was still very excited over my air combat and was very happy over my success. For us, it was not done to embrace someone after a successful combat, but he did so spontaneously. He said proudly, 'I saw your *Abschuss*, and it was great.' I asked him where he had been. He just said that Russian fighters had forced him towards the East, but then he was able to get away and due to shortage of fuel he had landed on a field base. His aircraft had been refuelled there, and then he took off to return to us.

Our Hungarian flying comrades visited us often later on and invited us to visit them also. We soon found out that their red wine was first class and that they had a good supply thereof. Wicked tongues later suggested that we received our Hungarian decorations and pilot's wings from the air marshal of the Hungarian Air Force only due to our ability to drink large amounts of red wine. The friendship was however genuine and soon the first invitations to Hungary came. The Hungarian pilots were almost all nobles and had volunteered for frontline duty. Only *Hauptmann* Kirschner was able to attend a get-together in the Looping-Bar in Budapest. However the city commandant had something against the fact that the celebrations went on until the morning, and *Hauptmann* Kirschner was provided with a free ticket and pass to return to his unit at Kharkow.

The Critical Air Battle over the Kuban

On 15 March, *III/JG 52* left Nikolayev for Kerch, in the Crimea, and later flew from Taman, across the Straits of Kerch on the western point of the Taman peninsula (from 1 April 1943)[37] for operations over the Kuban bridgehead. Here Gerd Schindler remembers most missions being Stuka escorts, but he was able to shoot down a Pe-2 and was transferred to the *9/JG 52* before the move to Taman. Here he shot down an Airacobra and was himself hit twice but managed to put his aircraft down in one piece at the difficult Anapa airfield where *II/JG 52* lay (and which had to be approached from over the sea, with a cliff right where the field started) with his red fuel warning lamp burning brightly.

The next day he had to do this again after an unsuccessful tussle with three Laggs 100 km behind the lines. His friend Bertl Korts returned from home leave and they flew together over the Novorossiysk bridgehead where the Russians had landed, but soon after in April 1943 Schindler was posted to France as an instructor. He remembers an improved Russian enemy over the Kuban:

> Over the Kuban the Russians' tactics had already improved, their fighters were faster and flew in a more disciplined way. They had learnt from us. During the war in the East the Russian fighter tactics improved continuously and also a number of aces appeared. Regarding morale in our own units, I cannot really say that *JG 52* had especially high morale and fighting spirit, as for most of the war, probably till the end of 1944, this was the case in all *Geschwadern*. And there were famous and beloved leaders in all as well.

Another pilot who served with *III/JG 52* over the Kuban bridgehead was *Unteroffizier* Wilhelm Hauswirth, who flew as an instructor after his training before finally joining *8/JG 52* in October 1942, by which time they were operating deep in the Caucasus.[38] Hauswirth was a very successful pilot, arriving in *III/JG 52* at a time when their Soviet opponents were implementing widespread reforms in strategy, tactics, operational control (and use of radio), already starting to become evident on a large scale during the ongoing Stalingrad struggle. From the unit history of *III/JG 52*,[39] Hauswirth's early successes can be traced: first claim on 30 October, followed by nine more by mid-December 1942, all relatively inferior opponents to the Me 109 G-2 he was flying: Lagg-3s, Il-2s (few yet had rear gunners although this would soon change), Mig-1s and the last of the victories, on 16 December, a Jak-1, which was a dangerous opponent in competent hands. He flew mostly as wingman to the highly experienced *Unteroffizier* Schuhmacher, who already had well over 30 victories to his name. These air battles were mostly in PQ ('*Plan Quadrat*' or grid square) 44 and 54, around the area of Mineralnye Vody,[40] compatible with the furthest advance eastwards that the *Wehrmacht* managed. By early January 1943 he had been awarded the EK 1 (Iron Cross First Class), having brought his score to 10 victories.[41]

By March 1943, the retreat of the German troops from the Caucasus into the Kuban bridgehead had been going on for several months and *III/JG 52* was operating from the Kerch peninsula in the Crimea and from Taman on the opposite side of the straits; missions were flown mostly over the western Kuban (PQs 75–76, 85–86).[42] Hauswirth's first success in this area was on 21 March 1943, again flying with Schuhmacher, followed by a Lagg-3 six days later, by which time he was flying as a *Rottenführer* himself. By 23 April he had amassed a total of 19 victories, the last two in company with his *Staffelkapitän*, the famous ace Günther Rall.[43] In the further Kuban operations summed up in the table below, between 24 April and 30 May 1943, Hauswirth raised his score from 19 to a total of 50 victories, no mean achievement for such a difficult battle. He was awarded the *Frontflugspange Gold* on 5 May.[44]

From 4 April to the end of May 1943 over the Kuban, for the first time and on a large scale, and strongly influenced by leading Russian ace Pokryshkin's tactical innovations and use of Lend-Lease Spitfires, Airacobras and the new Soviet Lag-5 and La-5 aircraft, the first successful challenge to the *Luftwaffe*'s fighter pilots was offered.[45] Also, a consistently applied tactical doctrine was used at unit level, tailored to the characteristics of the particular Russian fighter being used, and with pairs and finger-four fighter formations, and also the use of height-staggered Russian fighters, protecting them against the German bounce tactics and in fact applying these equally to their German opponents.[46] Fighter casualties on both sides were very high; the days of German dominance were over, at least where good tactical Russian leadership was applied. It is within this framework that the tabulated summary below for *Unteroffizier* Wilhem Hauswirth should be seen.

Example of a fighter pilot's operational life, Eastern Front, 1943, based on flying logbook, 24 April 1943–30 May 1943: *Unteroffizier* Wilhelm Hauswirth, 8/JG 52 (Source: logbook and other documents).[47] All flights in Me 109 G-4 aircraft. (Operational flight or 'op.' = *Frontflug*; PQ refers to grid square on operational maps; Il-2mH = Il-2 ground attack aircraft with rear gunner [*mit Heckschütze*]). 8/JG 52 based at **Taman**, western Kuban peninsula

APRIL

24:     Free chase, 07h04–08h10 (96th operational flight); Kabardinka–
        Gellendshik area
        Stuka escort and free chase, 12h44–13h53 (97th op.); over
        Novorossiysk beach-head
        Stuka escort and free chase, 15h55–17h15 (98th op.); met Bostons &
        Airacobras over Novorossiysk beach-head, shot down two Bostons
        (20th and 21st *Abschüsse*)

25:     Free chase, 06h02–07h15 (99th op.), Kaberdinka–Gellendshik area
        Free chase, Stuka escort, low-level attack, 14h45–15h40 (100th op.),
        PQ 8772

27:     Ju 88 and He 111 escort, 13h30–14h42 (101st op.); met Laggs in
        Krymskaya area, shot down one Lagg (22nd *Abschuss*)
        Ju 88 escort, 16h35–17h46 (102nd op.); met Spitfires, Laggs and
        Airacobras in Krymskaya area, shot down one Spitfire, one Airacobra,
        one Lagg (23rd, 24th, 25th *Abschüsse*)
        (That evening transferred only for one night to **Kertsch 4**)

28: Stuka escort, 07h45–09h02 (103rd op.), over Krymskaya area (landed at **Taman**)

Free chase, 17h12–18h12 (104th op.), met Spitfires in Krymskaya area, shot down one Spitfire (26th *Abschuss*)

29: Stuka escort, 06h05–07h05 (105th op.), met *c.* 30 Laggs and bombers over Krymskaya, shot down one Lagg (27th *Abschuss*)

Free chase, 12h40–13h50 (106th op.), met Il-2s with Lagg escort in Krymskaya area, shot down one Il-2 (28th *Abschuss*)

Free chase, 15h08–16h22 (107th op.), met Spitfires, Laggs, Bostons in Krymskaya area, shot down one Spitfire, two Laggs (29th, 30th, 31st *Abschüsse*)

30: Ju 88 escort, 08h00–09h08 (108th op.), met Laggs and Mitchells over Krymskaya, shot down two Mitchells (32nd, 33rd *Abschüsse*)

Fw 189 escort and free chase, 16h15–17h28 (109th op.), met Laggs in Krymskaya area, shot down one Lagg (34th *Abschuss*)

MAY

1: Weather reconnaissance and free chase, 09h05–10h16 (110th op.), in Krymskaya area

2: Stuka escort and strafing, 06h22–07h25 (111th op.), in northern area

Free chase, 17h38–18h38 (112th op.), met Laggs in Krymskaya area, shot down one Lagg (35th *Abschuss*)

3: Stuka escort, 08h50–10h10 (113th op.), in northern area

(Data on next page not shown on webpage; 12 operational flights made from **Taman**, 4–19 May; three *Abschüsse* (36th–38th))

20: Weather reconnaissance and free chase, 04h06–? (126th op.), in operational area

Weather and general reconnaissance, 06h42–? (127th op.), over beach-head

21: Ju 88 escort, 06h55–08h05 (128th op.), met Laggs in Kholmskaya area, shot down one Lagg (39th *Abschuss*)

Free chase, 11h25–12h35 (129th op.), met Laggs in Krymskaya area

22: Free chase, 06h32–07h40 (130th op.), in Krymskaya area

Stuka escort, 13h08–14h15 (131st op.), in northern area

23: Stuka escort, 08h23–09h18 (132nd op.), in northern area

Scramble and free chase, 10h40–11h35 (133rd. op.), in operational area

(Mid-afternoon of 23 May transfer to **Saki** and early next morning flew three convoy patrols in Sevastopol area (didn't count as *Frontflüge* as over own territory and no enemy contact) and just after mid-day 24 May back to **Taman**)

26: Free chase, 06h15–07h25 (134th op.), met Laggs and Airacobras in Krymskaya area, shot down one Airacobra (40th *Abschuss*)

Stuka escort, 09h08–10h15 (un-numbered op.), met Laggs and Il-2s in Krymskaya area, landed at **Anapa** (40 minutes later, returned to **Taman**)

Stuka escort, 12h47–13h55 (135th op.), met Laggs in Krymskaya area, shot down one Lagg (41st *Abschuss*)

Stuka escort, 18h07–19h00 (136th op.), met Spitfires in Krymskaya area

27:     Weather reconnaissance and free chase, 03h42–05h00 (137th op.), met Laggs and Il-2s in Krymskaya area, shot down one Lagg and one Il-2mH (42nd and 43rd *Abschüsse*)

Free chase, 08h15–09h25 (138th op.), met Laggs and Il-2s in Krymskaya area, shot down one Lagg (44th *Abschuss*)

Free chase, 15h40–16h55 (139th op.), met Laggs and Mitchells in Krymskaya area, shot down one Mitchell (45th *Abschuss*)

28:     Stuka escort, 06h05–07h08 (140th op.), met Ratas in Krymskaya area, shot down one Rata (46th *Abschuss*)

Stuka escort, 17h13–18h18 (141st op.), met Il-2s in Krymskaya area, shot down one Il-2mH (47th *Abschuss*); another claim, for a second Il-2mH was only '*nachbestätigt*' (confirmed later, at *Geschwader* level) as his 50th *Abschuss*

29:     Free chase, 14h32–15h20 (142nd op.), met Laggs in Krymskaya area

30:     Ju 88 escort, 14h46–15h30 (143rd op.), met Laggs and Mitchells in Krymskaya area, shot down one Lagg and one Il-2 (48th and 49th *Abschüsse*)

During the period covered in the table (37 days from 24 April to 30 May 1943) Hauswirth had flown an average of 1.3 missions per day, and for 21 of those days he recorded an average of 1.1 encounters with enemy aircraft per diem. The two continuous periods recorded in the table (10 days from 24 April to 3 May, and 11 days from 20 to 30 May) show daily missions decreasing slightly from 1.8 to 1.7, but enemy encounters increasing from 1.0 to 1.2 per day; combat intensity was thus on the increase, something that would mark the character of the air war on the Eastern Front from the Kuban period, through Kursk and onwards. The German fighter pilots found themselves in a situation where they could not hope to win the war of attrition, and had to content themselves with preservation of their force as far as possible, combined with maximum casualties to the enemy. This raised scores for the few lucky and skilled survivors, killed off most of the rest, and played only a negligible role in affecting the progress of the Russian war effort; truly a strategic misunderstanding and misapplication of available air power.

In early May 1943, *Unteroffizier* Peter Düttmann, who was to become in time a very successful pilot, and who was famous for his humour and in leading post-war sing-songs at veterans' get-togethers, was posted to the front, where he was thrown into the Kuban air battle, meeting his first Russians (in Spitfires!) two days after joining *5/JG 52* at Anapa airfield in the Taman peninsula. His account, below, of these first few days is an absolute classic and provides a vivid insight into what it was like to be a newly qualified front-line pilot flying against a resurgent Russian air force over the Kuban.

On 6 May 1943, *Unteroffizier* Düttmann reported to the headquarters (it was an earth bunker) of the 5th *Staffel*, *II Gruppe* of *JG 52* in Anapa, as having been 'transferred to the *Staffel*'. Now I had finally managed to get myself to the front after two and a half years of training (one year of elementary flying school, including fighter pilot pre-school, then fighter school and *Ergänzungsgruppe*) – and in addition to join the then-leading German *Jagdgeschwader*! The two men in the headquarters (not wearing shirts), who were busy with clerical duties – as I later established, they had to keep the pilots' logbooks, the aircraft records and those of the engines etc. up to date – did not seem very impressed with me. Only one replied to me, telling me to put my baggage down.

At that moment the telephone rang, and one of them had a very short conversation and said to me 'come along'. The three of us went outside, then turned left and entered into a trench. 'Duck your head, it will come crashing down now!' And immediately I heard engines howling and one could hear shots being fired – that was my 'baptism of fire'. The airfield at Anapa, a port city on the Black Sea, lay directly on the coast where almost vertically sloping cliffs fell away to the sea below; it was often attacked, always from the sea, by ground attack aircraft (Il-2s) with fighter escort (mostly Jak-1s) – for the two men in the headquarters thus nothing out of the ordinary.

About half an hour later (minor damage had been caused at the airfield) a *Kraftfahrzeug Zwei* (a small four-seater 'Stöwer' vehicle) with two pilots in it drove up to the headquarters, where they climbed out and the 'Stöwer' took me and my baggage to the *Staffel*'s office, that was in a small house on the edge of Anapa. I reported myself to the '*Spiess*' (=Hauptfeldwebel – Sergeant Major) and was instructed to leave my clothes bag there, as one didn't ever need that much baggage at the front. After my particulars had been recorded I was sent to the equipment store where I was carefully fitted out with the right size of flying jacket and flying suit, as well as a net-helmet with headphones and throat microphone. Then it was off to the parachute store – also here it was carefully fitted on (every pilot received his own personal seat-type parachute) and thereafter to the armoury. There my heavy 7.65 mm FN pistol was changed for a Walter PK (of the same calibre, but lighter and more handy) and I got two magazines each with six rounds of ammunition. The weapons *Feldwebel* counted out the bullets individually and remarked drily: 'Watch out, that you keep the last one for yourself in case you have to come down!' For someone not yet even 20 years old these were unexpected sentiments!

Then it was back to the *Staffel* office and the *Spiess* took me personally to a small house in the neighbourhood, where some of the pilots were quartered, and showed me to one of the four field beds standing in one of the rooms – this was where I would live and here I could unpack my things. In the meantime it had been gradually getting dark, several pilots returned from the airfield and I got to know my future comrades. They accepted me in friendly fashion and we went next door to the mess ('*Casino*'). There we would all eat the evening meal together. After a short while the *Staffelkapitän* also appeared (a *Leutnant* from Vienna), to whom I reported. He looked at me briefly, told me that I must report to him the next morning at 06h00 and that I should now join him and the other comrades at the table for the meal (there were about 10 to 12 pilots altogether). There was (canned) bread, sausage, cheese and a good white wine from the vineyards next to the airfield.

After the meal, smoking was permitted and in a haze of tobacco and cigarette smoke a lively conversation began on the day's events. There had been several combats, also some victories, and thank God no losses to ourselves. Everybody around the table was allowed to (and indeed was expected to) give his own opinion of what had happened and I wished I had a second pair of ears to make sure I understood all the events discussed correctly and fully! About two hours later the *Kapitän* broke it up and we went to bed. That ended my first day at the front. How different this all was compared to the barracks life in the homeland! I felt somewhat at home amongst these total strangers (who also mostly outranked me) right away.

Next morning, reporting to the *Kapitän*, he asked me about my training and then if I had already flown the 'Gustav' (Me 109 G). I answered 'Yes, but only a couple of take-offs!' 'Right, then you take the "Black Two", which is a G-2, fly some circuits and then familiarise yourself with the bird!' Wow, that was some order! About one and a half hours later I reported to him 'orders carried out' and was detailed for 'area introduction and airfield defence' as wingman (*Katschmarek*) for the afternoon. On the next day the assignment to be airfield defence repeated itself, and on the following day 'expanded area introduction' and with that, familiarisation with the most modern Me 109, the G-4. During this we flew along the coast towards the northwest. About 25 km from the airfield there was an old shipwreck that I was supposed to shoot at using only the cannons (in training we had only shot with the machine guns, never with the cannons!). This I did and

123

was glad that I apparently managed to get a few hits (the cannons were the MG151/20, 2 cm calibre).

On this day (8 May) the *Staffel* had to provide two aircraft at cockpit readiness. That meant two hours sitting in the machine ready for immediate take-off if the alarm went off (red flare) – in the glaring sun this was not much fun. As the alarm was anyway seldom given, I was assigned as *Katschmarek* but with the most experienced pilot in the *Staffel*, as a precautionary measure. As luck would have it after about 100 minutes of cockpit readiness, the alarm went off, we took off and flew towards the front (Kuban bridgehead near Krymskaya), climbed to 6,000 m – and then already over the radio came the message 'attack'. Suddenly we were in the middle of a combat and suddenly I saw how elliptical wings with red stars flew vertically in front of me from right to left – I shot wildly at this target, but naturally hit nothing. Then the combat was already over as suddenly as it had begun and on the return flight we heard over the radio that our *Kapitän* had taken off.

Then we landed and my *Rottenführer* asked me what I had been able to notice. I replied that except for the 'Spitfire' (elliptical wings) that I had seen right in front of my nose, and for the nice little clouds (fair weather clouds), nothing else had really attracted my attention. As everyone else laughed heartily I was corrected: the clouds were not only white, but also reddish, blueish and greenish-yellow – thus from Russian flak of various calibres. In addition we had met Jak-1s and Airacobras; however, I had kept station well on my leader's wing! Then I had the same thought as I had had on my first flight in training – 'you will never learn all this'!

Shortly after this a single 109 landed – it was the *Katschmarek* of our *Kapitän*. His aircraft had been hit several times and he had lost sight of his leader. After some time we received the sad news that our *Kapitän* had been hit and had crashed in flames near the front. In accordingly depressed mood that evening we sat together. The *Kapitän*'s chair remained empty, and on the table in front of it a single candle burnt! Thus the day ended very sadly, on which I had flown my first *Feindflug*. My *Rottenführer* took over leadership of the flying activities of the *Staffel* and for the next day I was assigned as *Katschmarek* to the next-most experienced pilot – but only when free chases were to be flown. This in fact occurred at midday. In the meantime my *Rottenführer* spoke to me at length and gave me some basic principles for survival: never climb with the sun behind you, never fly straight and level, but rather fly continuous gentle turns to left and right and through those observe carefully in all directions with your eyes wide open – particularly behind you.

Thus we took off in perfect weather, this time with 109 G-4s, climbed to *c.* 7,000 m, flew far into enemy territory and then reversed course. All the time I was supposed to report if I believed I had seen anything in particular, and then immediately the answer came from my *Rottenführer*, sometimes positive, sometimes however also negative. In this way I learned to keep my eyes open and to observe, and when we saw some Lagg-3s near the front and my *Rottenführer* attacked (and sent one of them down in flames into the ground), the entire event seemed crystal clear and logical to me; that's how an inexperienced beginner was introduced to the front!

You can see that these initial experiences at the front have remained perfectly clear in my memory. I believe that at that time the basis for my own later successes was laid – when one and a quarter years later I myself had to lead a *Staffel*, I laid great emphasis on introducing young pilots in exactly the same fundamental way, even when practice flights were forbidden due to fuel shortages (one could always find some excuse for practice flights, without one being vulnerable to punishment as a result!). In the meantime we received an *Oberleutnant*, wearing the *Eichenlaub* to the *Ritterkreuz*, as *Staffelkapitän* (this in fact was *Oberleutnant* Batz who only received his *Ritterkreuz* and *Eichenlaub* later)[48] who really took very great trouble to mentor his young pilots – mostly even having long private conversations with them. In this way I learned some new tricks: when your machine is hit, determine whether oil or coolant is burning; is the aircraft still completely controllable?; when someone is shooting at you, hit the rudder pedal, immediately to turn to the left (because of the propeller's rotation in the same direction, for most Russian aircraft the propeller rotated in the opposite direction); use the radiator flaps to align your course by opening and closing them, and so on. In this way I gradually accustomed myself to the various tasks, learned how to fly escort missions (very different and dependent on the machines to be escorted), *Schwarm* operations, low-level attacks etc. I also received the first hits in my aircraft, thank God with no serious effects.

After a month I had already flown 40 *Feindflüge* 'in harness'! (A *Feindflug* was defined as any mission with aerial combat and any mission across the lines.) Of those only half at most were free chases, all the rest were escort missions, especially for Ju 87 units. Mostly these missions resulted in tough combats and more than a third of my comrades who were already there from the beginning of May 1943 had already been killed or were in hospital. I had also scored my first *Abschuss* – still today I believe that I did not actually hit my opponent directly, but rather that he made a crash-landing from sheer surprise, and this was far within Russian territory near Krasnodar. In the meantime occasionally a Ju 52 arrived with which the young pilots (mostly about 20 years old) from the entire *Gruppe* were flown to Odessa, Nikolajew amongst other places to fetch new aircraft. In this way I acquired my first personal aircraft, 'Black Twelve', to which a permanent crew chief was assigned and which I was able to fly exclusively from then on. This was very important as the differences between individual 109s, even from the same factory, were often quite marked and with an unknown machine it took some time for one to learn its foibles and get used to it.

I think I have described adequately the problems which a newly qualified fighter pilot could be faced with. Up until the war's end, this became harder and harder, as the training quality of the newly arrived replacement pilots got increasingly worse. This reality has been known for a long time but for me as a unit leader it was a reason to introduce the 'youngsters' as carefully as possible to their required duties. I have never before told so much and that's the way it will stay as well.

Leutnant Walter Bohatsch similarly began his career as a fighter pilot flying against the VVS in the Kuban bridgehead, an exceptionally tough area for any beginner. He also describes a supportive introduction to combat flying at the front.

As a member of *5/JG 3*, to which I belonged for *c.* 18 months, I enjoyed an exceptionally good comradeship in the unit. In this time *Oberleutnant* Archim Kirschner was *Staffelkapitän*; pilots included: *Leutnants* Dohse, Myrrhe, Fürst, *Oberfeldwebel* Jupp Schütte, *Feldwebeln* Hans Grünberg (known as 'Specker'), Traphan, Notemann, Kloss, *Unteroffizieren* Mohn, Dahms and my insignificant self. *Uunteroffizier* Kurt Wüster fulfilled the function of *Staffel* clerk (*Staffelschreiber*); my lead mechanic was *Obergefreiter* Gräfe who looked after my 'Black Six' extremely well. As far as I know only Grünberg, Notemann, Mohn and Bohatsch survived the war. Operations flown were typically free chases, protection over tank columns, fighter-bomber missions, escort for Ju 87s and He 111s. These missions all took place in the southern part of the front, in the area from Bjelgorod to the Kuban. The *Gruppe* was used tactically as a fire brigade in the southern front and field bases were changed often. 14 days on one field was already an exception.

When I joined 5th *Staffel JG 3* in Russia (mid-April 1943)[49] and reported to the *Staffelkapitän Oberleutnant* Kirschner, I was straight away assigned to fly the next day as *Rottenflieger* (*Katschmarek*) of *Oberfeldwebel* Schütte, and this was to be of critical importance for my further career as a pilot. Jupp, as *Oberfeldwebel* Schütte was known by his first name to all, had then already over 30 *Abschüsse* and thus a significant experience at the front. I claimed my first *Abschüsse* under his guidance, and this was like a father showing his son how these things were best achieved. In the 5th *Staffel* there was a very marked comradely atmosphere, largely due to the good relations between officers and NCOs.

On the Kuban bridgehead one can only report that operational activity was very intense. I can still remember flying eight operations on one day. We were stationed in Anapa, and the airfield lay directly on the sea with a steep coastal slope between the two. The landing area of the airfield was surrounded by a *c.* 50 m-wide belt of mines. Landings from the sea side were very problematic as the landing area sloped downwards and one had to really watch out not to overshoot into the mines. Our missions were mostly free chases, escorts missions and low-level strafing attacks. At night we were often attacked by Russian bombers. For this reason we often flew to Gostagajevskaia in the evenings and returned to Anapa in the early mornings. A Russian officer landed with a Jak-9 in Anapa. *Leutnant* Myrrhe of the 5th *Staffel* was shot down near Noworossisk while attacking a Russian speedboat. In the Kuban bridgehead American aircraft, Airacobras, were also operational.

On 13 April 1943, flying the Black Thirteen, I was wounded for the first time, in the Kuban by 2 cm flak and landed up in the hospital at Symferopol in the Crimea. After about 14 days I had recovered and I rejoined the 5th *Staffel* of JG 3 that had moved to Kharkov in the meantime (moved there on 2 May and returned to Anapa again on 7 May).[50]

The Battle of Kursk

For the Kursk offensive, the Germans concentrated most of their available fighters for the battle, including *I/JG52* (Belgorod area 4–17 July 1943) and *III/JG 52* (Kharkov area 3–14 July), along the southern front of the salient.[51] The latter *Gruppe* moved to the northern face of the salient as the Russian counter-offensive towards Orel got under way, being stationed in that area until 2 August 1943.[52] From now onwards the German fighter *Geschwadern* would increasingly be shunted around the Eastern Front from one area of crisis to another; quite how proper maintenance could have been done is very questionable, and the disruption to their efficiency must have been marked. As an example, *I/JG 52* experienced 21 moves in area of operations and/or base from 17 July till the end of 1943.[53]

Wilhelm Hauswirth, 8/JG 52, whose operations over the Kuban based on logbook excerpts were recorded earlier, later flew over Kursk as well. After its successful time over the Kuban, *III/JG 52* was transferred north to Ugrim on the southern part of the Kursk salient on 3 July 1943[54] to take part in the massive battle about to begin there. Further logbook entries[55] indicate that he shot down a Lagg in a free chase over the Belgorod area (51st *Abschuss*) the next day. When the great Kursk battle began on 5 July 1943, *Feldwebel* Hauswirth flew his first operation in the very early morning (take-off at 04h27) during which he claimed a Lagg shot down (52nd victory). At 07h50 he was off again for his second mission of the day (his 145th *Frontflug*), shot down two Il-2mH for his 53rd and 54th claims, and did not then return to base.

Although posted as killed by his unit, and thought to have fallen victim to flak behind Russian lines, Hauswirth did in fact survive as a prisoner and eventually returned to Germany in 1947. Many months after his disappearance, in late 1944, his suffering wife, who remained unaware of his survival until his return from Russia, received a package with the *Abschussanerkennungen* (victory confirmation certificates) for his first 48 claims from *Oberleutnant* Friedrich Obleser[56] who had replaced Rall as *Staffelkapitän 8/JG 52* on the day after Hauswirth was shot down.[57] These included confirmed victories over four Spitfires, two Mitchells, four Airacobras, two Bostons, two Mig-1s, 26 Laggs, six Il-2s, one I-153 and one Jak-1. The German Cross in Gold was awarded to him, supposedly posthumously, on 16 July 1943.[58]

After leaving the Kuban bridgehead, *II/JG 3* had a short stint at Kharkov (2–7 May). Following this, they moved to the area around and north-west of Kharkov for the Battle of Kursk.[59] Walter Bohatsch recalls the atmosphere in the *Gruppe* during this period.

Typical for *5/JG 3* at this time was that the *Oberfeldwebels* and *Feldwebels* were the backbone of the *Staffel*. Personally, I have Schütte and 'Specker' (*Feldwebel* Grünberg) to thank for my career as a fighter pilot; they introduced me gradually into this life. I am still a close friend of Specker today (writing in 1990). Both on the ground and in the air the pilots of *5/JG 3* were mostly addressed by their nicknames. Some of these nicknames originated in very special circumstances. On a mission in Russia I was flying a free chase with a *Rotte* and heard on the radio that Specker was also about with his *Rotte*. He had contact with the enemy and let his wingman *Feldwebel* Kloss know that an 'Indian' (enemy) was sitting behind him. He told Kloss to carry on flying straight and level, as he was busy getting ready to shoot this enemy down. Shortly after that I heard Kloss encouraging Specker to get on with it, as the 'Indian' was getting really close behind him; Specker again let him know he was almost ready. Then shortly after that Kloss was told, 'Get the hell out of there, my guns are jammed.' Soon after I had landed the *Rotte* of Specker and Kloss also landed and taxied to our dispersals, where Kloss jumped out of his aircraft and hurried up to Specker whom he choked off about his experiments and told him very directly, 'I am not after all your sacrifice.' After that Kloss was known as the 'sacrifice'.

III/JG 3 flew over the Kursk salient from the Belgorod area from 5 July until 15 July.[60] *Feldwebel* Hans Grünberg ('Specker') of *5/JG 3* was airborne on the first mission of the first day of the Battle of Kursk, as related below.

At the beginning of July the *II/JG 3* lay in Rogan near Kharkov. On the evening of 4 July 1943 bomber and Stuka units landed at our airfield. Now we pilots and the ground crew knew that next day the large and decisive battle of the Kursk salient would begin. *Hauptmann* Kirschner received the order to take off on 5 July at dawn with myself as *Rottenflieger* for a weather reconnaissance, and to report on the weather by radio, so that the bomber formations could be sent in to their respective targets. In the darkness I could see over our own front areas the exhaust flames everywhere of aircraft, flying in a westerly direction. I immediately reported to *Hauptmann* Kirschner by radio, that everywhere below us there were Russian aircraft. The airfields at Kharkov and surroundings were stuffed full of our bombers, Stukas and ground attack aircraft. Suddenly we saw that in Kharkov-North, where the airfields were already being attacked by Russian ground attack machines, there was strong flak fire. *Hauptmann* Kirschner alerted by radio all airfields, told them what we had seen and warned of strong formations of Russian ground attack Il-2 aircraft. Then he said to me: 'Specker, now we are going to get us some Russians.'

The air combat occurred at an altitude of about 200 m near our own airfield. Our ground crews saw from close to how we flew in between hundreds of Il-2s and sent the first flaming to earth. *Hauptmann* Kirschner and I were the only German aircraft in the skies at the beginning, and could thus shoot at everything that was flying. The success was thus great. *Hauptmann* Kirschner scored three and I got four victories on this mission. My good Me had of course received many bullets through its wings and in the fuel tank – and these were not just enemy bullets – so that my flight ended after scarcely an hour due to fuel shortage. I have to say that our infantrymen could shoot very well with rifle and machine gun and knew the necessary deflection to score hits. My beloved Black 1 with its red nose had to go into the workshop to be repaired. At that time I anyway had a second Me 109, as due to many low-level strafing attacks on enemy airfields, one aircraft was almost always being repaired in the workshop.

This first day of the Battle of Kursk I will never forget. The Russians had sent in all their ground attack and bomber aircraft. From morning to evening wave after wave rolled over our tank and infantry advance columns. From our side, every Me 109 that was serviceable was immediately sent back into battle, even alone as combats took place almost everywhere. All pilots of *II/JG 3* scored victories on this day. After a hard yet successful day we counted over 75 *Abschüsse*, without having suffered any losses ourselves (in reality, total claims: 77 victories; losses were four damaged aircraft, one destroyed and four wounded pilots).[61] Our greatest ace, *Hauptmann* Kirschner, claimed nine, myself seven and our *Kommandeur*, *Major* Brändle, five victories. This day's victory haul was unique for the German *Luftwaffe*.

Leutnant Walter Bohatsch, a colleague of Grünberg's in the same *Staffel* at Kursk, was also in the air on the opening day of this vast struggle on the ground:

Jupp Schütte was wounded on a flight in the Kharkov area in 1943 (5 July)[62] and was sent to hospital in Germany. This happened on one of the two operations flown by *II/JG 3* against a large Russian attack laid on against the tractor factory in Kharkov where German tanks were repaired. This attack came in in two waves, mainly of Il-2s with fighter escort, and *II/JG 3* was able to claim *c.* 70 victories (77 victories over the entire day noted in the unit history)[63] in the two missions. After that I flew a lot of missions with Grünberg on the southern front from Bjelgorod and south-south-westwards. The most successful pilots in the 5th *Staffel* were Kirschner, Schütte and Grünberg. Losses in Russia during this time in the *Staffel* encompassed Myrrhe (*Leutnant* Lothar Myrrhe, missing 21 April 1943 in combat over the Kuban),[64] *Leutnant* Dohse (on 31 July in the aftermath of Kursk),[65] Dahms and another *Unteroffizier* whose name I no longer recall (also killed were: *Feldwebel* Horst Lüdtke, 5 June 1943 in combat in Obojan area; *Obergefreiter* Heinz Welsch, missing on 8 June in combat with Lagg-3s west of Bjelgorod; *Leutnant* Herbert Fürst, killed on 16 June after an accident-related belly-landing near Kharkov).[66]

II/JG 3 remained in the Kharkov area till 2 August 1943, apart from a detachment stationed west of the Mius River; they then returned to Germany to serve in the increasingly over-strained Home Defence.[67] Once more, Walter Bohatsch is the witness to these events:

Shortly before our transfer to Germany from Russia in the middle of August 1943 – we were then stationed on the Mius front at Kuteinikowo where we flew many Stuka escorts – the 5th *Staffel* suffered another big loss. Hartwig Dohse already had his leave pass in his pocket, when another operation was announced. An escort for He 111s had to be flown. As Hartwig Dohse had no chance of catching a Ju 52 on the way to Germany on this day (31 July 1943), he insisted on flying on this mission. After the mission was completed and all the He 111s were safely on the way home again, this escorting *Schwarm* flew a free chase. This led to contact with the enemy, meeting a formation of Il-2s and Jak-9s. 'Specker' Grünberg was able to shoot down an Il-2. It is presumed that Hartwig Dohse was in all likelihood shot down by a Jak-9 as he did not return. In the flying units it was customary that no more missions would be flown once someone had a leave pass in their pocket.

On 15 July *III/JG 3* were moved back south again from Belgorod to the area north of and near Stalino itself, until 1 August 1943, when their move back to Germany began.[68]

In May 1943 *I/JG 51* were transferred to Orel once again for the Kursk battle, till 2 August when it was back to Bryansk.[69] A move to Orel by *III/JG 51* (May 1943–15 July 1943) for the Kursk offensive was also followed by a period at Bryansk (15 July–30 August 1943).[70] After a break from combat as an instructor at *Jagdergänzungsgruppe Ost* (1 April–beginning of July 1943), *Leutnant* Günther Schack was posted back to 8th *Staffel* of *III/JG 51* just in time for the Kursk offensive.[71] He was glad to be back among old friends in *III/JG 51*: 'I felt especially close with my old 7th *Staffel* and particularly with "Benjamin", as Weber, the new chief and successor to *Hauptmann* Wehnelt, is known in the air. He and the (*Gruppe*) Adjutant *Oberleutnant* Gudehus, are often guests in my quarters.' Schack also had nothing but praise for the hard-working ground crews. 'Our good ground crews are really efficient in their various tasks. Only seriously damaged aircraft end up in the repair depots, all other damage is handled with excellent results right on site. An engine change hardly lasts more than six to eight hours. The hole in my wing had to be handled by a large workshop facility far behind the lines; for the transfer flight immediate repairs are first made.'

By mid-July 1943, the German attack along the northern face of the Kursk salient had already been brought to a stop and the Russians counterattacked towards Orel. Günther Schack was one of those who was rapidly transferred to meet this new threat. 'Once again (on 15 July 1943)[72] we had to go to Bryansk on short notice to meet a new need, and where we were placed under command of a *Gruppe* of *JG 54*. The *Kommandeur* of this mob is *Hauptmann* Rudorffer, an old acquaintance, who had shown me the night life of Paris only a few weeks ago! *Oberleutnant* Weber has jaundice, and so I temporarily (on 20 August 1943) took over my old *Staffel* (7/JG 51), in which I had originally begun as a *Gefreiter*.'

Günther Schack was one of the most successful German fighter pilots during the Kursk–Belgorod battles of July–August 1943. 'In the event, due to the high number of missions daily, this was a very turbulent experience. We were stationed together with *I/JG 51*. The three most successful pilots

(*Oberleutnant* Thiel, *Oberfeldwebel* Jennewein [Skiing World Champion] and I) were photographed together at the front by the press. We had to fly six to seven missions per day.' By mid-1943 Schack had progressed very far as a fighter pilot due to his long accumulated experience in the aerial frontline:

> In the beginning of my career I was praised particularly by, amongst others, *Kommodore* Nordmann when I was still a *Feldwebel*, because of my 25 *Abschüsse*, 20 were bombers. However, this was largely due to my being unable to hit anything when turning in a dogfight. It was only during the course of the war due to experience that this situation with me improved. In a steep turn one does not see the enemy machine at all any more, as it is covered by your own machine, because of the deflection one must allow. I have often seen a Russian fighter sitting behind me when sitting in my cockpit and shooting at me, knowing full well that he could not hit me if I could see him, only when I saw his belly did it become dangerous for me. As I read in the Mölders book, he was apparently of the opinion that one could not score victories when flying in steep turns.

For the Kursk operations, *I/JG 54* were transferred from Estonia to Orel (June–August 1943).[73] *Unteroffizier* Ernst Richter, who had begun his career flying convoy protection over the Gulf of Finland, had suffered injury on his third operation there already, but had recovered in time to briefly take part in the enormous air battle over the Kursk battlefield which began on 5 July:

> My third *Feindflug*, on 1 June 1943, ended with me in hospital. But already on 2 July I was flying a Fw 190 again and on 5 July 1943 I flew my fourth *Feindflug*. This day was the beginning of the Orel offensive which was supposed to cut off the Kursk salient, and thereby also shorten the front line. Four *Jagdgeschwadern* were involved in this offensive; from the north *JG 51* and *JG 54*, and in the south it was *JG 3* and *JG 52*. It was said that these *Geschwadern* shot down about 400 Russian fighter aircraft on the first day; of this total the *I Gruppe* of *JG 54* got 52. I only flew one more mission there, on 6 July 1943 and shot a Lagg-3 down during it. After that I was given leave, also because of my earlier stay in hospital.

Another member of *I/JG 54* was *Unteroffizier* Ulrich Wernitz, who had joined *3/JG 54* in May 1943 aged 22, when they were flying the convoy protection missions over the Gulf of Finland, based at Esel Island off the coast of Estonia.[74] When the *Gruppe* transferred to Orel as part of the build-up for the Kursk battle in June 1943, he was left behind in the Leningrad area[75] to get more experience before being sent into the intense air battle of the Kursk offensive. In an excerpt from a shortened version of his *Leistungsbuch* (performance record) there is a record of nine operations flown over the Volkhov–Schum–Mga–Kolpino area (all in the German Northern Front region) between 17 June and 6 July 1943.[76] Interestingly, he was still in the north when the Kursk battle had already begun on 5 July, demonstrating the care typically accorded to the introduction of new pilots into the fighting along the Eastern Front by the *Luftwaffe*. Of his nine recorded operations around Leningrad in this period seven were bomber escorts (for Ju 87s, Ju 88s and Do 217s), one a free chase and the last a combination of weather reconnaissance and free chase. The enemy was met on four of the operations, comprising, respectively: assorted Lagg-3, Lagg-5 and Yak-1 fighters; two Lagg-3s and one Yak-1; six 6 Lagg-3s; five Airacobras; as was common for the Eastern Front flak opposition was intense on all missions.[77] He scored his fifth claimed victory when he dispatched a Lagg-3 on 18 June 1943.[78]

However, the high pace and serious losses suffered by the German fighters over the Kursk–Orel battlefield necessitated employing all available resources, and Wernitz was soon sent southwards to Kursk, where he was put temporarily in the *Geschwader Staff* flight of JG 54 (where his *Kommodore, Major* Hubertus von Bonin, could keep an eye on him) flying over the Orel area; his first three missions (14, 15 and 16 July 1943) there were recorded in the copy of his *Leistungsbuch*.[79] These encompassed two Ju 87 escort missions and one free chase, the Russians being met twice, once consisting of eight Jak-9s and on the other occasion made up of 20 Il-2s escorted by six Jak-9s. A later excerpt from the *Leistungsbuch* showed four free chase missions in the Orel region between 31 July and 4 August, where the Soviets were driving forwards to the north of the Kursk salient; on two of these missions, respectively, two and six La-5 fighters were met, and on the other two, Il-2s escorted once by La-5s and on the other mission by Airacobras. Wernitz claimed a La-5 for his 10th victory on 1 August and another the next day, but without a witness this one could not be added to his score.[80]

After Kursk

After the Battle of Kursk, *III/JG 52* flew in the Stalino area (18 August–8 September 1943) and then retreated steadily from Stalino westwards to the Kirovograd area up till 31 October; for the rest of the year they operated over the Nikopol region and west thereof.[81] After having had a break from the Eastern Front as an instructor in *Jagdergänzungsgruppe Ost* in La Rochelle, France from April to September 1943, *Leutnant* Gerd

Schindler was posted back to *III/JG 52* in October 1943, to serve in the East again till March 1944 when he was transferred to Germany to join *IV/JG 27* in the Home Defence.

His great friend *Leutnant* Korts had been killed on 29 August 1943 while Schindler was still in France, having got the *Ritterkreuz* after bringing his score to 108 victories. While Gerd Schindler missed this period, when many of his friends and comrades greatly enhanced their scores, and missed out on any chance of the *Ritterkreuz* (RK) himself, the posting to instruct might also have saved his life, giving him the rest to continue fighting successfully again later. Schindler recalled the loss of his friend:

> Bertold Korts became my friend and especially comrade on whom I could depend, in a short time after we met; we were known as the *Stabsrotte* (they flew together in the *Gruppenstab III/JG 52*) and were even mentioned in dispatches once (on 20 October 1942 for an action the previous day).[82] We always protected each other in action and both of us had several times shot away an enemy behind the other. We competed for victories, were inseparable and in more favourable circumstances (without my being transferred to La Rochelle) in the 'hot summer of 1943' would likely both have achieved the RK. Korts (a sports teacher at a political school in Upper Bavaria) went missing with his wingman on the day of his *Ritterkreuz* announcement; for me the news, which I received in La Rochelle, was a heavy blow.

Schindler detailed his further adventures in the East in correspondence with the author. In October 1943, when Gerd Schindler returned to the Eastern Front, he was lucky enough to find a Ju 52 to fly to Kirovograd (via Krakau) where he found his *Gruppe* by chance, being assigned to the 9th *Staffel*, the '*Karaya-Staffel*' first made famous by Hermann Graf. Here he acted as *Staffelführer* when *Oberleutnant* Hartmann, its *Kapitän*, was away. Soon he was once again flying mission after mission, but found that much had changed in the six months he had been absent, including many new faces. He shot an Il-2 down from the side, but now these aircraft had also acquired a rear-gunner. They flew in the Kirovograd area and then over the German bridgehead on the eastern bank of the Dnieper River at Nikopol.

Here he was himself shot down and wounded on 22 November 1943 for the first time. Over enemy territory a Jak had sneaked up behind him and shot at a slight angle, past his armour plate, hitting the dashboard and his right upper arm. Despite losing a lot of blood, with tattered clothing and a failing aircraft, he managed to get back to base, where the ambulance was already waiting and the *Gruppe* doctor attended to him, after which he had to stay in bed for three weeks. After recovering he took over 7/ JG 52 as *Staffelführer* in place of the incapacitated *Oberleutnant* Walter Krupinski.[83] At Nikopol he also forgot once to lower his undercarriage while landing after a hectic dogfight, despite being a highly experienced pilot already; *Gruppenkommandeur* Rall was not amused. He was shot down for the second time on 17 December and force-landed with a dead engine due to strikes in his radiator, touching down smoothly in the snow, and was rescued by the *Waffen-SS*, who wrapped him up snugly in a thick fur coat and returned him to his comrades.

Just as Schindler was experiencing greater difficulty fighting the Russians in late 1943, his fellow pilot in 9/JG 52, *Leutnant* Hermann Wolf, remembers that after 1942 things had become much harder in the East:

> In 1942 we had the better aircraft but this changed with time. The Russian aircraft became better; apart from that more and more American machines appeared. Then it was far more down to the flying ability of the pilots. The Russians also had good and ruthlessly fighting pilots. However as they continuously appeared with new and better types of aircraft my impression was that they were often not yet that familiar with them. I flew only the Me 109, for example, from beginning to end (1 May 1942–27 February 1944 on the Russian Front) that, one must admit was often upgraded with new models, but I was totally familiar with this aircraft. In total I flew 587 *Einsätze* over Russia, achieved 51 victories there and was promoted to *Leutnant* for bravery in the field.

II/JG 52 remained on the Kuban front until 1 September, then operated for a short while over the Poltava (1–18 September 1943) and Kiev (18–30 September) areas, before putting in almost a month in the region of Zaporozhye (1–25 October); for the rest of the year they were back in their earlier stomping grounds in the Crimean region.[84] The poor pilots and presumably skeleton ground crews of I/JG 52 were shuttled from north to south, east to west after the Kursk–Orel battles: Kuteinikowo (17 July–6 August 1943), Kharkov area (6–16 August), the Donets basin (16 August–6 September), Poltava area (6–12 September, and again from 15–18 September), Kiev region (12–15 September and again from 18–19 September), the eastern Crimea–Kuban region (22 September–11 October), then Zaporozhye (11–27 October), Crimea (27 October–14 November) and Kirovograd (to end of year) regions.[85]

These rapid perambulations of the thinly spread fighter *Gruppen* would not have led the Russians to think that German fighters were everywhere (prisoners kept them well enough in the real picture of the dire *Luftwaffe* situation) but do underline that the Germans had lost control of the strategic airspace over the Eastern Front. However, at least one *Gruppe, I/JG 54*, felt it worthwhile to employ two *Schwarms* of their limited numbers of Fw 190s to try and fool the Russians into thinking they were more numerous and widespread than they were, as related below by Ernst Richter. While the Russian ground offensives swept rapidly and inexorably westwards, only local tactical successes of a few *Luftwaffe Experten* could be held up against a panorama of endless defeat. The importance of the topmost airborne scorers in the East to Goebbels' propaganda empire also became much more critical, emphasising the superiority of the German fighting man in the face of endless Russian hordes (the latter in itself not a true reflection of reality either; the Russians also had significant manpower problems).

After the Kursk battle had ended on the northern part of the salient, *I/JG 54* was transferred south to Poltava (August–October 1943), later to Vitebsk (October–December 1943) and finally, Orsha (December 1943).[86] After flying out of Orel (May till August 1943), *II/JG 54* moved to Kiev (August–October 1943), Shitomir (west of Kiev; October–December 1943) and Vinnytsia (south-west of Kiev; December 1943).[87] *Unteroffizier* Ernst Richter, who had missed most of the Kursk battle due to leave granted after being wounded and hospitalised earlier, returned to operations in the *Gruppenstab* of *I/JG 54* where he became wingman to the great Walter Nowotny.

> When I returned to the *Gruppe* (*c.* August 1943) I finally became the wingman (*Katschmarek*) of *Kommandeur* Walter Nowotny. Apart from short breaks I flew on his wing, until 'Novy' got his 252nd victory. On one particular mission he got seven victories and on the same day in a further mission he shot down three more. Of his 250 *Abschüsse* I was the witness to about 100 of them. On these missions, only two *Abschüsse* were left for me. I did not consider this very serious, more important for me that I never had the feeling that I was about to be burned. I also learned a lot and this gave me self-assurance for later missions where I had responsibility on my shoulders. 'Novy' was our example and our buddy (*Kumpel*)! He and I had our aircraft serviced and armed with the 1st *Staffel* of *JG 54*.
>
> On the quality of the Russian fighters: they appeared mostly in large masses and up to and including the Jak-9 their machines were inferior to the Fw 190. They also mostly did not cross the front line into our territory; this they only did when they thought there were no German fighters in the area of the front. Seeing as the German fighter *Geschwader* had to guard an enormous front, from Leningrad to the Crimea, they attempted to deceive the Russian pilots. Thus, for example, the *I Gruppe* of *JG 54* kept two *Schwarms* (eight aircraft) whose only task was to show themselves on the widest possible extent of the front. To achieve this they landed at

various field bases and took off from there again. The main task of I/JG 54 was to escort bombers, Stukas and also reconnaissance aircraft. Escorting reconnaissance aircraft was not very exciting!

During the Orel offensive we flew in the main free chases looking for Russian bombers. During my time in Russia I got to know the front from Leningrad to Charkov; I can no longer count all the airfields where we operated from. I achieved 12 *Abschüsse* on the Eastern Front, three Lagg-3s, four La-5s, one Airacobra, one Curtiss P-40, one Il-2, and two Jak-9s. Having been promoted to *Feldwebel*, at the beginning of April 1944 I was transferred to *JG 11* in the Home Defence at Wunsdorf near Hannover.

Walter Nowotny was the successor to the preceding 'greats' among the *Jagdflieger*, Werner Mölders (first to score 100 victories), Gordon Gollob (first to 150), Hermann Graf (first to 200), and was also to be awarded the Diamonds to the *Ritterkreuz* and to become a propaganda figure of note. In his case the focus was on *Schwarm Nowotny* rather than an individual flier; teamwork had become a key to survival on the Russian Front. Richter commented as follows on this expert's tactics:

I can say little about specific tactics Nowotny used when attacking Russian aircraft, from my side. One always tried to attack from a higher altitude so as to surprise the enemy, and if possible also out of the sun. When things got too hot, one pushed the aircraft into the vertical and dived away. Most Russians could not follow such a manoeuvre and with a steep climb back up from the speed attained in a dive, we could rapidly put ourselves behind them again. Later the Russians came up with a new tactic. They flew in a protective circle. When it was big enough, our aces were able to slip into this and shoot enemy aircraft out of the circle. On Nowotny one can add that he did nothing with excessive force when flying! He always said when one asked him what the secret of his success was, 'my machine shoots and hits on its own'.

One of the armourers in *I/JG 54*, *Waffenmeister* Ernst Brunns of the *Gruppenstab*, remembers Nowotny with affection; he was obviously very popular with all ranks in his *Gruppe* and his fellow pilots regarded him as much as a *Kumpel* (pal) as they respected him as their commanding officer.

Herr Nowotny was a first-class chap, grew up in the Hitler Youth but that was so common then; an outstanding officer, he was respected by everyone, even by the *Führer*, Adolf Hitler! Once he came back from a *Feindflug* with nine victory claims, and we thought that his magazines would all be completely empty, but he only used two or three rounds of cannon ammunition, two incendiary rounds and one explosive shell for each. He said farewell to us (*I/JG 54* which he commanded) in Orsha; we were very sorry to see him go.

On 13 November 1994 I accompanied *Herr* Ernst Richter to Bramsche-Epe, where *Major* Walter Nowotny had crashed due to unknown causes 50 years before (he appears to have been shot down by American fighters while flying an Me 262 jet fighter, as the *Kommodore* of *Kommando Nowotny*, an experimental unit testing this unique new machine in combat);[88] one only found a hand at the site. The local farmer built a memorial at the crash site that is carefully tended still. The officers from the airfield at Rheine/Westfalen laid a wreath at the memorial in 1994, where the speech was given by Peter Bremer (who had gone missing at Orel, and served seven years as a POW; he flew with Nowotny in Russia) who spoke very moving words. In the local inn '*Zur Linde*' we sat down together with the officers. Ernst Richter had a combat report with him from Orel, signed by *Hauptmann* Jung, also a successful fighter pilot (68 victories), with whom I enjoyed a very good and friendly relationship, an outstanding officer and man.

Later in August 1943, *Unteroffizier* Ulrich Wernitz, who flew with *Stab/JG 54* and *I/JG 54*, had moved to the Poltava area of the Ukraine, and his *Leistungsbuch* here recorded eight missions between 6 and 25 September, encompassing five free chases, one reconnaissance and two Stuka-escorts.[89] The Russians were met on three of them: 11 Jak-9s on one; a large formation of 30 Pe-2s escorted by 20 Yak-9s and La-5s on another; six Lagg-3s on the third, of which Wernitz shot down one (16 September) for his 11th *Abschuss*. He himself was wounded lightly in the head on 25 September when flak hit his cockpit.[90] By October 1943, *I/JG 54* were flying out of Vitebsk over the already old Kursk salient battle area, where Ulrich Wernitz's *Leistungsbuch* recorded 12 missions between 9 and 17 October: 11 were escorts to Ju 87s and He 111 formations with only one free chase.[91] The enemy was met on three of these operations: ten Airacobras on 11 October of which Wernitz claimed one probable; some La-5s next day when Wernitz scored his 15th victory; a large formation of 18 Pe-2s escorted by six Jak-9s on 13 October from which Wernitz knocked down a Jak-9 for his 16th claim.[92]

Clearly the *Luftwaffe* fighter arm had lost control of these air battles, with almost all missions necessitating escort of their own bombers and little opportunity for the free chase operations they preferred; additionally, only modern Russian aircraft were met and their formations were increasing in size. *IV/JG 54* flew in the Leningrad region during August–September 1943, then from Idritsa, north-west of Vitebsk (September–December 1943) and from Dno, south-west of Lake Ilmen

(December 1943).[93] *Feldwebel* Georg Füreder, who had been part of *I/ JG 26* earlier in the year when they were flying over the Staraya Russa, Smolensk and Orel areas, and had returned to the Channel front with this *Gruppe* in early June 1943, found himself back in Russia soon after, as told below.

In July 1943 the East reclaimed me once again. I joined the *IV Gruppe*, 11th *Staffel* of *JG 54*, in East Prussia which was in the process of being set up, and in the same month we moved to Krasnowardejsk, south-west of Leningrad. In this unit, to which I belonged until my transfer to *JG 11* in March 1944, I collected the majority of my Eastern Front experience. Our *Gruppe* was the only fighter unit in this northern area during this time. Somewhat later we relocated to Siverskaya and from there we operated as needed in *Schwarms* of four aircraft from forward field bases. The airfield at Siverskaya was an established Russian military airbase with brick-built quarters and with hangars large enough for fighter aircraft.

Directly next door in the forest lay the largely wood-built dachas of the Leningrad Russians, in which the wives and children of the owners lived, who during the original advance of our troops either did not want to flee or could not leave. There was no fence between the airfield buildings and these houses. Relations between us and the inhabitants of the dachas as well as the population of the area generally were friendly. Many of the people worked on the airfield. There were no acts of sabotage during this time. There was also no theft by cleaning staff in our quarters. As a pilot, who operated from an airfield protected by ground troops, one lived an unmolested life protected from the ground battles.

However, the aerial battles were another matter. Here I restrict my remarks to the time from July 1943 to March 1944. Quantitatively the Russian air force had already recovered from its previous losses. Qualitatively the majority of its aircraft, including the Airacobras and P-40s delivered by the Americans and the British, were inferior to both the Fw-190 and the Me-109 G-6. The La-5 and Jak-9 were about equal. The majority of the pilots were imperfectly trained (especially in shooting skills) and lacked experience. The leadership of the Russian air forces concentrated at that time on supporting ground operations. Their air armies always operated where they themselves were attacking. In this way over time there existed areas along the front without any meaningful Russian air activity.

From 1943 onwards the Russians no longer tried to use large combined fighter units (of *Staffel* or *Gruppe* strengths) over the front. They now split up for operations (*Schwarm*-sized formations) and applied our own tactics that we had perfected through experience. Their operational morale was not better or worse than our own. However they preferred to break off combat before it was necessary, largely due to a lack of experience, successes and self-confidence. As a result, despite our being inferior in numbers, we were everywhere able to cover our ground troops in the year 1943 and the beginning of 1944. However, it became necessary to strengthen the escorts for our own bomber formations.

The assignments for free chases became scarcer as the Russian ground attack aircraft (Il-2) became more numerous. They operated in small formations (four to eight aircraft), directly over the front. Due to their heavy armour they were rather slow. To hit them in vulnerable places, one had to get close and as they flew at low altitude, you yourself entered the zone of the Russian flak defences that mostly fired without caution within range of their own aircraft to get at us. On such operations I was hit twice by flak within a period of twelve hours, but each time was able to reach our own lines before force-landing. I can say little about the battle at Kursk–Orel. We pilots knew of course about the intention of our leadership to strive for a decisive battle there, before we fell too far behind quantitatively. This battle had to be won before the invasion in the West. Whether Kursk was the right area is at least doubtful, as it had been very well prepared for defence by the Russians.

Hauptmann Rudolf Sinner commanded *IV/JG 54* on the Northern Front from September 1943 till February 1944[94] and commented on this period: 'In the winter 1943/1944 the air war over Northern Russia was not very active due to the bad weather and the shortness of the days, and was essentially restricted to operations close to the front lines. It was noticeable that the enemy had caught up both technically and in the standard of training.' These two witnesses from *IV/JG 54* bear out an overall significant improvement in the standard of both VVS aircraft and crews, especially bearing in mind that this *Gruppe* was operating on a relatively quiescent frontal segment.

In August 1943, *I/JG 51* moved south (from Bryansk) to the Poltava area till October when a move to Orsha/Kirovograd followed; in December they were moved to Bobruisk.[95] *III/JG 51* were also stationed at Poltava in Ukraine (30 August–October 1943), and finally at Orsha till the end of the year.[96] *Leutnant* Günther Schack, *Staffelführer 7/JG 51*, recorded some of the adventures he experienced in Ukraine in the summarised post-war version of his diary, excerpts from which follow. Much reduced in numbers by now, his *Staffel* lost several of the few pilots it still had, as the retreat of the German air force and army continued unabated across the plains of the Ukraine.

26 August: The *Gruppe* moves to Gluchow in the Ukraine. A really nice town, especially when compared to poverty-stricken nests in the Central

Front. Naturally, nothing has been prepared for us, so that as always the first few nights and meals were really primitive. At present the 7th *Staffel* of *JG 51* has only five pilots and the same number of machines. *Leutnant* Hamer, an ex-student of mine from Toulouse, has proved himself amazingly and in the past few months has scored over 30 *Abschüsse*. The oldest and most experienced in the *Staffel* is now May, with 45 victories to his name he belongs amongst the most successful pilots of the *Gruppe*. As a result he has advanced from *Unteroffizier* to *Oberfeldwebel*.

27 August: This month has really been something else, but we can definitely not complain of a lack of enemy air activity. Unfortunately the front is moving backwards slowly but surely to the West. When the Bolshevists have succeeded in breaking through at one point, then the entire sector of the front wavers. One also has the impression, at least from the air, that this slow yet steady advance of the Russians is not solely due to their quantitative superiority. At present at Sewsk there are large aerial incursions which almost invariably are associated with large-scale ground operations. In only ten minutes more than 120 incoming Russian aircraft are reported. Three of us were escorting a reconnaissance aircraft in this area, when near the end of the mission a large formation of bombers with at least 20 fighters barrelled in, and fortunately or more likely prudently, our charge went home. We still had enough fuel for a bit and I was able to shoot down one of the bombers, but then we ourselves had to dive away fast, as the Russians were cross having seen one of their own go down in flames. That was my 90th claim.

Soon after, on the next mission, there was a drama. During combat, just as I had shot down a fighter, May rammed my aircraft and crashed. Gläser shouted: 'Günther has been shot down, *Leutnant* Schack has been shot down!' Now only did I realise that it was May, falling out of the sky below me from 4,000 m. I screamed to him 'Get out, get out!' but no parachute showed. I thought I heard faintly, 'I can't', and then I saw two machines hit the ground right after one another: my Russian and poor May. With the collision there was a heavy vibration but I was able to regain control of my spinning machine again. May must have attacked the same machine as I from above and behind, without seeing that I was already going for him. In any case as one of the wingmen in my vic he should have kept that sort of thing in mind. Totally depressed, we turned for home. May and I had become good friends, although this quiet and somewhat private person only gave little away. My aircraft was seriously damaged in the right wing, which had to be changed. There was no time to brood, as two more operations followed.

On the fourth mission of the day my engine suddenly started running irregularly. I broke off my combat and flew homewards. The aircraft became slower and slower, I could not understand what was wrong with it, as all the instrument readings looked fine. Near our field my bird had become so slow that I could no longer risk a turn. With great difficulty I was just able to get over the town and then I slid along the ground onto a field. Despite the hard forced-landing everything went well. I grabbed my chute and stopped the first vehicle on the nearby road. Brown uniforms made me think they were Russians, as there were many Russian auxiliaries in this area. But in answer I found out that they were Hungarian officers. A *Hauptmann* introduced himself. I saluted and told my little story. They were happy to take me along and let me off in front of our base headquarters. A notably heavy day.

28 August: My machine had a typical engine seizure, most likely the engine could not take the wild dogfighting. As the *Staffel* had no other *Schwarmführers*, I took another machine and flew on. Today also my hunting luck was bad. After all else, in landing I found that as the aircraft slowed down it veered to the right, and I could not hold it. I thus quickly retracted the undercarriage and she slid on her belly, and that way the damage was not as great as when an undercarriage leg broke off on one side. In most such cases the aircraft normally got away with just a change of airscrew. The hit on my aircraft had come about due to my sitting behind a low-flying opponent and our good infantrymen had once again shot too far behind him.

29 August: Once again we had to get moving, the Russians were close to home once more. With a few panzers he rolled unopposed towards Gluchow. On that evening we flew to Konotop; two years before we had already been here. How the picture had changed in the meantime! Then we were advancing, today we are in unbridled retreat. The Konotop airfield had changed very much for the better in these two years. The mess would not have been out of place at a field in the middle of Germany. Quarters and food are outstanding. Overall since the general retreat started the provisions have often been extravagant. In Konotop also, the supply dumps are being emptied as fast as possible.

1 September: The past month has seen the *Gruppe* change completely. Never have the losses been so high, but the successes also in these four weeks. Against 40 *Abschüsse* I had to belly-land four times. Today claim number 99 fell.

3 September: In the last two days and even before that I have been allowed to fly many free chase operations, so that I can bring my 100th victory home. Over Gluchow, that already lies almost 20 km behind the front lines and where the Russians are already landing, I finally got my wish! I announced

my 100th *Abschuss* loudly over the radio. The *Kommandeur* who was in the air at the time, called: 'Günther from Hannibal, congratulations on the 100th!' The non-flying adjutant congratulated me also, from the ground by radio. With the last of my fuel I waggled my wings over base and rolled my aircraft close to the ground. Flares flew up from the dispersals as I parked my machine, and the entire *Staffel* had collected there. A huge wreath was placed over my head and the good ground crews congratulated me with a beautiful bunch of flowers. Already the first champagne corks were clanging against my machine. At the headquarters more champagne flowed, but the celebration was very short as the Russians were close to Konotop. Almost hastily we had to leave the place.

Our new base lay about 100 km south-west of Bryansk on the River Desna, near Trubschewsk. *Leutnant* Hamer and *Unteroffizier* Gläser were to have flown two slightly defective aircraft to the new base from Konotop; 15 minutes after taking off Gläser came back alone and reported to me that Hamer had made a smooth belly-landing just east of the Desna. I got a huge fright, as the entire area east of the Desna had become Russian territory a few hours before. Immediately I sent a small communications aircraft there and led the escorting *Rotte* myself. We circled over the belly-landed aircraft and saw nobody anywhere around. The unopened parachute lay next to the aircraft. Hopefully he would still be able to make his way back to our own lines, as there was no question of a firm front here for the moment.

While we were circling over the force-landed machine, a strong Boston formation flew above us towards Konotop. I immediately let the ground station know that all aircraft should take off as a big attack on Konotop was imminent. Their target would definitely be our airfield. Over the city I was finally able to catch up to this formation. We each attacked a somewhat separated bird three times, and both engines caught fire. He must soon fall; suddenly the *Kommandeur* appeared and also shot at him. As he now tumbled from the sky we heard on the radio that the old man claimed the *Abschuss*. Our airfield was burning brightly, and 13 people had been killed. Fortunately our *Gruppe* suffered only one loss. Several Ju 52s sent in to help evacuate the field had gone up in flames.

We quickly refuelled, packed our stuff into the aircraft and flew to the new base where we landed in the rain and almost complete darkness. My nerves almost reached breaking point as I came in to land as the last one and had to go round again, as it was now so dark that it was very difficult to see even a few outlines. Eventually I got my aircraft down. For an hour we sat down again in pleasant company, just three pilots still left. The *Spiess*, *Oberfeldwebel* Ruscher and the chief mechanic also joined the party. But we didn't stay long as after this stressful day our beds were calling. We were quartered in a school. The next day I could again give some attention to the *Staffel*, as the weather was bad. The many geese in this area, the 1,700th victory of the *Gruppe* and my 100th, were the occasion for a communal supper.

<u>6 September</u>: Sadly we never heard anything again about *Leutnant* Hamer. A pleasant relationship had developed with a neighbouring reconnaissance section. Before every mission the comrades from the other fraternity landed on our airfield and asked for escort. Whenever humanly possible they got it too but unfortunately it was not always possible. Our main task is to escort particularly the Stukas. We became particularly friendly with the Wolf-crew, and mostly I flew their escort myself. But it was terribly boring flying circles around a tired reconnaissance aircraft, but we did it for this crew gladly. Today I even had some luck in this task and caught a long-range reconnaissance machine at 4,000 m that went down in flames next to our charge.

<u>9 September</u>: A crate with ten bottles and 300 cigarettes arrived for me by air from the *Kommodore*, with a congratulatory note on my one hundredth. Along with two chickens and a goose shared between four of us – in the meantime *Leutnant* Katlun had returned hale and hearty again – we sampled the gift. Some bottles went to the mechanics also. Our stay here would not be very long (they moved on 12 September 1943 to a new base west of Roslawl).[97]

IV/JG 51, who had been at Orel for a long time (February 1943–2 August), moved back to Bryansk (August), south to Poltava in the Ukraine (August–October 1943), then north again to Orsha (southwest of Smolensk; October–December 1943) and finally to Shitomir, west of Kiev, Ukraine.[98] In late November 1942, *6/JG 51* had been detached from its parent *Gruppe* (by then transferred from Russia to Tunisia, where it formed a new 6th *Staffel*) and became, in time, *Stabstaffel/JG 51*.[99] This was a full-strength *Staffel* and not comparable with a *Geschwaderstab* formation, and by early 1943 had become more and more a *Jabostaffel* specialising in ground attack operations.[100] *Unteroffizier* Horst Petzschler, who was to become successful in both Eastern and Western theatres in time, began his career in this unusual *Staffel*:

Fresh from training school, from 23 August 1943–1 April 1944 I served with *Stabstaffel, Jagdgeschwader Mölders*, in the Smolensk–Terespol (Terespol lay just over the Polish border, southwest of Minsk, on the main Moscow-Warsaw freeway route) area. My missions in my first shift in Russia comprised 126 *Jabo*-operations with 500 kg bombs, attacking pin-point targets: bridges, tanks and troop concentrations; we also flew escorts for *Oberst* Rudel's '*Panzerknacker*' (panzer-crackers)! Compared to other parts of the *Wehrmacht*, we fighter pilots enjoyed first-class treatment and we even had a Ju 52 transport aircraft at our disposal that brought back many luxuries, including things to drink also, from Spain and France, apart from ferrying those going on and returning from leave. Lice, bugs and flees affected everyone who was in Russia, they were free and gratis! We were mostly stationed on field bases close to the front, just behind the infantry divisions. The (Russian) artillery bothered us continually!

During this first period on the Eastern Front, Petzschler claimed his first three victories: a Jak-7 (5 November 1943), and two Il-2s with rear-gunners (both on 10 November), all three in the region of Newel (north-north-west of Vitebsk and south-west of Velikiye Luki).

It is perhaps fitting to conclude this account of German fighter operations over the Russian Front in this fateful year with some comments by Hermann Buchner, a notable *Schlacht* (specialist ground attack) pilot who experienced the retreats through the Ukraine in the second half of 1943. These pilots often had the worst of it, facing the very dangerous Russian ground defences, normally at low level, and being expected to tackle any Soviet fighters on their own. *Schlachtgeschwader 1* re-equipped with the Fw 190 from late 1942 through to May 1943.[101] *Feldwebel* Hermann Buchner rejoined this *Geschwader* on 10 July 1943 at Varvarovka in southern Ukraine, south of Kharkov and then retreated with them through the Ukraine to Kiev where they were based from August to October 1943, after which they were sent to the Crimea.[102]

After Stalingrad my *Geschwader* were equipped with the Fw 190 A-4. As far as I recall the Fw 190 A-4 was not armoured. We had two 13 mm MGs mounted on top of the engine and two 20 mm cannons in the wing roots, under the fuselage an ETC for 250 or 500 kg bombs and under the wings 4 ETC's for 50 kg bombs. From 1943 onwards the Russian pilots improved in their training and then also received the Jak-9, an outstanding aircraft. When we had got rid of our external payload there were no longer any disadvantages in performance of the Fw 190 compared to our opponents. The pilots of the Jak-9s were very good and aggressive soldiers. We ground attack fliers were now often forced to drop our bombs in order to take on aerial combat against the superior numbers of Russian fighters. If there were no enemy fighters in the area we completed our ground attack tasks. If there were enemy fighters about, a part of our formations took them on as fighters. In October 1943 a reorganisation was made of the *Schlachtflieger* units, the *III/SG 1* (his *Gruppe*) becoming *II/SG 2 Immelmann*.

Hermann Buchner then became a member of *6/SG 2*.[103]

As the fighters available to the *Luftwaffe* over the Eastern Front decreased with significant transfers to the Home Defence (illustrations 7, 8 and 9), it became impossible for the *Jagdflieger* to strive for any semblance of air superiority anymore. With valuable fighter aircraft in short supply, in particular the popular Fw 190s, these went increasingly to the *Schlachtgeschwadern* (illustration 12) which were expected to do their ground assault jobs, defend themselves and also to provide a modicum of fighter activity over the front as well. This reflected a hard expectation and the chances of survival of these ground attack pilots in the East were correspondingly low. As an example of *Schlacht* casualties, *I/SchG 1* lost 16 Fw 190s in combat and another 14 operational/accidental losses in July 1943; for the same month, the figures for *II/SchG 1* were 13 and 14 Fw 190s lost, all in the Kursk battle and in the succeeding Russian advances.[104]

7

Endless Retreats; the *Bagration* Debacle (January–August 1944)

A massive Russian winter offensive from December 1943 to April 1944 ushered in this phase of the air war on the Eastern Front. Senior, highly experienced witnesses remark on the much improved capabilities of Russian pilots and their aircraft, making the aerial operations in this period much more dangerous. *Hauptmann* Erich Rudorffer, a highly experienced fighter pilot who began in 1940 as a senior NCO and who had attained 74 victories in the West, was appointed to lead *II/JG 54* in the East from 1 August 1943 till February 1945[1]; he flew against the Russians in northern Russia, from Finland, the Kurland pocket, and is an authoritative voice. He had this to say about the Russians in the later war years: 'As I only flew operationally with the Fw 190 in the East from August 1943, I can only express an opinion on this time period. A good Russian pilot was as good in air combat and in perseverance, as any of us. After better Russian fighter aircraft such as the Jak-11 and La-7 were used, the aerial struggle became very hard!'

Oberstleutnant Günther Scholz, an equally experienced opponent of the Soviets, flying in the Far North where he led *Jagdgeschwader 5* for a long time (from June 1943 to May 1944, and again from February 1945 till the end of the war), found the Russians to be a lesser threat than the Western Allies: 'Particularly the Jak-3 was at least equal to the Me 109-G. In general one can say that the battles against the Soviet fliers were easier than those against the English and American fighters and especially those against the large bomber formations, the "Flying Fortresses" of the Americans, that had to be attacked head-on, in order to incapacitate the pilots.'

To *Major* Wolfgang Späte, who came from the Home Defence in that fateful year of 1944 to fly once again on the Eastern Front (as *Kommandeur* IV/JG 54) for the first time since his last experiences there in 1942, a distinct change was immediately obvious: 'When I returned to the East in early summer 1944 – after a two-year break – and resumed operations on the Russian Front, the Russian fighters were equal to some of our own, the Il-2 compared favourably with the Ju 87 and the Pe-2 had the defensive power of a Ju 88 or Do 217. Quantitatively by then the Russians outnumbered us twenty-fold. A considerable improvement in the level of training on the Russian side was also noticeable.'

While it was one thing for an experienced and veteran unit leader to fight against a revitalised opponent, for a newly arrived and inexperienced youngster, the realities of the Russian Front air war must have been staggering. One such was *Unteroffizier* Albrecht Licht, who flew briefly with *I/JG 54* and then with 6th *Staffel* of *II/JG 54* from December 1943 right through until the end of the war. He provides an overview of his experiences below:

In December 1943 I went from the *Ergänzungsgruppe* to *II/JG 54* in the southern part of Russia (Belaja–Zerkow). In March the *Gruppe* moved to the northern section of the front (Petseri). Here the *I* and *II/JG 54* were deployed along a front length of *c.* 630 km between Finland and Polozk (Central Front, Russia). As soon as the Russians attacked one sector of this long front, we as a *Staffel* or in *Gruppe* strength often had to move to the new crisis point for one or more days. After a serious flying accident on 2 May 1944 in Polozk, I was unfit for operational flying until July 1944. In total I scored nine *Abschüsse*, eight of them over Kurland. As the front was continually moving in the time I was with *JG 54* (from December 1943), and as the crisis points were constantly changing, we often had to move from one base to another. The Fw 190 used 600 litres of fuel in about 55 minutes at full throttle. However, full throttle was only used in aerial combat. With normal flying the fuel would allow about 100 minutes in the air. Because of this reason the fighter bases were always near the front, so that we had only short distances to fly to and from the front, leaving us enough time for the operation itself.

As a result I experienced a gypsy lifestyle this whole time. We often had a more permanent base where we landed in between and where our belongings lay (for example at Petseri in Estonia). For most of the time I travelled with only a briefcase which contained the most urgently needed things. Often we had moves that only lasted one day. In such cases the chief mechanic was taken with us in the rear fuselage of the Fw 190 (this was not possible in the Me 109 without considerable alterations, leaving it generally unserviceable also), so that the aircraft could get minimal servicing between operations. However there were also transfers where we sat for one or two weeks on the same field. We were on standby from dawn till dusk every day, during which time we were on the airfield itself at our dispersals. Only if the weather was really bad (mist, snowfalls, a saturated runway, etc.) was readiness cancelled. After the day was over or readiness cancelled we went to our quarters, and after supper we had the time to ourselves. Then we played cards, attended to our possessions, or wrote letters to our parents, wives, fiancés, girlfriends and friends. A good comradeship existed amongst the pilots, and thus we experienced no melancholy; we laughed a lot and when the weather was bad such that we could not fly, then we also celebrated. Only when a comrade had failed to return from an operation was there a widespread sadness amongst us.

Our operations encompassed: free chases – here we could look for our own targets within a specified airspace; escorts – for bombers, Stukas or also for ships, to protect them against enemy aerial attacks; low-level attacks – against ground or ship targets, strafing with our cannons and machine guns; fighter-bomber missions – although these were sometimes flown I did not experience them; reconnaissance missions – these were to reconnoitre the frontlines and also for a certain distance behind those lines; weather reconnaissance – the weather *Rotte* normally took off just before sunrise and reported the weather conditions along the front and its hinterland (flown at heights of 2,000–3,000 m); airfield protection – cockpit readiness of a *Rotte*, that could take off immediately when there was a surprise attack (*Alarmrotte*), in general this readiness lasted for two hours, but in extreme conditions (very cold at 20°–40° of frost) pilots were relieved every 20 minutes.

1944 was to be a fateful year for the *Luftwaffe* and for Germany altogether. During the first five months of the year over Germany, where the majority of the *Jagdflieger* was deployed, the preponderance of Allied airpower was to see their defeat and consequent effective impotence during the invasion of Normandy. In the East, where a much-reduced German fighter presence met ever better-equipped, better-trained, more experienced and much more numerous opponents, only a modicum of protection for the sore-tried ground forces could be provided as they struggled to survive many onslaughts against a background of rapid transfers enforced by a continuous need to withdraw in the face of Soviet pressure. In the far north, Finland would pull out of the fight in September, Army Group Centre would be destroyed utterly in the Minsk salient in June–July (Operation *Bagration* of the Red Army), the siege of Leningrad was broken early in the year, and both Romanian and Polish territory were reached by the surging Russian forces. The first few months of 1945 saw the final defeat of Germany in both West and East, with the weight of the fighter arm finally deployed in the East, but it was a case of too little too late.

In the Far North; Finland Makes Peace

The situation on the ground did not change significantly in the Far North until the autumn of 1944, and the pilots of JG 5 were often troubled as much by the weather and tough living conditions of the *Eismeerfront*, as they were by their Russian enemies. *Oberleutnant* Rudolf Gloeckner had originally joined I/JG 77 in Norway in mid-1941 and was a very experienced pilot by the beginning of 1944, which found him in 6/JG 5; in May 1944 he was appointed *Staffelkapitän 8/JG 5* (part of III *Gruppe* and later renumbered to 11/JG 5) which he led till February 1945.[2] Most of his victories (a total of 32 claims, 31 of them Russian aircraft) were scored between February and September 1944 on the *Eismeerfront*.[3] He remembers tough enemies and equally tough weather conditions. 'The Russians were good flyers, especially towards the end of the war. They were tough opponents equipped with good fighter planes (La-5 and Jak-9) and of course quite a few American planes like Airacobra and Kingcobra as well as some Spitfires. One of our greatest enemies in Northern Finland and Norway of course was the weather which gave us considerable difficulties.'

III/JG 5 was stationed in northernmost Finland–Norway along the White Sea (*Eismeerfront*) from the beginning of the year until 8 November 1944, IV/JG 5 serving in the same area between August and 6 November 1944.[4] II/JG 5 had been transferred south to Pleskau (at the southern end of Lake Peipus, on the Estonian–Russian border) in late 1943 and operated from there until March 1944, when they went to Alakurtti (northern Finland, *c.* 300 km south-west of Murmansk) until April 1944, when they moved again, this time to Latvia (April–31 May 1944 when transferred, once more, to Germany).[5] *Oberleutnant* Günther Schwanecke flew in both II and III/JG 5 on this front, till January 1944 in Stab II/JG 5 and then from February till September 1944 was a member and later *Staffelkapitän* of 4/JG 5, shooting down six Russian aircraft in the latter *Staffel*.[6] From September he led 7/JG 5 (later renumbered 10/JG 5) until October 1944, before being transferred to Germany and the Home Defence.[7] He remembers the Me 109 as being generally superior, for an experienced flier:

In North-Finland the Russians were not aggressive, and when we appeared they immediately formed protective circles, to cover each other. In the north of Finland and of Norway there were only German fighter units (i.e. no Finnish aircraft). As far as I recall, we always maintained air superiority. The Soviet fighter aircraft were lighter than our Me 109 and in dogfights were about equal, but inferior in diving. This applied to all types of Russian fighters. The Me 109 was also superior in climbing ability at high altitudes, from about 5,000 m upwards, and also generally in its fire power.

On 10 June 1944 the Russians launched a strong offensive against Finland across the Karelian Isthmus (north of Leningrad), and the Finns, although holding together, were driven back and in trouble, and asked the Germans for help.[8] As a result, an informal assembly of *I/SG 3* (Ju 87s), *I/SG 5* (Fw 190s), *II/JG 54* (Fw 190s) and a reconnaissance and a transport unit in support, informally termed *Gefechtsverband Kuhlmey* after the senior officer, *Oberstleutnant* Kurt Kuhlmey, *Kommodore* of *SG 3*, operated in support of the Finns, from 13 June till 23 July (with *I/SG 5* staying on till 13 August 1944).[9] In contrast to the deliberate widespread destruction of many *Luftwaffe* records at the end of the war, some of the records of *Gefechtsverband Kuhlmey* have survived in Finnish military archives, and make interesting reading; there follow two daily summary reports (file number and secret designation – geh. – given in heading; ground attack bomb tonnage dropped in parentheses) from July 1944.[10]

Gefechtsverband Kuhlmey. Total day sorties 14 July 1944 (Br. B. Nr. 173a/44 geh.) Ground attack: three missions with 50 Ju 87s (26.3 t.) and four missions with 13 Fw 190s (6.5 t.); targets: pontoon and wooden bridges at Äyräpää, assemblies of pontoons and crossing points; successes: several direct hits on bridges, and again disrupted in evening; probably three pontoons and 10 to 12 lorries destroyed. Fighters: three escort missions with 24 aircraft, one free chase with four aircraft, one scramble with two aircraft, total of 30 Fw 190 sorties; *Abschüsse*: three Jak 9s; no losses. Signed 'Kuhlmey'.

Gefechtsverband Kuhlmey. Total day sorties 15 July 1944 (Br. B. Nr. 180a/44 geh.) Weather resulted in only one mission in evening (and second by 35 Ju 87s[15.8 t.] and third by 12 Fw 190s[6 t.]). Ground attack: targets bridges at Äyräpää and crossing points; success: bridges persistently destroyed at landing zones, explosions. Losses: missing Ju 87 crashed near Utti, thought to be accident, crew dead. Fighters: two escort missions with 16 aircraft, one weather reconnaissance with two aircraft, one free chase with four aircraft, with total of 22 Fw 190 sorties without meeting enemy; losses: nil. Postscript: 'Congratulatory message! I thank all ranks who took part in the tough defence of the bridgehead at Vuoksen and the battles at Vuosalmi which exhausted the enemy. You have ensured that the enemy's attacks have been thrown back. These achievements will inspire you to new victories in the future. *Generalleutnant* K.L. Ösch.'

One has to wonder whether the rather bombastic message from the commanding German general had much effect, but *Luftwaffe* morale tended to be maintained right through to the end of the war, especially in the East. With the Germans retreating after the greater *Bagration* offensives, and the Russians advancing successfully deep into Estonia during August 1944, the position of Finland rapidly became untenable. Consequently, on 4–5 September a ceasefire was implemented, with an armistice becoming effective from 19 September; the Germans were granted 14 days to remove all forces from Finland, but as they did not fully meet this deadline, some conflicts did take place.[11]

January–21 June 1944; before the Bagration Offensive,
from Leningrad to the Black Sea
By 1 December 1943, the massive Russian advances following their victory at Kursk–Orel had produced a frontal situation wherein the Kuban peninsula in the western Caucasus had been liberated, and to the immediate north of the Crimean peninsula the Russians had advanced quite far westwards to the mouth of the Dnieper River, thus cutting off the Germans in the Crimea, where an epic air battle would be fought in April–May 1944. From there the front ran north-westwards (and lying mostly west of the Dnieper River) up to Kiev, also liberated, and then on to the south-eastern part of the Pripet Marshes, to the north-west of Kiev. A large German salient was left as a result to the north of Pripet, centred on the Belorussian capital of Minsk, and with Orsha, Vitebsk and Polotsk lying close to its north-eastern border. Swinging briefly north-eastwards again north of Polotsk, the front then continued northwards to Lake Ladoga's southern shore, with Leningrad still besieged.

This situation was followed by the Russian winter offensive, so that by the end of April 1944 a new situation had arisen. In the north the siege of Leningrad had finally been broken, and the Russians had advanced westwards to Narwa in the north, the front running south along Lake Peipus and then further down to north-east of Polotsk. A much larger advance was made in the south by the end of April 1944, past Odessa on the Black Sea coast, into the north-eastern corner of Romania further north, the front running west of Tiraspol and east of Lvov in Poland, and then north again to east of Brest-Litovsk. From there it turned sharply eastwards again along the Pripet Marshes to greatly deepen the southern arm of the Minsk salient, now projecting dangerously far eastwards.[12] This situation did not change meaningfully until the launch of the massive Russian

Operation *Bagration* (22 June–19 August 1944), to eliminate the Minsk salient and all the troops therein. Dispositions of the various *Jagdgruppen* during the first half of 1944 reflected this new and changing frontal reality.

While *I/JG 54* spent part of January 1944 in the Minsk salient, the same month they were transferred to northern Estonia near the national capital of Tallinn, staying there until 23 June 1944.[13] In contrast, *II/JG 54* found themselves in the Ukraine, based to the south-west and south of Kiev from December 1943 till 5 March 1944.[14] This *Geschwader*'s newest recruit, *Unteroffizier* Albrecht Licht, saw service in both *Gruppen* in December 1943 and early 1944. In the space of about a week at the forward base of Orsha in the Minsk salient he was to face a very stark introduction to what life at the front could mean; one really has to wonder at his state of mind and his view of his own future with this sort of start.

I arrived by train in Königsberg/East Prussia on 5 December 1943. From here according to the telegram I had received that called me back from leave, I was supposed to take a Fw 190 to the front. Of course this never happened. At the station headquarters and also at the flight control centre in Königsberg-Devau, nobody could tell me where *JG 54* was located. At flight control I was advised to wait, as every week a Ju 52 came from Borrisow and then flew back again. On 6 December travelling on this Ju 52 I reached Borrisow and on another day flew with another Ju 52 to Orscha. Here at flight control I learned that *I/JG 54* and the *Geschwaderstab* were stationed on that field.

Temporarily, I was transferred to the *I Gruppe*, in the 1st *Staffel*. I had to wait until the rest of the pilots from the *Ergänzungsstaffeln* arrived also. In this interval I was very strongly confronted with the events of frontal reality that shocked me emotionally. On 8 December I reported to *Staffelkapitän Oberleutnant* Fischer at 1st *Staffel* as temporarily transferred to it. Shortly after that he took off on a mission and did not return. I had befriended myself with a *Gefreiter* Karl Maul. On 9 December 1943 he also did not return from an operation. On 11 December I reported myself to the *Geschwaderkommodore Oberstleutnant* von Bonin as transferred to *JG 54*. He commented that the events of the past few days must have depressed me. He comforted me and said, 'That is an unfortunate coincidence!' On 15 December 1943 he also was shot down. It took me a long time to digest this.

The loss of *JG 54*'s *Kommodore* was keenly felt by all ranks, as witnessed by senior armourer Ernst Brunns, who served on the *Stab* of *I/JG 54* at Orsha at this trying time. 'Hubertus von Bonin was the best type of officer, from a family that had produced a number of high-ranking officers including a Prussian minister of war. He came from Stolp in Pommerania and was a quiet and prudent man. He was also very popular with the fairer sex. We laid this good man to rest in Orscha in the USSR; a military band was flown in from Pleskau in a Ju 52. The tears ran down our faces underneath our helmets when they played "Guten Kamderaden". *Frau* von Puttkamer, a close friend of the family was flown in from Warsaw.'

However, life and the war had to go on and *Unteroffizier* Albrecht Licht's next experiences included not only a change of unit within *JG 54* but also another tedious journey to reach the frontline base of his new *Staffel*, 6/*JG 54*; for him the conversion on to the Fw 190, which he was expected to fly in combat almost immediately, was a very rushed affair. In about mid-December 1943, Albrecht Licht was uprooted from *I/JG 54* and the Minsk salient part of the front, to join *II/JG 54* far to the south in the Kiev region of the Ukraine, as he relates next.

In the meantime all the pilots from the schools had arrived and now we were all assigned to the different *Staffeln*. A *Fähnrich* Haase and I were transferred to the *II Gruppe* in the southern part of Russia to Bejala–Zerkow (south of Kiev). I was sorry about this as I had already somewhat accustomed myself (to 1st *Staffel*). On 20 December 1943 the two of us flew in a Ju 52 to Wilna to the rear command of the *Geschwader*. On 22 December 1943 we got our marching orders and took the train for the *c.* 650 km to Kasatin, and thus we celebrated Christmas on the train. From there we travelled with a lorry on a railway flat car further, at *c.* 18° to 22° of frost. In the afternoon of 26 December we finally reached *II/JG 54*.

On 29 December in very poor visibility we moved to Koskov, as the front had penetrated to within 3 km of the field. On 4 January 1944 and on 6 January I made a total of four flights to convert onto the Fw 190 A-4, which I had not yet flown. Up till 27 January I had flown three *Feindflüge*. On 28 January I flew as *Rottenflieger* with *Feldwebel* Wernicke over the front. Here I was hit by a 3.7 cm flak shell. This ripped open the left wing from wingroot to the aileron and also ripped open the wing up to its middle. I flew this aircraft back to our base and made a successful wheels-down landing, instead of a belly landing. For that I received an impressive choking-off and deservedly so. The landing had occurred with only one flap and one aileron. In this incident my guardian angel had sat right next to me. Later on a comrade had only the aileron rod shot through and he had to bail out as the Fw 190 was no longer controllable.

By this stage of the war, incoming pilots would have none of the easy pickings typical of the beginnings of *Barbarossa*, and were faced with modern Russian aircraft and pilots better trained and more experienced than they were themselves. Albrecht Licht recalls meeting some of these new Russian machines. 'The La-5 and La-7 were further developments of the Lagg-3. I only met the La-5 twice. Once was in the Winniza area (southern Russian front) where I only saw it at a distance of *c.* 1,500–2,000 m flying away from me, back over the front.'

By early March 1944, Licht was back in the north again, after a brief detour via Latvia, flying out of a field base at Petserie (also spelled Petseri, and of uncertain exact location) from 12 March until June;[15] back in the north again, another loss of a leader must have hit home hard once more for Licht. 'Our *Staffelkapitän* Albin Wolf (a post he occupied only from 4 February to 2 April 1944 when he was killed)[16] was an example for us, as a pilot and as a *Staffelkapitän*. He only asked of us what he was also prepared to do. We had a good relationship with him.'

Exactly where the forward base of *II/JG 54* at Petseri was located remains somewhat puzzling as various options exist. Another new recruit, *Unteroffizier* Kurt Beecken, who joined Licht's 6th *Staffel* when it was based there, places it on Lake Peipus, which itself lies along the Russian–Estonian border:

> After completing training I was ripe for the front. I received two days home leave and then travelled by train via Berlin and East Prussia to Dorpat in Estonia, where the *Stab* of *Jagdgeschwader 54* lay, where I was to report. I was assigned to the 6th *Staffel II/JG 54* that was then stationed in Petseri on Lake Peipus (northern Russia). (Beecken joined them in the first half of 1944, sometime between March and June).[17] Here I flew my first operations initially as wingman (*Katschmarek*) of highly experienced frontline pilots. I do not wish to detail *Abschüsse*, being shot down myself and other experiences.

Many place names in the East have changed since the war and the *Luftwaffe* also tended to use historical more Germanic names if available, or even gave their own names to more isolated field bases. One candidate for 'Petseri' is Pechory, which lies close to but not on the shores of Lake Peipus at its southern end close to Pskov; another 'Petseri' lies *c.* 50 km west of Pskov, and a third place of the same name is in Valga on the Estonia–Latvia border even further west. Yet another choice, a known wartime airfield, lies on the small island of Piirissaare in Lake Peipus itself, close to its western shore and was a forward base for the major German airfield at Tartu, west of the lake.

Any of these choices, with the possible exception of the one at Valga, would fit what is told by Kurt Beecken of *6/JG 54*; however, the problem of identifying the field base of 'Petseri' becomes more acute when the return of *II/JG 54* from their part in *Gefechtsverband Kuhlmey*'s operations in Karelian Finland (*c.* 13 June–*c.* 23 July 1944), as described above, is considered. Upon this return they were situated at 'Petseri' once more, but Pskov, a major town nearby at the southern end of Lake Peipus, had fallen to the Russians on 23 July,[18] which suggests that the Valga choice of 'Petseri' would have been the only appropriate one of the four possibilities discussed above. Albrecht Licht rather vaguely placed 'Petseri' in Estonia. This geographic digression merely goes to illustrate the problems which can beset those wishing to reconstruct historical events, especially when dependent at least partially on witness accounts from long after the war. Perhaps there was more than one field base with this or a similar name.

Up till the end of 1943 the Germans still besieged Leningrad, but in an operation from 14 January to 1 March 1944 the Russians advanced westwards to Lake Peipus and the Narva River.[19] By then, *I/JG 54* lay in northern Estonia (at Wesenberg, January 1944–23 June 1944).[20] A short excerpt summarising details gleaned from the *Leistungsbuch* of Ulrich Wernitz, serving with *3/JG 54*, provides a window into the details of an operational pilot flying in that area and at that time.[21] *Feldwebel* Wernitz flew mostly as a *Rottenführer* on these missions, only occasionally as a *Schwarmführer*, as befitted his level of experience (a not inconsiderable 116 *Feindflüge* and 24 claimed victories). Interestingly here, the more normal German term of *Feindberührung* (enemy contact) is replaced by *Luftkampf* – things were obviously getting tougher! In all, a total of 36 *Feindflüge* is recorded over a period of 82 days, of which 15 resulted in his meeting enemy aircraft. This relatively quiet period, summarised in the table below, would come to an end with the tidal wave of Operation *Bagration* in June 1944.

Example of a fighter pilot's operational life, Eastern Front, 13 March 1944–2 June 1944: *Feldwebel* Ulrich Wernitz *3/JG 54* (Source: handwritten, shortened copy of *Leistungsbuch* of pilot, from web page advertising militaria for sale)[22]

Operating from Wesenberg, near Tallinn in northern Estonia

MARCH

13:     Fw 189 escort (117th *Feindflug* – operational flight)
23:     Ju 87 escort and airfield protection (118th op.); met Lagg-3s
25:     Fighter patrol (119th op.)
26:     Ju 87 escort (120th op.)
28:     Fighter patrol (121st op.)
29:     Ju 87 escort (122nd op.)
30:     Ju 87 escort (123rd op.); combat with six Jak-9s, shot down one Jak-9 (25th *Abschuss*)
        Scramble (124th op.); combat with 12 to 16 La-5s, shot down one La-5 (#26)

APRIL

1: Free chase (125th op.)

Free chase (126th op.); combat with four Il-2s

2: Scramble (127th op.); combat with 15 Lagg-3s, eight Il-2s, shot down one Il-2 (#27)

4: Scramble (128th op.); combat with eight Jak-9s, shot down one Jak-9 (#28)

6: Ju 87, Fw 189 escort (129th op.); met four Jak-9s over target

7: Ju 87 escort (130th op.)

17: Scramble (131st op.); against lone Pe-2, this shot down (not confirmed), own aircraft hit

19: Ju 87 escort (132nd op.)

Scramble (133rd op.), combat with seven Il-2s, six to eight Jak-9s, shot down one Il-2 (#30)

21: Escort 35 Ju 87s (134th op.)

Escort 35 Ju 87s (135th op.)

MAY

8: Scramble (136th op.); combat with nine IL-2s and varied fighters, shot down one P-40 & one Jak-9 (#s 31, 32)

11: Escort Fw 189 (137th op.), to Narwa bend

12: Escort 16 Ju 87s (138th op.)

13: Escort Fw 189 (139th op.)

16: Scramble (140th op.); combat with 25 Il-2s, 30 to 40 Jak-9s and La-5s, shot down one Jak-9 (#33) at 20 m

26: Escort Do-24 (141st op.), to Narwa Bay

28: Escort Fw 189 (142nd op.), to Narwa

Ju 87 escort (143rd op.), combat with four Lagg-3s, shot down one Lagg-3 (#34)

27: (retrospective entry) Scramble (144th op.), to Narwa Bay, combat with four fighters

29: Scramble (145th op.); combat with 30 Il-2s, 40 Jak-9s and La-5s, shot down one La-5 and two Jak-9s (#s 35-37)

30: Fw 189 escort (146th op.)

Ju 87 escort (147th op.); combat with 11 Jak-9s over Narwa Bay

Scramble (148th op.); combat over Narwa Bay with six Jak-9s and four La-5s, shot down one Jak-9 (38th *Abschuss*)

31: Free chase (149th op.)

Fw 189 escort (150th op.), Narwa

JUNE

1: Fw 189 escort (151st op.)

2: Ju 88 escort (152nd op.)

With the *Eismeerfront* being comparatively quiet next to the rigours imposed by the Russian winter offensive further south from December 1943 to April 1944, *II/JG 5* had been sent to Pleskau at the southern end of Lake Peipus from the beginning of the New Year to March 1944 (followed by a month back in Finland at Alakurrti, *c.* 300 km south-west of Murmansk, March–April 1944) and was then at Jacobstadt (modern Jakabpils) in Latvia (April–31 May 1944).[23] *Leutnant* Ernst Scheufele, *5/JG 5* was with them and recorded his impressions.

In November 1943 we were transferred (from *Eismeerfront*) to northern Russia (Pleskau–Idritza). Our main duties were Stuka escorts; till May 1944 I scored another 10 victories (after his 1st scored over the *Eismeerfront*). In general the Russians tried to avoid combat because they knew that we were superior to them with the Me 109. This applied first and foremost to the Lagg-5, Airacobra, and Hurricane. The Jak-9 was better. However all this applied only to the average pilot; an outstanding Russian in a Jak-9 could make life very difficult for one. Until May 1944 we had to fly far over the Soviet lines to meet the enemy.

But to comment on this question more exactly I do not feel it is my place to do so. There are still some men alive (writing in 1989) who can give a fundamental judgement. I am thinking of Walter Schuck (over 200 *Abschüsse*), Rudolf Glöckner (30 *Abschüsse*), Werner Gayko, Dietrich Weinitschke. But in thinking of these men I realise for the first time that actually hardly anyone else is left alive who is more experienced than me. But I should add that I always felt that I was still a learner. I do not think of myself at all as an ace, as my total time at the front only lasted for a year and my time in Finland and Russia only from November 1943 till May 1944. All those I have just named belonged to the *III Gruppe* of *JG 5* that had stayed in the Far North till the end. My comrades in the *II Gruppe* were all lost in the Home Defence (after May 1944). Of the old experienced pilots, only Günther Schwanecke and Jupp Kunz are still alive.

One of the major aces in *JG 5* on the *Eismeerfront* was Theo Weissenberger. Ernst Scheufele of *5/JG 5* knew him well and details a memorable mission they flew together early in 1944 near Lake Ilmen, after the transfer of *II/JG 5* to northern Russia.

After leaving middle school Weissenberger learned the trade of gardener and was an early glider pilot and then later a gliding instructor. After his training as a military pilot, he flew initially in a Me 110 *Staffel* in northernmost Norway. He was so successful with this relatively unmanoeuvrable machine that he was transferred to a Me 109 *Staffel* in the same *Geschwader*. Already on 13 November 1942 he was awarded the *Ritterkreuz*, and on 2 August 1943 the *Eichenlaub* for 125 *Abschüsse*. In the meantime he had been promoted from *Oberfeldwebel* to *Oberleutnant*.

On 1 February 1944 we flew an escort mission for Ju 87s near Lake Ilmen, when we were attacked by 20 to 30 Lagg-5s. Within four minutes Theo Weissenberger shot down five of the Russians. As if in a fury, he swept about between the Russian machines, turning so tightly that short condensation trails showed at his wingtips, and mostly required only two to three short bursts of fire until the Laggs went down smoking. I had never experienced anything like this before and did not think it possible. But his greatest achievement still lay ahead, on the Invasion Front.

Theo Weissenberger had his own inner core, was without any complexes, and was full of warmth, charm and kindness. Whether as commander or as comrade he had a natural authority. After the war he was lucky enough to get a position in the grocery business of his father-in-law. He used this position to help all his ex-comrades who were hungry and freezing in post-war Germany in any way possible. He was in all ways a huge example to me, even though he had never experienced a high school certificate or any further study. He was a real personality.

I/JG 51 spent the entire year up to the beginning of *Bagration* in the Minsk salient, being accompanied by *III/JG 51* there until 27 March 1944; thereafter *III Gruppe* was stationed in eastern Poland (not far west of Brest-Litovsk) until *Bagration* burst upon Army Group Centre.[24] *IV/ JG 51* spent the first two months of the year west and south of Kiev in the southern part of the front, was moved to the Minsk salient until 1 April 1944, and then to the Lodz area of south-east Poland until the great offensive began.[25] *Stabstaffel/JG 51*, the full-strength and independent *Staffel*, seems to have had the same areas of operation as *III/JG 51* prior to the *Bagration* offensive.

Feldwebel Erich Rahner joined *III/JG 51* early in 1944 and recalled his time in this unit until transferred to the West. 'In the middle of February 1944 I joined *III/JG Mölders*, 8th *Staffel* at the field base of Bobruisk (Russia). From Bobruisk we were sent to the field base at Deblin–Irena in Poland for conversion from the Fw 190 onto the Me 109. At the beginning of March we became operational from the field airbase at Terespol on the Bug. At Whitsun 1944 three or four pilots were taken from each *Staffel*. From them the 7th *Staffel* of *JG 51* was made up and transferred to *JG 1* in the Home Defence.' He was among these pilots so transferred and was seriously wounded in July 1944 on the Normandy front; he would later return to the Eastern Front once more.

Feldwebel Günther Granzow was another new arrival in the *Geschwader* in early 1944, and flew with *Stabstaffel/JG 51*; he reported on his terrifying introduction to combat in a new aircraft prior to the major offensive in June 1944.

Unfortunately, unlike many of my comrades, I am not in possession of my logbooks or any similar documents, as I came from the eastern part of Pomerania (today a part of Poland) and only a few photos have survived. I joined *Stabstaffel/JG 51 Mölders* at the beginning of 1944. When I was ordered to join *Stabstaffel/JG 51* I got to know the Fw 190 for the first time, the aircraft with which our *Staffel* was equipped as it flew mainly fighter-bomber missions. After a short oral introduction (it was a single-seater) I took off for familiarisation: to get used to its behaviour in flight and flying qualities; after about 20 minutes I landed. There followed a short debriefing, and then the *Staffel* took off for a mission. I never even had any training for dropping bombs.

I certainly had mixed feelings for the first few operations. I did not know the aircraft, and thus had to fly mainly depending on the instruments and still try and maintain my position in the fighting formation of the *Staffel*. After about 40 missions I started to get the hang of things. Often the operations were most definitely almost suicide missions. On these one flew as far as 100 km into the Russian hinterland. Targets to be attacked were things like bridges and railway lines to disrupt the enemy's supply lines. These pinpoint targets were always defended with massive flak units. When we then dived down to attack them and flew into the waves of flak, we always had to think about the aircraft only having one engine ... and the flight back was long. Despite this we had relatively few losses. If someone was hit, we suffered heavily from anxious thoughts and feelings. Due to the weather the operations were periodical. Sometimes for some days it was quiet, and then there were days of intense operations.

In the southern parts of the Eastern Front where *JG 52* was the principal fighter *Geschwader*, a nomadic lifestyle of almost continuous retreat and rapid changes of frontline airfields became the norm. *III/JG 52* began the New Year in Apostolove in the Nikopol bridgehead (which stuck out eastwards into the Russian lines) and then moved steadily north-westwards, via Uman and ended up in Vinnitsa in the first part of March 1944; from there it was on to Proskurov airfield about 100 km further west.[26]

Leutnant Gerd Schindler described (letters and accounts sent to the author) an unusual experience while flying out of Proskurov, as *Staffelführer 7/JG 52*. On 17 March 1944 a very high-flying aircraft with

1. Karl-Heinz Erler, who later flew with *JG 5* operationally, in a Fw 56 *Stosser* at a *Jagdfliegervorschule* (fighter pilot introductory school); these aircraft were flown also at *AB Schule* (basic training school). (Karl-Heinz Erler)

2. Karl-Heinz Erler (later flew with *JG 5*) at *Jagdfliegervorschule*, sitting in a Heinkel He 51, the first German fighter to serve in the *Luftwaffe*, vintage *c.* 1936. Trainee fighter pilots were exposed to obsolete fighters such as this before graduating to older marks of current models such as the Me 109 and Fw 190. (Karl-Heinz Erler)

3. *Feldwebel* Otto Schmid, instructor at *Jagdergänzungsgruppe West* (operational training unit for fighter pilots intended for the Western fronts), June 1943–January 1944, commented on this photograph: 'A practice flight with five pupils in a fighting formation – here two vics of Fw 190 A-3 and A-4 aircraft, Cazaux. I took the photo from my own aircraft.' (Otto Schmid)

4. *Feldwebel* Otto Schmid: 'Practice flight with Me 109 G-4, *Jagdergänzungsgruppe West*, Cazaux.' (Otto Schmid)

Above left: 5. Oberstleutnant Günther Scholz at left, who led a *Staffel, Gruppe* and eventually an entire *Geschwader* against the Russians on the Leningrad/ Northern and Far Northern/*Eismeer* fronts in the East from the invasion on 22 June 1941 till May 1944. (Dr Max Clerico)

Above right: 5A. Feldwebel Alfred Rauch, 5/JG 51, experienced NCO with the *Mölders Geschwader* in the East. (Alfred Rauch)

Right: 6. Major Günther Rall, *Staffelkapitän 8/JG 52* (24 July 1940–28 November 1941 and after recovery from a very bad crash, 28 August 1942–5 July 1943) and *Gruppenkommandeur III/JG 52* (6 July 1943–18 April 1944). (Günther Rall)

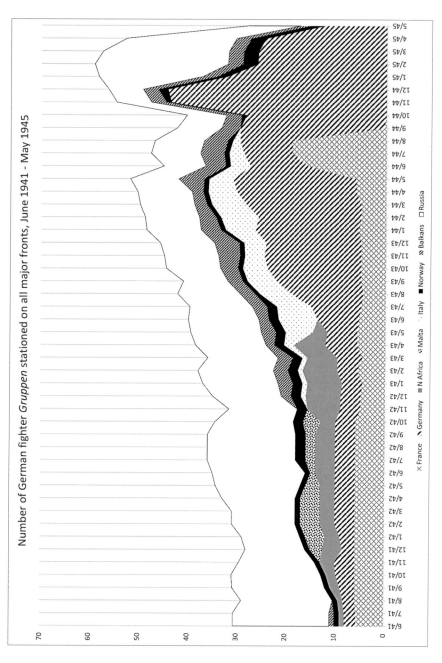

7. Chart showing the number of *Luftwaffe* fighter *Gruppen* stationed on all major fronts from June 1941 to the end of the war. Despite a gradual increase in fighter *Gruppen* from June 1941 onwards, these were mainly taken up by greatly increased commitments to the Battle of Germany from early 1943 and prior to that, from late 1941, and to a much lesser extent, by reinforcement of the Mediterranean theatre, after which time this commitment basically maintained its scale. Part of the Balkan units from 1944 onwards were also facing the Russians (and western enemies simultaneously) in south-eastern Europe. Commitments in France remained basically the same, with a major spike during the June 1944 invasion and the following few months. In fact, fighter *Gruppen* assigned to the Eastern Front slowly decreased during the war, despite the increase in total fighters available, reaching its lowest point in late 1944, before a big reinforcement in 1945 which was too late to be effective.

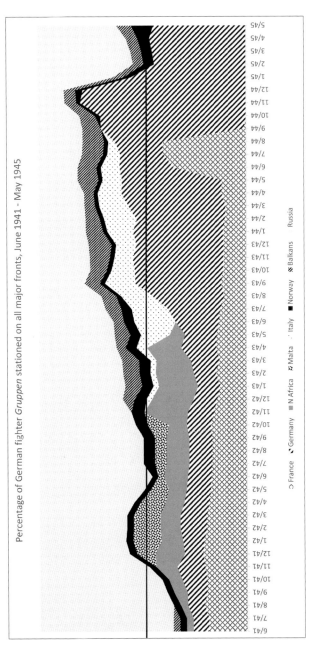

Percentage of German fighter *Gruppen* stationed on all major fronts, June 1941 - May 1945

↻ France ✈ Germany ▓ N Africa ✕ Malta ⋯ Italy ■ Norway ✿ Balkans Russia

8. By expressing the same data as in the previous illustration as percentages of total fighter *Gruppen* assigned to each major front, it is clear that the bulk of the available fighters was only assigned to the Russian front during its opening few months. During the Soviet counter-offensive in winter 1941/42, the Mediterranean theatre swallowed up significant fighter assets previously stationed in the East. Once the German summer offensive of 1942 began, only a proportion of these *Gruppen* returned to the East. During summer to early autumn 1942 German fighters assigned to Eastern and Western spheres of conflict were basically equal at 50 per cent each; from October 1942 onwards a relatively rapid reduction of fighter *Gruppen* in the East reflects mainly German home defence requirements. Even in July 1943 for the Kursk battle, German commitments of fighters in the East showed no significant increase, and within a few months, only about 25 per cent of available fighters were stationed on the Russian front and even gradually shrunk until the end of 1944. Finally, too late, major reinforcement of the Eastern Front occurred in 1945.

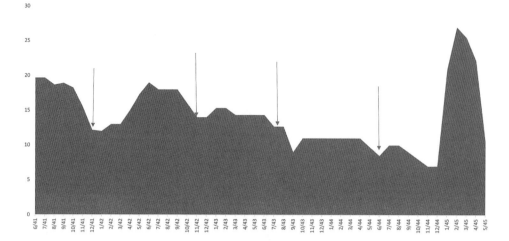

Number of German fighter *Gruppen* stationed on the Eastern Front, June 1941 - May 1945

9. This graph clearly shows a steady decline in German fighter *Gruppen* posted on the Eastern Front. Notably, allocations of fighters to the East were high for the two summer offensives of 1941 and 1942. It is interesting that for four of the major battles on the Eastern Front (arrows, from left to right: number one = December 1941 Soviet winter offensive; two = November 1942 Stalingrad encirclement; number three = July 1943 German Kursk offensive; four = June 1944 Russian *Bagration* offensive) there was even a reduction of *Jagdgruppen* just prior to each one. Also interesting are the small upticks in fighters after the first two such major battles. A plateau of eleven German fighter *Gruppen* was maintained in the East from October 1943 till April 1944.

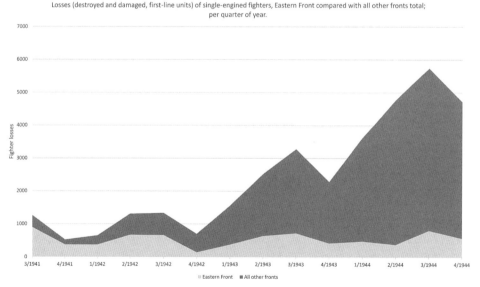

Losses (destroyed and damaged, first-line units) of single-engined fighters, Eastern Front compared with all other fronts total; per quarter of year.

10. Comparison of German single-engine fighter losses on the Eastern Front, compared to such losses on all other fronts (destroyed and ≥ 10 per cent damaged aircraft). It is apparent that *Luftwaffe* fighter resources were concentrated on the Russian Front in 1941 and early 1942, with approximate parity of fighter losses in the East and West/South in the second and third quarters of 1942. Losses against Western enemies became predominant from the fourth quarter of 1942 and thereafter grew enormously. In contrast, *Luftwaffe* fighter losses in the East remained almost static and vastly fewer than those suffered against the Western enemies. (Loss data from US Strategic Bombing Survey; see Bibliography).

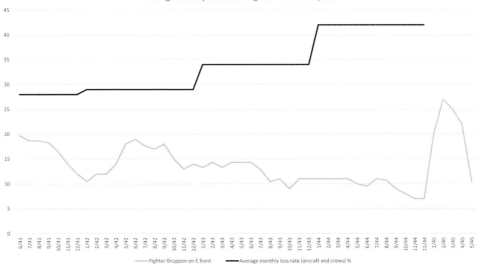

Number of fighter *Gruppen* stationed on the Eastern Front, per month, June 1941 - May 1945 and annual average monthly loss rate of fighter aircraft and pilots

Fighter Gruppen on E front   Average monthly loss rate (aircraft and crews) %

11. Graph of number of *Jagdgruppen* stationed on Eastern Front against average monthly loss rates per annum, 1941–1944, of single-engined German fighters. Quite clearly, annual German fighter loss rates were climbing as Russian numbers and quality grew, and as *Luftwaffe* fighter numbers were steadily decreasing. Author's own data for fighter *Gruppen* stationed on Eastern Front; loss data from US Strategic Bombing Survey (see Bibliography).

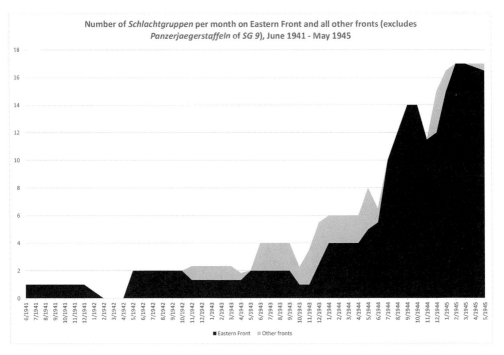

Number of *Schlachtgruppen* per month on Eastern Front and all other fronts (excludes *Panzerjaegerstaffeln* of *SG 9*), June 1941 - May 1945

Eastern Front   Other fronts

12. The huge growth in *Schlachtgruppen* (ground attack units) in the *Luftwaffe* from mid-1943 onwards and particularly from mid-1944 is obvious in this graph. It is also noticeable that the vast majority of these units were assigned to the Eastern Front. Equipment of these units was with Hs 123, Me 109, Hs 129 and Fw 190 aircraft.

13. Tough conditions on field bases were endemic to the Eastern Front. This photograph shows a Me 109 F (engine-mounted 20 cm cannon firing through propeller hub, and two nose-mounted machine guns clearly visible) of *JG 53* (note the *Pik-As* emblem prominent on the engine cowling) stuck in the mud at Lubno-South, a field base near Warsaw, not even at the front. It might well have nosed over as it slowed on landing as sticky mud grabbed at the main wheels, as the propeller blades have been bent. Presumably this was a replacement aircraft on its way to the front. (Josef Ederer)

14. *Oberleutnant* Günther Scholz, *Staffelkapitän 7/JG 54* said of this photograph: 'Tented camp of the *Staffel* – 7/JG 54 – in Dünaburg, Latvia.' Good camouflage was provided by both tent material and use of trees. (Günther Scholz)

15. *Oberleutnant* Günther Scholz, *Staffelkapitän 7/JG 54* (beginning of war till February 1942) described this photograph as showing: 'Entrance to the *Staffel*'s quarters in Siverskaya. The Dutch wooden clog with wings (white on a blue background) was the *Staffel* emblem.' Such quarters were unusual in Russia for the *Luftwaffe* and reflect also the more fixed nature of the front lines around Leningrad at the time. (Günther Scholz)

16. *Oberfeldwebel* Josef Ederer (centre, with two mechanics) who served with *3/ JG 53* in Russia, 1941–1942, shown here later in the war, while engaged in flight testing aircraft to be issued to frontline units, March–June 1944 in Athens. The aircraft is a Me 109 G-6/N with flame dampers on the exhausts. (Josef Ederer)

17. Adolf Glunz flew as an *Unteroffizier* in *4/JG 52* in the first few months of Operation *Barbarossa*. This photograph was taken later in the war by which time he was an *Oberleutnant* and had been awarded the *Eichenlaub* for his achievements with *JG 26* on the Channel front. (Adolf Glunz)

18. *Major* Hanns Trübenbach, *Kommodore* of *JG 52* in the ubiquitous fighter pilot's deck chair, Romania. He described this photograph as: 'Summer 1941 at Mamaia near Constanza on the Black Sea.' (Hanns Trübenbach)

19. *Feldwebel* Helmut Notemann who flew over both Demyansk and Rzhev salients in September to November 1942, before moving to the Stalingrad pocket in December. Shown here as an *Oberfeldwebel* sometime in 1943. (Helmut Notemann)

20. *Feldwebel* Helmut Notemann of *5/JG 3* posing on his Me 109 G during 1942, on the Russian front; note the *Udet Geschwader* emblem on the engine cowling, and the flare gun ammunition around his waist. (Helmut Notemann)

21. Some tired-looking pilots of *III/JG 52* who appear to have just completed a mission (not wearing any decorations while flying in action); all were from *Stab III/ JG 52* except for Rall. *Leutnant* Gerd Schindler described the scene as: 'From left: *Oberleutnant* Schinke, Technical Officer, *Oberleutnant* Rall (*Staffelkapitän 8/JG 52*), *Oberleutnant* Dickfeld, *Fahnenjunker-Unteroffizier* Schindler; *Stab III/JG 52*, field base Gonstakowka, Terek bridgehead, Caucasus, October 1942.' (Gerd Schindler)

22. *Leutnant* Gerd Schindler, a member of *III/JG 52* who flew over the Caucasus and then for a short while over the Kuban bridgehead in late 1942-early 1943 before being posted as an instructor to *Jagdergänzungsgruppe Ost* in La Rochelle, France; he is shown here with a Me 109 F at La Rochelle in July 1943. The emblem on the nose of the aircraft is that for *Jagdergänzungsgruppe Ost*. In October 1943 he returned to the East for two months before moving to the Home Defence after recovering from being wounded over Russia. (Gerd Schindler)

23. Post-war photograph of the survivors of *II/JG 3*. *Feldwebel* Helmut Notemann noted those shown: 'From left to right, Bilek, Notemann, Grünberg, Bohatsch, Bode, Mohn; those from my operational time in the *5/JG 3 Udet* who are still alive today (1990): Grünberg, Bohatsch, Brinkmann, Mohn and myself. Rudi Scheibe is thought to also be alive, living in the DDR (German Democratic Republic, before German reunification).' (Helmut Notemann)

24. *Leutnant* Gerd Schindler, who flew two tours of duty with *III/JG 52* on the Eastern Front, in the Caucasus, Kuban and southern Ukraine 1942–1944; photograph taken in Graz, Austria. (Gerd Schindler)

25. *Unteroffizier* Ernst Richter, last wingman of the famous ace Nowotny, *Kommandeur* of *I/JG 54* over Russia when Richter joined them in May 1943, pictured here after promotion to *Feldwebel* in 1944. (Ernst Richter)

26. Post-war (1983) photograph of ex-*Unteroffizier* Albrecht Licht, who flew against the Russians with *1* and *6/JG 54* from the end of 1943 till the end of the war, finishing up over the Kurland pocket. (Albrecht Licht)

27. *Leutnant* Ernst Scheufele, *5/JG 5* described these two photographs as 'two pictures from my Me 109 time'. He served with *IV/JG 5* over Norway, and then in *II/JG 5* on the White Sea front and in the Leningrad region flying against the Russians, before transferring to the Home Defence, where he ended up in *JG 4*. (Ernst Scheufele)

28. Three members of *Stabstaffel/ JG 51*, the specialist ground attack unit of *JG 51*. *Feldwebel* Günther Granzow in 1990 described the picture as follows: 'In front of the Fw in Russia; from left: *Leutnant* Willi Hübner (killed April 1945), *Leutnant* Günter Heym (living in München), Günther Granzow.' Hübner was killed on 8 April 1945, after scoring 62 victories and receiving the *Ritterkreuz*; Heym scored over 20 victories and was awarded the *Ehrenpokal* (Honour Goblet). (Günther Granzow)

29. *Oberfeldwebel* Hermann Buchner, who flew as a ground attack (*Schlacht*) pilot in *SG 1* and *SG 2*, and then flew the Me 262 jet fighter in *JG 7*. The *Krim-Schild* (Crimean Badge), awarded for active service in this difficult theatre in 1944, is just visible on his left upper arm. (Hermann Buchner)

30. The ex-wartime *Oberfeldwebel* and proud father Horst Petzschler, who served in the Home Defence and over the Eastern Front, respectively in *JG 3* and *JG 51*, said of this photograph: 'Horst and family (children Patrick and Nora), Wichita/ USA, March 1992.' (Horst Petzschler)

31. *Oberfeldwebel* Horst Petzschler, *III/JG 51* recalls of this photograph: 'Taken in January 1945 in Berlin, and then I flew with an Fw 190 into the Danzig pocket.' (Horst Petzschler)

32. *Feldwebel* Erich Rahner, who flew with the 8th and 10th *Staffeln* of *JG 51* on the Eastern Front and with *JG 1* over Normandy; seen here in a photograph taken while he was still an *Unteroffizier*. (Erich Rahner)

33. Post-war (*c.* 1989) photograph of ex-*Fahnenjunker Feldwebel* Lothar Busse, who flew on the Eastern Front in *Stab/JG 51* and *Stabstaffel/ JG 51* from August 1944 to February 1945. (Lothar Busse)

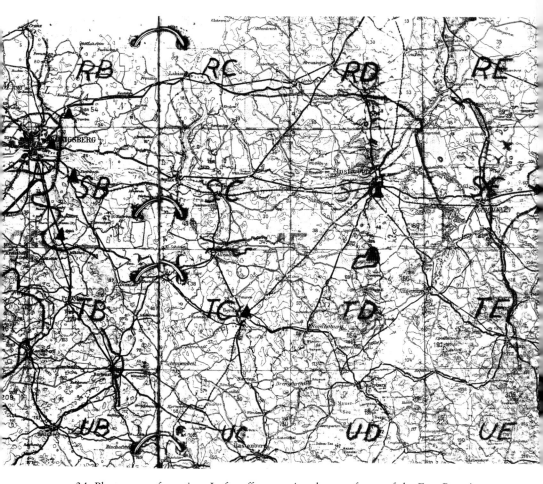

34. Photocopy of wartime *Luftwaffe* operational map of part of the East Prussian combat zone. Lothar Busse said of this map: 'Photocopy of part of the last preserved *Frontflug*-Operational Map, used by *Fähnrich* Lothar Busse previously of *JG 51 'Mölders'* – *Geschwaderstab* and *Stabstaffel*. Time period of the notations on the map: first half of February 1945.' Symbols noted on map: black triangle = operational base; curved solid lines = front line; Y-symbols = tank battles (e.g. left of grid square TB); X = *Abschüsse* claimed by Busse (see grid square SE); city of Königsberg at northwest (top-left) corner of grid square SB. (Lothar Busse)

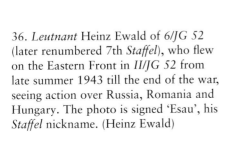

35. Photocopy of wartime map showing approximate front line and airfields of *II/JG 54* in the Kurland pocket, in about February 1945; *Unteroffizier* Licht of *6/JG 54* has marked the front line in light-grey dashes and shown *JG 54* bases with light-grey dots. Memel is on the west coast south of the front line, and Riga lies east of the termination of the front on the Gulf of Riga. (Albrecht Licht)

36. *Leutnant* Heinz Ewald of *6/JG 52* (later renumbered 7th *Staffel*), who flew on the Eastern Front in *II/JG 52* from late summer 1943 till the end of the war, seeing action over Russia, Romania and Hungary. The photo is signed 'Esau', his *Staffel* nickname. (Heinz Ewald)

BESITZZEUGNIS

Im Namen des Führers
hat
DER OBERBEFEHLSHABER
DER HEERESGRUPPE KURLAND
dem

........Unteroffizier........
Dienstgrad

Albrecht L i c h t
Vor- und Zuname

II./Jagdgeschwader 54
Truppenteil

DAS ÄRMELBAND „KURLAND"

verliehen.

O.U., 20. April 1945
Ort und Datum

Unterschrift

Dienststempel

Oberst u.Geschwaderkommodore
Dienstgrad u.Dienststellung

37. Certificate confirming award of the Kurland armband to *Unteroffizier* Albrecht Licht, *6/JG 54*. These were not mere campaign medal equivalents as only certain battles and specific combat areas where really hard fighting occurred were so recognised, either by an armband (known in the *Luftwaffe* as an *Ärmelband*) or a shield or badge (e.g. Crimea Badge – *Krim-Schild*). (Albrecht Licht)

38. It was a young man's war. *Leutnant* Erich Sommavilla, *Stab I/JG 53*, returns from a mission over Hungary, early 1945. He is showing the typical joy at having survived another mission and another day at war, rather than just reflecting a pleasant and relaxing time at the front. (Erich Sommavilla)

39. Ernst Schröder captioned this photograph as: '*Feldwebel* Ernst Schröder, 5th *Staffel JG 300*. Last wartime photo of a soldier, taken about end of March 1945 in Löbwitz bei Bitterfeld.' Like almost all successful *Luftwaffe* fighter pilots he saw himself as nothing more than an ordinary soldier, doing his duty. (Ernst Schröder)

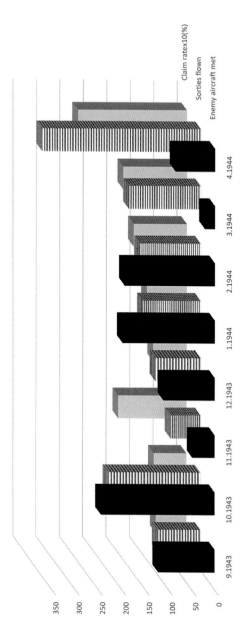

Summary of some operational parameters (per month),
7/JG 51, 13 September 1943 - 18 April 1944

■ Enemy aircraft met   ▥ Sorties flown   ▨ Claim ratex10(%)

40. Chart showing sorties flown, number of Russian aircraft met, and victory claims made against them by 7/JG 51 per month (or portion thereof for September 1943 and April 1944). Where figures were not recorded for the number of Russian aircraft met on certain missions, in the *Startkladde* (detailed record of all flights), no other parameters are included in the chart's data either. The claim rate is simply the percentage of Russian aircraft met which were claimed as victories, and is shown at 10 times real values for visibility. While there is a general trend of increasing monthly sorties (exception for October 1943) and claims made (exception for November 1943) over the period covered by the *Kladde*, the number of Russian aircraft met (only where these numbers were in fact recorded) is more variable. Incomplete data might be responsible for at least part of this. It is doubtful if the noted variability is any reflection either of Russian sorties or operational intensity.

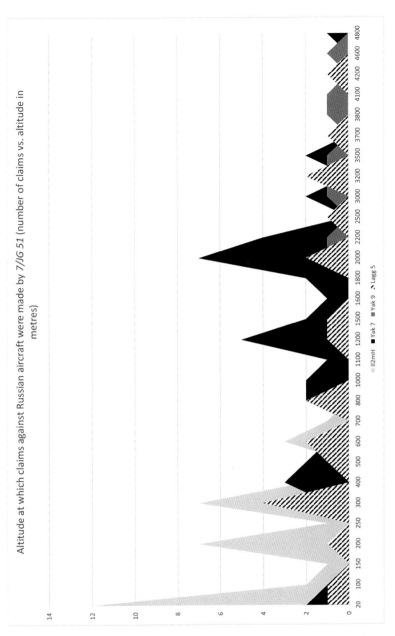

Altitude at which claims against Russian aircraft were made by 7/JG 51 (number of claims vs. altitude in metres)

Il2mH ■ Yak 7 ■ Yak 9 ＼Lagg 5

41. This chart shows altitudes recorded for confirmed claims against the most common Russian aircraft shot down by *7/JG 51*. It shows clearly that the Il-2s operated essentially at 800 m and below, escorted at medium level by Yak-7s, with high cover given by Yak-9s (and occasionally by Yak-7s); the Lagg-5s operated at all altitudes. Lower altitudes shown for some Yak-7s suggests their diving down to protect Il-2s under attack and then being attacked in turn by diving German fighters from above. When attacked, the Il-2s probably dived down to near the ground to protect their vulnerable oil coolers from damage from underneath. The versatility of the Lagg-5 (though named as such in the *Kladde*, these would in fact have been La-5s) fighter is also indicated by its use at all altitudes. The chart also shows very clearly that the great majority of attacks and successes were achieved by the German fighters at altitudes of about 2,000 m and less, with little action above that and then only up to about 5,000 m.

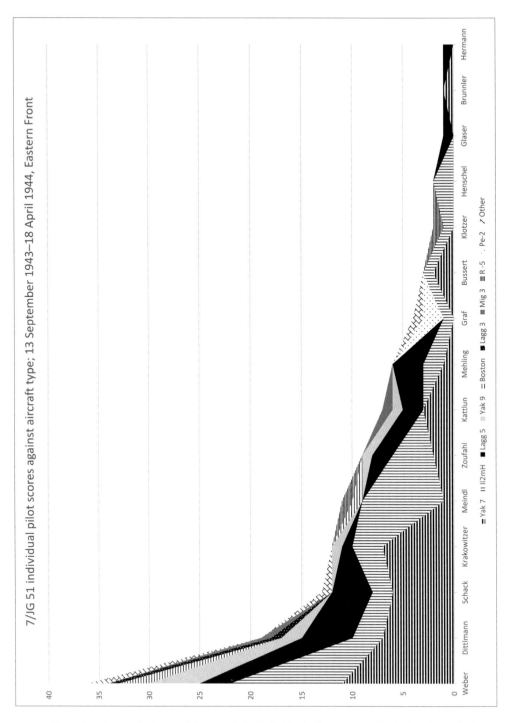

42. Chart showing total victory claims made by individual pilots in *7/JG 51* during the period covered by the *Startkladde*, and also broken down into the main Russian aircraft types shot down. Of the 127 victory claims made by the entire *Staffel* over the period covered by the *Kladde*, the *Staffelkapitän* was responsible for 28.35 per cent and the top five pilots for a massive 71.5 per cent of all claims – this is typical of all air forces, theatres and wars, in general. Note also that most claims were made against Yak-7s, Il-2s and Lagg-5s.

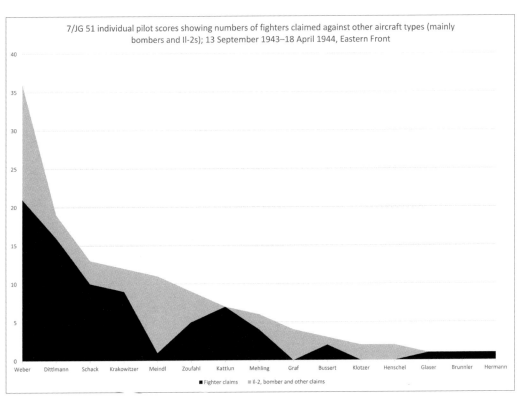

7/JG 51 individual pilot scores showing numbers of fighters claimed against other aircraft types (mainly bombers and Il-2s); 13 September 1943–18 April 1944, Eastern Front

■ Fighter claims ■ Il-2, bomber and other claims

43. This chart shows very clearly that most fighter pilots made claims against Russian fighters. The average for *7/JG 51* for the entire *Kladde* period was 61.4 per cent of claims being made against Russian fighter types; the balance were mainly Il-2mHs and bombers. Only a few individuals concentrated on shooting down Il-2mHs and bombers: Meindl, Graf, and to a lesser extent, Weber.

44. Günther Schack figures prominently as a *Leutnant* in the *Startkladde* of *7/JG 51*. He kept a diary through the war and served on the Eastern Front from the beginning to the end of *Barbarossa*. A major ace with 174 victory claims, and awarded the *Eichenlaub* to the *Ritterkreuz*, he ended the conflict as a *Gruppenkommandeur* and *Hauptmann*, as shown in this photograph. (Günther Schack)

45. *Hauptmann* Alfred Grislawski, highly successful ace in both East (109 victory claims in *JG 52*) and West (23 victory claims including 17 four-engined bombers in the Home Defence and Invasion Front, *JG 50*, *JG 1* and *JG 53*) and decorated with both *Ritterkreuz* and *Eichenlaub* by the end of the war. The tail of his personal fighter shows his first 40 claims, which brought the *Ritterkreuz*, as indicated by the top rather ornate symbol which included his initials also. Below are a further 69 Eastern claims and his first three Western claims. The highly visible top decorations (grades of the *Ritterkreuz* or Knights Cross) worn prominently at the neck were the aim of many German fighter pilots (*Halsschmerz* – 'throat pain'), but were seldom achieved. Showing your personal score, irrespective of any subsequent administrative confirmation procedures (often regarded with some contempt) on your personal aircraft was the right of the experienced pilot who enjoyed a personal machine. (Alfred Grislawski)

46. Copy of *Abschussmeldung* (claim reporting form) submitted by *Feldwebel* Georg Hutter on 10 May 1942, for an aircraft claimed as 'probably destroyed' (*Wahrscheinlicher Abschuss* clearly typed into form at top; form printed for *JG 1*) on the previous day. The form is very detailed regarding aspects of the aerial action, including also witnesses as well as ammunition expended. Note also that the final fate of the aircraft was not seen due to continuing air action, hence presumably the probable nature of the claim. (*Bundesarchiv-Militärarchiv* Freiburg, copy via Otto Schmid)

47. Copy of *Gefechtsbericht* (combat report) submitted by *Feldwebel* Georg Hutter on 10 May 1942, for an aircraft claimed as probably destroyed (*Wahrscheinlicher Abschuss*) on the previous day. For an *Abschuss* to have been claimed more extreme damage would have had to have been visible, hence the probable claim (many sources claim the *Luftwaffe* had no such thing as a probable claim!). (*Bundesarchiv-Militärarchiv* Freiburg, via Otto Schmid)

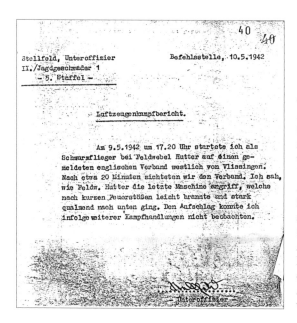

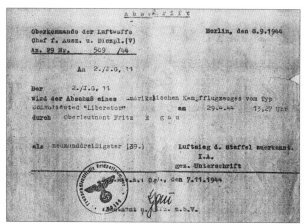

48. Copy of *Luftzeugenkampfbericht* (aerial witness battle report) submitted by wingman (*Rottenflieger*) *Unteroffizier* Stellfeld of *5/JG 1* on 10 May 1942, for an aircraft claimed as 'probably destroyed' (*Wahrscheinlicher Abschuss*) by *Feldwebel* Hutter on the previous day. (*Bundesarchiv-Militärarchiv* Freiburg, via Otto Schmid)

49. *Abschussanerkennung* (victory confirmation) certificate for *Oberleutnant* Fritz Engau, *Staffelführer 2/JG 11* for a claim made for a Liberator on 29 April 1944. Such certificates are hard to find, and most of those in books or on websites are facsimiles of copies rather than of the original document. The victory was officially awarded to the unit (always the *Staffel*, except for where the claimant was a member of either *Gruppen-* or *Geschwaderstab*) and not the pilot, and the unit concerned would forward copies of the original to the pilot concerned, to his family (if he was killed or missing) or to the personnel files held by the military unit where he was first recruited. As can be seen, this is a copy prepared by the unit, as denoted by *Abschrift* at the top, and is signed by the IA of the *Gruppe*. The *Briefbuch* number here is 509/44 (file number 509 for year 1944) and is issued by the Air Ministry's (*RLM's*) Chief of Personnel and Discipline. Very importantly, the victory number (here, 39th *Luftsieg* of *2/JG 11*) is that as given at the date of award (8 September 1944) and not at the date of the claim – there was always a several months-long delay between these two dates. In the original document version of an *Abschussanerkennung*, there is an official form number and a printing date (year and month) in the bottom-left corner. The official stamp here is for *Feldpostnummer* 00134, which is the field post number for *2/JG 11*. (Fritz Engau)

G e h e i m !
===================

2007/III/7a.

Luftflottenkommando 1   Samp. 9.1.43   H.Qu.,den 3.1.1943.
Führungsabteilung / Ic   ILB.Nr 33/Ek/1c

Br.B.Nr. 206/43 geh.

F.V.O.

Feindnachrichtenblatt der Luftflotte 1 Nr. 1/43
vom 16. - 31.12.1942
─────────────────────────────────

I. F l i e g e r t r u p p e :

1.) Stärke:

Wegen der anhaltenden schlechten Wetterlage war e i n e Lb.-
Aufklärung nur an wenigen Tagen möglich. Die Feindauswertung
vom 16.12.42 zeigt eine fast unveränderte Flugzeuganzahl. Nach
den Ergebnissen des H-Dienstes ist die Stärke der russischen
Luftwaffe vor Luftflotte 1 gleich geblieben.

Der Raum 3a ist für die Betrachtung ausser Acht gelassen, da die
dort untergebrachten Verbände zumindestens in der angegebenen
Zeit nicht gegen Luftflotte 1 bzw. Heeresgruppe Nord wirken. In
dem übrigen frontnahen Raum vor Luftflotte 1 ist weiterhin mit
etwa 600 Flzg. zu rechnen, von denen etwa 400 in der Front angenommen werden.
In der zweiten Monatshälfte nachts 1214, tags 1001, insgesamt
2215 Einflüge.

Unterlagen über die Belegung der rückwärtigen Räume war infolge
der Wetterlage nicht zu erbringen. Unveränderte Stärke wird je-
doch angenommen.
In der Berichtszeit wurden 84 Abschüsse erzielt, 79 durch Jäger,
5 durch Flak.

2.) Gliederung und Befehlsverhältnisse:

Die laufend fortschreitende Umgliederung der Flieger-Führer bei
den Fronten und Armeen in Luftarmeen bzw. Div.-Stäben läßt das
Bestreben zur Herauslösung der Luftwaffe aus der bisherigen engen
Bindung an das Heer erkennen. Im Raum Leningrad ist seit 15.12.42
die 13.Luft-Armee mit unterstellten Divisionen bestätigt.
Weitere Einzelheiten siehe Karte Anlage 1.

3.) Einsatz:

Die Einflugtätigkeit leidet unter der Wetterlage und lebt bei
Einsetzen auch nur geringerer Wetterbesserung sofort auf. Alle
Wetterlagen und Tageszeiten, die geringere Wirkungsmöglichkei-
ten für Jagdkräfte mit sich bringen, werden für Einsätze ausge-
nutzt (Einflugmeldung über Il-2 und U-2 bei niedriger Wolken-
höhe und bei Nacht). Die Luftwaffe des Gegners wirkt unverändert
vorwiegend gegen HKL und den Raum hinter den Stellungen. Bei
geeigneter Wetterlage und besonders bei Nacht Einsatz gegen die
Bodenorganisation der eigenen Luftwaffe und gegen lohnende Ziele
im rückwärtigen Raum (Nachschublager). Hier richten sich die
Angriffe überwiegend gegen das rückwärtige Gebiet der 16.Armee.

Die Lb.-Aufklärung in der Berichtszeit läßt nach der Flugplatz-

- 2 -

50. Intelligence report (*Feindnachrichtenblatt*) for *Luftflotte 1* for the period
16–31 December 1942, *Briefbuch* number 206/43; interestingly, all 79 victories
claimed in this report by *Luftwaffe* fighters appear in Tony Wood's victory
lists (see Bibliography, under websites) – none were rejected in any form.
(*Kansallisarkisto* (National Archives of Finland) via Juha Vaittinen)

51. No Nazi supporter, Alfred Grislawski came from a left-leaning miner's family and had not joined the Hitler Youth. He was never awarded the German Cross in Gold as a consequence, despite achieving the *Ritterkreuz* and *Eichenlaub* for his 132 victory claims. A long-serving NCO before attaining officer's rank, he ended the war as a *Hauptmann*. (Alfred Grislawski)

a long condensation trail came over from an easterly direction. Schindler was leader of the *Alarmrotte* and they were scrambled after what was thought to be a Russian reconnaissance aircraft. When they eventually reached the aircraft at a height of 8,000 m, to their great surprise it turned out to be a Ju 88 with German markings. There was no reaction from the pilot or crew even when they approached so close that they were almost ramming into the Ju 88. Recognition flares were no longer used in the East at this stage of the war, so they had to assume it was one of theirs, and they turned away and left it. After they had been ordered to land and were on the ground again, they saw the condensation trail make a 180 degree turn and fly back eastwards. With hindsight it was easy to work out that this must have been a captured Ju 88 put back into commission by the Russians, and anyway if really a German-crewed machine it would not have survived alone over Russian air space, nor would it have turned back towards the east either.

Soon after this incident Russian tanks came close to their base at Proskurov, and after waiting very nervously for a day of bad weather to pass, they managed to get off the ground, for the next base at Kamenz–Podolsk (arrived there 23 March 1944)[27] but lost planes and pilots due to the terrible weather conditions. After only a single night of miserable and freezing conditions there, they were off to Kolomea, the next base where on their first evening low-level attacks had to be flown against Russian forces closing in on the new base, where they remained only till 26 March[28] before looming Russian armour again forced them to leave. Their destination, Lemberg in south-eastern Poland, at least offered a short respite to collect themselves again, for the space of nine days (27 March till 5 April)[29] before it was time to move again. From Lemberg, Gerd Schindler and his comrades from *III/JG 52* flew missions in support of army units surrounded at Ternopol and Kamenz, before leaving for the long haul to Roman in Romania (6–9 April)[30] before departing for the Crimea. Schindler did not accompany them but was posted instead, with some of his comrades, to the Home Defence.

The majority of *III/JG 52* flew in to the besieged Crimea where a critical situation existed, where the *Gruppe* fought a losing battle from 10 April till exactly a month later when they returned to eastern Romania, where they remained till 26 June.[31] In contrast, *II/JG 52* spent many months in the Crimean peninsula, from 2 November 1943 till their departure for Romania on 9 May 1944, as the Crimea fell to the Russians.[32] Newly minted fighter pilot Heinz Ewald joined *II/JG 52* in the late summer of 1943, first flying in 6th *Staffel*, and quite soon after became wingman to his famous *Gruppenkommandeur Hauptmann* Gerhard Barkhorn (second highest-scoring Luftwaffe ace on 301 victories) with whom he flew 138 *Feindflüge* including many over the Crimea in late 1943–May 1944.[33] Ewald recalled: 'As fighter pilots some of the Russians were very aggressive, as they were egged on by their ground control stations. In dogfights the Me 109 was slightly better than their fighters, that is it did not fall out of a tight turn so fast due to the airflow over the wings not being cut off so abruptly.'

Ewald began his career as a *Gefreiter*, and progressed to officer cadet and finally *Leutnant* in *6/JG 52* (*Staffel* later renumbered *7/JG 52*).[34] *II/JG 52* especially but also *III/JG 52* claimed heavily over the Crimea (respectively 281 and 110 victories claimed between 8 April and 12 May 1944)[35] as did the ground attack pilots of *II/SG 2*, but Russian loss figures (179 over the same period)[36] suggest that approximately two and a half German claims were made for each Soviet loss. This is hardly surprising given the intensity of the aerial fighting above the peninsula at this time, and the numbers of Russian aircraft involved.

II/SG 2 supported *II/JG 52* for much of their time in the Crimea, performing as both ground attack and fighter pilots. Hermann Buchner of *6/SG 2* (later promoted to *Staffelführer 4/SG 2* in this battle) describes what it was like to be there in the first half of 1944:

> As a ground attack pilot, I shot down 23 Russian aircraft in defensive battles over the Crimea in the period 12 February–9 May 1944; 13 of these victories were fighters, and I also destroyed several tanks. In 1944 our unit (*II/SG 2 'Immelmann'*) flew Fw 190 A-4 and A-6 aircraft. After reaching the figure of 500 *Einsätze* (operations), and having flown as *Rottenflieger*, *Rottenführer* and *Schwarmführer* I was recommended for the *Ritterkreuz* in February 1944 and was decorated with this on 20 July as *Oberfeldwebel*. In the East I flew a total of 613 *Feindflüge*, scored 46 *Luftsiege* (confirmed victories) and amongst other ground targets destroyed 46 tanks.

The operations over the Crimea were a perfect example of the symbiosis between *Jagdflieger* and *Schlachtflieger* on the Eastern Front; ground attack had become a more important function than maintaining anything more ambitious than temporary and local air superiority to enable attacks to be made on advancing Russian ground forces. The number of *Schlacht* or ground attack *Gruppen* would outnumber ordinary fighter Gruppen as 1944 wore on (illustrations 11 and 12). *I/JG 52* essentially spent the first three months of 1944 in a region stretching from the Crimea in the south-east to Uman in the north-west before moving to Romania and remaining there until 26 June 1944.[37]

Operation Bagration

Not only did *Bagration*, launched on the third anniversary of the German invasion of the Soviet Union on 22 June 1944, smash the Minsk salient but it also led to a Russian advance further westwards: to the south-west of Lake Peipus and close to Riga in the north, and then with the new front line running from south of Riga, south-west to just east of Warsaw in the centre, and to east of Krakow in southern Poland.[38] With the launch of this massive Russian offensive, which was to smash Army Group Centre in the salient almost entirely, both *III* and *IV/JG 51* (and *Stabstaffel/ JG 51*) were transferred immediately to the Minsk region, while *I Gruppe* was already there.[39] A chaotic situation followed as the operations on the ground followed quickly, leading to rapid base changes for all units: *I/ JG 51* had four bases within the space of 10 days (22 June–1 July) before retreat to Poland; *III/JG 51* operated from three airfields (21 June–2 July), and *IV/JG 51* also flew from three field bases (22 June–1 July) before both *Gruppen* were also pulled back to Poland.[40]

There are few survivors from the hectic days that followed as they tried to stem an unstoppable tide. The specialised ground attack pilots of *Stabstaffel/JG 51* were thrown into the maw and expected to perform as *Schlacht* and 'pure fighter' pilots, as experienced by *Feldwebel* Horst Petzschler: 'In summer 1944 (23 June) I returned to *Stabstaffel/JG 51*. In the West the Invasion had begun! *Jagdgeschwader Mölders*: we operated from Minsk, Warsaw, Okecie, Jürgenfelde near Insterburg, Lobellen near Tilsit (now Sovetsk) in Kurland–Libau–Memel, and over the Ostsee (Baltic). In Minsk, the capital of Byelorussia (today Belarus) we provided strong opposition to the advancing "Bolshevists" once more, but with American aid they had become so strong, that we were forced ever further backwards, we could do nothing against their masses of materiel and men.' Petzschler here lists the bases he flew from in this *Jabo-Staffel* and later in *I/JG 51* from the time of *Bagration* till early 1945. In June 1944 Petzschler was able to claim victories over a Jak-9 and a Pe-2 in the Baranowice area (south-west of Minsk).

Another pilot caught up in the massive *Bagration* offensive was *Feldwebel* Günther Granzow, also a member of *Stabstaffel/JG 51*, who recalled this very turbulent operational period:

When the massive Russian offensive began in June 1944 (Operation *Bagration* against the German Army Group Centre), I had already flown over 100 fighter-bomber missions, but not a single operation as a 'fighter'. Turbulent days and weeks followed, with up to ten fighter-bomber missions per day, and on the ground helping even to fill the aircraft's fuel tanks by hand, and to load up the bombs etc. Sometimes it was 250 kg bombs, sometimes 500 kg. We regularly moved to new bases as well. Now we received ever more orders to fly free chases. The operational palette varied from cockpit readiness (ready for an alarm take-off) through protective free chases to fighter-bomber missions and escort operations. Joy and sadness followed close upon one another, as there were days when we, because we were young, could celebrate happily. Compared to the army units we mostly had a bed to sleep in, to say nothing of the good rations we enjoyed.

Reinforcements were rapidly deployed to help the units of *JG 51*. With the simultaneous crisis in Karelia, *II/JG 54* could not be spared from their deployment in Finland (where 1st *Staffel* from *I/JG 54* were also operational, from Turku in the south-west of the country), but the balance of *I/JG 54* flew against *Bagration* from the shrinking Minsk salient from 27 June to 1 July.[41] *IV/JG 54* was also rushed in, from Germany, flying from Baranowici within the salient from 27 June till 3 July[42]. *III/JG 11* also flew in from Germany, arriving at Dukodowo, *c.* 150 km west-south-west of Minsk on 24 June where they remained till 3 July 1944.[43]

A set of rapid moves followed for *III/JG 11*, to the Kaunas area in southern Lithuania, and then three different bases in south-eastern Poland; on 1 August they moved to East Prussia where they remained till 2 September when they flew back to Germany.[44] In this brief period, *III/ JG 11* claimed about 125 victories for the loss of 12 pilots and 11 more wounded during active operations.[45] A final fighter reinforcement was *III/ JG 52*, who flew up from Romania to operate in the Minsk salient from 1 to 3 July – the flight from south to north took five days, longer than they actually saw action in the salient.[46]

In the Immediate Aftermath of Bagration: July–August 1944
In the Baltic States, just after *Bagration* had consumed Army Group Centre and torn a huge hole in the German lines, giving access into eastern Poland, a major Russian operation was launched to conquer the Baltic countries of Estonia, Latvia and Lithuania. This was intended to cut off and/or destroy the German Army Group North and prevent it interfering with advances further south into East Prussia and Poland.[47] Starting in the south of the Baltic region, on 5 July 1944, the 1st Baltic Front advanced westwards into the northern half of Lithuania and, having taken Shaulyai in the central-northern part of the country, turned north and made for Riga in Latvia.[48] Unable to take this city, they managed to reach the Gulf of Riga at Tukums by 30 July, thereby forming a northward-narrowing north–south salient to the gulf and cutting off Army Group North from the Memel–East Prussia region.[49]

Next in the line to the north, on 10 July, the 2nd Baltic Front advanced westwards from Russian territory into the central part of eastern Latvia, but were held up in the Madona–Plavinas region there by the end of July and into August. The 3rd Baltic Front's westward-directed offensive was launched on 16 July into southern Estonia, took Ostrov and Pskov south of Lake Peipus, then also took Pechory (11 August 1944) and Tartu on 25 August, west of the central part of Lake Peipus. By late August they were held there and at Valga on the Latvia–Estonia border to the south-west.[50] Finally, the northernmost arm of this offensive into the Baltic States was launched by the Leningrad Front, north of Lake Peipus against Narwa on 25 July and took the town the next day but was then also held.[51] A major attempt by the Germans to cut off the Gulf of Riga salient took place from mid-August and though it failed to take Shauylai it did retake Tukums, opening up a narrow link once more to the previously cut-off Army Group North.[52] By the end of August 1944, the front thus ran from Jalguva–Shauylai in Latvia–Lithuania down to Suwalki in the north-eastern corner of Poland.[53]

Within this ground operations framework, *I/JG 54* were stationed in south-east Latvia near Daugavpils (1–25 July) and then near Plavinas in central-eastern Latvia until sometime in August 1944 when they retreated to the Riga area.[54] *II/JG 54* returned from their sojourn in Karelian Finland about 23 July 1944, to Petserie once again.[55] However, by this stage Russian advances would have made the possible locations of this airbase south and south-west of Lake Peipus fairly untenable. A final possible location of a place by this name (albeit one using a different, Finnish language-influenced yet equivalent name) lies on the northern coast of Estonia (i.e. on the southern side of the Gulf of Finland), near Tallinn. From the experiences noted by Albrecht Licht of *6/JG 54* below, a base near Tallinn seems a distinct likelihood. As Licht recalled:

The second time I met the La-5 was in Estonia in the Wirtzsee area (*c.* 60–70 km west of Lake Peipus); unusually we were flying in a vic formation. The La-5 fled from us in the direction of its base. Upon following it we experienced a definite superiority in the speed of the Fw 190. On 6 August 1944 we scrambled against a Pe-2 formation with escort, which was attacking our shipping in Kunda Bay (Gulf of Finland). After a few minutes we reached the enemy formation and immediately became involved in intense fighter combats. There was a wild dogfight. I saw a Jak-9 sitting behind my *Rottenführer*, and I turned in on him. He immediately turned away, and now I made a mistake, I followed this Jak-9, but did not catch up with him. When I now turned round and looked at the airspace around me, it was totally empty; not an aircraft was in sight, neither friend nor foe.

Now I didn't feel so good, as a *Rottenflieger* was not allowed to just abandon his leader and then return to base alone. Thus I had another good look around before flying back home. Then I saw two Jak-9s *c.* 100 m above me; now followed my next mistake, I flew alone after these two aircraft. The two had not seen me. As I lacked experience, I opened fire at 200 m range already. That was of course somewhat too far. The two Russians dived away, and I shot for all I was worth with all weapons. The Jak I was shooting at showed a white trail that got ever larger. We had now reached the Gulf of Finland and here I turned away and flew back to base. As I did so I saw the Jak-9 getting ever lower. With that damage the Jak-9 would no longer be able to reach his base on the Island of Lavaassari (this island actually lies off the north-west coast of Estonia and was still firmly in German hands at this time; probably he means one of the Russian occupied islands in the Gulf of Finland, which are seldom named on maps).

When I reported myself back to the *Staffelkapitän* (*Oberleutnant* Wettstein) I was thoroughly bawled out as I had left my *Rottenführer* and the *Abschuss* was not recognised, as there was no witness thereof. Very likely the marine units had seen this *Abschuss*, but no enquiries were made, at the end of the day my mistake could not also be rewarded. One thing I have to also note here, I was not amongst the fighter aces.

Interestingly, this *Abschuss* claim was not followed up as a punishment or, better put, necessary lesson, a severe disciplinary action within the victory-obsessed *Luftwaffe* fighter arm. Other claims by *II/JG 54* on this day give grid square locations close to Kunda Bay as well.[56] In the period from 3 to 15 July, after leaving the Minsk salient, *III/JG 52* served briefly in Lithuania (Vilnius and Kowno) with an interregnum in Dubno, south of Bialystok, Poland.[57]

By the end of July 1944 Russian forces (1st, 2nd and 3rd Belorussian Fronts) had pushed on into eastern Poland and established an essentially V-shaped front towards Warsaw, with heavy fighting in the Praha suburb on the eastern bank of the Vistula. This front then bent back south-eastwards in a direction west of Lublin and also north-eastwards from Warsaw, in a direction west of Bialystok.[58] *I/JG 51* had retreated westwards as the Russians advanced, from east of Brest to west thereof, to the Warsaw area by August 1944.[59] *III/JG 51* was stationed briefly at Pinsk (150 km east of Brest; 2–8 July) before spending the next week till 15 July at Kaunas in southern Lithuania; six days in the Lvov area was followed by a move to Dubowo, east of Suwalki in north-eastern Poland, until sometime in August.[60] *Stabstaffel/JG 51* were in East Prussia at this time; one of their pilots, *Feldwebel* Günther Granzow, had witnessed an unpleasant event there at the time. 'In August 1944 I had to watch while my *Schwarmführer* was shot down by German flak and, just before an emergency landing, was torn to bits by an explosion.' This was *Feldwebel* Fritz Lüddecke, winner of the *Ritterkreuz*, 50 victories to his name; he was killed on 10 August near Wilkowischken, East Prussia.[61]

IV/JG 54, which had left the Minsk salient on 1 July 1944 for a three-day respite in southern Poland, returned to Lida (100 km west of Minsk; 3–9 July), thence to west of Brest for two days, and finally to Lublin (11–15 July) before dispatch to the Lvov area on the latter date.[62] They were to remain around Lvov and west thereof till 23 July, and then moved westwards to Krakow in southern Poland in August before being stationed near Warsaw from August 1944 till early in 1945.[63] *Luftwaffe* fighter concentrations in the Lvov area were in response to the massive Russian Lvov–Sandomierz operation (1st Ukrainian Front; 13 July to end of August 1944) in south-eastern Poland.[64] Apart from *IV/JG 54* (and *III/ JG 51* briefly) other fighter *Gruppen* sent in to reinforce the Lvov area included *I/JG 52* (26 June–31 July), *II/JG 52* (10–25 July) and *III/JG 52* (15–24 July).[65] Following this German defeat, the *Gruppen* of *JG 52* were moved westwards, to the Krakow area: *I/JG 52* (31 July–31 October), *II/ JG 52* (25 July–21 August) and *III/JG 52* (24 July–8 August).[66] During mid-August, *I/JG 52* flew north to East Prussia where they handed over their aircraft to *JG 51* at Tilsit on 16 August 1944.[67]

The Fall of Romania (August 1944)

While Army Groups Centre and North had been hammered in the Minsk Salient and further westwards and in north Russia and the Baltic States respectively, events also continued apace in the southern regions of the Eastern Front. *I/JG 53* flew in defence of Romania from May 1944 till 26 August while *III/JG 77* had been stationed in the country from October 1943 until late August 1944. Their duties encompassed the aerial defence of this country and particularly its Ploiesti oilfields against attacks from the US 15th Air Force, stationed in the Foggia area of Italy; until 19 August they performed these duties and then there was a sudden change in their fortunes.[68]

Early the next day *III/JG 77* moved to north-eastern Romania (Husi and Jassy airfields on the Pruth River) to defend against the Russian offensive along the southern parts of the Eastern Front.[69] Here they scored 30 victories against Russian aircraft between 20 and 23 August 1944. On the evening of the latter day, King Michael I of Romania led a coup which ousted the fascist regime of Marshall Antonescu, allied to the Germans, and the next day, following a German raid on Bucharest (during which *III/JG 77*, while escorting bombers, claimed four Romanian Me 109s), Romania declared war on Germany.[70]

Shooting down planes piloted by folk who had been your allies till the day before must have been a strange experience. By the evening of 25 August the *Gruppe* was in Mizil, north of Bucharest, and from here they departed for Hungary on 28 August.[71] *Oberfähnrich* Erich Sommavilla was one of the pilots in *III/JG 77* who experienced these dramatic changes.

After the capitulation of Romania the US incursions over Romania ceased and we flew along the ever closer advancing Eastern Front against the Russians and Romanians, once again operating together with *I/JG 53* and a *Gruppe* of *JG 54*, in the area of Focsani, Jassi and Husi. When the frontline approached too close to our last field (Mizil), we flew over the Carpathians to Hungary, having cut open our Bf 109s behind the cockpit to at least take with the remaining few ground crew, but left behind a lot of materiel. Through this action the aircraft were naturally no longer serviceable and were sent home for repairs. Vehicles, equipment and tools were largely lost and thus *III/JG 77* moved to Germany to be built up again. Prior to this *Major* Harder (*Gruppenkommandeur* of *I/JG 53*) came to us – he had sent his perfectly motorised *I/JG 53* ground component by road in time and they managed to get over the different Carpathian passes to Hungary after some skirmishes – and chose some pilots for himself from *III/JG 77*.

II/JG 52 also flew briefly over eastern Romania at this time, from 21 to 28 August 1944.[72]

8

Late 1944–1945: The End of the Campaign in the East

By August–September 1944, and consequent upon the *Bagration* disaster, Russian forces had advanced rapidly westwards. They stood deep in Poland already, had advanced to the boundaries of East Prussia (then part of Germany, separated from the main German territory by the Polish Corridor) and taken Romania following the coup there as already described above. They had been on the boundaries of the Slovak state since quite early in 1944 already. German forces in time became trapped in an East Prussian pocket, and the remnants of Army Group North were similarly trapped in the Kurland pocket in north-west Latvia, which managed to hold out till the end of the war.

Once Romania had fallen, operations shifted to adjacent Hungary. Like most of the other Nazi-aligned small nations of eastern Europe, Hungary also tried to depart the German camp; however, after signing an armistice with the Russians they were taken over by the Germans and fighting raged there till the end as well. The final massive Soviet offensive was that from western Poland and the River Oder line; it swept on to Berlin and brought an end to the conflict in Europe, in concert with Anglo-American advances into western Germany in 1945. It is these various eastern European theatres and battles that will be dealt with in this chapter.[1]

East Prussia (September 1944–End of the War)
East Prussia had been part of Germany during the Second World War, and Russian troops had now reached its boundaries. The 3rd Belorussian Front attacked East Prussia from the south-east on 16 October 1944 and took Goldap (north-east of Suwalki) but were held on a line to the north-west of that town, running north-east to south-west through Gusev

(= old Gumbinnen), and the battle was called off by the end of October.[2] The next major battle over East Prussia was launched in January 1945, the 3rd Belorussian Front attacking from the east from 13 January and taking Tilsit on 19 January and advancing into Gusev soon after.[3]

The greater blow was struck by the stronger 2nd Belorussian Front, which advanced westwards and north-westwards from the Bialystok region on 14 January; by 19 January they had taken Mlawa, Przasnysz and Plonsk to the north of Warsaw and then turned north-north-westwards for East Prussia.[4] After taking Tannenberg (south-east of Ostroda; 21 January) and Allenstein (now Olsztyn; 23 January) they punched through to the sea to the east of Elbing (now Elblag) and by 24 January had reached the south of the Frisches Haaf, and took Marienberg (now Malbork) on 26 January.[5] Despite desperate break-out attacks from 27 to 30 January 1945 by the trapped German forces in East Prussia as they tried to escape the pocket westwards through the Elbing area, the pocket remained closed and was to last for another two and a half months, finally surrendering on 9 April 1945.[6] *Luftwaffe* fighter units also flew out of the Danzig area, another smaller pocket along the coast to the west, until it fell on 30 March 1945.[7]

The main German fighter units which served in East Prussia (and also in the Danzig area to the west) were from *JG 51*: *I/JG 51* (August–November 1944; 23 January–23 April 1945), *III/JG 51* (August 1944–20 August; 1 November 1944–May 1945), and *IV/JG 51* (23 January–20 March; first half of April 1945).[8] *I/JG 52* (16 October–9 November) and *III/JG 52* (8 October–7 November) provided short-term reinforcements during the heavy Russian attacks of October 1944.[9] Prior to that *IV/JG 54* were stationed in the area also (August 1944; 6–14 September 1944), while *I/JG 54* flew over East Prussia from March 1945 till the end of the war.[10] The *Luftwaffe* thus devoted considerable fighter resources to trying to protect the first German territory invaded by the Russians.

Feldwebel Horst Petzschler flew with *Stabstaffel/JG 51* in the early days of defending East Prussia and commented on his Russian opponents. 'Equal to us, and always getting better, in numbers greatly superior to us, we had a hard time coping with the strengthening of the Russian air force. We loved to fly, but hardly had the fuel anymore, which lack affected our operations the most! That our leadership paid little attention to logistics was also our loss!!' In September 1944 Petzschler was able to bring down two Pe-2s, one Il-2mH, one La-5 and a Boston, in the Memel–Autz (Memel = modern Klaipeda) areas. But then he was taken out of combat as an instructor.

In September 1944 I became an instructor and was transferred to Liegnitz in Silesia; this did not suit me at all, but the young pilots had to be trained and bomber pilots converted on to fighters (Fw 190, Me 109-G), and thus it was my duty to provide these people as well and as fast as I could with my operational wisdom. I did this to the best of my ability and all my 35 trainees within the five months I served as an instructor were very grateful to me. This (*Jagdergänzungsgruppe-Nord*) was an accelerated training school and some of them flew operations in the end, over Danzig and Königsberg, over the *Ostsee* in *Rotten* and *Schwärmen*. Many ships were escorted safely, as long as we were still able to fly, but when our fuel ran out, things changed totally!!

By February 1945 Petzschler had been posted back to *JG 51 Mölders*, this time joining the *III Gruppe*. 'From 13 February–24 April 1945 I flew in *III/Jagdgeschwader Mölders* from bases at Danzig, Langfuhr, Pillau, Brusterort, Littausdorf and Junkertroylhof (east of Danzig, now Gdansk) on the flats of the Weichsel (=Vistula) river. In East Prussia we protected the columns of fleeing refugees moving over the "*Haaf*" to Pillau as best we could, who were always being attacked by the formations of Russian Il-2 Sturmoviks and falling into the icy waters.' Pillau was the port serving the fortified city of Königsberg – today Kaliningrad – while *Haaf* refers to the bay lying between a long spit and the mainland. Pillau was inside the northern part of the spit, linked to the open sea by a narrow entrance; at this time in winter the *Haaf* was frozen over, allowing people to be borne by the thickness of the ice, but not stopping ship's passages. Horst Petzschler, now promoted to *Oberfeldwebel*, continues his recollections of this dreadful time. 'That (Russian attacks on refugees) was a war crime!! I will never forget those images! We older, experienced pilots flying the Me 109 and Fw 190 had no problem out-flying the Russians, but our young crews had too little flying experience and were most often the casualties.'

In the final days of the war Petzschler moved to *I/JG 51*, operating out of a small pocket east of Danzig. He particularly remembered details related to their escape to the West at the end of the war:

Then from 25 April to 4 May 1945 I flew in *3/JG 51 Mölders* from Junkertroylhof. On 4 May our *Gruppenkommandeur* (*Hauptmann* Joachim Brendel) gave us the transfer order to fly from this base to Copenhagen. Our *Gruppenkommandeur*, who was a shining example on all flown missions, spoke brief, hard words to us; we, that is all pilots of the *Staffeln* who still lay in Junkertroylhof, wrote our names in *Hauptmann* Brendel's book. We all knew that the war was over. It was a difficult farewell because this last flight was into the unknown. In trucks 15 pilots drove out to the airfield, each was in a hurry, as Ivan was again flying reconnaissance missions. Nobody wanted to let their aircraft be shot up at the last moment. The take-off followed at

13h00, very chaotically, as the airfield had been heavily bombed and two days of rain had made it very soft. Past Hela we flew on a course of 295 degrees. My drop tank did not behave, and with the last drops of fuel I managed to just reach the airfield of Malmö-Bulltoffa. Here I was interned. One hour after my landing I learned of the capitulation of the German forces in Denmark!

His claimed victories during this difficult period of the war encompassed one La-5 in February, then two Il-2mH, a Lagg-7, a Jak-9 and two Jak-3s in March, and finally two Pe-2s, respectively on 27 and 28 April 1945.

Another returnee to *JG 51* in East Prussia was *Feldwebel* Erich Rahner of *III/JG 51*, who had been transferred to the Home Defence before Operation *Bagration* in June 1944 and later flew over Normandy.

After recovery (from being seriously wounded over Normandy in July 1944) I returned to the Eastern Front on 11 November 1944, to *JG 51 Mölders*, 10th *Staffel*, at Insterburg, East Prussia. On 15 January 1945 in aerial combat a Russian Jak shot away my throttle control and put a bullet through my left arm. I was able still to make a belly landing on the field at Insterburg. After a 14-day stay in Domelkeil Hospital in Samland I rejoined my *Staffel* again in Neu-Kuren. From there, via field bases at Pillau, Klein Liedersdorf in Samland, Junkerstreuhof on the Vistula river lowlands, Peenemünde, Güstrow, and Ribnitz we ended up in Flensburg (Schleswig-Holstein) where the capitulation caught up with us on 8 May 1945. In the East I had flown the Me 109 exclusively. In the last year of the war the Russians had made big steps forward with their fighter aircraft, Migs and Laggs and also Jaks, in particular in their climbing ability, and also in their tactics and in radio technology. The Russians compared badly to the Western opponents, as in the West they were quantitatively, and in terms of training, superior.

Rahner managed to claim four victories over Russian aircraft and two over Normandy.[11]

Fahnenjunker-Feldwebel[12] Lothar Busse was posted to the Eastern Front shortly after *Bagration* and joined *Stabstaffel/JG 51* in August 1944 and remained with them and *Stab/JG 51* till February 1945, flying mainly over East Prussia, including the Königsberg region, where he scored six victories.[13] He learnt a lot there early on from experienced comrades already mentioned in this volume: 'Alfred Rauch was often my *Schwarmführer* in the *Stabstaffel/JG 51* "Mölders". I flew about 35 missions with him and scored a couple of *Abschüsse* on them also. I also knew Günther Schack well.' He offered some detailed comparisons of the fighter aircraft used by both sides in the East at this late stage of the war, and the consequent tactics applied by the *Jagdflieger*.

We flew the Fw 190 which due to a balanced rudder trim was more elegant to fly than the Me 109; maximum operational ceiling for the Fw 190 A-8 was 8,500 m and for the Fw 190 D-9 and D-11 it was 12,500 m (Me 109 G-14 ceiling was 11,500 m), maximum diving speed for the Me 109 G-16 to K and H models was 850 km/h as opposed to almost 1,000 km/h for the Fw models! Our operational duties included defence against enemy bombers and ground attack units, our own ground attack and low-level strafing attacks against enemy airfields, infantry support, protection missions for the refugee columns, convoy and ship patrols, attacks against enemy supply columns, and aerial combat against Russian fighters. The 'Ivans' were definitely brave opponents, but their emotional doggedness was often in direct competition with clever tactical practices. Their fighter aircraft La-7, Jak-9 and especially the late-war Jak-3 were good aircraft with good turning circle and climbing capabilities.

Despite this the victories scored stayed in favour of the German fighters. The tactics we used depended always on the position in which we found ourselves in the air when we met the enemy aircraft. Naturally one discriminated whether these were fighters (Jak-9, Jak-3, La-5, La-7 or Airacobras), ground attack aircraft (mostly Il-2s) or bombers (Pe-2s, Bostons and others). Furthermore it was taken into account what you yourself were flying, an Me 109 G-6, Me 109 G-14, Fw 190 A-8 or Fw 190 D. These German fighter types had distinct differences to each other and you had to adapt your approach to the air combat accordingly. In any case, one generally tried to attack from above and with superior speed. It would fill a book to describe all variations of possible aerial combats. High victory tolls were scored despite superior enemy numbers!

The living conditions for pilots on the ground (in the quiet intervals between your own operations, or at night) must be seen within the context of continuous nervous tension. One always had to reckon on the chances of attacks by bombers or low flying aircraft on our own airfields. As a result, during our quiet intervals between missions a *Rotte* was ready for emergency scramble all the time. The supply of fuel was very variable and one often had to disperse aircraft to neighbouring airfields to fill up with fuel. The ration supplies were relatively good right to the end, the delivery of field post, however depending on front line location, was often greatly delayed.

On the day Lothar Busse was shot down and seriously wounded in February 1945, a valuable historical document was saved quite by chance at the hospital: 'I am sending you a photocopy of probably the only remaining copy of an operational pilot's front line map. When I was seriously wounded on 18 February 1945 in Heiligenbeil, East Prussia, my last operational map was found in the knee pocket of my flying overalls.

It is very valuable as the daily front line locations of the first half of February 1945 are shown (and for me personally, as the locations of my last *Abschüsse* are also shown there).' This map is shown in illustration 34. *Feldwebel* Günther Granzow also flew in *Stabstaffel/JG 51*, and, like Busse, was shot down and seriously wounded over East Prussia, but had the consolation of having previously met his future wife there.

> After *c.* 180 *Feindflüge*, on 16 January 1945 I was shot down and seriously wounded, with third degree burns to my face, a deformed pelvis and a broken upper arm. I achieved 11 confirmed *Abschüsse*. In autumn 1944 we were operating from a variety of fields in East Prussia. Here I got to know my wife, she was a communications auxiliary. When I was shot down on 16 January 1945, she was on duty and received the reports on take-offs and landings: 15 aircraft took off, one did not return from the mission. What always impressed us, was that as the war went on for longer and longer, the dedication of the technical staff (i.e. ground crew) suffered not at all. One could always depend on the 'black men', also at night. This explains also that despite significant shortage of spares, the spirit of innovation took wing. Also, the comradeship within the flying personnel was very good, irrespective of rank, as we all depended on each other.

Kurland (September 1944–End of War)
In mid-September 1944, Russian forces of the Leningrad Front attacked in the Narwa area in northern Estonia and those from the 3rd Baltic Front northwards in the Tartu area and broke through in both areas, leading to the evacuation of German Army Group North units from mainland Estonia.[14] After the destruction of Army Group Centre in the Minsk salient, the 3rd Belorussian Front attacked westwards to Vilna (fell 3 July 1944) and Kaunas (fell 1 August) in southern Lithuania and by mid-August 1944 had begun to close up to the eastern border of East Prussia.[15] In late September the Russian forces of the 1st Baltic Front, which were aligned on what can be termed a 'Riga axis' facing northwards towards that port, were realigned to face west, creating a 'Memel axis'; in early October these forces made for Memel, reaching the sea to the north thereof on 10 October, and Memel was effectively isolated.[16] On 13 October Riga fell to the 2nd Baltic Front, and consequently the remainder of Army Group North was squeezed into the Kurland pocket in north-west Latvia.[17] The first battle of Kurland began on 16 October, and there were more to follow, but the pocket was defended successfully by the Germans to the end of the war; Memel (today Klaipula) fell to the Russians in January 1945.

Both *I* and *II/JG 54* were stationed at various field bases around Riga from August to October 1944, and from the fall of Riga were moved into the

Kurland pocket.[18] While the *I Gruppe* of the *Grünherzgeschwader* remained there until March 1945, *II/JG 54* stayed in Kurland till the end of the war.[19] They were reinforced by *I/JG 51* which flew in defence of the pocket from November 1944 till 23 January 1945.[20] Albrecht Licht of *6/JG 54* saw action over this hotly contested combat zone for the entire period of the existence of the pocket, and has provided a copy of a war-time map (illustration 35) of the Kurland pocket, and some vivid memories, detailed below.

My rank was *Unteroffizier*, and I flew the Fw 190 A-6. For the last few months I operated as a *Rottenführer*. I was no *Experte* (ace). The *Kurlandkessel* had a depth of *c.* 150 km and a front-length of 250 km. The biggest city was Libau and the front ran as close as 15 km to this city. From September 1944 until 8 May 1945 there were six major Kurland battles. The Soviet air force opposed us with *c.* 3,000 aircraft, while *I* and *II/JG 54* together had about 100 fighters. Due to fuel shortages we mostly operated as *Rotten* from 1 January 1945. As a result these pairs of aircraft often had to face 80 to 150 enemy aircraft. Despite being thus vastly outnumbered our losses were small. Our *Staffel* was newly constituted in September 1944. By 8 May 1945 for 150 enemy aircraft claimed shot down we ourselves had suffered six pilot losses: *Unteroffizier* Koch, killed 16 October 1944; *Flieger* Carstens, killed 24 October; *Unteroffizier* Böschl, killed 21 November; *Oberfeldwebel* Mahlan, killed 23 December 1944; *Gefreiter* Handke, killed 17 February 1945; *Oberfeldwebel* Bienicke, killed 21 February. In the other *Staffeln* the ratios were similar and in some cases even better.

In this same time period a total of 722 enemy aircraft was claimed by *JG 54* over Kurland. On 14 and 15 December 1944 the Russian air force lost 100 aircraft to *JG 54* and 11 to flak. We suffered no losses, apart from some aircraft hit and destroyed or damaged by bombs on the ground. When there were large raids on the harbour, airfield and city of Libau, mostly both *Gruppen* would take off with all serviceable Fw 190s. On 15 December I was not able to take off as my Fw 190 had got stuck in a muddy hole. I thus had to experience the bombing attack on the airfield on the ground. Generally, after our fighters had intercepted the bomber formations, the heavens were full of parachutes within a few minutes. It looked like paratroopers had been dropped, but they were all pilots or crew of shot down aircraft. On this day (15 December) the two *Gruppen* of *JG 54* shot down 54 aircraft and the flak eleven Russians. Eleven of our own aircraft were destroyed by bombs on the ground. We had no losses in the aerial combats.

When we took off only as a *Rotte* (which happened mostly when trying to save precious fuel) and met a large formation of enemy aircraft with a strong escort, then we tried as far as possible to attack from above, to pick one Russian out and shoot him down, then to dive away, pull up once more and attack again. This was a tactic naturally that could only be used under specific circumstances. One could only survive with good luck and a guardian angel, who always warned us in time. Edward H. Sims has written in his book entitled *Jagdflieger die grossen Gegner von einst*[21] that the later versions of the Jak-9 and La-7 were actually faster than us; but apparently the German pilots in the Me 109 and Fw 190 were that much better, that it made little difference to them which type of aircraft the Russians were flying. But I prefer not to comment on these published views; from the material I am sending you, you can make up your own mind. (Quite obviously Albrecht Licht is not fully in accord with Sims' rather scathing view of the Russians met over Kurland.) On the award of the EK 1 (Iron Cross, First Class; awarded to him on 28 February 1945[22]) there is nothing special to report (this is in reaction to a photo of this award in a book on *JG 54*)[23] as decorations followed as *Abschüsse* were achieved. Then one received the EK 1 for seven *Abschüsse*, when these included at least two bombers. With promotions, *Abschüsse* also played a role.

Libau city and harbour, the main base and supply point for critical shipping, was continuously raided by Russian bombers, largely Pe-2s and Il-2s. Licht relates further, on these versatile Russian aircraft:

The Pe-2 was almost exclusively used for bombing missions. From my own experience I know that they also dropped bombs with time delay fuses from low level. The Pe-2 was also used as a reconnaissance aircraft and for artillery spotting. In an attack on Libau harbour, on one occasion I saw that a Pe-2 formation dived down from a height of *c.* 4,000 m to 3,000 m before dropping their bombs. Thus an all-round aircraft. In general, the Pe-2 was an easy aircraft to shoot down compared to the Il-2. Both aircraft flew with a rear gunner; of these one can say the gunners still shot back, even when the aircraft was diving down to destruction. From prisoners' statements, on average the gunners did not survive more than three missions, but there were always enough replacements at the squadrons. With the Pe-2 units in Kurland there were also fully trained female pilots, but after some accidents, mainly at take-off, they did not fly operations. I do not know if these women flew operations later; in the Russian flak units women were in frontline service.

Albrecht Licht put together a compilation of the shipping destroyed or damaged in Libau harbour and its approaches between October 1944 and the end of the year, shown in the table below. This is included here to illustrate the effectiveness of the Russian raids on Libau, using ground attack aircraft (Il-2s) and light bombers (Pe-2s) against a heavily defended target. This also serves to gainsay at least to a degree the derogatory views given in the Sims book[24] discussed briefly above.

Ships (transports and supply vessels only) destroyed or damaged by Russian air attacks on Libau harbour, 1 August–31 December 1944[25]

Date	Time	Vessel	Fate/damage	Cause
12 October		*Brake*, steamer	Damaged	Bomb in hold four
27 October	13h00–14h00	*Vakuum*, Luftwaffe tanker	Capsized	Direct bomb hit
		Gotenland, transport	Partly burnt out	Direct bomb hit
		Askari, target ship	Light damage	Bomb splinters
		Deike Rickmers, steamer	Heavy damage, rudder and engine out	Bomb(s)
28 October (80 aircraft attack city and port of Libau)	11h30–12h30	*Gotenland*, transport	Light splinter damage and fire	Bomb splinters
		Braunsberg, freighter	Large hole in side, took on water, serious fire, some cargo saved	Direct bomb hit
30 October (Pe-2s attack Libau harbour)	12h00–13h00	*Stubbenhuk*, hospital ship	Structural damage, leaks, needs repair	Bomb salvo near-miss
1 November	Morning	*Warthe*, transport	Heavy list, no longer serviceable	Hit two mines outside Libau
20 November	Morning	*Mimi Horn*, target ship	Minor damage	Unexploded bomb (defused)
22 November (Il-2 raid on Libau city and harbour)	14h40–15h10	*Eberhart Essberger*, transport	Damaged on one side	By bomb shrapnel or dud bomb
		Adele Traber, steamer	Two holds flooded, ship beached	Two direct bomb hits
		Wischhafen, freighter	Two dead, one wounded crew	Strafing attack

Date	Time	Vessel	Fate/damage	Cause
27 November (raid Libau harbour)	11h40–11h47	*Eberhart Essberger*, transport	Seriously damaged	Il-2 dropped armour-piercing bomb, direct hit
		Memelland, tanker	Seriously damaged, pumping needed to keep afloat	Bomb hit
		Wischhafen, steamer	One dead	Strafing attack
		Max Bornhofen, steamer	Seriously damaged outside port of Libau	Drifting mine or torpedo hit(?)
14 December (heavy attack, harbour, 60 Pe-2s with escort)	11h58–12h52	*Otterberg*, freighter	Sank at dockside	Bomb exploded between quay and ship
		Trude Schünemann, steamer (carrying ammunition)	Light damage	Strafing attack
		Bore VI, steamer	Fire and bomb damage; captain and first officer dead	Bomb hit midships
		Klara L.M. Russ, steamer	Ship caught fire	Two bomb hits
		Lütjehörn	Bomb splinter damage	Bomb exploded on adjacent quay
		Hamburg, tug	Light damage	Bomb splinters
		Michael Ferdinand, steamer	Light splinter damage	Bomb splinters

Date	Time	Vessel	Fate/damage	Cause
14 December (second heavy attack, city and harbour of Libau; 60 Pe-2s with escort)	16h57–18h48	*Erika Schünemann*, steamer	Exploded	Bomb hit, munitions carrier
		Minna Cords, steamer	Burnt out	Bomb(s)
		Inka, tanker	Burnt out	Bomb(s)
		Lappland, transport	Damaged	Direct bomb hit
		Masuren, steamer	Small fires, put out by crew	
		Corona, steamer	Light damage below waterline	Bomb hit in water nearby
15 December (heavy attack on city and harbour of Libau)	10h50–11h53	*Lappland*, transport	One hold burnt out, no longer operational	Direct bomb hit
		Tanga, transport	Serious fire	Direct bomb hit
		Wappu, steamer		
18 December (raid on Gotenhafen)	Morning	*Unitas*, whaling ship	Heavy fire damage, sunk at moorings	Several direct bomb hits
		Virginia, steamer	Temporarily unserviceable	
		Ginnheim, steamer	Temporarily unserviceable	
		Theresia L.M. Russ, steamer	Sunk at moorings	Direct bomb hit
		Trüde Schünemann, steamer	Sunk at moorings	Direct bomb hit

By this stage in the war, the German *Jagdflieger* would often be confronted with the most modern Russian aircraft. Albrecht Licht of *6/JG 54* describes an interesting encounter with the latest La-7 fighters, and also stresses the importance of the German radio interception intelligence service, below.

The La-5 and La-7 were further developments of the Lagg-3. I met the La-7 twice, over the Kurland pocket. The first time was just before overflying the harbour and the airfield at Pelangen. Here we flew in a *Schwarm* and sank two Russian speedboats. After we had shot off all our ammunition on this task, the La-7 appeared behind us. Of course then we could not let ourselves be caught up in any combat so we fled. The second time, I was ordered to take off with a *Rotte*, as 60 enemy aircraft had been reported south-west of Libau. When we got closer I saw that the formation was made up of 60 La-7s. I flew with my *Rotte* into this formation and then they flew in all directions in confusion. I picked on one opponent flying ahead of me. But in this dogfight I pulled the stick too hard and my Fw 190 landed in a spin (which could happen with the Fw 190 if handled thus). So the two of us disappeared below and were now *c.* 1,500 m lower than the bunch of La-7s. I flew up in the direction of the sun. Once we had gained a superior altitude I flew towards this bunch a second time. Apparently the Russian fighters had seen us and also began to climb, and thus we ended up in a hopeless attacking position, with the superior numbers of the La-7 formation. I broke off the mission then as our fuel was not sufficient for a third attack.

My overall experience: the La-7 was the equal of the Fw 190. It was better at climbing but the Fw was better at diving. This was explained by the La-7 being of mixed construction (metal and wood) while the Fw 190 was built entirely of metal. According to official data the La-7 was supposed to be faster than the Fw 190, which was quite possible. But in its armament the Fw 190 was superior to all types of Russian aircraft. There was no fighter control system like in the Home Defence for the Russian theatre. The *Gruppe* headquarters received the report of any enemy aircraft flying across the lines. Reported were the number of enemy aircraft, their height and their position (on the grid square system). After this either the *Gruppenkommandeur* or his deputy let the individual *Staffeln* know and ordered the number of fighters to be assigned to that mission. The leader of the *Staffel*, *Schwarm* or *Rotte* so assigned received further directions from the headquarters until he sighted the enemy formation. But often, by then the enemy aircraft had disappeared again. There was another support for the German pilots, from radio posts close to the front, which sighted and reported enemy aircraft. We marked these radio posts on our maps; they had names such as Adler, Eule, Sperber, etc.

After the mission we had to use our maps to find our own bases again. We did not have good contact over the radio with our bases. We also had the problem that our radios only had a range of about 40 km and often reception between ground and aircraft, and even between aircraft themselves, was bad or it was even impossible to understand what was being said. At that time advanced radio technology was still in its infancy and was still very unreliable. Thus the pilots almost always had to be self-sufficient. They had to fly, find the enemy from low level up to heights of 10,000 m, shoot them down, keep an eye on the airspace around them so as not to be surprised themselves, and also to confirm enemy aircraft shot down by our side as witnesses, and finally to provide information on our own losses (e.g., parachute seen); after the combat was over the exact location of our victories had to be noted (grid squares) and then we had to map-read our way back home.

Then there was another system, the early recognition of attacking units of Russian aircraft: a radio interception system where Russian-speaking comrades listened in on enemy radio communications. Especially in Kurland this helped us a lot. We almost always knew two hours in advance, which targets were going to be attacked. We could get information from these radio intercept posts whether it was army or navy air units (they had different frequency identifications). We were also informed when these units took off. With the large attacks at that time, we took off ourselves early enough and waited for these formations at heights of *c.* 6,000 m, while the enemy bombers flew in at *c.* 4,000 m. Our attacks then followed before these formations had reached their targets.

In the *Luftwaffe* cuff titles on uniform sleeves were worn by pilots flying in a unit bearing an honorary title following the *Geschwader* number (e.g. *JG 26 Schlageter* or *JG 51 Mölders*). In addition, participation in specific campaigns was rewarded with similar arm bands, but only in a few exceptional cases: for example, the airborne invasion of Crete resulted in such an *Ärmelband* for the paratroopers concerned but not the fighter pilots involved. For the Crimean defence of April–May 1944 a *Krim-Schild* (Crimean shield or badge) in metal was worn on the upper arm, being awarded to troops on the ground and *Luftwaffe* fighter and ground attack pilots involved – one of these can just be seen in the photo of Hermann Buchner on his upper left arm (illustration 29). Similarly, active service in the Kurland pocket gave ground and air participants the right to wear the *Ärmelband Kurland* as shown by the award certificate belonging to *Unteroffizier* Albrecht Licht (illustration 37).

JG 54's top ace of the war was Otto Kittel, who began as an *Unteroffizier* and ended up as an *Oberleutnant,* with the Swords and Oak Leaves to his Knights Cross.[26] Despite his great experience of air combat (583 *Feindflüge* and 267 eastern victory claims) he fell victim to the gunner of an Il-2 over Kurland on 14 February 1945.[27] Albrecht Licht, who knew him, recalls: 'Otto Kittel was a very good comrade, just as we all enjoyed a very good comradely relationship amongst the pilots and also with the ground staff. This comradeship still exists today (writing in 1990). We still meet every year, at least those of us who survived the war and are still alive.' JG 54's ability to defend the airspace over Kurland was severely limited by shortages of fuel, also experienced by the ground attack pilots, also flying the Fw 190 on this front. This shortage of fuel generally for the entire *Luftwaffe* by this stage of the war, and specifically in the Kurland pocket, is graphically illustrated by an excerpt from the logbook of *Feldwebel* Ernst Scotti of *8/SG 3*, a ground attack pilot who flew there from 25 December 1944–11 March 1945, recording only 16 *Feindflüge* in this period.[28]

As the war came to an end, the pilots of *II/JG 54*, the sole remaining *Jagdgruppe* still operational in Kurland, made great efforts to rescue as many of their mechanics as possible when they flew out to the 'safety' of Germany to avoid capture by the Russians. Albrecht Licht, *6/JG 54*, was one of those pilots.

> How we got out of the Kurland pocket: I previously wrote an account of this and I am enclosing a photocopy of that. I have some additions to make to that account. All the Fw 190s were equipped with a 250 litre drop tank except for my Fw 190. At a *Geschwader* reunion in Memmingen I talked to our former *Geschwaderkommodore* about the escape of *II Gruppe* of *JG 54* from the *Kurlandkessel*. There I established that it was not known that I reached Germany without a drop tank. But now to other boasts. All pilots were assigned ground crew members, whom they were to take with them in the single seat Fw 190s. Thus most of the Fw 190s flew with the pilot and two ground crewmen, a few even with three extra men. Two of the men were in the rear fuselage and one man immediately behind the pilot. *Oberleutnant* Gerd Thyben shot down a Pe-2 on 8 May 1945 with his chief mechanic in the fuselage. Noticeably in the Russian account of this particular combat, 40 Fw 190s are supposed to have attacked, and there is mention of a thick cloud layer. It was actually a beautiful sunny day. What is a fact is that this was the last victory of *Oberleutnant* Gerd Thyben and also of *JG 54*.

In his published account (in *Jägerblatt?*) of leaving Kurland on 8 May 1945, Albrecht Licht recalls *Staffelkapitän* Helmut Wettstein informing all pilots of *6/JG 54* that the armistice would come into effect at 18h00, and that they were to leave Libau-North airfield at 11h00 and to fly to Flensburg in Schleswig-Holstein, a trip of *c.* 800 km. All Fw 190s were to carry 250-litre drop tanks and each pilot was assigned ground crew to take with on the flight. Licht's chief mechanic Ero Martin and an armourer were to be flown out by him, but the former told him that the connection of the drop tank to his aircraft was faulty and that there were no spare parts. He instructed his mechanic to strip the aircraft of all unnecessary weight, and reported the situation to his *Staffelkapitän*, who told him to only take his chief mechanic. Once airborne with his

Schwarm, Licht found that the pump for the built-in 110-litre extra tank would not work, so he was down to only the 600 litres of fuel in the main tank. Then he examined the circuit breakers on the side of his cockpit and found one was out, but he could not reach it to reset it as the breaker was behind a panel and only accessible via a small hole of *c.* 6 mm; he managed to reset it with a nail file and could then use the urgently needed extra 100 litres of fuel.

By this time Licht had lost some height and was a bit off course, and had lost the other three *Schwarm* members, so it was on with the flight on his own. At low revolutions he flew on over the Baltic, past several islands, and with his fuel warning red light burning brightly he managed to get the plane safely down at Grossenbrode airfield with 15 litres of fuel left. His luck had held! Licht also recalled a final tragedy at Libau after *II/JG 54* had left:

> The airfield at Libau was very heavily bombed after we had left. Actually this was hard to understand, as the capitulation was imminent. The damage from this attack would have to be cleaned up by the Russians themselves. A Ju 52 unit that had come from Norway and intended to pick up more soldiers and take them to Germany suffered heavy losses there, as we fighters had already left. As far as I know, 32 out of the formation of 36 Ju 52s were shot down. We had not known that more aircraft from Norway would come and land at Libau to take soldiers back to Germany.

Czechoslovakia (September 1944–End of the War)

The German annexation of the *Sudetenland* before the war had already reduced Czech territory, which then became a protectorate (of Bohemia and Moravia) of the *Reich*, while the Slovakian part of Czechoslovakia became an independent Nazi-allied vassal state. Russian troops had reached the eastern boundary of Slovakia in April 1944 but did not progress further, apart from vigorous support for partisan operations within that territory.[29] A Slovak rising in late August 1944 led to a full German occupation before Russian troops began operations against Slovakia in December 1944 and invaded during January 1945; Prague in the western (Czech) part of the country only fell right at the end of the war, in May 1945.[30] *I/JG 52* was posted into the protectorate in January 1945 and stayed there and in the adjacent *Sudetenland* till the end of the war.[31]

Right at the end of the war *JG 7*, the Me 262-equipped *Jagdgeschwader*, moved to the Prague area to escape the chaos of Germany just before hostilities ended. *Unteroffizier* Kurt Beecken was there at the end, as related next.

I can briefly state: on 14 January 1945, I was shot down for the third and last time. This was my last mission in the Fw 190, in the Home Defence (probably he was then in the *IV/JG 54*). With some others I was chosen for conversion to the Me 262. Via some intermediate stops the conversion took place in Lechfeld near Augsburg. Via Brandenburg–Briest I managed shortly before the end of the war to join *JG 7* at Prag–Rusin. After one mission, a low-level attack on a Russian truck column in the area Forst–Cottbus–Guben, my Me 262 had been damaged. No replacement aircraft were available. I was placed into the infantry and experienced ground combat, with nasty experiences, and fled on my own from Prag–Rusin and managed to get through to where the Americans were in the neighbourhood of Karlsbad.

Hungary (September 1944–April 1945)

The rapid change of events in Romania at the end of August 1944 led to political upheavals in neighbouring Hungary, and as Soviet troops (who had entered Hungary in September) advanced deeper into eastern Hungary at the beginning of October, the Hungarian government sought an armistice with the Russians (and the Allies) which was signed on 11 October 1944.[32] However, before Hungary could depart the Axis camp, the Germans moved first and took over the country, and installed a fully pro-Nazi puppet government that repudiated the armistice.[33] German and many Hungarian troops fought on; Budapest was surrounded by the end of December 1944 but held out until 13 February 1945, but by early April Hungary was fully occupied.[34]

The three *Jagdgruppen* that had been stationed in neighbouring Romania all moved north-west to Hungary with the defection of Romania from the Axis. *II/JG 52* and *I/JG 53* transferred to Hungary on 26 August and *III/JG 77* two days later.[35] While *III/JG 77* only remained in Hungary for a short time (till 15 September), the other two *Gruppen* flew over Hungary until late in March 1945, when Russian advances forced moves to Austria, where they saw out the end of the war.[36]

Heinz Ewald was already a successful fighter pilot by this time, and would score exactly half of his final claims total for the war (84 victories) over Hungary. While this section will only examine German fighter operations against the Russians, there was extensive and bitter combat also against escorted American four-engined bomber formations over Hungary (as had also been the case in Romania); these latter operations will be dealt with in a third planned volume – *Alarmstart South to North* – in a chapter there dealing with the Balkan air war from 1943 onwards. Ewald, known to all his friends in *II/JG 52* as 'Esau', recalls difficult conditions in the air and on the ground.

Living conditions on the Eastern Front were often terrible, as we had to fight against a superiority of 1 to 20 in Russian numbers and against the Americans at 1 to 40 (over Romania); apart from that we also had to deal with pesky partisans in the form of lice, bugs, flees etc. (he refers here to conditions within Russia itself, prior to the Hungarian period), and also bitterly cold weather conditions. I flew a total of 396 *Feindflüge* in the East, scored 84 confirmed *Luftsiege* and *c.* 25 more lacking witnesses. On 1 March 1945 while coming in to land at my base at Vesczprem airfield in Hungary, with a damaged aircraft from combat against American aircraft, I was shot down by the German flak and wounded, bailed out at 300 m height. For 42 *Luftsiege* achieved over Hungary I was awarded the Grand Cross of the King's Decoration on 17 February 1945.

During his service in the East (Russia, Romania, Hungary), Heinz Ewald was, successively, a *Gefreiter*, *Unteroffizier*, *Fähnrich* and finally *Leutnant*, mostly in *6/JG 52* (*Staffel* later renumbered *7/JG 52*) and also flew in *Stab II/JG 52*. *Unteroffizier* Gerd Hauter joined Heinz Ewald's 7th *Staffel*, *II/JG 52*, somewhat later, and his vivid description of his first operation encompasses pretty much all the potential mistakes a novice was likely to make:

Finally, on 12 November 1944 I joined *II Gruppe* of *JG 52* at Budaörs near Budapest, and was assigned to the 7th *Staffel* of *Leutnant* Ewald. My reception by the old hands was very friendly, the quarters in private lodgings and the food were outstanding. We lived in the town immediately adjacent to the operational airfield, which we went to daily for readiness and to await orders at the command post. Only after about three weeks of daily waiting was I ordered on an operation with *Leutnant* Ewald. Ewald lead, I flew at a distance of 60 m and to the side, towards the East; we climbed to 5,000 m, then to 6,000 m when Ewald suddenly dived down and when I followed him, only then did I see that he had just shot down a Russian fighter that I had not seen at all before that. Ewald pulled his machine back up high after the *Abschuss*, with me behind, but I lost sight of him.

In my excitement I had forgotten to put on my oxygen mask above 4,000 m and I was thus badly confused, and apart from that the red light had gone on, indicating that there was only 10 to 15 minutes of fuel left in my tank; I also did not know where I was. So I flew a course of 270 degrees and hoped for the best and eventually spied Budapest and behind it my field base of Budaörs. As I was still feeling unwell due to lack of oxygen, I had to go round again twice due to my speed being too high to land, the whole time worried whether the fuel would last, to eventually on the third attempt manage to get down on the ground again. Ewald, who had landed long before me, stood at the edge of the field, I reported back to him and he delivered himself of an impressive choking-off. This was one small episode from my operational time. After this I flew another 20 operations and received the *Frontflugspange* in Bronze for that. The Russians were also good pilots, but their machines were still inferior to ours. I cannot give an opinion on the La-5 fighter as my memory is no longer so good; regarding living conditions on the ground, these were very good. Throughout we had outstanding rations and the best of accommodation. After the war I flew gliders and powered aircraft until 1990.

The bounce and immediate pull-up described above shows that Heinz Ewald had fully mastered the typical and deliberate fighting method used by most *Jagdflieger* in the East, certainly from about 1943 onwards. *II/JG 52* and *I/JG 53* served alongside each other through much of the Hungarian campaign and enjoyed friendly relations. *Leutnant* Erich Sommavilla had transferred to Hungary from Romania along with the rest of *III/JG 77*, but was invited by *Gruppenkommandeur* Harder of *I/JG 53* to join that unit when his own *Gruppe* departed the theatre in mid-September 1944. He describes some of his experiences flying in *Stab I/JG 53* with three successive *Kommandeurs* of his new *Gruppe* below.

Due to very good reports on my flying and military abilities *Major* Harder took me into the *Stab* of *I/JG 53* as his *Rottenflieger* (*Katschmarek*), and I retained this post as wingman of the *Kommandeur*, first under *Major* Harder, then under *Hauptmann* Hartmann, and following that until the bitter end under *Hauptmann* Lipfert. I flew almost all my operations as the wingman of the *Kommandeur* in only a *Rotte*, only very seldom were we part of a *Schwarm*. But often several individual *Rotten* or even *Schwärme* were used in the same area.

When we were not flying a free chase, but took off on an emergency scramble, we heard just before take-off or even only once airborne, over the radio, what our targets would be. There was no fighter control system, as used against the four-engined bombers, when flying against the Russians. Our radar units would pick up incoming Russian aircraft and report them to us. In those cases, a single controller, normally an experienced higher-ranking officer, decided if we took off or not.

Our operations were spatially limited due to our bases lying close to the front. From October 1944 until March 1945 we were stationed in Veszprem (north-west of the northern end of the *Plattensee*, Lake Balaton). From there we witnessed the fall of Budapest, the Russian advance south of the *Plattensee* and the battles of the Gran bridgehead in northern Hungary. Our main targets were the Russian ground attack aircraft Il-2, that both without escort and then again with very large escorts attacked our army positions in large formations. Thus we shot down mostly Il-2s and Russian fighters, we saw very few twin-engined bombers. Almost always in these operations, the *Kommandeur* and I flew in a *Rotte*.

In February 1945 *Major* Jürgen Harder became the *Kommodore* of a *Jagdgeschwader* (*JG 11*) in the Berlin area, where sadly on a flight without having met the enemy and for no known reason, he crashed and was killed. I experienced few commanders who had such a distinguished disposition, who demonstrated such qualities as a formation leader in murderous air combats, and who enjoyed the affection which our ground crews, whom we called the 'Black Men' (*Schwarze Männer*), had for him to the extent that they hung pictures of him in their quarters. *Major* Harder scored 64 victories, 10 of them against US four-engined bombers, and sank a British submarine in the Mediterranean Sea. He scored several victories while flying over the *Afrikakorps* and also shot down the first US four-engined bomber over Africa, a B-17 Flying Fortress.

After *Major* Harder, *Hauptmann* Hartmann was *Kommandeur* of the *I/JG 53* for a short time, and then *Hauptmann* Lipfert, who raised his victory tally in the last few months of the war from 180 to 203 in the *Gruppe*. We on the Eastern Front also had to fight against large enemy superiority in numbers and had the requisite losses as a result. I can remember that towards the end of 1944 we received 18 young pilots from the training schools, of whom none experienced the end of the war with us – dead, missing or wounded.

Among the Russian fighters I experienced the Jak-9, the La-5 and then the La-7. These Russians fighters were not bad aircraft, but because of our experience over long periods in defensive operations and through our definite feeling of superiority, especially as concerned the superior tactics of our experts, we maintained ourselves as an effective force right to the end despite the large numbers we were opposed by. In general, the Russian fighters, starting already with the legendary Rata, were more manoeuvrable than the 109, they were after all lighter in their construction, but from about the beginning of 1945 we could in emergency apply 1.8 atmospheres of boost pressure and use the methane-water injection to cool the engine internally, and then no Ivan could keep up with us, as I myself experienced personally. When we did this we had about 1,800 to 2,000 horsepower available for a short time period, no one knew exactly how much extra power.

In Hungary, which was a farming country, we could always get food supplies easily, in the shops and restaurants there were still delicatessens and every form of alcohol was easily obtainable. At Veszprem we served alongside the famous *II/JG 52* for months at the same airfield. A young *Ritterkreuz* winner from this *Gruppe*, from which quite a few experts had come, wrote a relatively unknown book on his experiences that I can recommend strongly (referring here to Heinz Ewald's book).[37] Within the context of the general war situation, *I/JG 53* was dissolved in about the middle of April 1945, their materiel and a few pilots being taken over by the successful *II/JG 52*, and the rest of the pilots and the ground crew being transferred to ground forces. *Hauptmann* Lipfert now became my *Staffelkapitän* in place of my *Kommandeur*, but we flew only a very few missions. In the last few days of the war we lay in Zeltweg in Steiermark (Austria) and to avoid falling into the hands of the Russians, we flew to München–Neubiberg on 8 May 1945, where the Americans were.

On 20 December 1944, Erich Sommavilla had three very lucky escapes on a single mission, suffering a direct hit to his fighter's windscreen, a collision with a Russian fighter, and a belly-landing:

On 20 December 1944 I shot down a Jak-9 above a closed cloud cover north of the *Plattensee*. Despite several witnesses being available, the crash of the Jak could not be fixed due to the dense cloud cover. On the same flight a few minutes later a Jak-9 shot at me from head-on, fighter against fighter, with a closing speed of about 900 km/h. I was hit by some of his bullets, one of them on the small armour glass windscreen panel of my Me 109. Luckily this hit was an explosive round from the nose cannon of the Jak-9. I thus saw only the flash of the explosion, about 40 cm in front of my face, and the armour glass was about half destroyed. From close range and using all my guns and with our very effective ammunition, I obtained several hits in his engine and cockpit. Through all this we had now come so close to each other that our wings touched and the entire left wing tip of my aircraft was torn away, and the wing, leading edge slats and rudder were also damaged. I was able to see that the Jak-9 spun down with about a third of the one wing of the Russian broken off.

During a rather difficult flight home with my partially wrecked machine, I saw a lone Il-2 which was getting ready to attack a train. With the last of my ammunition I was able to hit the relatively small oil cooler, so that the Il-2 had to belly-land only a few kilometres away from my base at Veszprem. In February or March 1945 at a height of 8,200 m I shot down a lone reconnaissance aircraft in flames, a twin-engined Pe-2 that plunged down like a torch into the frozen *Plattensee*. In addition I damaged ('*wirksame Beschüss*') several other aircraft, Il-2, Jak-9 and La-5 types. On 25 December 1944 I shot down an Il-2 from a formation that was attacking our positions north of Stuhlweissenburg that crashed in flames and disintegrated on the ground. Otherwise I experienced about 60 *Feindflüge* in total!

His recorded victories in the *JG 53* unit history are[38]: two Jak-9s and one Il-2 on 20 December 1944; one Il-2 on 25 December; one Pe-2 on 23 January 1945; one La-5 on 20 February.

Having flown as the regular wingman of three great aces who led *I/JG 53*, Sommavilla was able to observe their tactics at close range.

The leadership abilities of the only 24-year-old *Major* Harder were unique, but cannot be compared with the special tactics of Hartmann or Lipfert, which were applied against the Russians under totally different circumstances and where they utilised their own very successful methods. These two scored their successes based on deliberately planned surprise attacks from above, and then pulling up underneath the unsuspecting enemy at high speed, allied to the most accurate shooting at very close range. Lipfert brought back from almost every successful fighter combat, due to our very effective ammunition and due to only opening fire from a few metres away, splinters of his victims that literally exploded in the air, caught up in the air intake of his radiator. Hartmann was able to shoot down opponents with a few rounds from the MG 131 machine guns and perhaps 5 rounds from the cannons, MG 151/20.

Later we received aircraft with a 3 cm cannon, Mk 108. With this weapon I saw *Abschüsse* of the strongly armoured Il-2s that were normally so hard to shoot down, such that the engine, wing parts and fuselage fell out of the cloud from the explosion of the aircraft. Especially the armour-piercing munitions shattered everything into pieces. Of the three aces I had so much to do with, *Major* Harder was the absolute 'Sir'. Lipfert was an honourable, genuine '*Landsknecht*' (difficult to translate fully – literally a 'son of the soil' but also implies something of the concept of the 'naughty boy' and the American expression of 'good ol' boy'), cordial, caring and someone to be depended on. He always gave me comradely advice, in the air and on the ground, and in many ways was like an older friend to me. He is ten years older than me. With Harder and Lipfert one enjoyed a feeling of belonging, the shared dangers and being dependant on each other in combat, making this feeling marked.

Like all the German pilots who met the iconic Il-2 ground attack aircraft in the East, *Leutnant* Erich Sommavilla had to use specialised tactics himself to attack them successfully, and also saw how others approached the same problem.

When attacking Il-2 formations we attacked one after the other the rearmost or the outermost aircraft. The Il-2 was able to absorb a large number of strikes, as all the German experts have also reported in their books. The radiator was placed behind the engine, and cool air was channelled in from outside on the top of the engine, passing then through the radiator and out again below the aircraft, so that the chances of hitting the cooling system were practically nil. The fuselage was protected by armour plate and if one attacked from behind and slightly below in the typical German fighter fashion, you could see the explosive rounds exploding harmlessly on the armour and the tracer rounds also flew off again in all directions, equally without effect. It only worked if the attack was made very steeply from behind and above so that the rounds hit the strongly armoured cabin at a steep angle and then could penetrate, or when one hit the open cabin of the rear gunner, destroying this or, using the Mk 108 cannon, ripping the cabin apart.

I observed from very close range, about 30 m, how *Major* Harder shot down an Il-2, using a burst from all weapons (two MG 131s, one Mk 108 cannon) from behind and above into the cabin, with the enormous power of the 3 cm armour piercing rounds literally tearing the Il-2 apart, so that the engine, the tail assembly and the wings emerged separately out of the cloud of smoke of the explosion. I did not personally fire on an Il-2 with the Mk 108 cannon, and my hits on the Il-2 oil cooler (underneath the aircraft) on 20 December 1944 with my MG 151/20 cannons were probably just chance or lucky hits. There were specialists amongst our pilots who used the wing cannons while attacking from behind and above to shoot at the wing roots, when the entire wing would break off.

Unteroffizier Heinz Hommes had joined *JG 53* in December 1942 already, flying initially with the 9th *Staffel* in the Mediterranean theatre, and in early 1944 had moved over to 2/*JG 53* where he remained for the rest of the war.[39] He had scored his first six victories with I/*JG 53* over Romania in June to August 1944, five American and one Russian aircraft, and then scored another eight Soviet victories over Hungary up till April 1945.[40] He recalls his time flying over Hungary next.

With the retreat from Romania we moved to Hungary where we got to know the Russians, the ground attack aircraft Il-2, the fighters La-7 and Jak-3. We were able to catch our breath again, as the Russians were easier to get at than the fighters of the Western powers. That does not mean that the Russians were without courage or not full of fight. However they were unimaginative in their tactics. The Russian aircraft also got better while the Me 109 declined as it became ever heavier armed, in order to achieve better successes in the battle against the four-engined bombers. As a result the Me 109 became slower and less manoeuvrable in dogfights. In the meanwhile we called the 109 '*die Beule*' (the 'Bump', referring to the bulges in the engine cowling on both sides due to enlarged breechblocks of larger-calibre nose-mounted cannons fitted in many G-models). However, despite this we flew our missions daily.

Unfortunately – for us – the numerical superiority of the enemy got ever larger and the losses of our pilots, especially those new to the front, grew more and more. However, we did not mutiny, in contrast, there was a comradeship amongst us, despite daily bad news, that was beyond compare. Our *I Gruppe* formed a united community with the ground staff. We lacked for nothing. Up till the last minute we had our special flying rations that included: money, chocolate, cigarettes, wine, coffee and more. Hermann (Göring), Commander in Chief of the *Luftwaffe*, looked after us splendidly. Only as a prisoner (thank God only for five weeks) did I get to know hunger. As we lacked for nothing, we in our *Gruppe* were a happy bunch, thought little about life or death. We often took off for operations a bit under the weather, but this disappeared when we saw the tracer from our own guns. In the evenings, each amused himself according to taste. Despite the lead-rich skies it was a wonderful, carefree time. One could tell so many stories, they would fill a book. That we stuck together, is shown also today by the '*Jägerblatt*' (official publication of the veterans association, *Gemeinschaft der Jagdflieger*; has been re-named as the *Fliegerblatt*).

The association has also been renamed: *Gemeinschaft der Flieger deutscher Streikräfte* – Association of German Aerial Forces.

The Oder Front, and the Russian Advance to Berlin
The Soviets opened up a massive offensive on 12–14 January 1945, from the approximate Vistula River line (including the eastern suburbs of Warsaw), and by the end of that month had advanced spectacularly to the north–south running River Oder line, right on the eastern boundary of Germany proper.[41] Several isolated defended towns and cities remained behind in Soviet territory, with Breslau (now Wroclaw) being the main one, and to the south the Silesian industrial area had also been conquered.[42] In late February and early March 1945 the Russians turned north and on 25 March reached the Baltic Sea between Stettin to the west and Danzig (Gdansk) to the east; Gdynia fell on 26 and Danzig on 30 March.[43] A small pocket remained east of Danzig–Gdynia, including the airfield at Junkertroylhof, from which pilots remember operating in defence of the Königsberg pocket further to the east.

As a result of this catastrophic development, which brought the Russian armies from central Poland to within less than 80 km of Berlin, there was a major shift of *Jagdgruppen* to the main Eastern Front along the Oder River line: all three *Gruppen* of JG 1 and II/JG 300 (latter for January 1945 only); all three *Gruppen* of JG 11 (I/JG 11 till March and the other two till the end of the war); all three *Gruppen* of *JG 6*, *I* and *II/JG 301* till March–April 1945; all four *Gruppen* of *JG 4* till April 1945; three of the four *Gruppen* of *JG 3* (*I/JG 3* was there from January only to March 1945), *EJG 1*, and all three *Gruppen* of *JG 77* till the end of the war.[44] However, all of this effort was a case of too little too late, and despite many of the fighter units being employed essentially as ground attack formations, they were not able to influence the outcome in any significant way. The final act in the Eastern Front drama was the advance from the Oder line to Berlin and past it westwards to link up with the Allied armies along the River Elbe.[45]

As noted above, *I/JG 3* was among those *Gruppen* moved in haste to the Eastern Front in January 1945; the *Kommandeur*, *Oberleutnant* Alfred Seidl, recalled: 'At the beginning of January 1945 we moved to the Eastern Front, to Stettin–Plathe. Our task was to stop the Russian advance with bombs and cannons/machine guns. Then we retreated to Neu-Brandenburg in March 1945 for the dissolution of the *Gruppe*. The pilots were sent to other units and I was sent to *JG 7*.' One of his pilots describes these last desperate missions trying to stem the Russian advance across the Oder River and to Berlin, in considerable detail. Having survived flying Ju 52s in the Stalingrad airlift as well as the tough missions as a fighter pilot in the later part of the Home Defence, *Oberfeldwebel* Rudolf Hener, *2/JG 3* was able to get through these final encounters in one piece, and demonstrated that the almost universally high morale of the *Jagdflieger* was finally beginning to crack as they realised that the war really was finally and irretrievably lost. His recollections appear below.

In the first days of January 1945 after days of bombardment, the Russians over-ran our entire front on the Weichsel (Vistula River). There were no more reserves available behind the lines then and the Russians were almost everywhere able to intrude across the borders of the German Reich almost unhindered. As a result troops were pulled out of the Western Front, to stop the Russians in the East. Some fighter units were also transferred to the East, including ourselves *I/JG 3* 'Udet'. We flew from Paderborn, first to Jüterbog, where we had to stay put for a few days due to continuing heavy snowfalls. Then it was on further, to Gabbert near Schneidemühl on the previous Polish border. This airfield lay in the middle of a large forest. Already on the second night there we heard the Russian tanks driving past us, without having discovered us. As a result we took off immediately the next morning and flew back to Pyritz. Our ground crews drove back with their vehicles surreptitiously along back roads and also came through safely.

When four days later the Russian tanks had advanced again, to within 10 km of the field at Pyritz, we once more had to depart quickly and moved back further to Stettin. We remained there for two weeks, but then again had to leave, flying to Pinnow which lay south of Kolberg and after about three weeks had passed, and once Russian tanks once more appeared a few kilometres away from this field and had also shot up all the villages around our airfield into flames, we finally retreated behind the Oder to Neubrandenburg. There the *Gruppe* was dissolved in the middle of March 1945. The pilots went to other fighter *Gruppen*, the mechanics, those outstanding specialists, without whom we could never have flown at all, were employed as infantry. Many of them were killed.

Naturally through all of this we flew many operations, during which at take-off and landing the iced-up, snow-covered runways and the very low temperatures (minus 20–25°C) provided enormous challenges to be overcome; missions were against tank formations and supply columns of the Russians. At least through these attacks the Russians were forced to march at night only. The high command of the *Luftwaffe* in the beginning had no idea at all of the location of the frontline. Due to this, and as I had flown from Stettin for years as an instructor and 'knew every tree and shrub in Pomerania', I was sent out on daily reconnaissance flights between Danzig and Frankfurt/Oder. Thus almost daily (when there was enough fuel available) in the earliest morning I flew reconnaissance missions with my wingman, and sometimes with an entire *Schwarm*. On these missions we often surprised Russian horse-drawn and motorised supply columns, which we attacked immediately, but also the Russian infantry that were riding on their tanks. We shot them off the tanks. But when the Russians forced German women to sit with them on top of the advancing tanks, we had to cease these attacks.

During one such attack on a Russian horse-drawn supply column, the oil cooler on my machine exploded, presumably from having been shot at, and my *Rottenflieger* Alto Sittler had to belly-land. I saw him running away from the aircraft in the direction of the edge of a forest. Six days later he managed to return to us. He had hidden himself in the forests during the daytime and only at night did he walk westwards, very carefully. Without any food or anything to drink after about 50 km he reached the Oder once again where he came across some German soldiers and had saved himself. During a free chase mission (17 February 1945)[46] behind the Russian lines I saw a lone Russian fighter that had apparently lost contact with a *c.* 40-strong fighter formation ahead of him. He noticed nothing when I manoeuvred myself behind him and the *Abschuss* was easy. It was a Jak-9. I left the rest of them alone. Why should I risk my own life and that of my comrade, while the war had been lost for a long time already? To knock some more Russians out of the heavens was not decisive for the war, but to have been responsible for the loss of one or the other of my comrades was too much for me. No, it was about surviving the end of the war, and explicitly for myself and for all my comrades who flew with me and for whom I was responsible.

Hener claimed a total of six victories against the Russians in February–March 1945 including three Lagg-3s, one Jak-9, one P-39 and one Il-2, to end the war with a score of nine.[47] The *Gruppe* as a whole claimed 14 victories over the Eastern Front in January–March 1943, for the loss of eight pilots in action.[48] These figures reflect the changed situation in combat between the *Luftwaffe* and the VVS; the days of massive German claims and minimal casualties were long over. *Unteroffizier* Ernst Schröder flew in the *Sturmgruppe II/JG 300*, in the 5th *Staffel*, where he claimed five confirmed victories, one probable and a few damaged, all in the Home Defence. In early 1945 his unit was also briefly ordered to fly ground attack missions on the Oder front, as summarised in the table below. His ongoing problems with the *Kommandogerät* (which was an early type of computer controlling many engine functions) on his Fw 190 are notable.

Example of a fighter pilot's operational life, Eastern Front, 1945, based on flying logbook, 23 January–2 February 1945: *Unteroffizier* Ernst Schröder *5/JG 300* (Source: Ernst Schröder).

JANUARY

23:   *II/JG 300* moves from **Löbnitz** to **Schönfeld–Seifersdorf**
24:   Low-level attack on Russian columns, 11h40–12h40 (operational flight); in Steinau area
Took off for mission, landed early, 15h25–15h50; early return due to faulty *Kommandogerät*
26–27: *II/JG 300* moves from **Schönfeld–Seifersdorf** via **Grossenhain** to **Löbnitz**

FEBRUARY

1:    Low-level attack on Russian columns, 13h00–14h25 (op. flight); in Küstrin area; *Kommandogerät* gave trouble
2:    Low-level attack on Russian columns, 11h35–13h10 (op. flight); in Frankfurt a.d. Oder area
Took off for mission, belly-landed due to faulty *Kommandogerät*, 15h30–15h45

As an instructor in *Ergänzungsgruppe-Süd* in Straussberg, east of Berlin, *Obergefreiter* Pay Kleber was also caught up in the catastrophic situation in the East late in the war, seeing action there in another training outfit, *2/EJG 1* (second *Staffel* of *Ergänzungsjagdgeschwader 1*).

From 30 January 1945 I flew operations with the Me 109 in the Frankfurt/Oder area against the Russian army as a fighter-bomber pilot, about 195

Feindflüge until the end of March (in only two months!). Then I returned to 7/JG 2. On 29 January I led a *Schwarm* in a high flying exercise in the direction of Posen. We flew back at low level. Above the airfield at Posen we were fired on by flak. We made out some T-34 tanks and reported this. Overnight some of the Me 109s were equipped with bomb racks (EDC). From 30 January we flew fighter-bomber attacks continuously with four 50 kg bombs each. The river Oder was covered by a permanent ice layer. Soon this became the main front line and we attacked it at low level. Our targets were tanks, artillery positions, supply columns and infantry units. At that time the Soviets had only a few Jak-7s and Mig-4s in operation, but lots of Il-2s flying backwards and forwards. Until the end of March we maintained air superiority.

After we had dropped our bombs we strafed mainly supply columns, flew 'free chases', and Stalin's Guards units north of Küstrin (Königsberg/ Neumarkt, Mohrin) were reduced to 30% of effectiveness. The forests looked like those at Verdun, it was a real inferno. We had hardly any losses, just bullet holes from infantry weapons. The high number of sorties I flew resulted from the fact that I was an instructor and had two machines at my disposal and after twenty minutes on the ground took off again leading a new *Schwarm* into the air. Flying time to the front was about ten minutes. Later we also flew escort for Stukas. My *Staffel* chief was *Hauptmann* Goedert.

The number of combat missions (*Feindflüge*) he carried out in only two months was very high, but reflected his experience and the emergency situation with the unstoppable Russian advance. Exactly what he means above by 'Mig-4' is unclear – possibly this refers to Mig-5 fighters, which are known to have seen action in small numbers.[49]

9

The *Startkladde* of 7/JG 51: Understanding German Fighter Tactics and High Claims in the East

Andreas Zapf, who runs a very interesting and valuable historical website on the *Luftwaffe* with emphasis on the fighter pilots,[1] maintains a large collection of original documents, mainly flight logs of individual pilots. In November 2013 he noted on his website that he had also obtained another document as a surprise, namely the *Startkladde* of 7/JG 51 for the period 13 September 1943 to 18 April 1944, covering operations over the central part of the Eastern Front. Andreas very kindly provided a scanned copy of this valuable document to the author. This is the first time such a document has surfaced, and, thanks to Andreas Zapf, also become available to aviation historians to study; most *Luftwaffe* documents were destroyed at the end of the war, hindering detailed studies in many ways. This document thus enables, for the first time, a detailed operational study for a small German fighter unit on the Eastern Front. In this chapter a detailed analysis will be presented and this will be used to address the vexed question of the very high-scoring German fighter pilots on the Eastern Front. It is essentially the lack of such documentation which has been responsible for much of the controversy surrounding the victory totals of the top aces on this front.

This surviving war-time record details all flights made by individual pilots of the *Staffel* during the period, including planned operations, scrambles, weather reconnaissance flights, transfer flights and test flights after repair work and servicing of aircraft. The *Startkladde* of the 7th *Staffel* of JG 51 is a handwritten document of almost 100 pages, written in the German *Sütterlinschrift* script and can be read well enough after some study and getting used to the handwriting of the recording clerks and the script itself. This script (or handwriting style) was taught in German schools from the First World War until *c.* 1941. In the German *Luftwaffe* a clerk was tasked with keeping such records, and would also have written up individual pilots' logbooks (with additions and comments added by the pilots too, particularly of details from active combats). The *Kladde* record also details where the *Staffel* was based.

Data given in the *Startkladde* equates strongly with the so-called RAF Form 541, and includes: aircraft number (such as 10w, which means 'white ten'; different *Staffels* in a *Gruppe* used different colours to distinguish them); rank and surname of pilot; times of take-off and landing; duration of flight; purpose of flight; in the final column some remarks about the flight if contact with the enemy occurred – in other words, was it a *Feindflug*, defined as one where the enemy was met in the air or on the ground, or where flight occurred over enemy territory, or even over own territory with the chance or certainty of meeting the enemy. Additionally, claimed victories and losses are also given; while the former are clearly given, being written across all columns on separate lines, the losses tend to be squeezed in between filled-in columns and no percentages are given with the losses – the Germans always gave aircraft losses in percentage terms, with 60 per cent or more being a write-off with decreasing salvage of components as 60 per cent was exceeded, until at 100 per cent nothing could be reused or the aircraft was missing or known to be down behind enemy lines.

They were stationed in the so-called Central Front, in the general area of Vitebsk–Smolensk–Bobruisk–Gomel for the most part, with short stays on the Southern Front around Korosten. They moved often, sometimes after only a few days, and were never at any one base for long. Movements were mainly as part of the entire *III Gruppe* of *JG 51*, as a *Staffel* on its own lacked any real servicing, medical, administration or supply capability. By this stage of the war in the East, the Germans had totally lost the initiative and were in almost constant retreat, particularly in the Central and Southern Front areas. Up until approximately the end of 1943 on the Central Front, they lost one town, one city and one base after another regularly; the logistics of keeping even a small unit like a *Staffel* on active service were extremely challenging, bearing in mind also the poor rail and road communications in Russia.

In the first part of 1944 the Central Front line was more stable as the Russians prepared for the giant and catastrophically effective *Bagration* offensive, which in a few days in June 1944 destroyed Army Group Centre. Quite simply, after the failed Kursk attack in July 1943 the Germans lacked adequate troops and equipment (particularly the very powerful armoured divisions) to stem the Russian advance – there was no frontline as such, just a series of fortified positions, or towns and cities with areas between strongpoints only lightly held or just patrolled. If the Russians advanced in strength with armoured support, only armour would suffice to stop them and lots of it – it was just not available in the quantities needed, and armoured divisions once committed to serious battle rapidly became worn out, both the men and the equipment, and thereafter needed considerable time before they could operate again at full strength following training, re-equipment, etc.

The *Luftwaffe* was as stretched as the ground forces, if not more so, and was used as a sort of fire brigade, desperately trying to make an impact everywhere it went but never being able to stay long enough to really do so or to establish longer-term air superiority. The inherent attrition related to establishing air superiority was beyond the means of the *Luftwaffe* fighter force in Russia from 1943 onwards. The demands of the Italian and forthcoming Normandy fronts kept eating up reinforcements and the mass of the German fighter force was concentrated at the centre, fighting the Battle of Germany.

The life and very survival of the few fighter units in the East was thus a very unique experience and very specific methods and approaches were applied, totally different to the air war in the West by this stage of the conflict. An air war of attrition in the East was totally out of the question and maintenance of the existing fighter units remained paramount. Casualties were continuous but had to be kept down as supplies of new pilots (novices of little use until experienced) and even of the Fw 190 aircraft they flew (in the case of 7/*JG 51* at this time) were always limited. The details offered below, based on this very valuable document, provide a small window into the reality of fighting the air war in the East in the face of the demoralising and continual retreats and the obvious conclusion that this could not end well for Germany or any of them.

The Pilots

When the record begins on 13 September 1943, the *Staffel* was led by *Staffelkapitän* Karl-Heinz Weber. He had joined the *Luftwaffe* in 1939 while still some months short of his 18th birthday and joined 7th *Staffel* of *JG 51* at the beginning of October 1940 as the Battle of Britain wound down, scoring his first success in June 1941 as Barbarossa began.[2] His 100th victory was claimed on 13 August 1943[3] and he was on leave during September 1943 when the *Kladde* begins. In the absence of its 21-year-old leader, the *Staffel* was led in action by an equally famous pilot, Günther Schack. Schack was five years older and had joined 7th *Staffel* of *JG 51* in March 1941, scoring his first success in July 1941 in the East.[4] A year later he shot down his fifth victory and had brought this to 48 victories by the beginning of April 1943, when he was posted to *Jagdergänzungsgruppe Ost* (the OTU for Eastern Front fighter pilots) for a rest.[5] He was back in July 1943 in time for the Kursk battle, joining the 8th *Staffel* and then 7th *Staffel* again.[6] By 13 September 1943 he had 103 victories to his name and was awarded the *Ritterkreuz* at the end of the following month for this feat, by which time he was back with the 8th *Staffel* again.[7] He was to shoot down 13 more victories during his time in 7/JG 51 from 13 September 1943 till leaving for 8th *Staffel* in late October.

There were a number of other experienced pilots with the *Staffel* in September 1943, as listed in this paragraph. *Leutnant* Heinz Kattlün had scored his first success in March 1943 and his score now stood at five.[8] *Unteroffizier* Martin Gläser had shot down nine Russians starting from his first success on 6 July 1943.[9] *Unteroffizier* Kurt Graf, 21 years old in 1943, had previously flown with the 9th *Staffel* of JG 51 and had brought his score to six in August–September 1943 before joining 7th *Staffel*.[10] The highly experienced *Feldwebel* Franz Meindl had claimed 15 victories in 7th *Staffel* already, going back to at least February 1943 and probably earlier also[11] (unit unknown for his additional, first two successes). Another old salt was *Feldwebel* Heinrich Dittlmann, one year older than his *Staffelkapitän* at 22,[12] and whose first victory of the 40 he now had to his name dated back to early September 1942,[13] before the Stalingrad debacle had changed everything in the East. *Leutnant* Friedrich Krakowitzer had shot down 11 aircraft in Russia since the beginning of operation *Zitadelle* (Kursk) on 5 July 1943,[14] a very creditable performance for a relative beginner.

Unteroffizier Walter Klötzer had also begun his career as a fighter pilot during *Zitadelle* and now had three victories to his name in September 1943.[15] Another three-victory relative novice with 7/JG 51 on 13 September 1943 was *Oberfeldwebel* Johann Bussert,[16] who only flew one mission during September 1943 in the period covered by the *Kladde* and then was away till January 1944 before rejoining the *Staffel* in the depths of winter. Four more recent arrivals yet to open their scores against the Soviets were 24-year-old *Feldwebel* Herbert Riegel, *Unteroffizier* Hans Hermann, *Unteroffizier* Günther Henschel and *Feldwebel* Helmuth Heidemann.[17]

On 13 September 1943, when the *Kladde* record of all operations flown by 7/JG 51 on the central part of the Russian front opens, the *Staffel* thus had 14 active fighter pilots. With the *Staffelkapitän* away during the 13–30 September period, and others not flying or also away (Dittlmann and Klötzer), only 11 pilots shared the combat missions of September. The inexperienced pilots were not called upon to fly more than between one and five operations in the part of the month under examination, and most of the *Feindflüge* were done by only four pilots: Schack, Gläser, Kattlün and Graf (see table showing monthly operations by individual pilots, below). During the latter part of September several more novice pilots joined the *Staffel*, who would only see action from October onwards: *Flieger* Armin Mehling, 26-year-old *Feldwebel* Kurt Kästner and 24-year-old *Unteroffizier* Georg Orth.[18] Alas, both Kästner and Orth would soon disappear, Orth going missing in October after flying only six missions during which he also crash-landed once, and Kästner surviving 26 missions before being reported missing in January 1944.[19]

As was typical for all nations and theatres, the young and inexperienced made up most of the casualties. However, neophyte Armin Mehling did survive the war, becoming the primary wingman of *Staffelkapitän* 'Benjamin' Weber, while also scoring six victories during the period covered by the *Kladde* – quite a performance for a newcomer. His rank, the lowest possible, suggests some serious disciplinary breach during his earlier training or military induction and he remained an *Unteroffizier* until the end of the war and a successful career as a fighter pilot during the really hard years of the conflict, in both eastern and western combat zones.[20]

In January 1944 two new pilots joined 7/*JG 51*: *Feldwebel* Franz-Josef Zoufahl, previously with 8th *Staffel*, where he scored 10 victories from July 1943 onwards,[21] and the much less experienced *Leutnant* Johann Brünnler, who had one victory to his name (with an unknown unit). Neither would survive the 1944 mid-year battles on the central Eastern Front, by which time they had moved to 8/*JG 51*. Zoufahl scored another nine successes with 7/*JG 51* during the time covered by the *Kladde* and Brünnler one more. Finally, in March 1944, towards the end of the time covered in the records of the *Kladde*, two more pilots, both raw novices, joined 7th *Staffel*: *Leutnant* Ultsch and 22-year-old[22] *Unteroffizier* Johann Klupp. Both joined just in time for the intense activity of April 1944, with its many more missions and also many *Jabo-einsätze* (fighter-bomber attacks); Klupp flew 28 missions in April, a very tough beginning for a newcomer, but was killed in a force-landing in early May 1944, by then flying with another unit in *III/JG 51*.[23] It has not been possible to find any trace of Ultsch's activities after April 1944.

As can be seen from the table summarising pilots' missions, four further pilots flew single or very few missions with the 7th *Staffel*: a *Leutnant* Busse (probably Heinz Busse, who flew normally as part of *Stab III/ JG 51*),[24] who logged three operations in September–October 1943, and *Feldwebel* Paul Hollmann, *Feldwebel* Schmidt and *Oberfeldwebel* Alexander Slomski (also a member of *Stab III/JG 51*),[25] who each flew a single mission. Surprisingly, both Slomski and Hollmann survived the war, but Busse died in August 1944 in the East;[26] of Schmidt nothing further could be determined, particularly reflecting the lack of a first name recorded for him in the *Kladde* and the common surname he bore.

Operations flown per month by individual pilots, with 7/JG 51, 13 September 1943–18 April 1944, Eastern Front

	Sept.	Oct.	Nov.	Dec.	Jan.	Feb.	Mar.	Apr.	Total
Oblt./Hptm. Karl-Heinz Weber		32	6	3	18	23	20	42	144
Lt. Günther Schack	19	15 (crl)							34
Lt. Heinz Kattlün	17	18	6	9					50
Uffz. Martin Gläser	19								19
Uffz. Kurt Graf	13	8	3	4	13 M 24th				41
Fw. Franz Meindl	4	25	7	14			19	32	101
Fw./Ofw. Heinrich Dittlmann		22 (crl)	10	11	19	18 (f) M 23rd			80
Lt. Friedrich Krakowitzer	5	23	8	14	15	12 (crl)	20	33	130
Flg. Armin Mehling		4	3	11	14 (crl)	12 (acc)	17	27	88
Lt. Johann Brünnler					8	10	17	38	73
Uffz. Walter Klötzer		1				1	14	2	18
Ofw. Joachim Bussert	1				9	12	8	37	67
Ltn. Busse	1	2							3
Fj. Fw. Herbert Riegel	5	3	3 M 11th						11
Uffz. Hans Hermann	4	6 (crl)	7	11	8		12	39	87
Uffz. Günther Henschel	3	6		7	6	8 (dam)	1	7	38

	Sept.	Oct.	Nov.	Dec.	Jan.	Feb.	Mar.	Apr.	Total
Fw. Helmuth Heidemann	1	15	6	5	4	11 (fl)	8	18 (crl)	68
Fw. Kurt Kästner		9	6	9	2 M 5th				26
Uffz. Georg Orth		6 (fl) M 24th							6
Fw. Paul Hollmann		1							1
Fw. Schmidt		1							1
Fw. Franz-Josef Zoufahl					9	23	14	29	75
Ofw. Alexander Slomski						1			1
Lt. Ultsch							4	8 (fl)	12
Uffz. Johann Klupp							1	28	29
Total operational sorties per month	92	197	65	98	125	131	155	340	
Number of pilots flying operations per month	12	18	11	11	12	11	13	13	

<u>Notes</u>: crl = crash-landing; dam = damaged; acc = accident; M = missing followed by day of month loss occurred; grey shading indicates leadership of *Schwarm* size or larger formation in action. Operations all indicated as *Einsatz* in the *Startkladde* of 7/JG 51 and weather reconnaissance missions also included here (not always indicated as an *Einsatz*), plus any transfer or test flight which led to enemy action; also, any missions where there were early returns are included – the *Kladde* varies in its labelling these as *Feindflüge* depending on length of flight. Missions numbers thus exceed slightly officially designated *Feindflüge*. An *Einsatz* in *Luftwaffe* usage equated to operations in general and included *Frontflüge/Feindflüge*, which are specifically combat either over enemy territory or in contact with enemy aircraft over your own territory or the sea separating enemy and own territory.[27]

The leadership of the small formations typically used by the German fighter arm on the Eastern Front are shown by the grey shading (indicates a pilot leading a formation in action comprising four or more aircraft at least once during the month in question) in the table above. From these it is seen that *Staffelkapitän* Weber led many missions when at the front; the same applies to the highly experienced Schack, and also to Dittlman, a senior and seasoned NCO with a high victory total. This is typical of the *Luftwaffe*, where an experienced NCO would often lead less experienced officers in the air, where rank counted for nothing and experience and victory totals counted for everything. NCO training in the German forces was much more thorough than that of any of their opponents, and their responsibilities, rank for rank, were that much greater as a result. As in all armed forces, senior and experienced NCOs were the backbone of the fighting units, 7/JG 51 being no exception.

Other formation leaders included *Leutnant* Kattlün, who often led while with the *Staffel*, and *Feldwebel* Meindl who led less often. *Feldwebel* Zoufahl only led during one month. *Leutnant* Krakowitzer is a more interesting case – while experienced, he was also often placed as wingman to Weber in October and November 1943, before starting to lead from December onwards. Despite being a much-used formation leader from then onwards, he still sometimes flew as wingman to the *Staffelkapitän*; perhaps he was still being assessed by the 'boss' for a subsequent leadership role, and in fact, on Weber's departure in June 1944 from the *Staffel* to lead a *Gruppe* in JG 1, Krakowitzer took over 7/JG 51 as *Staffelführer*[28] (a term equating with acting *Staffelkapitän*).

A Brief Operations Summary of the Startkladde 7/JG 51
The brief operational summary presented in this section is derived directly from the *Kladde* and also includes inferences which may reasonably be made from the data in the *Kladde*.

Record starts 13 September 1943; *Einsatzort* (cf. base) Ponjatowka: Only there for two days and flew three operations on 13 September involving five sorties in total and five operations next day involving nine sorties. Fw 190 formations used of two aircraft and one of one aircraft. Missions involved escorting Stukas, bombers and Fw 189 reconnaissance aircraft and a few free chases. One transfer flight for two aircraft combined with a free chase (more efficient use of aircraft and fuel). Met the enemy on only two sorties (once versus one Yak-5, and second time against ten Il-2mHs [Il-2s with gunner] and six fighters), resulting in one Yak-5 being claimed and one Il-2 *wirksam beschossen* (effectively or efficiently shot-up; equates to a damaged aircraft). *Leutnant* Schack acted as *Staffelführer* while the

Staffelkapitän Oberleutnant Weber was on leave. Victories: *Leutnant* Schack one Yak-5. Losses: nil.

<u>*Einsatzort* Smolensk; 15–20 September 1943</u>: Only three Fw 190s transferred and one was already at Smolensk on 15 September. These four aircraft flew all the operations for the next three days with one additional aircraft coming on line on 18 September, and another four next day, giving a total serviceable line up of nine aircraft by 19 September. A total of 16 missions flown here, comprising 53 individual sorties. Six missions escorting Stukas, bombers, an Hs 126 short range reconnaissance aircraft, and a Fw 189 longer-range reconnaissance machine; four free chases, two combined with transfer flights; six scrambles. Formations used were mostly of four Fw 190s, some of only two and one scramble with a single aircraft. The enemy was met on 11 of the 16 missions resulting in 10 victory claims, and one Il-2mH and one Yak-7 *wirksam beschossen*. Notable missions follow.

On <u>18 September</u> *Leutnant* Schack led four aircraft against 15 Russian fighters and shot down one Lagg-5 at 3,000 m and a Yak-7 at 1,000 m 16 minutes later. Schack thus stalked this relatively large Russian formation and twice shot out a single aircraft. This illustrates the effectiveness of the German fighter battle tactic, to score steady successes at little risk to self, with the small numbers of German fighters bouncing the more numerous Russians from a higher altitude where their aircraft had a decided performance edge, followed by a zoom climb back to altitude where no enemy could follow such a high-speed climb. Thereafter, as so often happened, the Russian formation continued on its way and mission, and sometime later another attack from above could be launched.

On <u>20 September</u> *Leutnant* Schack led four aircraft against six Lagg-5s; in a single bounce just after 09h30 by the leading *Rotte*, his wingman shot down one Lagg-5 and one minute later Schack got another, both at 3,000 m. The second *Rotte* stayed up as high cover. Later the same day Schack led four aircraft to attack an Il-2mH formation with mixed fighter escort soon after 16h00. He made two bounce attacks with his own *Rotte* first, seven minutes apart, and shooting down first a Yak-7 at 2,000 m and then an Il-2mH at 600 m. After another seven minutes had passed the second *Rotte* got their chance with the leader getting a Lagg-5 at 2,500 m and his wingman damaged an Il-2mH. Total victories from this base: *Leutnant* Kattlün one Yak-9 and one Lagg-5; *Leutnant* Schack four Lagg-5s, two Yak-7s and one Il-2mH; *Unteroffizier* Gläser one Lagg-5. Losses: nil.

<u>*Einsatzort* Mogilev; 21–24 September 1943</u>: Aircraft already being transferred from 19 September to the new base and flying back and forth

between Smolensk and Mogilev for several days. 10 aircraft serviceable and operational during the first few days. Only one operation involving four sorties flown from Mogilev, escorting Ju 87s; no victory claims or losses.

Einsatzort Novo Zybkov; 25 September–3 October 1943: Eight aircraft did the transfer flight over several days from 25 September onwards. Only eight missions flown, involving 23 sorties: four weather reconnaissances (not always counted as *Feindflug* in the *Kladde*), two free chases (first one on 25 September combined with an area familiarisation flight), and two Ju 87 escorts. Formation sizes varied from two to four Fw 190s. No victory claims or losses.

Einsatzort Korosten; 4–8 October 1943: 10 Fw 190s transferred far southwards to Korosten, north-west of Kiev, on 4 October. 13 missions flown from here, encompassing 47 individual sorties: nine Ju 87 escorts, four free chases, three of them towards the end of this assignment combined with transfer flights away from Korosten. Formations used between two and six Fw 190s, but operated mainly in flights of four. The enemy was met on six of the missions, with two large interceptions on 4 October; other interceptions were against pure fighter formations, comprising between four and 12 Russian fighters. Notable missions follow.

On 4 October *Leutnant* Schack led a *Schwarm* into action against 15 to 30 DB-3 bombers accompanied by 15 Russian fighters shortly before 13h00. Schack's *Rotte* made the first bounce (Schack shooting down a Yak-7 at 3,500 m) with the second pair just behind them, the wingman of this second *Rotte* getting a DB-3 two minutes later, at 2,500 m. The *Schwarm* made a second attack five minutes later, with Schack's wingman getting a Mig-3 at 1,800 m. The leader of the second *Rotte* also damaged two Mig-3s. Perhaps *Schwarm* attacks, rather than by one pair with the second providing top cover, were preferred due to the relatively large size of this formation, despite the risks involved.

In a second mission on 4 October, at *c.* 15h30 *Leutnant* Schack took six Fw 190s up to engage 25 Il-2mH escorted by 12 fighters. The first *Rotte* attacked first, Schack getting an Il-2mH at 600 m, and as they zoom-climbed up again, *Rotte* two dived down, its leader shooting down another bomber at 400 m, five minutes later. The leader of the third pair damaged a Lagg-5 while the wingman forced an Il-2mH to crash-land. The latter however did not count as an *Abschuss* for the pilot, *Leutnant* Krakowitzer and also does not appear at all in the *Luftwaffe* general claims lists of Tony Wood.[29] Seven victories claimed flying from Korosten, as well as four *wirksam beschossen*: *Leutnant* Schack two Yak-7s, one Il-2mH; *Unteroffizier* Graf one DB-3; *Leutnant* Kattlün one Mig-3; *Feldwebel* Meindl one Il-2mH; *Feldwebel*

Dittlmann one Mig-3; *Leutnant* Krakowitzer one Il-2mH forced to land (not counted!). Losses: *Leutnant* Schack crash-landed at Korosten on 5 October following battle damage picked up in a fight against 12 Russian fighters during which he shot down a Yak-7.

<u>*Einsatzort* Vitebsk; 9–16 October:</u> Starting on 7 October already and continuing till 9 October, a total of 11 Fw 190s transferred to Vitebsk, mostly via Novo Zybkov and a few via Smolensk. 24 operations encompassing 71 individual sorties were flown from this base: nine free chases (six combined with transfer flights); six Ju 87 escorts (one combined with a transfer flight); three Ju 88 escorts (one combined with a free chase and one with a transfer flight); three He 111 escorts (one combined with a transfer flight); one escort to formations of Ju 87, Ju 88 and He 111 bombers; one unspecified escort mission; one transfer flight counting as a *Feindflug*; one *Jabo-einsatz*. The combination of transfer flights with active duty assignments clearly indicates the *Luftwaffe*'s weakness, due no doubt to small numbers of aircraft available and low fuel reserves. Fw 190 formation sizes varied between one and five machines, but mostly comprised either two or four aircraft together. The Russians were met on 11 occasions, 10 of them being fighter formations only, numbering between four and 15 aircraft. Notable missions follow.

On <u>10 October</u> *Oberleutnant* Weber led two Fw 190s against a Yak-4 escorted by five Yak-9s. The formation was bounced twice – on the first, Weber shot down an escorting Yak-9 at 3,200 m and 19 minutes later bounced the formation again and got the Yak-4 at 3,500 m. Again a masterly example of the perfect *Jagdwaffe* repeated bounce tactics. This waiting between two such attacks took a cool head, superior leadership, lots of experience and patience, but yielded results at little risk to their own limited forces. Later on <u>10 October</u> *Leutnant* Schack led four aircraft against six Yak-7s. Schack attacked first (with wingman presumably) and got one Yak-7 at 3,000 m, and five minutes later the second *Rotte* attacked the Yaks again and the *Rotte* leader claimed a Lagg-3 shot down.

On <u>14 October</u> *Oberleutnant* Weber led five aircraft against six Yak-7s and he and his wingman attacked once, each shooting down a Yak, Weber's at 4,100 m and the wingman's at 3,000 m one minute later – presumably the Yaks were trying to dive away after being bounced, which bearing in mind the much superior diving abilities of the Fw 190s, was not very advisable. Later on <u>14 October</u> *Oberleutnant* Weber led four Fw 190s against eight Yak-7s and let the second *Rotte* make the bounce while he and his wingman provided top cover; the two pilots of the second *Rotte* each made one claim at exactly the same time and altitude (1,800 m). This is good leadership, allowing less experienced pilots a chance at scoring victories; excellent for morale and ensures experience being built up among the *Staffel* pilots. Nine victories were claimed (and four *wirksam beschossen*) in total while flying from Vitebsk, without any losses: *Oberleutnant* Weber one Yak-4, one Yak-7, one Yak-9; *Leutnant* Schack two Yak-7s; *Feldwebel* Dittlmann one Lagg-3, one Yak-7; *Leutnant* Krakowitzer one Yak-7; *Leutnant* Kattlün one Yak-7.

Einsatzort Korosten; 17–18 October: While most of the *Staffel* transferred to Novo Zybkov and some further south-west to Ovruch ('Owrutsch' in *Kladde*) preparatory to flying on to Korosten between 14 and 15 October, only four Fw 190s actually flew to Korosten on the 15 October; no missions were flown from this base at all over the two days these aircraft were based there.

Einsatzort 'Korsinka' (illegible in *Kladde* – possibly Khoyniki; definitely to west of Lojew area and also close to Retschinka district; could also be Kalinkavichi which is west of Lojew); 19–27 October: Eight Fw 190s flew in on 19 October and one more next day, four from Korosten, four from Ovruch and one from Novo Zybkov. 21 operations encompassing 56 individual sorties were flown: eight Ju 87 escorts; three Ju 88 and 1 He 111 escort missions; one non-specific escort; two escorts to single Fw 189 reconnaissance aircraft and one to an Hs 126 short range reconnaissance aircraft; two free chases and two weather reconnaissance flights; one non-specific operational flight. Formation sizes were between one and five Fw 190s, mostly either two- or four-strong formations. Contact was experienced with Russian formations 10 times, all with fighters, with strength thereof varying between two and 15 enemy aircraft. Three victories were claimed for three losses. Notable missions follow.

On 20 October *Oberleutnant* Weber led five of his *Staffel* against Russian aircraft and a bounce of two *Rotten* was made, Weber shooting down a Yak-9 at 3,800 m, with the second *Rotte* coming down behind the lead pair and the number two man shooting down another Yak-9, at 3,500 m, three minutes later. Presumably the fifth Fw 190 stayed up as top cover. Total victories from this base: *Oberleutnant* Weber two Yak-9s; *Feldwebel* Dittlmann one Yak-9. Losses: *Feldwebel* Dittlmann crashed landing back at base after the action noted above on 20 October; *Unteroffizier* Orth force-landed away from base on 21 October following engine failure; on 24 October Orth was missing from an operational flight as one of a pair of Fw 190s which had been escorting Ju 87s and which had engaged six Yak-7s.

Einsatzort Novo Zybkov; 28 October only: Seven Fw 190s flew in on 27 October (two having earlier flown to the new base on 24 October). In the single day they were stationed there, three missions totalling

10 sorties were flown – one scramble and one Ju 87 escort each by a pair of Fw 190s – and in the afternoon six aircraft were flown back to 'Korsinka' again. The latter mission resulted in the only enemy contact while operating from this base on 28 October – they met 14 Yak-7s of which one was claimed shot down by *Leutnant* Kattlün.

Einsatzort 'Korsinka'; 29 October–5 November: In addition to the six aircraft flown in the previous day (one of which was flown back to Novo Zybkov on that same day), five more came in on 30 October – total thus at the new base by this date was 10 Fw 190s. Only four missions (14 sorties) were flown in the eight days at this base: four free chases, one of which was combined with a weather reconnaissance. The Russians were only met once, on 30 October, when *Oberleutnant* Weber led a *Schwarm* up, losing his wingman to an early return with mechanical trouble before combat began. The remaining three Fw 190s abandoned their normal cautious doctrine and made a single bounce on the Russian formation and Weber shot down an Il-2mH at 700 m, and the remaining *Rotte* leader got another at 300 m two minutes later. These were the only victories and no losses were suffered throughout the period at this base.

Einsatzort Vitebsk; 6–19 November: Eight Fw 190s transferred via Novo Lybkov to Vitebsk on 5 November, joined by one more which was already at Novo Lybkov; another aircraft also already at Novo Lybkov flew on to Vitebsk the next day. Total number of Fw 190s at Vitebsk thus nine (one had returned to Novo Lybkov on 6 November) on 7 November. 10 operations (totalling 31 sorties) flown from Vitebsk: four Ju 87 escorts; four free chases; one scramble and one unspecified operation with air combat involved. Formation sizes varied between one and four aircraft, but were mostly four. Russian aircraft were met on nine of the 10 missions, involving mostly enemy fighters (between four and 10 in number) but 7th *Staffel* twice engaged unescorted formations of Il-2mHs on 11 November. No operations flown between 13 and 19 November at all. Notable missions follow.

On 10 November *Leutnant* Kattlün led four Fw 190s against eight to 10 Russian fighters, he and his wingman making two bounces five minutes apart, Kattlün shooting down a Yak-7 at low level on the first and a Lagg-5 at 800 m on the second. No chance was given here to the second *Rotte* to score.

On 11 November *Feldwebel* Meindl led a *Rotte* against four Il-2mHs and made two bounces 15 minutes apart, shooting down two of the Il-2s, one at 300 m and the other at 250 m. His wingman (*Feldwebel* Riegel) went missing during this action. Although an experienced NCO pilot with a good victory total to his credit, Meindl possibly exercised less than ideal leadership in this case; for a single *Rotte*, a single surprise attack would have been seen by many as safer. Seven victories were claimed (and one *wirksam beschossen*) from this base: *Oberleutnant* Weber one Yak-7 and one Lagg-5; *Leutnant* Kattlün one Yak-7 and one Lagg-5; *Feldwebel* Meindl two Il-2mHs; *Leutnant* Krakowitzer one Il-2mH. Losses: *Feldwebel* Riegel missing.

Einsatzort Novo Zybkov; 20–24 November: Nine aircraft flown in on 19 November to add to one already there, for a total of 10 available Fw 190s at the new base on 20 November. Only three operations (10 sorties altogether) flown here, all on 22 November: two free chases and one escort to He 111s; two *Schwarms* and one *Rotte* of Fw 190s used on these. Both *Schwarm* missions met Russian aircraft. *Feldwebel* Dittlmann led the first mission against Russian aircraft but lost his wingman before that due to an early return for a technical problem. The remaining three aircraft bounced the enemy with Dittlmann shooting down an Il-2mH at 2,000 m, and the leader of *Rotte* two another at 1,500 m three minutes later, as the bombers dived closer to the ground to protect their vulnerable oil coolers beneath the planes' bellies. Again a more risky procedure used, with another even more experienced NCO pilot leading the formation. Later the same day *Oberleutnant* Weber led the second interception, of Bostons at high altitude; he made two attacks six minutes apart, shooting down a Boston each time, one at 3,600 m and the second at 4,000 m. Victories claimed from this base: *Oberleutnant* Weber two Bostons; *Feldwebel* Dittlmann one Il-2mH; *Feldwebel* Meindl one Il-2mH. Losses: nil.

Einsatzort Bobruisk; 25 November 1943–7 January 1944: A comparatively long stay at one base for this period in the war: 44 days! Nine Fw 190s transferred to Bobruisk on 25 November, via Novo Zybkov. 40 operations were flown from Bobruisk (involving a total of 144 sorties; formation sizes used were between one and seven Fw 190s, mostly *Schwarm*-size but with several larger formations of six to seven aircraft used): 11 Ju 87 escorts, one of them combined with a transfer flight and one involving also escort of Ju 88s; one Ju 88 escort and one escort for He 111s and Ju 88s followed by ground strafing attacks by the Fw 190s (*Feldwebeln* Meindl and Dittlmann shot up several vehicles, setting two armoured cars on fire); eight weather reconnaissances and three scrambles; 14 free chases (one combined with a transfer flight); one enemy contact during an air-test flight. Russians were met on 15 of the 40 operations: involving both Russian fighters (up to 20 in number) on their own and fairly large escorted Il-2 or bomber formations – up to 20 Pe-2s and 12 Bostons, apart from the common Il-2mH formations. Notable missions follow.

On 8 December *Leutnant* Krakowitzer led off a pair of Fw 190s on a scramble, meeting three Lagg-5s only three minutes later at 50 m; while he damaged one his wingman destroyed one and damaged another. This time there was no finely timed ambush from altitude but a wild fight at low level straight after take-off. On 15 December *Feldwebel* Meindl led four aircraft of 7/JG 51 against a Russian formation of 12 Bostons and 15 fighters and a single attack was made by the entire *Schwarm*, Meindl shooting down a Boston at 1,800 m one minute after the leader of the second Rotte had got an escorting Yak-7 at 1,600 m. Once again with an NCO leading, doctrine was abandoned (no top cover left at altitude); the contrast with the leadership shown by both Schack and Weber is noticeable.

On 23 December *Oberleutnant* Weber took up a *Rotte* that intercepted Il-2mHs and Yak-9 escorts and in two attacks; he got one of each six minutes apart, a Yak-9 at 800 m and an Il-2mH at 300 m thereafter. Presumably he left his wingman up as top cover on each bounce as *Luftwaffe* practice dictated for a single *Rotte*; however, still a risky procedure when done twice, but he was a highly experienced pilot and formation leader.

On 28 December *Oberleutnant* Weber led a *Schwarm* which ambushed two lonely Il-2mHs, Weber allowing the second *Rotte* to do the first bounce during which the number two claimed one of the bombers at 300 m followed by his leader getting the second two minutes later at 200 m. Another example of the *Staffelkapitän* letting his pilots enjoy opportunities to obtain victories and experience; this *Staffel* must have enjoyed high morale with such a supportive leader. Altogether while flying from Bobruisk 12 victories were claimed (plus four *wirksam beschossen*) as well as one Yak-7 *ohne Zeuge* (unwitnessed victory claim) for *Feldwebel* Kästner – this is not listed as a normal claim in the *Kladde* neither does it figure in Tony Wood's claims lists.[30] *Feldwebel* Kästner himself was the sole casualty while flying during this period from Bobruisk – missing in action on 5 January 1944 while on a mission to escort Ju 87s and a concomitant transfer flight. Victories claimed from this base: *Feldwebel* Dittlmann two Yak-7s; *Flieger* Mehling one Lagg-5; *Leutnant* Krakowitzer one Yak-7, one Il-2mH, one Lagg-5; Feldwebel Meindl one Boston, one Il-2mH; *Oberleutnant* Weber one Yak-9, one Il-2mH; *Unteroffizier* Graf one Il-2mH, one Pe-2; *Feldwebel* Kästner one Yak-7 oZ (*ohne Zeuge*).

Einsatzort Orsha; 8–11 January: Four Fw 190s flew in on 6 January and four more on 8 January. Four operations were flown while stationed at Orsha (involving a total of 15 sorties): one Ju 87 escort combined with the 8 January transfer flight of four Fw 190s; a He 111 escort, a free chase and a weather reconnaissance (Fw 190 formation sizes were two to five aircraft strong, but mostly four to five machines). Russian aircraft were met twice on 8 January, the one mission involving an enemy formation of 20 fighters and 18 Il-2s – *Flieger* Mehling crash-landed at Orsha returning from this operation. No victories were claimed during the brief period at this base.

<u>*Einsatzort* Bobruisk; 12 January–5 February:</u> Seven Fw 190s flew in on 12 January and one more the next day. 22 operations were flown from Bobruisk (involving 105 individual sorties): nine Ju 87 escorts (one combined with a transfer flight); nine free chases; one scramble and three weather reconnaissance missions. Fw 190 formation sizes used varied from two to eight machines, with quite a few *Schwarm* formations and larger formations of six to eight aircraft operating (used eight times). Enemy contact experienced on 11 operations out of the 22: apart from the normal fighter formations of one to four enemy aircraft, several large formations of Bostons/Pe-2s (eight to ten bombers and six to 20 escorting fighters) as well as several escorted Il-2mH formations were met – the largest was 15 to 20 Il-2mHs and 20 fighters on 24 January. On 12 January Weber and his inexperienced wingman met a lone Lagg-5 and Mehling was allowed to shoot this down. Notable missions follow.

On <u>14 January</u> *Feldwebel* Dittlmann led off a pair of Fw 190s who met a formation of five Il-2mHs and five Lagg-5 escorts. Dittlmann made the first bounce and shot down two Laggs a minute apart, at 300 m and 200 m, with his wingman following up two minutes later, getting a third at 600 m. It is possible that the wingman stayed up during Dittlmann's attack and came down to attack one of the Laggs that was climbing for height and thus posing a danger for his leader.

On <u>25 January</u> *Staffelkapitän* Weber led off eight aircraft who sighted four Yak-9s at altitude. Three attacks are made just after 08h30: by the lead *Rotte*, three minutes later by the third pair and after two more minutes by the fourth pair, the leader of each picking off one of the hapless Jak-9s as the fight continually descended as these combats tended to do, with the victims being dispatched, respectively, at 3,800 m, 3,000 m and 2,000 m. The second *Rotte* stayed up high for cover the whole time. Later the same day *Oberleutnant* Weber took up another large formation of eight aircraft which sighted two unsuspecting Yak-7s at altitude, no doubt out for a free chase themselves. Weber allowed his fourth *Rotte* to do the first bounce shortly before 13h00, and its leader got one of the Yaks at 3,500 m, after which the other dived down but five minutes later was dispatched by the *Staffelkapitän* at 1,200 m. Weber, the consummate leader and ace pilot, had ensured a classic double-bounce attack.

On <u>30 January</u> *Oberfeldwebel* Dittlmann led four aircraft which encountered two Il-2mHs escorted by two Yak-7s, all at low level. Dittlmann dispatched one of the Yaks at 300 m and the other one probably took off, leaving the two bombers to their fate. A couple of minutes later the leader of the second pair shot down both bombers, still flying at 300 m, falling one minute apart. 16 victories were claimed in total from Bobruisk during the time spent there and one *wirksam beschossen* for the loss of *Unteroffizier* Graf, shot down on 24 January by Russian fighters escorting an Il-2mH formation – his fate is unknown (missing). Victories: *Flieger* Mehling one Lagg-5, one Yak-7; *Unteroffizier* Graf one Pe-2; *Feldwebel* Dittlmann two Lagg-5s, one Yak-7, one Yak-9; *Unteroffizier* Herrmann one Lagg-5; *Leutnant* Krakowitzer one Yak-7, one Yak-9; *Oberleutnant* Weber one Yak-9, one Yak-7; *Feldwebel* Zoufahl one Yak-9, one Yak-7, two Il-2mHs.

Einsatzort Polotsk; 6–19 February: Eight Fw 190s flew in on 5 February. 19 operations flown from this base (totalling 61 sorties): 10 Ju 87 escorts; one scramble and three weather reconnaissance missions; one Fw 189 reconnaissance aircraft escort; two free chase operations; one escort for three Fi 156 light aircraft; formations used comprised two to six Fw 190s but mainly used *Schwarm*-strength formations. Enemy met on 11 missions: mostly fighters, between six and 12 of them at a time, and one unescorted Il-2mH formation of nine aircraft met on 9 February, and eight Il-2mHs escorted by 10 fighters later that same day. Notable missions follow.

On 6 February *Oberleutnant* Weber took up four aircraft who found a formation of six to eight Yak-7s at about 2,000 m; Weber attacked first and shot down one of the Russian fighters. After stalking the remainder for a further 14 minutes he let his wingman lead a second attack on a low-flying Yak from the formation, shooting it down at 100 m. Two minutes later Weber let the second *Rotte* pounce on the rest of the Yak formation still up high, the leader of this pair getting one at 2,200 m.

On 7 February *Oberleutnant* Weber led four aircraft against four P-40s and eight Lagg-5s, and he and his wingman bounced them twice, 14 minutes apart, Weber getting a P-40 at 2,500 m on the first and one of the Laggs at 4,200 m on the second. This is the very epitome of the German approach to fighting an enemy superior in numbers to themselves at fairly low levels above an active frontline battlefield (as they commonly did in Russia and North Africa). This methodology and the small Russian formations met at frequent intervals above the frontlines ensured that expert and experienced pilots could build up very high scores. Later the same day, *Feldwebel* Dittlmann led up a *Schwarm* against eight Lagg-5s and carried out the classic double bounce, his own *Rotte* followed five minutes later by the second, each *Rotte* leader getting one of the Laggs, Dittlmann's first at 2,000 m and his comrade's next at 500 m as the Laggs dived for cover after the first attack. Dittlmann's wingman force-landed out of fuel.

On 9 February *Oberleutnant* Weber led a pair of Fw 190s to find nine Il-2mHs flying low and without escort. He made two attacks eight minutes apart, shooting down a bomber on each, one at 150 m and the other at 200 m; he also damaged a third.

On 12 February Weber took up a *Schwarm* and made two bounces on a formation of eight Yak-7s, 13 minutes apart, getting a first Yak at 400 m and the second on the second bounce at 1,200 m, covered by his remaining *Rotte*. The leader of this second *Rotte* force-landed due to a flak hit. In total, while operating out of Polotsk, 14 victories and one *wirksam beschossen* Il-2mH were claimed for three losses of own aircraft. Victories: *Feldwebel* Zoufahl two Lagg-5s; *Oberleutnant* Weber three Yak-7s, two Lagg-5s, one P-40, two Il-2mHs; *Leutnant* Krakowitzer one Yak-7; *Oberfeldwebel* Dittlmann one Yak-7, one Lagg-5, one Il-2mH. Losses: *Leutnant* Krakowitzer turned over landing at Polotsk on 6 February returning from a Ju 87 escort and contact with eight Lagg-5s; on 7 February *Oberfeldwebel* Heidemann force-landed out of fuel after action with eight Lagg-5s met while escorting Ju 87s; on 12 February *Oberfeldwebel* Dittlmann force-landed due to a direct flak hit on an operation escorting Ju 87s which were intercepted by eight Yak-7s.

Einsatzort Bobruisk; 20 February–6 March: Nine Fw 190s flew into Bobruisk from Polotsk on 19 February, two having done a weather reconnaissance on the way. 19 missions were flown from Bobruisk (totalling 73 sorties): 12 Ju 87 escorts; six free chases, one of them combined with ground attack mission; one weather reconnaissance. Formation sizes varied from two to six Fw 190s, but mostly *Schwarms* were used. Russian aircraft met on ten of these missions: mostly included only fighters (two to eight strong) but also met larger formations four times, of escorted Il-2mHs and in one case a really large formation of 20 Bostons, 15 Il-2mHs and 15 fighters. Notable missions follow.

On 21 February *Oberfeldwebel* Dittlmann led four Fw 190s up and found a formation of Il-2mHs escorted by Yak-7s with the latter flying at only a few hundred metres (400–500 m and the bombers even lower). There appear to have been three attacks on this formation at intervals of four and 13 minutes; the first attack was by the lead *Rotte* (leader got a Yak-7, his wingman an Il-2mH) and was followed by two more of all four German aircraft. In the second attack, two Il-2mHs fell to Dittlmann and the number two man of the second *Rotte*; in the third attack, the leader of the second pair got an Il-2mH and Dittlmann's wingman a Yak-7. This formation was stalked and repeatedly attacked for a period of 27 minutes. Although the last two attacks appear to have been carried out without leaving a top cover, this might also reflect a low-flying enemy and one who reacted poorly to the initial attack, thus posing less danger for the Germans.

On 22 February a very large formation of 20 Bostons, 15 Il-2mHs escorted by 15 Russian fighters was seen by *Oberleutnant* Weber and three other Fw 190 pilots. Another long stalk and repeated attacking manoeuvres followed, for 21 minutes. The first attack was by the lead *Rotte* with Weber getting a Boston at 1,000 m, and then nine minutes went by before the second attack, which seems to have been by the two pair-leaders (each shooting down an Il-2mH, at 600 m and 400 m respectively), their wingmen staying up as top cover. Another nine-minute pause was followed by the third attack when Weber's wingman claimed a Lagg-5 and an Il-2mH in the space of two minutes at 300-200 m altitude. It is possible that this attack was made by the two wingmen with their pair-leaders staying up for cover.

On 23 February *Oberleutnant* Weber once again led a *Schwarm* into action and the two *Rotten* bounced a group of Russian aircraft in close succession, the second *Rotte*'s leader getting a Yak-7 at 1,100m, and the *Staffelkapitän* shooting down a second Yak at low level four minutes later. The leader of the second *Rotte* was missing from this mission upon return to base. Doctrine was not followed as no top cover was left in the attack and the loss of a very experienced pilot, *Oberfeldwebel* Dittlmann with 59 victories to his name, was likely the consequence. 17 victories were claimed plus one *wirksam beschossen* in this period of flying from Bobruisk. There were three Fw 190 losses in the same period. Victories: *Oberfeldwebel* Dittlmann two Yak-7s, two Lagg-5s, one Il-2mH; *Unteroffizier* Henschel two Il-2mHs; *Leutnant* Krakowitzer one Il-2mH; *Leutnant* Brünnler one Yak-7; *Oberleutnant* Weber two Yak-7s, one Boston, two Il-2mHs; *Flieger* Mehling one Lagg-5, one Il-2mH; *Feldwebel* Zoufahl one Il-2mH. Losses: Fw 190 of *Unteroffizier* Henschel damaged in action against large Boston – Il-2mH – fighter formation on 22 February; *Flieger* Mehling had a fuel-related accident on 24 February; after shooting down two fighters in an action on 23 February, *Feldwebel* Dittlmann failed to return, after his wingman had returned early after a 35-minute flight.

Einsatzort Orsha-Süd; 7–21 March: Nine Fw 190s had actually taken off for the transfer flight from Bobruisk to Orsha on 5 March but had to return due to bad weather; they actually transferred on 7 March. 14 operations were flown from Orsha (encompassing 64 sorties): five free chases; three Ju 87 escorts; one Hs 126 escort; two scrambles, one followed by a free chase; one weather reconnaissance; on 19 March there was a new type of operation – two fighter-bomber low-level attacks against partisans – on the first all bombs landed in a village and 15–20 houses caught fire, and thereafter a column was strafed; on the second, a village was bombed and 10–15 houses set on fire. Fw 190 formation sizes varied between two and 10 aircraft, but mainly operated in *Schwarms*;

eight and 10 aircraft used in the two fighter-bomber attacks. Met Russian fighters (respectively two and six of them) twice in the 14 operations. On the second contact, against six Yak-7s on 10 March, a Yak-7 was claimed shot down by *Leutnant* Krakowitzer, and two more were seen to collide during the action and were not credited to any particular pilot in the *Kladde*. Interestingly, in Tony Wood's victory claims lists[31] they are given to *Oberleutnant* Weber, the *Staffelkapitän*. No losses during this period.

Einsatzort Baranowitschi; 22 March–21 April: On 20 March 11 Fw 190s transferred from Orsha to Bobruisk and on 21 March eight of them went on to Baranowitschi; also on 21 March, four more flew from Orsha to Bobruisk, and two of these plus two new aircraft went on to Baranowitschi later the same day – total strength at Baranowitschi on 21 March thus amounted to 12 Fw 190s. A total of 63 operations was flown (totalling 406 sorties) – a much more intense period of operations than any time before in the entire *Kladde* record: one sector reconnaissance operation; nine Ju 87 escorts and five more *Erweiterte Stukaschutz* (meaning less direct Stuka escort); one weather reconnaissance; five free chases; four escorts to He 111 bombers; 27 fighter-bomber missions with nine more combined with Stuka protection, one more combined with a weather reconnaissance and one more combined with He 111 protection.

On one of the fighter-bomber (*Jabo*) missions combined with Stuka protection, the Fw 190's bombs had to be jettisoned when seven Yak-7s were met. The fighter-bomber operations were mainly against field positions, roads, bridges, guns, vehicles, sledges, troop columns etc., with two attacks on an airfield (Widnica?) on 15 April. In the second of these attacks, *Feldwebel* Meindl scored a direct hit with his bomb between parked aircraft. Combination of *Jabo-Einsatz* operations with other tasks like bomber escort shows a critical shortage of aircraft, pilots and fuel. Fittingly, on 7 April 1944, *Staffelkapitän* Weber claimed the 700th *Abschuss* of the *Staffel*, just after midday. Fw 190 formation size varied between two and 10 aircraft and many more missions were now flown with eight or 10 aircraft, especially the fighter-bomber missions. Russian aircraft were only met on 13 of the 63 operations, mainly just fighters, but also unescorted (twice) and escorted (once) Il-2mH formations were engaged. Notable missions follow.

On 1 April *Hauptmann* Weber (recently promoted) led off a large group of eight Fw 190s and was fortunate to encounter 15 unescorted Il-2mHs at 200 m. The German fighters, who broke away from their He 111 escort assignment, climbed in and in only five minutes eight bombers were claimed shot down (Weber two, his wingman one, leaders of *Rotten* two and three claimed one each, with two falling to the leader of *Rotte* four and one to his wingman), all at very low level. All four *Rotten* took part in this massacre and it seems likely that this time caution was thrown to the wind, with little attention paid to top cover and the possibility of attack from altitude by Russian fighters; perhaps a surfeit of confidence, a dangerous tendency. But in poor weather with the enemy unescorted and at low level, the danger might have been much lower than normal.

On 3 April *Hauptmann* Weber led six aircraft which intercepted a formation of 15 Il-2mHs escorted by 10 fighters; the bombers were very low at 100-odd metres with the escorting fighters at about 1,500 m, too high to do much in time. A very well-coordinated attack on the bombers (by the lead *Rotte*; Weber shot down two Il-2mHs within two minutes at ground level) and on the escort (by the third *Rotte*; leader got one Yak-7 within the same two minutes) was made, while leaving the second pair up as high cover. This marks a return to the careful and calculating tactics normally employed by this leader and most German fighter units in the East from about 1943 onwards, once they had totally lost the initiative.

On 5 April *Hauptmann* Weber led six of his aircraft in an encounter with 10 Yak-7s. The *Staffelkapitän* made the first attack and shot down a Yak at 800 m. 20 minutes later, having kept the Yak formation under close view all that time, the next bounce was by the lead and second *Rotten*, the two leaders shooting down two more Yaks within three minutes, at 2,000 m and 1,300 m respectively. Finally, after seven more minutes of following these hapless Russian fighters, it was the turn of the third pair to have a go and their leader got a fourth Yak-7 at 2,000 m.

On 12 April *Hauptmann* Weber led a maximum strength *Staffel* of ten Fw 190s who found four Yak-7s, and Weber let the third and fourth *Rotten* make the attacks, and within five minutes the leader of *Rotte* three dispatched one Yak and his colleague from the fourth *Rotte* claimed two, at altitudes varying from 1,000 m to 2,000 m. It would seem likely that the Yaks were flying in two pairs, one providing top cover to the lower. 23 victories were claimed in total while flying from Baranowitschi, with two more *wirksam beschossen*. *Feldwebel* Zoufahl also claimed a Yak-9 *ohne Zeuge* (oZ – unwitnessed) and this was not credited as a victory in the *Kladde* nor recorded at all in Tony Wood's lists.[32] Victories: *Oberleutnant* Weber five Il-2mHs, three Yak-7s, one Lagg-3; *Feldwebel* Meindl one R-5, two Il-2mHs, one Yak-7; *Unteroffizier* Klötzer one R-5, one Il-2mH; *Flieger* Mehling one Il-2mH; *Oberfeldwebel* Büssert one Il-2mH, two Yak-7s; *Feldwebel* Zoufahl one Il-2mH, one Yak-7, one Yak 9 oZ (didn't count!); *Leutnant* Krakowitzer two Yak-7s. Losses: on 3 April *Leutnant* Ultsch force-landed after an action against an escorted Il-2mH formation; on 8 April *Feldwebel* Heidmann crash-landed following an early return with a mechanical problem. The last operation from Baranowitschi was flown on 18 April 1944 and then no more missions followed for the next two days.

After this, the 7th *Staffel* of *JG 51* was transferred to Deblin–Irena in eastern Poland to convert from the Fw 190 (in chronic short supply) to the Me 109.

Deblin–Irena; conversion onto Me 109 – 25 April–15 May: At least 14 pilots took part in this conversion training.

Einsatzort Fernbigel; 16 May–2 June: 7/JG 51 transferred in on 15 May 1944. They did not fly many operations from here – apart from some sector reconnaissances, only a few scrambles, free chases, one escort for a Fi 156 and one for 16 *Jabo* Fw 190s – there were no contacts with Russian aircraft and no combats, victories or losses. On 2 June they were transferred back to Germany, to reconvert back onto the Fw 190.

A brief graphical summary of some operational parameters is provided in illustration 40. This gives, per month and for the period 13 September 1943 to 18 April 1944, the number of sorties flown by 7/JG 51, the number of Russian aircraft met on missions, and the claim rate (i.e. the percentage of Russian aircraft met which were claimed as victories). While there is a general trend of increasing monthly sorties (exception for October 1943) and claims made (exception for November 1943) over the period covered by the *Kladde*, the number of Russian aircraft met (only where these numbers were in fact recorded) is more variable. It is doubtful if the latter is any reflection either of Russian sorties or operational intensity, a point even more valid bearing in mind that data are not complete in the *Kladde*.

The table below provides fuller statistics for the operations flown by 7/JG 51, grouped on a monthly basis. As can be seen, the most common missions encompassed escorting Ju 87s, followed by free chase missions, and then in third place by some distance came ground attack operations. These *Jabo-Einsätze* only began in the last two months, being mainly in April 1944. Early returns of Fw 190s from operations due to technical faults increased as the ground attack missions came in. Surprisingly, victories claimed did not decrease to any marked degree once *Jabo* missions began; however, *Feindberührung* (enemy contact) per operation did decrease significantly as did losses to the *Staffel*. This underlines the suitability of the rugged Fw 190s with their air-cooled engines for these ground attack missions, and the difficulty the VVS had in intercepting fast low-level attacks on ground targets relatively near the front lines. 7/JG 51 met the enemy in the air 118 times on 292 operations that is on about four operations out of every 10; in March and April 1944 enemy contacts decreased markedly. In contrast, from about December 1943 onwards, the number of victories claimed per *Feindberührung* showed an overall (though not directly linear) increase.

Monthly operational statistics for 7/ JG 51 for period 13 September 1943–18 April 1944, Central Eastern Front; taken from data in the *Startkladde* for this unit (record of all flights made by individual pilots of the *Staffel*)

Statistic or type of operation	Sept.	Oct.	Nov.	Dec. 1943	Jan. 1944	Feb.	March	April	Total
Begleitschutz Ju 87	7.5	24.33	5	8.5	10	22	15	7	99.33
Begleitschutz He 111	1.5	4.33	1.5		1		1	3	12.33
Begleitschutz Ju 88	1	6.33	1.5	0.5					9.33
Begleitschutz Fw 189	4	2				1			7
Begleitschutz Hs 126	1	1					1		3
Other *Begleitschutz* operations		2				1*			3
Weather reconnaissance	1	6	1	7	4	4	3		26
Freie Jagd operation	8	16	8	11	12	6	9	3	73
Alarmstart	6	1	1	3	1	1	2		15
Jabo-Einsatz		1					2	35	38
Unexpected *Feindberührung* – on *Überführung* (U), *Werkstattflug* (W)		2(U)		1(W)					3
Non-specific operation		1	1				1		3
Feindberührung (Fdbr.)	14	29	12	11	16	20	7	9	118

Early return from operation	5	9	7	10	7	4	17	16	75
Victories claimed	11	22 (+1 BL)	11	10 (+ 1 oZ)	18	31	6 (+1 oZ)	20	129 (+1 BL, 2 oZ)
Losses experienced	1 f-l 2 cr-l	1 PM	1PM		2PM 1 cr-l	1PM 2 f-l 1 cr-l 1 acc 1 dam		1 f-l 1 cr-l	5 PM 4 f-l 5 cr-l 1 dam 1 acc
Total operations per month	30	67	19	31	28	35	34	48	292
Monthly Fdbr. per operation (%)	46.6	43.3	63.2	35.5	57.1	57.1	20.6	18.75	40.4
Monthly victories per Fdbr.	0.86	0.79	0.92	1.00	1.125	1.55	1.00	2.22	1.13

Notes: Only from 13 September for September 1943; only till 18 April for April 1944. Fractions for *Begleitschutz* (escort) operations refer to escorting more than one aircraft type (if it's two types, each fraction is a half, etc.). BL = forced to belly-land; oZ = *ohne Zeuge* – unwitnessed victory claim; PM = pilot missing (aircraft then also a total loss); f-l = forced-landing away from base; cr-l = crash-landing at base; acc = accident at base; dam = aircraft damaged in action. *Freie Jagd* = free chase; *Jabo-Einsatz* = ground attack mission. *Begleitschutz* operations for both Hs 126 and Fw 189 each time was only a single aircraft escorted. * = escort of three Fi 156s.

Fw 190 Aircraft Available, Per Month
From the *Startkladde* the number of individual aircraft flying active operations is recorded, here a monthly time interval is used (or part thereof for September 1943 and April 1944). Aircraft numbers used went from White 1 through to White 14, but White 3 was never used (probably due to some association with a previous loss, airmen being noticeably superstitious); after the loss of noted and successful pilot *Oberfeldwebel* Dittlmann on 5 January 1944, who was flying White 7, this number was also not used again, and White 13 and 14 were added to the White 1–12 numbers already in use. Another number used was White 0 (the favourite mount of *Staffelkapitän* Weber from October 1943 onwards; however he also used many other individual aircraft on occasion and others sometime flew 'his' aircraft – such were the dictates of a chronic shortage of Fw 190s in the *Luftwaffe*). Also used were: Black 7, 5, 10 and Green 9 – these were numbers used only for a few days or missions and reflect replacement (and not new!) aircraft supplied with their existing unit numbers. Other such replacements carried:

< (Adjutant, *I Gruppe*); <o (*Technischer Offizier, I Gruppe*); <~ (Adjutant, *III Gruppe*); < l (Adjutant, *III Gruppe*) – these all reflect replacement aircraft passed down to 7th *Staffel* from *I* and *III/JG 51 Gruppenstab* formations.

Over the relevant monthly periods, the number of available and serviceable aircraft used in operations totalled the following:

September 1943: 12
October 1943: 17 (five replacement aircraft received and one aircraft missing)
November 1943: 13
December 1943: 12 (one replacement received)
January 1944: 12 (one aircraft missing and one shot down)
February 1944: 12 (two replacements received) (one aircraft turned over on landing and replaced with one of the same number, namely White 11; one aircraft missing)
March 1944: 16 (five replacements received)
April 1944: 16 (one replacement received)

From these figures it is clear that aircraft establishment was considered to be about 12 Fw 190s during the period and maximum serviceable strength as demonstrated by the log of missions never exceeded 10 aircraft. Obviously, if 15 aircraft were on hand and also all used over a month, this does not imply all 15 were serviceable each day.

Feindberührung: The Chosen Tactics

7/JG 51 met their Russian enemy (*Feindberührung*) 118 times on the operations they flew in the 13 September 1943–18 April 1944 period. They made no claims against these enemy aircraft on fully one-third of these missions with contact, which suggests no attacks were made or only unsuccessful ones. It is far more likely that on these 'unsuccessful' missions no attacks were made, as with *Luftwaffe* fighter doctrine on the Eastern Front it was imperative to preserve their own forces while causing maximum damage to the enemy. They could not afford a war of attrition against their much more numerous opponents, and in the German view of aerial warfare, chasing victories was a central theme (and sometimes an obsession). The German air force also never had enough fuel to waste large amounts of it on operations where successes were few and where they did not enjoy advantage.

Another aspect of *Luftwaffe* fighter operations on the Eastern Front was the high quality of signals intelligence, as can be seen from extensive documentation from post-war interrogations: there are nine volumes making up a large document entitled *European Axis signal intelligence in World War II as revealed by 'TICOM' investigations and by other prisoner of war interrogations and captured material, principally German*, published originally by the Army Security Agency, Washington D.C. and now available from the National Security Agency website.[33] German signals intelligence on the Eastern Front was highly successful, providing tactically useful information for almost the entire duration of the conflict.

Russian radio discipline at the lower levels was poor and application of security measures often neglected. Due to a shortage of land lines, radios were also used almost as telephones. About 85 per cent of Russian enciphered Morse traffic was readable; combined with intercepts of messages in clear (i.e. radio-telephony or R/T – plane-to-plane communications), traffic analysis and direction-finding, it was possible to provide timely warnings to German flak and fighter forces of impending Russian operations, especially by the long-range bomber forces, but also by fighters and fighter-bombers. This information was speedily passed to German fighter units as some of the signals intelligence units were actually stationed on their fighter airfields. German fighter units could thus be launched with knowledge of what forces to expect, and where to find them; often, they would even know numbers, height and composition in terms of aircraft types.

With some experience the signals personnel also rapidly became *au fait* with the Russian air force battle order, where units were stationed, who their leaders were, etc., and this information was also often provided to the defending German fighters in time for an intercept.[34] Optimum use could thus be made of limited German fighter resources.

This intelligence information combined with small *Luftwaffe* fighter resources and the almost inevitable resulting tactics all helped to support and even stimulate the scoring of relatively easy victories, and made talented German pilots into major aces. However, this does not imply that the Russians had inferior aircraft or pilots; they won the strategic battles and the war, while the German fighter pilots won many of the tactical combats and the more able built their scores, some to very high levels, as is well known. A very similar situation pertained also in the Western Desert aerial fighting, against the RAF and later the US air forces as well; analogous tactics were used by the *Jagdflieger*, their scores were much higher for the best pilots, but once again tactical success was at the price of strategic failure. Allied bombers were not targeted, but fighters and fighter-bombers were.

The dominant tactic thus remained the surprise attack from altitude, the classic 'bounce', opening devastating fire from close range and just below and behind their unsuspecting enemies following a dive from superior altitude. The German fighter aircraft were heavier than those of the Russians, with better higher-altitude performance, while their opponent's fighters (Yak-1, Yak-7, Yak-9, Lagg-5/La-5) were much more manoeuvrable, faster and climbed better at mid- to low altitudes. By diving down, the German pilots were very safe, and by zooming up to superior altitude immediately after a brief attack, still benefitting from the power dive velocity, they would easily out-climb their lower-flying opponents. Always, their dogma dictated leaving some of their aircraft at higher altitude as top cover, with attacking elements being in pairs. The wingman's job was exclusively to warn his leader and to protect him from danger during the attack, when the leader's full attention could be focused on hitting his target in the briefest of firing passes. This tactic favoured the *Rotte* leader in scoring victories, and mostly the first attack was made by the formation leader who thus enjoyed a distinct advantage in raising his score.

High scores and promotion to *Staffelkapitän* are an intrinsic symbiosis in the records of the majority of the German *Experten*. However, this did not necessarily imply the *Rotte* and *Staffel* leaders always dominating the opportunities to score victories; this was particularly the case for *7/JG 51* where *Staffelkapitän* Weber insisted that opportunities for scoring came to all (his own wingman Mehling being a good example): during the period covered by the *Kladde* fifty two percent of victories went to the formation leader and forty eight percent to other pilots making up the formation. The entire tactic rested also on discipline and control and obviously in keeping a cool head and exercising patience. German formations were typically only one or, less often, two *Schwarms* strong, and these tended to stay together under control of the leader throughout a mission and then to land back together afterwards. The wild dogfight with all pilots getting stuck into an enemy formation in an aggressive way was distinctly frowned upon in the *Luftwaffe* but emotions still commonly ran away with young pilots and particularly when the less experienced and also when NCOs led the small formations. This was also when the casualties were likely to occur to the Germans.

The statistics for 7th *Staffel* aircraft landing with the aircraft still together in formation after missions where combat was experienced make for very interesting reading. Summarising all their missions where claims were made against the enemy, 189 sorties landed back at base still in their full formation strength as they had taken off (the few early returns due to mechanical problems are not counted). Against this, sorties totalling 143 were characterised by original formations landing back no longer still together; however fully 95 of these 143 sorties had maintained smaller formations till landing. No other fighter arm during the war could have made similar claims and this remarkable method of fighting illustrates the discipline and systematic approach to air combat the German fighter unit leaders were able to maintain over an active battle front where the enemy greatly outnumbered them. And they maintained it over the weeks, months and even years that their careers lasted. In this way also, combat stress was lessened as the risks were greatly reduced, the chances of scoring victories were greatly enhanced, and many pilots with a burning case of *Halschmerzen* ('throat ache' – i.e. for the *Ritterkreuz*, which was worn around the neck) could keep going for incredible lengths of time. They also caused heavy losses to their opponents.

However – and this is a big contrast – the German fighter arm thus never really made serious attempts to win air superiority, even locally and for short periods of time, except for major battles such as at Kursk in July 1943; the Russians kept coming, kept hitting their ground targets, and were never seriously impaired in operating over the front and with losses which remained bearable for their much larger numbers. This apparent blind spot in *Jagdwaffe* strategy typified the later years over Russia (from about 1943 onwards) and also operations over the comparable active battlefront in the Western Desert in 1941–42, where the German fighters were outnumbered but flew aircraft generally superior to those they met.

The huge scores thus run up by the exceptionally able among the German fighter pilots in the East and to a lesser extent over Africa were not a war-winning strategy. The German tactic also favoured picking off lone or vulnerable aircraft at the fringes of a formation and enemy bomber formations with massed return-fire potential were generally avoided in favour of surprise attacks on fighters (see table of victory claims below: 37.5 per cent of claims against bomber types). In the East, the favoured German attack method and its resultant high scores underlined the assumed superiority of the German airman to his inferred Slavic racial inferior, and this Nazi-inspired doctrine was thus supported and reinforced as time went by, and must have played some role in ensuring high over-claim rates also, as more optimistic claims were easily assimilated by a mind already distinctly prejudiced against a supposedly inferior opponent. The German propaganda machine could easily make much of the apparent superiority of their ace pilots, man-to-man, over their enemies, and when you are outnumbered and suffering almost constant retreats, this is a message which is well received by the ordinary German fighting man.

Chances of meeting enemy aircraft can be related to operation type: when escorting bombers, Ju 87s or on a *Freie Jagd* (which together accounted for two thirds of all missions flown), the enemy was met on about one operation out of two; this dropped to one out of two and a half for emergency scrambles (*Alarmstart*), and was much lower for all other mission types.

Victories claimed 13 September 1943–18 April 1944; Russian aircraft types

Aircraft type	No. of confirmed claims	% of all claims	No. of claims for damaged aircraft	% of all such claims
Yak-5*	1	1%	0	0%
Yak-9	10 (+1 oZ)	8%	1	4.5%
Lagg-5	22	17%	9	41%
Yak-7	41 (+1 oZ, 2 coll)	32%	5	23%
Il-2mH	38 (+1 forced to crash-land)	30%	4	18%
DB-3	1	1%	0	0%
Mig-3	2	1.5%	2	9%
R-5	2	1.5%	0	0%
P-40	1	1%	0	0%
Yak-4	1	1%	0	0%
Lagg-3	2	1.5%	0	0%
Boston	4	3%	1	4.5%
Pe-2	2	1.5%	0	0%
Totals	127 (+5)		22	

* No such aircraft; probably a Lagg-5. oZ = '*ohne Zeuge*' – i.e. unwitnessed claim, not accepted. Coll = collided. The Il-2mH forced to crash-land also did not count as a victory in the German system as the aircraft was not destroyed and was likely easily repairable.

7/JG 51 was the most successful of the three *Staffeln* making up III/JG 51 during the period covered by the *Kladde*; 8/JG 51 claimed 96 victories and 9/JG 51 a total of 56 (and one probable) (data from Tony Wood's lists of *Luftwaffe* claims).[35] When the victories claimed by 7/JG 51 against the main Russian aircraft types are compared to the altitude at which the claims were made, some very interesting patterns emerge. These are shown in a graph in illustration 41. This chart shows clearly that the Il-2s operated essentially from 800 m and below, escorted at medium level by Yak-7s, with high cover given by Yak-9s (and occasionally by Yak-7s). The Lagg-5s (actually La-5s, the designation of Lagg-5 in the *Kladde* being an error) operated at all altitudes thereby demonstrating their versatility. Lower altitudes shown for Yak-7 claims probably reflect their descending to protect Il-2s under attack and then being attacked in turn by diving German fighters from above.

When attacked, the Il-2s would have dived down to low levels to protect their vulnerable oil coolers from fighter attack from below. The chart shows very clearly that the great majority of attacks and successes were achieved by the German fighters at altitudes of about 2,000 m and less, with little action above that and then only to a maximum height of about 5,000 m. The aerial war in the East was thus largely a lower-altitude one; this is in direct contrast to the Western theatres where high altitude combat was the norm but is similar to combat over the Western Desert in 1941–42. The freedom of action conferred on the German fighters by their high altitude performance in this combat scenario is very clear; they could thus choose when and where to fight and tactically, at least, held the initiative.

Individual Scores of Pilots
Of the 127 victory claims (excluding the five: two oZ, collided pair and one force-landed machine; table above) made by the entire *Staffel* over the period covered by the *Kladde*, the *Staffelkapitän* was responsible for 28.35 per cent and the top five pilots for a massive 71.5 per cent of all claims (see also illustration 42). This is typical for the *Jagdwaffe* on the Eastern Front overall (and for North Africa also), and is really in many ways the natural result of the chosen tactics (bounce with risks kept to the minimum; avoid messy dogfights; no real attempt made to achieve air superiority) once the Russians could no longer be beaten. Some individuals, those with experience or rare talents, did very well at this tactic and could keep it up for very long periods without undue stress. However, it was a strategic disaster and air superiority remained firmly in Russian hands and they were able to keep up their ground attack and bombing missions, with significant casualties only to their fighter units (cheapest to replace in terms of cost and crew numbers). It should also be pointed out that the pattern of a few aces making the vast majority of victory claims applies to all air forces and theatres, in the Second World War and other conflicts also. The most common victory claims were scored against Russian Jak-7s, Il-2s and Lagg-5s (see also illustration 42; table below).

Victory claims of all pilots flying missions with 7/JG 51, 13 September 1943–18 April 1944, Eastern Front, against aircraft type claimed

Name	Yak-7	Yak-9	Lagg-5	Il-2mH	Mig-3	Pe-2	Lagg-3	Other	Total
Hauptmann Karl-Heinz Weber	11	5	3	11			1	5a	36
Leutnant Günther Schack	6		4	2				1b	13
Leutnant Heinz Kattlün	3	1	2		1				7
Unteroffizier Martin Gläser			1						1
Unteroffizier Kurt Graf				1				3c	4
Feldwebel Franz Meindl	1		5	3				2d	11
Oberfeldwebel Heinrich Dittlmann	7	2		8	1		1		19
Leutnant Friedrich Krakowitzer	7	1	1	3					12 + 1 BL
Flieger Armin Mehling	1		3	2					6
Leutnant Johann Brünnler	1								1
Unteroffizier Walter Klötzer				1				1e	2
Oberfeldwebel Joachim Bussert	2			1					3
Leutnant Busse									0
Fahnenjunker Feldwebel Herbert Riegel									0
Unteroffizier Hans Hermann			1						1
Unteroffizier Günther Henschel				2					2
Feldwebel Helmuth Heidemann									0

Feldwebel Kurt Kästner	2					0 + 1 oZ
Unteroffizier Georg Orth						0
Feldwebel Paul Hollmann						0
Feldwebel Schmidt						0
Feldwebel Franz-Josef Zoufahl	2	1	2	4		9 + 1 oZ
Oberfeldwebel Alexander Slomski						0
Leutnant Ultsch						0
Unteroffizier Johann Klupp						0
Staffel (excluded from total)	2					2

Total:127 (+ two oZ, two collided, and one belly-landed)

Notes: oZ = 'ohne Zeuge' i.e. unwitnessed victory claim (counted as a probable only); BL = belly-landed but not destroyed enemy aircraft (also not counted as a victory). The two victories counted for the *Staffel* collided with each other during air combat. Other claims: a = one Yak-4, three Bostons, one P-40; b = one Yak-5 (Lagg-5?); c = one DB-3 and two Pe-2s; d = one Boston, one R-5; e = one R-5.

Illustration 43 shows very clearly that most fighter pilots made claims against Russian fighters; the average for *7/JG 51* for the entire *Kladde* period was 61.4 per cent of claims being made against Russian fighter types; the balance were mainly Il-2mHs and bombers. Only a few individuals concentrated on shooting down Il-2mHs and bombers: Meindl, Graf and, to a lesser extent, Weber.

The Later History of the 7/JG 51 Pilots

The fates of the pilots who flew the missions summarised in the *Kladde* were variable but seldom happy. *Hauptmann* Karl-Heinz Weber led *7/JG 51* from the East on their transfer to the Western theatre of operations, arriving at Paderborn on 3 June 1944.[36] The same day he was appointed to lead *III/JG 1*, with *Leutnant* Friedrich Krakowitzer taking over the *Staffel*. On the evening of 6 June 'Benjamin' Weber led his new *Gruppe* to their predetermined base in France to counter the Normandy Invasion, Beauvais-Tillé.[37] The very next day, on his first operation, Weber led *III/JG 1* into a fight with about 30 P-51s south of Rouen from which he did not return; he has no known grave.[38] His victory total still stood at the 136 Eastern successes achieved with *7/JG 51*. The same day, *Leutnant* Heinz Kattlün (12 eastern victories with *7/JG 51*), by then flying with *5/JG 11*, was killed at almost the same time in a combat with P-47s north of Caen.[39] Another 7th *Staffel* pilot (flying with *7/JG 51*, now assigned to operate under the command of *II/JG 1*) was lost that day when, on a transfer flight to Le Mans and shortly before landing, they were surprised by the appearance of a P-51 formation at low level; they formed a protective circle successfully, but *Leutnant* Johann Brünnler (two Russian front victories to his name) broke away and was immediately shot down and killed over Chateaudun.[40]

Ten days later another two old *7/JG 51* Russian hands were killed on a transfer flight from Le Mans to Essay, again surprised by Mustangs: *Unteroffizier* Günther Henschel (three Russian victories) and *Feldwebel* Helmuth Heidemann (whose mechanic died with him, being squeezed into the rear fuselage for the short transfer flight).[41] Heidemann appears never to have achieved a confirmed victory with *7/JG 51*. The 7th *Staffel* of *JG 51* was incorporated into *III/JG 1* as its 8th *Staffel* on 10 July 1944; *Staffelführer* Krakowitzer had already died in a combat over Saint-Lô on 4 July.[42] *Unteroffizier* Hans Hermann (one eastern victory to his name), ex-*7/JG 51* and now with *8/JG 1*, went missing over Mortain on 7 August 1944.[43]

Other ex-members of *7/JG 51* managed to survive longer before succumbing to the overwhelming superiority of the Allied air forces. *Feldwebel* Franz Meindl, a Tirolean, one of the senior NCO mainstays of

7/JG 51 (in the *Kladde* period and before), was promoted to *Oberfeldwebel* and awarded the German Cross in Gold; after a stint as an instructor in *Jagdergänzungsgruppe Ost* (during which he shot down a four-engined bomber), he joined II/JG 11 in the West in July 1944 after their withdrawal from the Invasion front.[44] He flew in the operations against the Arnhem air landings in September 1944 (shot down two fighters) and thereafter over Germany (one final victory, his 32nd, in December).[45] On 1 January 1945, in operation *Bodenplatte* (mass attack on Allied airfields in Belgium and Holland), flying with 8/JG 11, he was posted as missing in the Asch region after contact with American fighters.[46] Another dependable and experienced NCO, *Feldwebel* Franz-Josef Zoufahl (*Deutsches Kreuz in Gold*), remaining behind on the Eastern Front (in 8/JG 51) after 7th *Staffel* departed for the West, was killed on 24 July in a forced-landing after combat in the Kauen area, his score by then at 26 victories, all in the East with III/JG 51.[47] *Unteroffizier* Walter Klötzer, after bringing his eastern successes with 7/JG 51 to five, joined 2/JG 27 in the West and added one more victory before being killed in action on 5 April 1945.[48]

Only four of the 7/JG 51 pilots featuring in the *Startkladde* survived the war: Günther Schack, Martin Gläser, Armin Mehling and Joachim Bussert.[49] Gläser ended the war with at least 12 victories to his name (10 in 7/JG 51), two of them scored with I/JG 27 late in the war.[50] Armin Mehling, *Staffelkapitän* Weber's favourite wingman, who held the demeaning rank of *Flieger* and who shot down six Russian aircraft in the period covered by the *Kladde*, finally made it to *Unteroffizier*, and added at least three more Russian aircraft to his achievements, all on 23 March 1945 while flying with Stab/JG 11.[51] Bussert continued flying on the Eastern Front after 7th *Staffel* left, ending the war with a total of 14 victories, all with III/JG 51.[52]

A Personal Account of Flying With 7/JG 51: Günther Schack's Diary
Günther Schack was the most famous pilot to feature in the *Startkladde* of 7/JG 51, although he would have been the first to decry any such status and, indeed, all hero worship of the glamorous fighter pilots. Having begun his war with JG 51 in Mölders' time before the invasion of Russia in June 1941 as a *Gefreiter*, he stayed with his *Geschwader* and rose to become a *Hauptmann* and *Gruppenkommandeur* successively of I/JG 51, still on the Eastern Front in December 1944, and finally of IV/JG 3 a few days before the war ended.[53] He was highly decorated with the *Eichenlaub* (Oak Leaves to the Knights Cross) for his many victories in the East, where the majority of his successes came while flying the Fw 190 (100 sorties with 92 victories, out of totals of 800 *Feindflüge* and 174 claimed successes). During the war on the Russian Front he kept a diary

which he typed up and edited into a shorter document after the war; he was kind enough to provide me with some excerpts in September 1989,[54] and luckily these included some on his time with *7/JG 51* and overlapping with the period of the *Startkladde*. His relevant diary entry begins with the transfer of *7/JG 51* on 12 September 1943, the day before the *Kladde* record begins.

Three days later (12 September) we transferred to Poniatowka west of Roslawl. We could no longer settle down anywhere. Scarcely had we been able to settle in and make ourselves comfortable to at least some extent, than the Russians pushed us further to the west.

15 September: Again we found ourselves in Smolensk. In the evening the 7,000th victory of our *Geschwader* was celebrated at the *Geschwaderstab* in a light-hearted circle. I was the only *Leutnant* amongst all the stars and braid.

On the 19 September it became rather dangerous in Smolensk. We moved back to Mogilev, where we were finally reunited with our entire *Staffel*. After a long time we could again make ourselves reasonably comfortable, and especially with our vehicles being present we could continue with forward operations from Smolensk. Everything was in uproar in this former metropole of the Eastern Front. Everywhere demolitions were being prepared. How often did we not experience that the Russians did not let themselves be hindered by an airfield sown with bomb craters. It is simply astounding what a master the Russian is of improvisation.

20 September: We could still operate by day from Smolensk but the Russians were soon so close to the city that we could not risk leaving the aircraft there overnight. In the afternoon the commanding general (of the *Luftflotte*) Greim appeared at our headquarters. For half an hour he tried to make the serious situation appear as rosy as possible to us. He was already in the doorway ready to leave when the *Kommodore*, *Oberstleutnant* Nordmann, told him that I had today shot down my 109th victory and had still not received the *Ritterkreuz*. Greim congratulated me and immediately had an appropriate priority signal sent to Berlin about this. But as it still took longer without anything happening, Nordmann tried other means. Nordmann complained that he had eight recommendations for the *Ritterkreuz* currently submitted, three of these pilots had been killed in the meantime. The requirements for the *Ritterkreuz* had in the meantime been set higher again for the fighter pilots at between 75 and 100 victories. As I recall this was already the third time I had been recommended for this decoration. In the afternoon, I was overjoyed to see Ekart Schroeter (an old friend) standing in front of me. I quickly found something to drink and we discussed all sorts of things including his just having become a father.

Then we had to take off at short notice. I brought home two victories, and on reporting my new score, the answers from my uncomprehending *Schwarm*'s pilots one after the other gave the remaining litres of fuel they still had, but "Hannibal" (generally a euphemism for ground control at base) said: 'Victor (I have understood) one, one, one, (111), congratulations!' In full view of my old friend from Elbing, I was able once again to enjoy waggling my wings in victory.

25 September: We retreat some more. The *Geschwader* now sits in Orscha, we are still in Mogilev. In the late morning I was supposed to support a pilot at a court martial. A *Leutnant* of our *Geschwader* was charged with shooting down a friendly aircraft. As the weather was poor, I had to use the car for the journey. On the way we had a puncture, so that the case was almost finished when we got there. The *Leutnant* was found not guilty. Shooting at friendly aircraft in air combat will always happen, one cannot eliminate it through legal proceedings. There were really more important things to do.

On the return journey the car began to skid when overtaking a convoy and turned over at a high speed. Fortunately I was able to keep it on the road. Somehow I clambered out of the vehicle and saw my driving companion lying unconscious on the road. He was blue in the face and motionless, and I got a huge fright. However, then he eventually gave a big sigh; he had a light head wound and difficulty breathing. I let him be taken immediately to the field hospital in Mogilev in a lorry. The beautiful V-8 was so demolished that it had to be towed away. The accident only made its effects noticeable to me later, when lying in bed that night when suddenly all my limbs began to ache. Next day I could only drag myself crookedly around. Carefully I prepared the Adjutant to inform the *Gruppenkommandeur* about his car.

This recollection, coming from one of the 7/JG 51 veterans who served in that *Staffel* during the early part of the period covered by the *Startkladde*, illustrates very well the itinerant lifestyle that frontline pilots experienced in the later period on the Eastern Front (from after the Kursk battle had been lost in mid-1943). However, morale appears not have been significantly affected at all, and the striving for victories and the concomitant decorations were pursued as before.

It was only experience and a lot of luck that allowed a few pilots to survive – in the case of 7/JG 51 only four out of the 25 pilots who flew in this *Staffel* over the September 1943–April 1944 period covered by the *Kladde* made it through the war alive. The *Staffel*'s 129 victory claims (includes two Russian aircraft that collided during combat) made over a period of just over seven months is not excessive, nor are the top scorers' totals of 36 claims by *Staffelkapitän* Karl-Heinz Weber and the

19 racked up by *Oberfeldwebel* Heinrich Dittlmann. If such rare and gifted individual pilots could stay alive long enough, a significant score could be achieved; for Weber, this was in the end 136 victories claimed over a period of 34 months on the Eastern Front. In the early stages of the campaign, 1941 and much of 1942, with inferior Russian aircraft, often poor tactics and commonly rushed training of their replacement pilots, this is perfectly reasonable. Once Russian aircraft and training began to improve, allied to good tactics, which began from late 1942 (and particularly advanced over the Kuban in the first half of 1943), victories by German *Experten* largely reflected the adopted bounce tactics of these greatly outnumbered fighter pilots from then on.

The *Startkladde* of 7/JG 51 thus provides a detailed operational window into the activities of a single *Staffel* in the East, and also shows how relatively high scores of a few lucky and gifted pilots could be realistically achieved. However, high scores were most definitely not universally achieved – quite the opposite – and the vexed question of the over-claiming of the German fighter pilots over the Eastern Front (something endemic to all aerial combat in all wars and all air forces) will be addressed in the next chapter.

10

The Victory Claims Debate

In terms of victories claimed and 'official' scores since widely recognised (what this means is discussed below), the German *Jagdflieger* are certainly far ahead of anyone else from the Second World War (and any conflict since then, for that matter). While these scores need some clarification and also qualification, as discussed below, they have now assumed an almost unquestionable veracity in many views and publications. However, many others address this issue and conclude otherwise. Of course the latter authors are correct: in fact, everybody in all air forces of the Second World War has been subject to what is termed 'over-claiming'. The term itself implies some sort of dishonesty or deliberate obfuscation, which in most cases is untrue. In the majority of cases claims were made in good faith. But the nature of air combat, even at Second World War aircraft speeds, implicitly carries the seeds of confusion and error.

It is a great truth of air combat that the greater the number of aircraft involved, the higher the amount of over-claiming that normally results. There are many levels and nuances in such debates. By and large, fighter pilots – especially the successful ones – are like race horses; they are highly strung, with hair-trigger reactions. They tend to be aggressive, optimistic and also self-confident if not arrogant in some cases. It is also in human nature, especially in life-threating situations, to see what you want or need to see and for such images to impress themselves on the memory. Quite simply, all fighter pilots are thus susceptible to over-claiming. Data providing, when one investigates a specific pilot's victory claims against known and detailed enemy losses, it will always be found that some claims can be easily confirmed and some easily rejected, while some remain uncertain. Any major ace in any air force from the Second World

War will show such a combat record upon scrutiny. Although the various discussions that follow below are often closely linked to aerial combat, aces and victory claims on the Eastern Front, this is not an exclusive linkage and the topic is addressed generically to include *Jagdflieger* on all fronts also.

The Greatest Aces? A Complex of Documentation, Inferences, Nuances and Reality

For the German fighter pilots, the well-known emphasis on scoring victories as the prime means and measure of successful air war prosecution (and one has to admit that they do have a point, although this also commonly goes along with strategic errors to balance their tactical achievements) went along with the culture of the ace, the *Experte* who stands as a reflection of the German fighting man and his inherent assumed superiority. With decorations essentially given for demonstrated successes in individual combat (and to a much lesser degree, and then only till about the end of 1940, for leading a *Jagdgeschwader* in action), scores and their apparent veracity assumed much greater importance than to most other participating air forces. The graduated set of relevant decorations was correlated directly with specific scores achieved, scaled to specific fighting theatres, and the necessary scores changed over time.

As the war progressed, the required scores tended to rise as accumulated victories by the surviving big aces grew, but they dropped again towards the end of the war as big scorers fell in action or accident and as victories overall became much harder to achieve thanks to the quality and quantity of opponents. The scores and their rewards were major targets for the virulent propaganda machine of Josef Goebbels, and fitted well into the Nazi concept of the German 'superman' who was seen as so much better than the perceived *Untermenschen* met in aircraft especially over the eastern (Slavic) nations, such as Poland or the Soviet Union. The great heroes whose scores surpassed the 100 claims of the first tyro, Werner Mölders, namely Gordon Gollob (first to 150), Hermann Graf (first with 200), Walter Nowotny (first to reach 250) and finally the 'best of all', Erich Hartmann (first to 300, with a final score of 352), were all major propaganda figures and all Nazis of conviction, as already discussed earlier in this volume.

It has often been pointed out that such politically affirmed and politically correct pilots had their victories confirmed sooner than others, and their decorations awarded long before any confirmation process of their claims had taken place. This is essentially not true, as both statements in fact apply to all pilots within a framework of the meaning of 'confirmed victories' (a much misunderstood term).

It is important to realise that any *Luftwaffe* fighter pilot effectively had three scores to his name. First was the total that he himself claimed (1), and which would be his personal score as given in many post-war accounts, and which were also displayed on the tail of his personal fighter aircraft (illustration 45), and mostly also in his personal logbook. Second was his unit score (2), which would comprise all his claims that were officially submitted via his unit to higher authority and eventually the *Reichsluftfahrtministerium* (RLM – Air Ministry) for confirmation – these claims were annotated as *eingereicht* (in other words submitted officially via the unit channels, upwards, with checking at all unit levels from *Staffel*, through *Gruppe* and even *Geschwader* that there was no double-claiming within units, and that all relevant paperwork was submitted); such *eingereichte Abschüsse* were also described as *bestätigt* (a word which can mean 'acknowledged' or even 'confirmed'). This is an unfortunate word as it is often seen to imply early confirmation of the claim, which is not true – it merely really implies that checking at *Geschwader* levels has been successfully carried out and that the claim is submitted to the RLM with the *Geschwader*'s stamp of approval. *Bestätigung* of claims could also take place above the *Geschwaderstab*, at *Jagdfliegerführer*, *Fliegerdivision* or *Luftflotte* level, especially in the Home Defence. Finally there was his confirmed score (3), as reflected in *RLM Anerkennungs* (i.e. official Air Ministry confirmations, with certificate supplied); this process took months, with an average of about four being common. These three 'scores' of an individual pilot were also graded in the sense that (1) > (2) > (3) in almost every case.

The results of such 'scores' (often without distinction of which of the three was used) provides the raw material from which many unit totals (or parts thereof) have been reconstructed in published sources, and obviously immediately sets the scene for confusion and at least a measure of error. What the 'real score' (which is not possible to determine under any circumstances for a long set of victory claims, despite many attempts and inferred comparisons of claim with potential enemy loss) of any pilot might be will always be impossible to establish fully. One can well appreciate that the German focus on a pilot's score did indeed necessitate the complex and strict claim submissions procedure, but this does not mean that the score resulting from that procedure bore any relation to what the real score of any *Jagdflieger* may have been; that real score will always remain an unknown. In addition, trying to establish which famous ace on side A shot down which famous ace from nation B, thereby presumably making ace A better than ace B, is really a pointless exercise as it ignores the reality of the tactical situation before and during the combat, fuel states, mechanical problems, health of the pilots, and many more imponderables, plus also of course the element of luck which so often interposed in war.

It is also critical to realise that the role of the *Staffelkapitän* was of crucial importance in the first steps to official submission and eventual and possible *RLM* confirmation. For all line pilots, it was the *Staffelkapitän* who checked all the documentation was there, provided his own *Stellungnahme* (comment) on the claim/paperwork, who signed off on the *Abschussmeldung* (claim report), and who also signed off on *his own claims* as well. Several examples of such self-signed claims for *Staffelkapitäne* have appeared in published memoirs (one such photograph being in the autobiography of Helmut Lipfert, noted *Experte* from *II/JG 52*).[1] Interestingly, at *Geschwaderstab* level the *Kommodore* did not sign off his own claims, but his 1a (operations officer) did, as clearly stated by *Major* Hanns Trübenbach, leader of *JG 52* in 1940–41.

If one goes to the trouble of examining a large enough sample of aces who became *Staffelkapitäne* (or *Staffelführern* – acting capacity) and how their claims increased markedly thereafter, a trend can be seen in quite a number of cases. Also, some leaders apparently inhibited the progress of their subordinates' claims – for example in the claims of Theo Weissenberger in *JG 5*, where Heinrich Ehrler was his superior, until he was able to sign off on his own behalf; no details are given here as the exercise can easily be performed from widely available electronic data, and of course, despite observed trends, nothing can ever be proven as gospel truth either. The relevant documentation submitted via the unit for possible *RLM* confirmation included the *Abschussmeldung* (a standard form to be filled in, and signed off by the *Staffelkapitän*), the *Luftzeugenbericht* (witness report; not a form), *Stellungnahme* of the *Staffelkapitän* (his comment, also not a form) and finally the *Gefechtsbericht* (also called *Gefechtsmeldung*) which was the combat report of the claiming pilot. Each *Staffel* had a *Staffelschreiber* or clerk who handled much of this paperwork, but even so the time to complete the relevant 'administration' for those highly successful aces who managed multiple victory claims in a day can only be imagined.

Shown in illustrations 46, 47 and 48 respectively are three documents: the *Abschussmeldung*, *Gefechtsbericht* and *Luftzeugenbericht* for *Feldwebel* Georg Hutter of *5/JG 1*, claiming a Spitfire probably shot down on 9 May 1942.[2] The *Abschussmeldung* form is clearly denoted by the typed-in comment added below the form's title, namely '*Wahrscheinlicher Abschuss*', which translates as 'probable victory'. Quite clearly the *Luftwaffe* did allow 'probables', despite what is stated in many sources; in fact, as discussed below, probable claims were much more common than often realised – once again it comes down at least partly to the German language and subtle differences in meanings. The very close correspondence of the last two reports (*Gefechtsbericht* and *Luftzeugenbericht*), and of their language, shows the influence of a clerk writing both reports from details supplied by the participants. This particular claim was sent up by the *Geschwader* as a full victory claim but appears to have been downgraded to probable status by the *Jagdfliegerführer Holland-Ruhr*, whose decision was recorded in the *II/JG 1* war diary.[3] This is not surprising given the visible signs of damage described by the pilot himself and even more so from the witness.

Another claim made in the same action by another pilot, this time from *4/JG 1*, was classified as *nicht bestätigt* (not acknowledged) because its claimant had also not seen his victim hit the ground or sea (this illustrates the influence of the *Staffelkapitän*, with different decisions regarding claim classification of two relatively similar claims by two different leaders, for 4th and 5th *Staffeln*); this claim was also accorded probable status by the *Jafü*.[4] Even better for promoting confusion, the *RLM* may have accepted one of these two *II/JG 1* claims (a designation in surviving archive records 'RL 10/482' may reflect this;[5] this is a typical *Briefbuch* number given to a *RLM*-confirmed victory; *Briefbuch* numbers discussed below in detail), although the claims lists of Tony Wood[6] do not include either of these two claims. Ironically, after all this, one Spitfire was indeed shot down by *II/JG 1* in this action.[7] This example, and study of relevant data and surviving records, indicates that a good deal of caution should be exercised with simple approaches to accepting a pilot's so-called 'score', and also illustrates some of the complexity and therefore also potential for error in the German claims submission system.

Whatever the complexities of the *Luftwaffe*'s claim submission system, it cannot on its own inherently provide a better-constrained evaluation of victory claims, as is often asserted. Any system used by people is subject to human manipulation in certain cases. One only has to think about the role of the *Staffelkapitän* in all this, potentially influencing his subordinates' scores positively or negatively, and also signing off on his own victories. But there can be little doubt that the German aces did obtain higher victory totals during the war than other nations. There are a number of likely reasons why this was so, detailed below.

(1) In the early part of the war a strong *Luftwaffe*, experienced in battle already from the Spanish Civil War (whence stemmed tactical innovations like the *Rotten* and *Schwarm* fighting formations of two and four aircraft), took on a succession of weaker and less well-prepared air forces (Polish, Belgian, Dutch, French, to an extent British also, and then the Russians), and often in brief campaigns without declarations of war.

(2) In many campaigns the *Luftwaffe* was provided with large numbers of enemy aircraft to engage and possibly shoot down – the Eastern Front for almost its entire duration, over North Africa, in the Battle of Germany, and even over France and the British Isles in 1940, over Malta at times, and also in the Italian theatre in 1943–44. The British penchant for keeping Spitfires in the UK and allowing inferior fighters to battle the latest Messerschmitts over the Mediterranean theatres for so long, and the introduction of modern aircraft into the Soviet air force, which took time and many casualties, exacerbated all this. Once their opposing air forces had reorganised, re-equipped and started to fight back effectively against the *Luftwaffe*, German fighter numbers and sortie rates had already begun to decline on many fronts, reflecting also the critical fuel situation. Thus, chances of scoring on the Allied side remained lower than for the *Luftwaffe* for much of the war.

(3) The German obsession with the ace concept and support of major aces who were also promoted to leadership positions based on their scores, while unwise, put them in positions at the head of formations which in many cases provided some order of protection for them at altitude while the ace and his wingman (or a *Schwarm*) made an attack and zoomed back up again to their umbrella. *Halsschmerz* (literally 'throat pain'), the coveting of the *Ritterkreuz* and its higher degrees, was a real phenomenon – these were young men competing with each other, and if the *Schwertern zum Ritterkreuz* (Swords) could be won, there was a post-war estate reserved for them.[8] The obsession with scores is well illustrated by a page of *JG 2*'s *Abschussliste* from 6 to 7 November 1940, where the first three columns show, respectively, running score number for the *Geschwader*, *Gruppe* and *Staffel* for each victory therein.[9]

(4) German fighter pilots tended to serve for the entire war at the front, with only limited leave periods or recuperation interludes when wounded or sick; there was no organised system of duty tours with required rest periods in between as in the RAF or USAAF. This is another of those partial truths with no universal application to all pilots, as discussed further below.

While it is true that quite a number of German fighter pilots did remain at the front for the entire war, including a number of the noted and famous names, this was by no means the case for all. Some examples will illustrate, once more, a more complex reality in this regard. *Oberstleutnant* Günther Scholz began the war in *III/JG 54*, later moving to *JG 5* on the *Eismeerfront*; only with his appointment as *Jafü Norwegen* on 27 July 1944 was he removed from direct aerial combat.[10]

It was especially the more senior pilots in leadership positions who often experienced very long tours of frontline duty, like Scholz. Heinz Bär, a famous Swords winner who flew with *JG 51* and then *JG 77* before leading several *Geschwadern* over Germany, had only two breaks in his service across the entire war: just over two months as an instructor in 1942, and about another four months in 1943 when he was also off sick for some of the time due to combat fatigue – he got little thanks for having thus exhausted himself and was demoted by Göring for some time after this.[11] *Feldwebel* Otto Schmid served for just over a year in *II/JG 1* in the Dutch coastal area and flew 48 *Feindflüge* before being granted a rest for eight months as an instructor. During that period in south-western France he was also involved in a couple of interceptions of four-engined bomber raids, and within a few weeks of returning to *II/JG 1* over Germany was terribly wounded and saw no more combat. *Hauptmann* Rudolf Engleder, also from *JG 1*, served for eight and a half months at the front before being shot down and wounded; hospitalised for two months and then given recuperation leave, he served just over a further eight and a half months as an instructor before his final stint back at the front for about four months till the end of the war.

Often a pilot would put in two to three years of combat operations before being given a break; *Hauptmann* Karl-Friedrich Schlossstein put in 37 months in Me 110s (a less than optimum combat exposure) on the White Sea front, and was then given a nine-month break before his final eight and a half months of operations to the end of the war. *Oberfeldwebel* Richard Raupach flew with *JG 54* in the East from June 1942 till May 1944, and was then an instructor till the end of the war. Generally a pilot joining combat later in the war, from about the beginning of 1943 or later, could expect little relief, except if wounded. This rather tough system had some advantages – many a pilot was lost just after returning from leave or a rest assignment before they could be fully integrated back into operations mode again.

Equally, while long periods on operations would burn some out, this didn't apply to everyone. Someone like Erich Hartmann, the 'ace of aces', served relatively continuously from late 1942 to the end of the war (apart from short leave and recuperation breaks). This kind of pilot probably enjoyed being at the front, and the adrenaline highs of combat became a way of life almost. As discussed with the great ace Hans-Joachim Marseille over the Western Desert (in a follow-up volume, *Alarmstart South to North*),[12] the really superior pilots almost entered a state of ecstasy during operational flights, once they had reached a certain level of expertise. However, in his case, these intense, almost life-dominating periods of combat had to be interspersed with ever-longer intervals of home leave. His superior, *Major* Eduard Neumann, was perceptive enough and a good leader and made sure this happened in his case, but inevitably Marseille burned out and died in an accident. It seems that the rather variable treatment in this regard of the different pilots discussed here, rested to a great degree on their *Kommandeurs* and *Kommodoren* as well as higher officers in touch with their subordinate units, and that this informality and great variation in resting of pilots prevailed in the face of a lack of any formal combat tour system.

The Data Available for Research: Microfilmed Luftwaffe Claims Documents ('Tony Wood Lists')

In many ways this topic is almost a minefield of confusing data, with many gaps therein, a lack of explanation of the precise meaning of terms, and especially of abbreviations contained within the records, and at least some attempts from the German archives and some researchers to confuse the issue even further. A collection of 18 rolls of microfilmed *Luftwaffe* claims documents exists which was available from the German archives for German researchers for quite some time before their existence even became known by the rest of the interested international community. In time, seven of these films became widely available, and later all 18 of them. The relevant history and background information, as well as critical comments to improve any interested person's understanding of these records (published widely on the web as Tony Wood's lists – 'O.K.L. Fighter Claims...' and in various subsequent versions as their accuracy and clarification have improved)[13] is best explored through the discussion board of the website of the *Luftwaffe* Archives and Records Reference Group.[14] The service which Tony Wood rendered to *Luftwaffe* historians by transcribing and publishing freely on the web these huge lists from poor-quality, often handwritten original microfilms is enormous.

Essentially these records, available to the interested researcher, are large but have gaps (e.g., with reference to the Eastern Front the claims data for the first half of 1942 are very sparse). Many were handwritten and are thus often hard to read, and as a whole they appear to have been microfilmed in something of a hurry towards the end of the war. In addition they contain several different sets of records, discussed below.

(1) There is a ledger-type set of records which seems to run till about the end of 1941 (and some into 1942 also) where all claims submitted by a unit were registered as they came in to the *RLM* (*Reichsluftfahrtministerium* – Air Ministry), and then once they had been examined and adjudged within the *RLM*, resulting confirmations were supposed to have been added to the ledger – although this was mostly done, it was not always so. For any specific unit a sequential set of numbered claims is given, per *Gruppe* (after 1941, per *Staffel*), where the claim number is prefixed by a Roman

numeral numbering system where I (or often in the lists, '*Teil I*') indicates the Polish campaign, II denotes the Western Front (and North German coast) from the beginning of the war to 9 May 1940, III (normally given as '3', which is confusing) relates to claims made during the campaign over Norway (9 April 1940–30 October 1940) and the invasion of France and the Low Countries (10 May 1940–25 June 1940), and 4 (again not IV!) denotes claims for the Battle of Britain period and beyond (26 June 1940–21 June 1941). Logically the rest of 1941 in the West is prefixed by 'V' (the Roman numerals are back), but to add some more confusion this prefix also applies to claims made over Germany or Holland in the preceding Battle of Britain time period.

Presumably due to large numbers of claims from the Battle of Britain period, there is one added feature here, namely that after the '4' there is then either a I or a II viz. 4/I- or 4/II- (where 4/I- covers *JGs* 2, 3, 26, 27, *I* and *II/JG 52* and *I/LG 2*, *Erprobungsgruppe 210*, and 4/II- covers claims by *JG 51* and *I/JG 77*, *JGs* 53, 54, and *III/JG 52* [July 1940 only for this *Gruppe*]). As an aside, use of Roman numerals after the prefix '4' above explains why, for the Battle of Britain period noted, the IV had been replaced by a 4. Following these possible prefixes is the sequential *Gruppe* claim submission number from the ledger, which is either followed by a capital 'B' or not, e.g., 4/I-49B or 4/II-78. Comparison of accurate claims confirmation data from Don Caldwell's excellent *JG 26* history volumes,[15] indicates quite clearly that the 'B' after the number equates in almost all cases to the existence of a *RLM* confirmation number and certificate, while those claim numbers lacking the 'B' are most often shown in the Caldwell victory lists as claims for which the existence of confirmation certificate/number is 'unknown' – i.e. they have not been found in available records of any kind. This suggests strongly that numbers with the 'B' are *RLM* confirmed victory claims (B probably stood for *Briefbuch Nummer*, see below), while those shown as lacking this letter (i.e Caldwell's 'unknowns') are some sort of probable victory claim.

Comparison of the ledger-type lists with others contained in the films shows many of the 'unknown types' (in the Caldwell books sense) to equate to the 'ASM' classification of the *RLM*. ASM is the abbreviation for *Anerkennung später möglich* – confirmation possible later (once further supporting data are obtained) – this translates for most people to a probable victory in the *RLM* classification. Of course, one cannot in these circumstances take the running totals of claims per *Gruppe* in the ledger to indicate the unit's score – this running total number is effectively the total of *eingereichte* (submitted) claims (i.e. it includes *RLM*-confirmed claims *and* ASM-types) and will be radically different from the total of those claims confirmed by the *RLM*. For the Battle over

France (10 May 1940–23 June 1940) the ledger list indicates 864 claims to have the 'B' designation (thus presumably having *RLM* confirmation numbers) while 370 lack them (out of a claims total of 1,464 for the period). Similarly for the Battle of Britain (1 July 1940–31 October 1940) the ledger lists indicate 1,226 *RLM*-confirmed claims and 573 not confirmed (out of a claims total of 2,128 for the period).

There are also many other abbreviations and classifications applied to smaller numbers of claims in the various microfilmed records, which need not be detailed here, with one exception: a relatively common abbreviation is 'VNE.ASM', equating to *Vernichtung nicht erwiesen, Anerkennung später möglich* – destruction not proven, confirmation may follow in future. Despite the use here of the 'ASM' designation, such claims are not seen as probables. Claims adjudged by the *RLM* as VNE.ASM were documented in surviving paperwork by two separate but adjacently placed stamps (respectively, for VNE and ASM) at the top of the *Abschussmeldung* forms and in some cases by handwritten comments why that decision had been reached; presumably these forms (or more logically a copy thereof) were returned to the submitting unit (and the unit probably passed a copy on to the claiming pilot?) showing the result of the claim submission. Certainly no *Anerkennungs*-certificate could be issued for either ASM or VNE.ASM classified claims. The power of German bureaucracy to confuse still today in the rather fragmented and disorganised remnants of records available to the modern researcher, probably also applied to many fighter pilots during the war – one can quite understand their preferring their own claim totals as expressed in their logbooks and on the tails of their personal aircraft.

(2) A second set of records contained within many films is headed *Abschuss Übersicht Jagd Verbände* – claims summary for fighter units. These are clearly lists of *RLM*-confirmed victory claims, given normally per *Staffel* and where the *RLM* claim confirmation number is given also, as well as the *Briefbuch* number (of which more below). These numerical lists are also in sequential order, based on the date of the issue of the confirmation certificate – once again confusion will easily arise, as these numbers will in no way equate with those sequences discussed under (1) above. Also, these lists do not include the name of the claiming pilot and this information must be obtained from other records or sources, which can further increase confusion as different researchers reconstruct a fuller database in different ways. In some of the *Jagdgruppen* histories of Dr Jochen Prien and co-workers (see the *JG1* and 11, *JG* 3, *JG* 53 and *JG* 77 volumes in the bibliography of this book, for example) it appears that the correlation of pilots' names with specific confirmed victories in

the *Übersicht* lists are denoted in the unit claims lists by an asterisk (*). However, in the explanations for this symbol given in these volumes they are generally described as showing pilot's claims where the date is uncertain – this is again confusing as the date of the *RLM*-confirmed victories in the *Übersicht* lists is not the uncertainty, but the name of the claiming pilot is. However, there may also be another use of the asterisk annotation in some unit's victory lists as published in Dr Prien's books, as discussed further below.

(3) Other records in the microfilms include daily lists of claims of various types, with claims denoted by an actual *RLM* confirmation number, or only by a *Briefbuch* number, ASM, VNE.ASM and quite a few others.

By now it should be pretty obvious what kind of a minefield of confusing information is encompassed in the available claims data. Despite years of study, correspondence with veterans, and with Tony Wood himself, the author of this book remains rather uncertain about his understanding of these surviving records; the decades-old bureaucracy is still far ahead! Published victory claims lists in unit histories must also be investigated painstakingly before use of the data, to determine whether they reflect the surviving records implicit in Tony Wood's web-based lists, or are from unit war diary portions that have survived, from logbooks or photographs of fighter aircraft tails in some cases also; quite often such unit lists might reflect a mixture of all or some of these possible sources.

The Data Available for Research: Briefbuch Nummer
Now it is necessary to elaborate a bit on what the *Briefbuch* number might be. This word is no longer used in modern German and is generally missing in popular English–German dictionaries or on relevant translation websites. However, the two components, *Brief* and *Buch*, literally mean 'letter' and 'book', and clearly the term refers to a file; a *Briefbuch* number is, then, a file number. The term may be found at the head of many different types of *Luftwaffe* documents, and two examples are shown in illustrations 49 and 50. Documents which have been found in published and web resources with a specific *Briefbuch* number (mostly shortened on the documents to *Br. B. Nr.*) include:

(1) Combat report of a flak battery – e.g. Br. B. Nr. 1139/44 for two P-51 victories claimed by *Flakabteilung* 667 on 9 September 1944[16];
(2) A document referring to the transport arrangements for a captured American bomber co-pilot – e.g. Br. B. Nr. 189/44 for Second Lieutenant J. H. Mann, shot down and captured on the night of 5/6 July 1944[17];
(3) Daily combat summary report (*Gesamttageseinsätze* v. 11 July 1944)

from *Gefechtsverband Kuhlmey*, an informal short-lived unit operating in support of Finland in June and July 1944 when the Russians opened their offensive on that country – Br. B. Nr. 142a/44[18];

(4) Final daily report (*Tagesabschlussmeldung* 6 July 1944 20.00 *Uhr*) from *Gefechtsverband Kuhlmey* – Br. B. Nr. 104/44[19];

(5) Intelligence report (*Feindnachrichtenblatt der Luftflotte 1* Nr. 1/43 *vom* 16–31 *Dezember* 1942) for *Luftflotte* 1 for the second half of December 1942 – Br. B. Nr. 206/43 – first page shown in illustration 50[20];

(6) Most importantly for this particular discussion, *Briefbuch* numbers appear on all *Luftwaffe Abschussanerkennung* (victory confirmation) certificates, as shown in the example in illustration 49, for *Oberleutnant* Fritz Engau, *Staffelführer 2/JG 11* for a claim made for a Liberator on 29 April 1944.

Individual *Anerkennung* certificates were grouped together in a file, the *Briefbuch*, which then had a number denoted by two to six numerals followed by an indication of the year of issue, such as 450/44 for example, which would be file number 450 for the year of 1944. Each file or *Briefbuch* normally contained a number of *Anerkennung* certificates, varying mostly from one or two to about 20, between 10 and 20 being quite common, and occasionally a *Briefbuch* would have up to about 48 *Anerkennung* certificates in it, these much higher numbers being typical for the *Zerstörer* units over France and England in 1940. *Briefbuch* numbers were used already in the Polish campaign, so essentially right from the beginning of the war. Mostly *Briefbuchs* contained *Anerkennung* certificates from the same *Geschwader* or *Gruppe*, or even the same *Staffel* or individual, but not the entire set of claims for an individual.

Anerkennung certificates very similar to those used in the Second World War were already in use during the First World War; examples displayed on militaria sales sites show that these were issued by the office of the Commanding General of the Air Forces, signed by his chief of staff and counter-signed by the *Staffelkapitän*, who also signed off on his own claims! The tradition of conferring such influence on the *Staffelkapitän* thus predated the Second World War. The confirmation of the victory came through several weeks after the claim was made, and they each had a file number also, but the term *Briefbuch* was not used in the First World War examples; the confirmation (*Anerkennung*) was made to the pilot rather than the unit although the running total number of such accredited claims for the *Staffel* was also noted on the First World War certificates. Most interestingly the distinction between an *Abschuss* and a *Luftsieg* (this distinction is discussed in detail below) was neatly sidestepped in the earlier conflict by confirming a *siegreicher Luftkampf* (a victorious air combat)!

The most interesting aspect of the *Briefbuch* numbers and their associated *Anerkennung* certificates is that there seem to be two groups of them, one appearing to pre-date the period of late July 1942 to early August 1942, and the other to post-date the beginning of that period – thus for some units this distinction might be at the end of July and for others only in early August 1942. *Briefbuch* numbers for claims originally submitted from the period before July–August 1942 comprise either five or six digit numbers (and were issued by the *RLM* in 1939, 1940, 1941, 1942 or 1943), while those for claims made from July–August 1942 onwards all have two to four digit numbers before the year: 85158/42 for example would be a typical pre-July/August 1942 *Briefbuch* number while one typical of being made from July–August 1942 onwards would be, say, 750/44.

Of note here is that **all** *Briefbuch* numbers from late July – early August 1942 onwards, whether the relevant victory was claimed in the latter part of 1942, during 1943 or in 1944 up to about August 1944, were all issued only in 1944. This point will be further discussed below. The earlier group of *Briefbuch* numbers relate to *Anerkennung* certificates awarded for a confirmed *Abschuss* for the relevant *Staffel*, whereas the later group of *Briefbuch* numbers relates to *Anerkennung* certificates for a confirmed *Luftsieg* for the relevant *Staffel*. One final difference is that the *Anerkennung* certificate forms used for the earlier *Abschuss* confirmations have a different printer's reference number at the bottom-left-hand corner (B 1651, followed by the date of issue thereafter in the form of say 2/42 – February 1942) to that appearing on the *Anerkennung* certificate forms for the later *Luftsieg* confirmations (B 5221, again followed similarly by date of issue). Two separate forms were thus used, depending on the period of the war when the claim was submitted, namely prior to late July–early August 1942, or during that time and thereafter.

There is thus a clear distinction between the terms *Abschuss* and *Luftsieg*. For the suffering reader who has made it this far into the final chapter of this book, their elucidation will probably lead to more confusion rather than clearer understanding. While the two terms were quite distinct in their accepted meaning in the *Luftwaffe* in the Second World War, they appear to have been misused in the *Briefbuch* – *Anerkennung* numbers system. *Abschuss* (a shot-down aircraft) refers specifically to an aircraft attacked and hit, seen to be damaged and generally one that leaves the aerial battle and descends rapidly downwards and away, often streaming vapour or white or dark smoke trails. However, its final destruction through pilot bailing out, impacting the ground, exploding in the air or being consumed by flames is not observed by the claimant or witness; if the final destruction of machine and crew is seen and witnessed, then the *Abschuss* becomes a *Luftsieg* (i.e. total destruction).

The earlier type of *Briefbuch* number and *Anerkennung* certificates thus limited all claims to an *Abschuss* only; this was a conservative approach. In the later type *Anerkennung* certificates (for claims made from July to August 1942 onwards) it clearly states on each one that the *Abschuss* (submitted via the *Geschwader* to the *RLM*) is being confirmed as a *Luftsieg*, thereby elevating what is essentially a likely or probable victory to a definite one, implying confirmed and total destruction. Just to add a bit more complexity, *Anerkennung* certificates for the flak branch of the *Luftwaffe* had a different printer's reference number for the forms (B5230) and these were confirmed on the relevant certificates as *Abschüsse* later in the war, unlike the aerial victory awards, termed *Luftsiege* for the same later wartime period!

Probable Victory Claims (and Possible Manipulation by Higher Authorities?)

Use of the term *Luftsieg* for *Anerkennung* certificates from July 1942 onwards (with their distinctive *Briefbuch* number system compared to the earlier claims) seems to be unjustified as this later group of claims and recognitions appear to have been based on a much looser definition of what a claim (viz. an *Abschuss*) really meant. There is a published translation of an order from Göring issued by the *General der Jagdflieger*, Adolf Galland, on 16 April 1942 (his order number [*Briefbuch*] 582/42) to *JG 54* on the Eastern Front which clearly states that if there is no witness to the claimed destruction of the relevant enemy aircraft, the claim report will be treated as a probable and subject to further review if additional support is found later on.[21] These probable claims are only to be passed on for pilots already having at least three previously reliable claims.[22]

It is logical that such a change in the submitted claims procedure would take time to be made known to all the frontline units and for the change in bureaucratic procedures of the *RLM Anerkennung* office to be prepared in advance; this changed procedure thus logically ties in with known changes to *Anerkennung* certificates made from late July to early August 1942 onwards. Corroboration of less strict conditions for registering such probable claims with the *RLM* is given by no less a person than *General* Galland himself, in his well-known book *The First and the Last*;[23] in a footnote and with direct reference to the high-claiming *Luftwaffe* ace Nowotny, he says that claim certification in the *Luftwaffe* was more liberal than in either the RAF or the USAAF, and further that many kills by German pilots would have been rated as probable victories by the Allied air forces.

There is thus clear evidence from both documents and the *General der Jagdflieger* himself, that a relaxation of Luftwaffe claims procedures occurred, and this is reflected in the *Briefbuch* number – *Anerkennung* certificates as discussed above. There is also another aspect to this changed claims procedure from late July to early August 1942. In the three-volume history of *Jagdgeschwader JG 53* by Dr Jochen Prien, which represents a monumental contribution (along with many further volumes on other units published subsequently) to German fighter pilot history, the *Geschwader*'s victory list (termed *Abschussliste*, which is the correct use of the word) has a number of claims shown with an asterisk.[24] The explanation given in the history is that this reflects claims for a pilot where there is some uncertainty of the exact date of the victory.[25] However, as stated above already, with reference to the microfilms with *Luftwaffe* claims data, it is actually the other way round for certain films, where the date of an accredited victory is known but the name of the pilot has to be determined from other sources.

Mention of the 288th victory of I/JG 53 being claimed by noted ace *Oberleutnant* 'Tuti' Müller on 10 April 1942 over Malta, recorded in a history of air operations over that island,[26] provides a means of investigating what the asterisk symbol might mean. Totalling all claims made by this *Gruppe* of JG 53 from the beginning of the war till 10 April 1942 (this date inclusive; using the claims data from Prien's unit history), then the following facts pertain: total claims = 353 of which 65 are *claims; if the 65 *claims are subtracted from the total of 353 claims, then 288 is the difference. This strongly suggests that claims marked by an asterisk in the JG 53 history volumes might in fact represent probable victories *sensu* Galland, in other words, those lacking a witness (or possibly also inadmissible as a fully corroborated victory for some other imperfection in the claim paperwork). In that case, it would also suggest that for I/JG 53, *claims were not included in their *Gruppe* victory total up till April 1942.

Detailed study of the JG 53 *Abschussliste* in Prien's history shows claims marked by an asterisk to be relatively uncommon up till 9 August 1942, when they suddenly start to predominate in the claims list for operations of I/JG 53 on the Eastern Front through to their departure therefrom in late September 1942.[27] Thereafter, *claims become uncommon once more for JG 53 operations in various theatres for the rest of the war. This indicates the possibility that probable-type claims were more acceptable on the Eastern Front than elsewhere. This could be an important factor in adjudging *Luftwaffe* claims on the Russian front, and the implication is possibly that it was easier to get *confirmation* of a claim in the East than in the West, which is *not* the same thing as it being easier to *achieve a victory* over a Russian opponent than a Western one.

Dr Prien's subsequent volumes of *Jagdgeschwader* history unfortunately did not offer much chance for follow-up research on such (*) possible probable-type claims in the East, with one exception, the book on *III/JG 3*.[28] Here, once again, there were only a few *claims prior to 9 August 1942, and thereafter on the Eastern Front till the *Gruppe* left that theatre in early August 1943, such probable (?) *claims were very common.[29] The victory list in the fourth and final volume of the *JG 77* history[30] shows relatively low numbers of (*) probable-type claims prior to the onset of the war against Russia, but during their entire time in that theatre (June 1941 till late 1942)[31] although significantly higher numbers of such claims appear in the list, the date 9 August 1942 (or alternatively late July 1942) does not stand out in this context.

The three volumes written by Bernd Barbas, giving respectively the history of *I, II* and *III/JG 52* are somewhat different: while the claims lists for *I* and *III Gruppen* have relatively few claim confirmation numbers prior to late July 1942 (respectively, 31 July 1942 and 28 July 1942 for *I and III/JG 52*), from those dates forward till late 1944 virtually every claim has such a number and is also marked by an asterisk.[32] The claims list for *II/JG 52* is not complete and no such trends can be clearly seen therein.[33] Taken together, these (*) probable-type (?) claims in the various lists do provide some support for an easier victory claim confirmation procedure on the Eastern Front from late summer 1942 onwards. It should also be noted here that the various published volumes of *Jagdgeschwader* history produced by Dr Prien and his team, as well as those of Bernd Barbas on *JG 52*, represent major and very valuable contributions to *Luftwaffe* history; what is offered in this chapter is some discussion of their published data and what they might actually mean in terms of wartime practices and documentation, little of which apparently survived. Within history, debate on published material must always be allowed and a range of views might also lead to some small steps forwards in terms of understanding this complex and multi-faceted topic.

Some further comment on the *JG 52* history volumes and their contained victory lists and claims marked by * is necessary. If the claims made by 7th *Staffel* of *III/JG 52* are studied, then the change from only a few *Anerkennung* numbers (with * also) to essentially all claims becoming denoted by this combination of the *Anerkennung* number and asterisk falls on 28 July 1942.[34] Totalling all claims (and claim types) made in the war up till 27 July 1942 gives a figure of 343 claims, which is close to the first *Anerkennung* number on 28 July 1942, namely 360*.[35] The few claims marked by this combination (*Anerkennung* number and *) prior to 28 July 1942 have *Anerkennung* numbers sequentially numbered down from 360*, the lowest such number being 337* in 1941, marking the earliest claim of this type in the 7/*JG 52* list.[36]

The implications from these facts derived from the published victory list are: that all claims made from 28 July 1942 onwards were in fact *Anerkannt* (recognised) (and denoted by the * symbol), and we know from the relevant *Anerkennung* certificates that all claims in the East after late July–early August 1942 were for a *Luftsieg* and not an *Abschuss* for the relevant *Staffel*; also, the start of the numbering of the *Anerkennung* of this series of recognised claims is derived from the total claims made in the war up to that date. The claims, while not all recognised prior to late July–early August 1942, were all recognised after that. This strongly supports a more lax system for *Anerkannte Luftsiege* from late July 1942 onwards, and that system was also applied retrospectively to make *all* previous claims '*Anerkannt*' as well.

All of this is unfortunately rather complex, but to really understand the nature of German victory claiming and its recognition, and how these changed during the war, it is critical to be able to infer where possible over-claiming might have occurred and what its magnitude may have been. From the 7/*JG 52* victory list, it is thus clear that the asterisk symbol (*) denotes an *Anerkannte Luftsieg*, bearing in mind that from late July – early August 1942, this actually meant a probable victory, in fact an *Abschuss* in the true meaning of that word! Study of the victory lists for 8th *Staffel*, 9th *Staffel* and *Stab III/JG 52* strongly supports that the * symbol denoted this type of *Anerkannte Luftsieg* for all four units in *III/JG 52*, which usage is also seen in the claims list for I/*JG 52*.[37] Analysis of the 8/*JG 52* claims list[38] also indicates the same change at 28 July 1942 and the backward sequential numbering of *claims prior to that date, from the cumulative claims total at 28 July 1942, exactly as for 7/*JG 52*.

The same principles hold also for the 9/*JG 52* victory list but with one exception, namely that pre-28 July 1942 *Anerkannte**-type claims form part of a running total numbering system, covering all claim types, but those which were '*Anerkannt*', dispersed among the other claim types, were given an *Anerkennung* number equal to its position in the overall running total up till 27 July 1942.[39] In the example of * type claims discussed for I/*JG 53* earlier in this chapter, where their 288th victory on 10 April 1942 over Malta[40] was compared with the victory list published in the *JG 53* history of Dr Prien,[41] these probable-type claims (in the West) did not count in their total score, nor were they retrospectively added in after late July–early August 1942, unlike what was done for *III/JG 52*. Different units were thus apparently treated differently in the claims recognition system.

Unfortunately more complications have to be added to this already challenging story. While Russian front-based units from late July–early August 1942 ran up large scores of essentially probable-type victory claims, all the known *Anerkennung* certificates for these claims are dated with *Briefbuch* numbers in 1944, with none known for either the latter part of 1942 or for 1943. This suggests the possibility that no such certificates were issued until 1944, but this is another tangled story, detailed very briefly below. The large scores of Eastern Front units ran on until late in 1943, when there was a massive lowering of the cumulative *Anerkennung** number totals for all of them. Some examples will serve to illustrate what the victory claims lists (derived from Tony Wood, and the published unit history volumes already discussed above) show. For 7/JG 52, with their accumulated victory total having reached 1,057 claims (mostly * type victories) by 30 November 1943, their next victory in the list, on 7 December 1943, is numbered as 307* and from then on the claim numbers increase sequentially once more, but from this much lower starting point.[42]

It is noticeable that 307* is close to the 343 total claims of all types by 27 July 1942 before the new system started – assuming that some of the 343 would have been excluded (such as claims marked by nb [*nicht bestätigt* – not confirmed at unit level], ASM etc.). By the time of the Normandy Invasion, where 7/JG 52 found itself in mid-1944, their new claims total had reached 1,039,[43] close to the 1,057* number just prior to the big drop in numbers after 30 November 1943. Similar trends can be seen in the victory lists for 8th and 9th *Staffeln* of JG 52 also,[44] and for three of the four major Eastern Front *Geschwader* in fact (JG's 51, 52 and 54; data available for JG 5 are too few to reach any conclusion). Essentially, then, in late November–early December 1943, victory claim totals for these units in the East were reduced arbitrarily to levels close to those pertaining in late July–early August 1942, but were gradually restored again, close to their previous peaks by mid-1944. The victory list for I/JG 53[45] shows also a similar pattern reflecting their Eastern Front service in the second half of 1942 as does that for III/JG 3;[46] however, for II and III/JG 77 which also flew in the East at this time, the victory list data available in Tony Wood's lists[47] is too incomplete to analyse.

In the discussion thus far, it has been clear that what effectively amounts to manipulation by *Luftwaffe* high authorities of the claims scores of units occurred on a large scale for *Staffeln* and *Gruppen* flying on the Eastern Front. This raises the question of whether an equal concession or relaxation of victory claim procedures was also implemented on the Western and Mediterranean fronts. The answer is a qualified 'yes' – for example, analysis of Tony Wood's lists shows that analogous *Anerkannte* claims numbers trends apply for *1/JG 2*, 7th, 8th and 9th *Staffeln* of *JG 2*, as well as for *4/JG 26*, while the *JG 53* unit history indicates the same trend for *III/JG 53* in the West;[48] all of these units showed a distinct fall in total *Anerkannte* victory claims in late November–early December 1943, to levels close to what they had been in late July – early August 1942. However, the scale of this decrease in claim numbering in late 1943 was much lower than for Eastern Front *Geschwader*, and there was no apparent almost universal change to probable-type claims (*) in late July – early August 1942 for Western (including Mediterranean) *Geschwadern*.

The big change (decrease) in *Anerkennung* numbering at the end of November 1943, has been related to a large and successful RAF night raid on Berlin on 25 November 1943.[49] A large number of the *Reichsluftfahrtministerium* (*RLM*) records (apparently including all the confirmation numbering documentation) is supposed to have been lost in this air raid on Berlin.[50] While wishing no disrespect to the authors of the two excellent volumes[51] on the German night fighters where this document loss is thus discussed, some discussion might be apposite. The *RLM* building was one of only a very few in Berlin not significantly damaged during the war. Furthermore, if the dates of the last high *Anerkennung* numbers before the reduction are taken, they vary from 6 November 1943 to 30 November 1943 for all units (*Staffeln, Gruppenstab, Stab*) of *JG 51, 52* and *54*.[52] Similarly, the first dates of lowered *Anerkennung* numbers for the same group vary from 1 December 1943 to 19 December 1943.

Note also that all these decreased *Anerkennung* numbers, although much reduced, are still quite large (most *Staffeln* are in the 200–300s and even up to the 400s) – if all *Anerkennung* records had been lost in the air raid on 25 November 1943, and a new start had had to be made in reconstructing the destroyed records thereafter, with additions of numbers from operational flying units requested to send in lists of *Anerkannte* victories, then initial *Anerkennung* numbers in the first few days/weeks should have been effectively zero for most units, and thereafter should have grown by large numbers, which they did not. At least one *Staffel* (2/ *JG 53*) shows the large decrease in numbering on 3 November 1943,[53] well before the relevant Berlin air raid of 25 November 1943.

The author would thus venture to suggest here that some obfuscation (but not by any sources cited here) in terms of preservation/destruction of *Luftwaffe* war records represents another possible explanatory scenario. If all *Anerkennung* certificates had to be redone in 1944, what about the many copies (held by both *Staffeln* and by individual pilots, as is known from surviving such certificates) of all the thousands of pre-existing certificates, many of which would have been dated in late 1942 and 1943? Certificates prior to late July–early August 1942, as already noted, were all to confirm *Abschuss*-type victories and all had *Briefbuch* numbers denoted by five or six digits and the year of issue (the author has copies of 16 such certificates), whereas those issued after that all have three- or four-digit *Briefbuch* numbers and were all issued in 1944 (six such *Briefbuch* numbers do appear in *III/JG 52* claims lists for claims made during 1941;[54] they were probably only actually credited after late July–early August 1942, thus in time receiving 1944 type numbers).

In addition, the two different forms used for these two groups of certificates, as already stated, had different printer reference numbers as well. As an alternative postulate, perhaps all the certificates from late July to early August 1942 onwards were redone and also credited as *Luftsiege* (as opposed to the earlier ones which were all credited using the more conservative term *Abschuss*), thereby rather neatly disguising the fact that the vast majority of the Eastern Front claims from autumn 1942 onwards were essentially probables (remember here also Galland's order of April 1942[55] in this regard, and the remark in his own book[56] discussed earlier in this chapter). Perhaps, as an alternative theory, these probables did not receive confirmation certificates, and only in 1944 was this rectified.

As with much of serious research into *Luftwaffe* history the lack of records (real or apparent) makes reaching firm conclusions in such matters very difficult. An example of a puzzling feature is that for some Eastern Front (and even also some Western Front units), there appear in the victory *Anerkennung* lists several otherwise inexplicable increases in claims totals, and these tend to be on dates marking the start of months in late 1942. As an example, for *9/JG 52*, the *Anerkennung* numbers in their victory list went up at the end of July 1942 (from 460 to 584), at the end of August 1942 (from 672 to 782) and at the end of October 1942 it went up once more (from 917 to 967). In total, these three increases added up to 284 victories apparently added to the unit's total;[57] once again manipulation of claims totals by higher authority seems a possible explanation. It is within this framework that the words of some of the pilots involved become really important, and the next sections provide a range of views on the subject of victory claims, from a set of largely senior veterans who flew at the *Geschwader Kommodore* level during the war, and who thus speak with a good deal of authority. The topic below is addressed generically, not just in the Eastern Front context.

*The Views of the Veterans: Luftwaffe Fighter Pilots on Claiming
Victories, the Realities of Aerial Fighting*
As always in military history, terminology employed at the time of battles is important for later interpretations of what actually may have happened; the search for 'truth' (always difficult after the fact) depends on correct

usage of terminology by the later researcher and writer, and this should also correlate closely with use of terminology during the actual aerial battles and by their proponents themselves. An immediate problem in this regard is the term 'probable victory' or just 'probable' for short. During the Second World War on the Allied side, a probable was generally considered to be an enemy aircraft that you had definitely hit and damaged, and relatively seriously enough at that, that its destruction was likely. For a *Luftwaffe* fighter pilot a probable victory is basically defined as an *Abschuss* for which you do not have a witness nor a wreck on the ground in your own territory, but implicit also is the assumption that your claim is for an enemy definitely shot down (thus not a probable claim in the Allied sense) but you lack proof thereof. In the Allied definition of probable, it is uncertain whether the enemy was in fact shot down. The two sides' usage of this one term is thus not easily comparable.

As an example of the German understanding of a probable victory, we can consider a quote by *Oberleutnant* Victor Mölders (who flew in ZG 1 over France in 1940 and in the later part of the Battle of Britain in *JG 51*, led by his famous brother Werner) on his own claims: 'Seven *Abschüsse* were confirmed; two were without witnesses; thus nine altogether. These were *Abschüsse* achieved with the Me 110, *Zerstörer*, that later counted double.' Here it is quite clear that his two claims lacking witnesses were still considered to be *Abschüsse*; but they were also probables in the *Luftwaffe* context as confirmation was impossible. The double counting of *Zerstörer* victories alluded to in this quote will not be pursued further in this volume; the topic being discussed is complex enough as it is.

Major Gerhard Schöpfel, who was *Kommodore* of both *JG 26* and *JG 4* at different stages of the war, raised a very fundamental question regarding terminology to be applied to the situation when, after a successful combat, your opponent managed to put his aircraft down relatively intact: 'The question arises, did the British and the Germans consider a damaged aircraft, with a still propeller and that belly-landed, as an *Abschuss* or a forced-landing?' Hanns Trübenbach, at the time a *Hauptmann* leading I/ *LG 2* over northern France provides a perfect example of this dilemma.

Think again of my own case, when with Herbert Ihlefeld as wingman I was 'abgeschossen' by the French flak (in 1940), when I went down with a thick smoke trail that later extinguished itself and I made a perfect belly-landing, and being unwounded, was able to fly my next mission some hours later and shoot down a Fairy Battle with stuttering machine gun of the salvaged Me 109. There were also other mistaken reports, when for specific fighter operations, radio silence had not been ordered by the controlling *Jagdkorps* or *Jagddivision*. Then, as in my case over the Somme, Ihlefeld called out over the radio for example: '*Achtung, achtung*, the *Kommandeur* has been hit by flak and is going down on fire.' Many others heard this and once again a false report had been made. This is just the nature of aerial warfare.

For the German *Jagdflieger* the two terms used, *Abschuss* and *Luftsieg*, each had a very distinct meaning and these well-defined meanings were of course well known to these pilots. Hanns Trübenbach, who as just stated led *I/LG 2* over France and the early stages of the Battle of Britain before becoming *Kommodore* of *JG 52* over England and continued in that role later in 1941 over Romania and Russia, stresses something very important: 'And once more: an *Abschuss* was by a long shot not a *Luftsieg*, that meant the death of the crew and total loss of the machine.' In many publications the two terms are considered as synonymous, and even the veterans themselves quite often mix them up in their own opinions and statements. For example, Hans-Ekkehard Bob recalled: 'Up till the end of the war I achieved 59 confirmed *Luftsiege (Abschüsse)*.' This sort of statement lends itself to many possible interpretations, among them that he was actually correcting himself, in that not all 59 victories were confirmed as *Luftsiege* (which would have been very likely, bearing in mind he served from the beginning of the war onwards, scoring victories already well before the almost universal recognition of especially Eastern Front probable-type claims as being *Anerkannte Luftsiege* after late July–early August 1942) but all could definitely be classified as *Abschüsse*. If such was his actual meaning, then misuse of the terms would not apply, and certainly someone of his experience (he flew to the end of the war) would not have been at all ignorant of the distinction between the two terms.

However, this nicety would not necessarily apply to many later historians of the Second World War in the air, as well explained by *Major* (later *Oberst*) Trübenbach:

When previous enemies express doubts about the German *Abschussmeldungen* (reported claims), these are almost certainly to be explained by their confusing *Abschüsse* with *Luftsiege*. The attached example from my former adjutant Wiese, gives the best solution to this conundrum. With the common quantitative superiority of the Russian opponent, it was practically impossible to differentiate between a *Luftsieg* and a simple *Abschuss*. Reports like 'Rata dived vertically downwards with smoke trail' could not be classified as a *Luftsieg*, as neither the death of the pilot nor destruction of his aircraft could be determined. However, one could justifiably let it be confirmed as an *Abschuss* for the claiming *Staffel* or *Gruppe*.

It is in this context (wherein an *Abschuss* is an aircraft driven down visibly damaged and in obvious and serious difficulty while a *Luftsieg* is an aircraft seen to be fully destroyed and the crew killed), that the majority of Russian Front probable-type claims (marked by an asterisk – * – in several claims lists) from the late summer of 1942 onwards are so very misleading, as they were credited to the relevant units as *Anerkannte Luftsiege* when they were nothing of the kind. This practice, which was also applied on a limited scale in the Western theatres, even sometimes confused the German fighter pilots themselves, as shown in this statement by *Feldwebel* Otto Schmid of *II/JG 1* (who flew over Holland and Germany from April 1942 to May 1943, and on a second tour in early 1944): 'An *Abschuss* was confirmed as a *Luftsieg* only when the confirmation was available from the *RLM*.' Prior to late summer 1942, victory claims were confirmed on the relevant *RLM* confirmation certificates as *Abschüsse* and only after the late summer of 1942 as *Luftsiege*. Otto Schmid's operational service spanned this change-over and he made claims in both periods.

Many *Luftwaffe* veterans stress the inherent potential for confusion and error inimitable to aerial combat itself; in this context, over-claiming or perhaps better put as unintentional mistaken claiming was a common factor in World War Two aerial combat, and in fact, all aerial combat. *Oberst* Eduard Neumann, long-time *Gruppenkommandeur* of *I/JG 27* and *Kommodore* of *JG 27* lays emphasis on a fundamental character of aerial combat and claiming therein: 'I am fully aware that it is a universal problem, with over-claiming. Roughly, one can say that where many fighter units – irrespective of whether they are friend or enemy – fight within a restricted airspace, the error quota is understandably high; when fewer units are involved, means fewer mistakes are made in adjudging successes. In North Africa in 1941 it was most of the time, on the German side, only *I/JG 27* that was present.'

As *Kommodore* of a geographically widely spread *Jagdgeschwader* (*JG 52*) Hanns Trübenbach often found himself flying with only one wingman over southern Russia in autumn 1941, where he quite often met with large packs of the ubiquitous I-16 *Ratas*, and made the following statement.

I always approached it in this way that an *Abschuss* could only be equated with the confirmed loss of an enemy when this opponent was observed to crash in flames into the ground. Such an outcome to a battle situation meant the same thing to both friend and foe, a real loss, as it had been handled already in the First World War. With the mass air battles in the Second World War, however, this approach could no longer be applied fully, especially when small units, such as a *Geschwaderstabs-Rotte* (two aircraft *Rotte* from the Staff flight) fought alone against thirty-thirty five enemy fighters. As with my own experiences in Russia on the Odessa front, in aerial combat with large numbers of Russian Ratas one could almost never follow the shot down opponent to observe the impact with the ground, nor could the wingman do this either, as he had to protect his leader as well as himself. In such situations, that occurred a thousand-fold deep in Russian territory, it came to *Abschussmeldungen* being submitted, when the enemy machine went down with visible evidence of having been hit, e.g. with a thick smoke trail, that however did not necessarily imply the death of its pilot nor the loss of the aircraft.

Oberst Gustav Rödel, who rose from *Staffelkapitän* to *Kommodore* in *JG 27*, had this to say about that common human reaction of seeing their own success subjectively: 'Seen subjectively – in other words from my own perspective – I do not accept no-longer-verifiable *Abschuss* figures as realistic, as the relevant pilot making the claim often actually experienced the *Abschuss* success subjectively. For example, in aerial battles at great heights and then later at low altitudes with other pilots involved, a damaged opponent that was later attacked again and "shot down" (*abgeschossen*) was not always recognised as being the victim of two different combats, with the same enemy aircraft.'

The confusion that went hand in glove with large numbers of combatants involved reached even larger proportions in the great aerial battles over Germany. Hanns Trübenbach who was a senior fighter controller in that campaign, recalls: 'During the *Reichsverteidigung* many heavily or moderately heavily damaged four-engined bombers were reported as *Abschüsse*, when these were no longer battle-worthy and only got back home to England with great difficulty. Although the *Abschussmeldung* in approximately 8,000 m height was correct, it was not possible to follow diving bombers to the ground, especially when escorting fighters hindered this anyway, and thus in the event many damaged four-engined bombers flew home at ground level to England.'

It is out of this reality that the concept and term of *Herausschuss* (separation of damaged bomber from its formation) arose. *Oberleutnant* Otto Stammberger, long-time member of 9/JG 26 and later *Staffelkapitän* of 4JG 26, was among the first pilots on the Channel front to face the four-engined bomber menace. In the following quote he notes some of the realities and complexities inherent in multi-aircraft combat.

On the *Abschuss* figures of the American bomber gunners, no more needs to be said, one must bear in mind that from each machine four to six, even eight guns were firing at attackers, irrespective of the direction from which we attacked them. When one fighter showed even just condensation trails in a sharp turn, one, two or three gunners from a single bomber would shout 'Abschuss', multiplied by about twenty times – which was the average size of the bomber formations – with the gunners who had opened fire at about 1,500 m distance already – that must have been some noisy shouting over their radios. Certainly, we had our losses also, but their number was in practice one – two percent of the US bomber claims. With <u>our</u> Abschüsse the question was always in the foreground: who actually achieved the victory? A four-engined bomber does not fall with the first spread of fire, unless it explodes or collides with another bomber. We attacked mostly several times, and dived one behind the other on the same machine, one from ahead, the other from behind, all at the same time; the bomber now shows significant effects of the fire and turns away below. And who was now the successful pilot???? And when the bomber, near the ground, flew its last few turns, the light flak shot at the mortally wounded aircraft and reported the victory for itself!

The Views of the Veterans: Comparison of Luftwaffe Claims against Allied Losses

Oberst Hanns Trübenbach strongly supported accepting that reported losses from the Allied side be taken seriously when adjudging Luftwaffe claims:

> I personally am of the opinion that the German Luftwaffe in many cases reported more Abschüsse than their opponents admitted. All the Abschussmeldungen and any special happenings were sent from the Geschwader in the normal service way to the RdL (Reichsminister der Luftfahrt; Minister of Aviation) and ObdL (Oberbefehlshaber der Luftwaffe; Commander in Chief of the Air Force), so that Göring and Hitler were always informed in detail. Regarding the justifiable question about comparing German Abschuss-figures and relevant loss confirmations of the then-enemies, I can only say that I agree wholeheartedly with the statistics/data of the enemies concerned. The records of the enemy countries of their own losses were in all cases closer to the truth than the reported Abschussmeldungen of our fighter pilots. On the ground one cannot overlook a dead pilot in his machine.

However, he quite rightly makes the following caveat for losses reported by the Allied nations.

> In regard to the evaluation of all reported German Abschüsse, we probably should accept that with the losses reported by the previous enemies, these were exclusively the total losses. This means that in the enemies'

reported confirmations of losses, these always encompassed a dead pilot in his destroyed aircraft. The breakdown of the *Abschüsse* of Marseille (the leading German ace in North Africa; data that I had sent him) can be taken to reinforce my summation. Reported *Abschüsse* should not necessarily mean total losses for the enemy, because, for example, badly shot-up enemy machines, seen to descend with heavy smoke trails, could not be observed to their end-phase, also if the wingman himself became involved in further combat and was unable to confirm the *Abschuss* was in order, due to his being otherwise engaged. Thus it could also often occur, that other accompanying fighter pilots reported *Abschüsse* on the radio that were only 'seen'.

As I stated earlier, in most cases it was not at all possible to follow the inferred shot down enemy to the impact thereof or to his eventual escape over his own home turf. The two volumes I and II on *Jagdgeschwader 52* of Nico Fast contain war and *Abschuss* experiences that all relate to these problems and which in some cases illustrate hair-splitting occurrences in this regard. If one examines the entire *Abschuss* question from a moral/ethical point of view, then one can infer serious doubt on whether the awarding of decorations should not have been based on other criteria. In other words, was it only *Abschüsse* that counted, in their many different guises as simply destructive acts, in awarding decorations, then the victory claims should have been accepted at face value without further discussion. Not only in the East, but in all theatres, the *Abschuss* figures need to be questioned or doubted, when one today examines the records of the ex-enemy countries in comparison of their true losses with the German *Abschussmeldungen*. But our years-long practice of war has taught us that ex-enemy's confirmed loss reports can <u>never</u> be <u>identical</u> with the German *Abschussmeldungen*. That was simply impossible and will remain so, because the sum of air combat experience stands against this.

Several witnesses laid emphasis on the details of claims confirmation procedures in specific theatres. *Oberleutnant* Otto Stammberger (4th and 9th *Staffeln* of *JG 26*, 1941–1943) comments on the very strict procedures he experienced in his time with *JG 26* along the Channel coast and also the difference when operating over enemy or friendly territory. Stammberger also made some comments on the Eastern claims of *JG 26* during 1943.

All reported *Abschüsse* had to be 'touchable', or otherwise confirmed from the enemy's side, failing which one received no confirmation at all. The Liberator I had shot up on 31 March 1943 had asked for help over its radio and this distress call was intercepted by our radio specialists. Thus I had my claim confirmed on the evening of that day. The biggest differences occurred with *Abschüsse* over enemy territory when one most often was unable to observe the fate of an aircraft that had been hit due to ongoing combat. Indeed a second or third man (here referring to comrades in a single *Schwarm*) from one's own side who had seen the hits and pieces of the target breaking off could confirm this, so that according to obvious damage of the enemy aircraft an *Abschuss* could be confirmed, or the claims could be counted only as a *Herausschuss*, or judged as damaged, or even totally rejected.

This subdivision into *Abschuss* and *Herausschuss* was only adopted in 1943 after the appearance of the four-engined bombers; together with the fitted gun cameras, this enabled exact judgements to be made on *Abschuss* or not. From 1942 in the West we flew after all over our own territory and a reported *Abschuss* had to be physically locatable, it had to 'lie down below'! Practically this situation began already after the Battle of Britain, as already from summer 1941 we no longer flew over England, escorting *Jabos* (fighter-bombers), reconnaissance aircraft, shooting up trains, apart from exceptional missions. There were genuine aces, who also achieved their *Abschüsse* in the years 1943, 1944 and 1945; one of them was Hans Waldmann. There were *Experten* who even after 1942, in the East, achieved high *Abschuss* scores; they were simply geniuses. Our I/JG 26 was stationed for a period of three and a half months in the East, but of that at most two months were on operations, and then almost continuous escort operations for bombers on the northern part of the front, in other words they experienced hardly any free chases. But at the same time as the I *Gruppe*, the 7th *Staffel* was also transferred to the East and shot down, in these same three and a half months, 65 Russians, giving in total 190 *Abschüsse* for JG 26 in the East, in exchange for limited losses. Unfortunately we have no summary of the successes of individual pilots, but one of our pilots did get six *Abschüsse* in one day.

Major Gerhard Schöpfel, *Kommodore* of JG 26 (December 1941–January 1943) and thus also, for a time, Otto Stammberger's commanding officer, also stressed the difference in claiming over your own or enemy territory, as well as the role that German radio interception could play.

Definite *Abschuss* figures only occur for air combats over your own territory, as one can find the wreck-sites. Over enemy territory there is always a question mark. For a confirmed *Abschuss*, our pilots needed a witness statement. But often pilots from different *Geschwadern* attacked an enemy aircraft, one after the other, that went down damaged, and each considered, without further thought, that the *Abschuss* was their own. Differences in the information supplied also occurred in these various views. In my time as *Kommodore* of the *JG 26*, when this *Geschwader* was the sole unit in the Pas de Calais, we listened in on the British radio after aerial battles and could often determine, that more losses had been suffered than *Abschüsse* reported on our side. It was understood that some aircraft on their return flight had crashed due to the effects of damage suffered.

I can also remember one of the first attacks of the American four-engined bomber units with American and British escort, as I recall 1942 on Eindhoven. Listening in on British reports we were able for the first time to determine that the claims of the Americans and British were reported separately. The American bomber gunners' claims reported exceeded even the number of fighters we had put into the air. It was revealing for us that on the next day a British formation approached Northern France, caused my *Geschwader* to take off, and after reaching the coast however they turned away; in our opinion they wanted to show the Americans how many German fighters there still were. In reality we had lost something like three aircraft, and shot down *c.* nine. The US boys reported 150 claims.

Oberst Eduard Neumann, initially *Gruppenkommandeur* of I/JG 27 in the Western Desert and later *Kommodore* of the entire *Geschwader* there, recalls that confirmation of final impact of claimed *Abschüsse* on the ground was easier in the barren wastes of North Africa. He also reminds us of the fierce competition among the top *Luftwaffe* aces (something endemic to all top fighter pilots in all air forces) that ensured that a beady eye was always kept on others!

In North Africa in 1941 it was most of the time, on the German side, only I/JG 27 that was present. In addition, the ground surface lacked any forests or swamps which gave a good means of visual control on aircraft shot down and hitting the ground. In 1942 for a long time there was only the one *Geschwader*, JG 27, only three *Gruppen*. In the book of Shores and Ring[58] the victory claims of both sides are given and analysed – meticulously in my opinion – and the mistakes found were almost all of small import. For me also, I was always able to note that the good fighter pilots of my *Geschwader* were each other's hardest critics.

The Views of the Veterans: The Claims System and Victory Confirmation Procedures
In countless publications on the German fighter pilots, it is emphasised that their system for submitting claims and eventually potentially receiving an official confirmation thereof from the *Reichsluftfahrtministerium* (*RLM*) was complex, very thorough and much tougher than that applied generally by their opponents. While there is a good deal of truth to

this, the *Luftwaffe* claims system was also even more complex than often realised, at various times incorporating shifting goalposts, and also contained some inherent weaknesses as already discussed earlier in this chapter. These matters will be examined further below, based on reminiscences of some of the pilots themselves.

Oberst Hanns Trübenbach provides an overview of the well-known need in the German claims system for a witness to any *Abschuss*, and, having been a *Gruppenkommandeur* and *Geschwader Kommodore* himself, draws attention to who made the initial decision on any claim at the various levels within a *Geschwader*.

> Every pilot who had achieved an *Abschuss* in the air, had to ensure he had at least one witness. For this, basically, the wingman had the duty to perform this role, and mostly was also able to fulfil it. However, over the Russian war theatres massed battles occurred where fighting took place right down to ground level also! It thus happened that a *Rottenführer* hit and seriously damaged a Russian, and the wingman then finally destroyed the same Russian. Now, each could potentially claim the *Abschuss* for himself, but both were forced to come to a consensus as to who got the victory claim. Often when attacking and following an opponent, the *Rotten-* or *Schwarmführer* lost his wingman, so that other pilots who had observed these events, could confirm the *Abschuss* over the radio, which naturally often must have appeared questionable. Thus with this aerial fighting, there arose a tremendous number of situations, that were not unequivocally explicable.
>
> Basically, all *Abschussmeldungen* went via one's own *Staffel*, one's *Gruppenstab* or even via the *Geschwader IA* when the *Geschwaderschwarm* had scored *Abschüsse*. The real checking of each *Abschuss* lay, according to assigned duties, with the *Staffelkapitän* who then just reported successes upwards or sent the written *Abschussmeldungen* via courier to the higher post, when the relevant staff were not on the same airfield. In most cases, the *Staffeln* reported the *Abschüsse* by telephone to the respective clerks' offices. When the entire *Staffel* or even the entire *Gruppe* did not provide witnessing of the claim, then the wingman was practically always able to confirm the *Abschuss*, as in aerial combat only the wingman was in a position to do so, when he was not himself forced through self-defence to leave his *Rottenführer*. And that in fact did happen often, so that the *Rottenführer* did now achieve an *Abschuss*, but had no witness to this. To avoid such situations, one required each *Rottenführer* to approach his attacks in such a way that the wingman could remain in his assigned place!

What is important to note in the account of *Oberst* Trübenbach is the real and significant influence of the *Staffelkapitän* on adjudging claims at the lowest unit level, and one has to bear in mind that most claims would have been submitted at this level. The *Staffelkapitän* also signed off on his own claims, as did the *Gruppenkommandeur* as is clear above. However, interestingly, the *Kommodore* and his *Geschwaderschwarm* colleagues were subjected to approval by the *Geschwader 1A*, a non-flying staff officer! Hanns Trübenbach also drew attention to something which always impacts on any system, no matter how perfect it might be: human nature, which often has the ability to override any system's theoretical efficiency. With reference to the final link in the claims confirmation chain, Trübenbach notes: 'Even in the *RLM* there were people who worked exactly and those who simply worked in a slovenly fashion.'

Oberleutnant Otto Stammberger emphasised how often somewhat arbitrary decisions would be made in terms of victory allocations, based on wrecks locatable on the ground on the Channel front.

> In this respect it was seldom easy for us to even count our *Abschüsse* correctly, they had after all to be found on the ground, and then also where we had observed them crashing. When the wreck was found, and when the time correlated, or if possibly prisoners who had bailed out were found in the numbers we had seen them leaving the aircraft, then only was a victory allocation relatively certain. Sometimes we remained puzzled over a specific *Abschuss*, and then sometimes the *Kommandeur* after listening to the descriptions of the action during the discussion afterwards, would divide the *Abschüsse* amongst the pilots. In 1943 this led to gun cameras being installed in our aircraft that were coupled to the firing levers and worked together with the weapons. Now we were able to allocate the *Abschüsse* with certainty. Prior to this point in time, for example, 12 *Abschüsse* would be reported by 12 pilots, but only four could be found on the ground, so that eight pilots had to accept the disappointment.

While camera guns certainly improved the accuracy of the claims system, they would not have removed all potential areas of error.

Feldwebel Otto Schmid, as an ordinary pilot at *Staffel* level flying over Holland and Germany, expressed views which confirm the general *Luftwaffe* claims system, and also incorporated the normal tensions between NCOs and officers, found in all units in war (and indeed in peacetime for that matter also!).

> The reports on *Abschüsse* had to be written by the individual pilots themselves. The same applied to the reports of the air witnesses. As far as I can remember, in two- or three-fold copies. The combat reports (*Gefechtsbericht*) on the relevant mission was put together by the operations

clerk of the *Gruppe*; we had nothing to do with that. Confirmed *Abschüsse* had in each case to be confirmed by aerial or ground witnesses. Only then did one receive a confirmation of the *Abschuss* by the *RLM*. With officers, in exceptional cases the word of honour of an officer sufficed. But mostly witnesses were always available. When as an NCO one could not indicate any witness, which did occur sometimes, it was better not to even report the *Abschuss* at all. One could avoid a lot of paperwork by this. In any case one would be faced with the fact that the *Abschuss* would not be confirmed by the *RLM*.

How exactly it was with *Abschuss* witnesses in other units, particularly in Russia, I heard in conversations with comrades who had been there in *JG 3* (*I/JG 3*, returning from Russia at the end of 1941, became *II/JG 1*, Otto Schmid's *Gruppe*, in 1942)[59] that the word of honour sufficed, in order to get the *Abschuss* awarded. In our *Gruppe* in Holland everyone had to have the necessary witness, either in the air or on the ground. When I shot down the Beaufighter (claimed as a Beaufort, on 20 November 1942, near a German convoy) I had a witness in the shape of a ship's crew member. Otherwise one mostly had comrades who had seen the *Abschuss* and could confirm it.

As is almost always the case with hearsay evidence – victories being awarded in *JG 3* based on word of honour – this can be discounted in almost all cases. This is amply supported by *Oberstleutnant* Günther Scholz, who flew extensively in the East in *JG 54* and *JG 5*, rising from *Staffelkapitän* to *Kommodore* and beyond to *Jafü* Norway: 'I never heard of confirmation of an *Abschuss* on the basis of "word of honour", neither in *JG 54* nor in *JG 5* was this practised. There always had to be at least one witness for the *Abschuss*.' However, as will be detailed below, unwitnessed claims could be accepted within the German victory allocation system, and indeed were in some numbers.

The Views of the Veterans: The Reality of Unwitnessed Claims Being Accepted into the Luftwaffe System

Many published sources and many *Luftwaffe* veterans (also quoted in this volume) have emphasised that claims without witnesses could never be confirmed, but as is so often the case when discussing a system and then going to its practical implementation in real war situations, things were not so simple. *Oberst* Hanns Trübenbach provides some insight into how exceptions could be – and, in fact, were – made.

Now there were also officers in leadership positions, who were pure lone fighters and flew as a rule without a wingman. In such cases it became the business of the immediate commander, to recognise the claim or not.

This also occurred over England already, but only seldom. In Russia for example there was a case of a fighter pilot who reported a victory every day. This seemed strange to the newly appointed *Kommandeur*. When he shadowed the said pilot daily, then this pilot reported not a single victory and the untruth was revealed. However all these dubious cases remained exceptions; in the striving towards the *Ritterkreuz* however, they did occur. That there was a striving amongst the German pilots to be awarded the *Ritterkreuz* as fast as possible was also related to *Reichsmarschall* Göring's promise to award an estate after the war to those awarded with the Oak Leaves and Swords to the *Ritterkreuz*. One of my earlier adjutants did not want to stay with me when I had to take over the training *Jagdgeschwader 104* in Fürth near Nuremberg (late 1941). He was transferred to the *Nordmehr-Jagdgeschwader* and told me when we said goodbye in Mamaia, he was determined to get the *Ritterkreuz*. He achieved his ambition and he paid for it with his own death and the loss of his wife and child in Germany. So much for so-called war-psychology.

The *Nordmehr-Jagdgeschwader* referred to above was most likely *JG 1*.

Oberst Hanns Trübenbach was someone involved directly in fighter operations throughout the war, as *Gruppenkommandeur* and then *Kommodore* of a *Geschwader* up till late 1941, flying in action over France, in the Battle of Britain and then over the southern front in Russia. After this he commanded a fighter pilot training *Geschwader*, and then became a *Jagdfliegerführer* in the very eye of the storm of the Battle over Germany for the rest of the war. It was he, for example, who was the key controller (*Jafü*) of the night fighters responsible for the massacre of Bomber Command on the night of 30/31 March 1944 in the famous Nuremberg raid. He was also someone who began his professional flying career in the 1920s – he was no amateur but a highly experienced professional, and a very honourable man who provided the author with extensive material and personal reminiscences.

In his quote above, Trübenbach states quite clearly that lone wolf-type fighter pilots were allowed to claim victories for themselves when they had no witnesses, and these could be submitted to the *RLM* if the immediate commander approved them. Of course, that was no guarantee that the *RLM* would in fact allow them, but the door in the supposedly cast-iron *Luftwaffe* system was thus opened, for certain individuals at least. Presumably such individuals were already established *Experten* and their possible loyalty to the Nazi ethos might also have been a factor in some instances. One only has to remember that all the major aces who first achieved the ever-higher claims totals from mid-1942 onwards (Gollob 150, Graf 200, Nowotny 250, Hartmann 300 and later 350+) were demonstrably convinced Nazis, as discussed earlier in this book. The role of German propaganda can also not simply be left out of the picture, as also stressed by another highly experienced *Kommodore, Oberst* Gustav Rödel in correspondence with the author on the whole victory claims debate:

> You have done very fundamental analyses on this topic, regarding the *Abschuss* figures which fighter pilots of various countries have reported, and a comparison with determinable losses of the opponents is justified. You know just as well as we, that in history, as long as it is recorded in writing, such opposites will always keep occurring. In retrospect, one can say that it was seldom a mistake, to make the almost unbelievable *Abschuss* figures reported explicable. Thus also in ancient times figures reported were also multiplied, to have a propaganda effect. Already at school we read of Tacitus and his information in his book *Germania* and learned to judge this within this context. *Temporá mutantúr* (when the time is right, modify), and so the relation between truth and measuring of values becomes a mirror image of history, seen subjectively. Another example: *Die Niebelungen-Saga* repeats itself in modified versions over the centuries, in several countries. Similarly for the *Beowulf-Saga*, in which even my named ancestor is supposed to have played a role.

Hanns Trübenbach specifically refers to victory claims without witnesses during the Battle of Britain. Earlier in this chapter the ledger-type microfilmed lists of *Luftwaffe* victory claims that survived the war ('Tony Wood lists') include a relatively comprehensive list for the Battle of Britain period (1 July 1940–31 October 1940) wherein 1,226 claims are marked by a 'B' symbol after the ledger number, which equates to the existence of an *RLM* confirmation number.[60] In contrast there are also 573 claims in this same list without this symbol, equating with a probable-type claim (i.e. unwitnessed). There is thus documentary support for Trübenbach's assertion.

A good example of such a claim is provided by *Oberleutnant* Franz von Werra, adjutant of *II/JG 3*, who claimed (in addition to a Spitfire shot down in a preceding combat on the mission) two British fighters and probably a third shot down on 28 August 1940 in the landing pattern, as well as five destroyed on the ground, at an RAF fighter base.[61] There is no evidence to support any such attack in British records; the ledger claims list (Tony Wood)[62] gives von Werra (a self-styled Baron with little claim to a title, trying to emulate the image of von Richthofen of First World War fame)[63] three Hurricane victories for this date, but none have the 'B' symbol; in the *II/JG 3* unit history, the claims list gives him the Spitfire as well as three Hurricanes.[64] Three of von Werra's claims, at least, were thus included in an *RLM* ledger claims list as probable victories, despite a total lack of any witnesses.

However, while the previous paragraph amounts essentially to circumstantial evidence for unwitnessed claims being accepted by the *Luftwaffe* claims recognition system, there is also direct documentary evidence as well. *Oberst* Trübenbach obtained for me a copy of such a document, and sent it to me to study and comprehend, but with the proviso that it be returned and not used directly in any publication; the same condition was imposed on him by the (anonymous; known to author) provider of the document. Obviously these conditions have to be respected (for this reason, no copy is shown here, nor are details as to claiming pilot or unit, or date of claim provided below). The document in question is a one-page printed form (printer reference S 7945/42 – thus printed in 1942) headed by the relevant *Geschwader* number, and also carrying the notification that it was '*Im Felde*' (i.e. in the field and close to the front line); the form itself is entitled '*Stellungnahme*' (opinion) on the *Abschuss* of a Jak-1 fighter claimed on a date in late 1943 over the eastern part of the Crimean peninsula. Interestingly, the details of the relevant combat and claim are made by the claimant's *Staffelkapitän* (once again the influence of this position was paramount), and approved and supported by both *Gruppenkommandeur* and *Kommodore* of the *Geschwader*, the former requesting *Anerkennung* for the *Gruppe*.

The *Staffelkapitän*'s account can be translated as follows:

On .... in the area of Kertsch, I attacked four Soviet fighters with a *Schwarm* of Bf-109s[65] and at 07h10 in grid square PQ 66814, I brought one of the Jak-1s down in flames. In the meantime, the *Rottenführer* of the second *Rotte*, *Unteroffizier* X (+7 white) placed himself behind the Jak-1 flying on the left outside and shot at him in a right turn from the right rear quarter. His wingman saw how pieces fell off the Jak-1 which turned away with a light smoke trail. Due to his own attack on the enemy fighters his *Rottenflieger* was not able to observe how the Jak-1 – according to the claimant (*Unteroffizier* X) – was attacked a second time, over Taman (07h15, PQ 66821) and dived down in flames. The veracity of the account of *Unteroffizier* X, who has already scored 14 witnessed ('*bezeugte*') *Luftsiege*, is undoubted as is his *Luftsieg* over this Jak-1. I request recognition ("*Anerkennung*") for the *Abschuss*, whose submission would just be delayed by searching for a further witness, for the 1st *Staffel*. Signed, *Hauptmann* and *Staffelkapitän*.

Below this, the *Gruppenkommandeur* has added: 'I have no doubts at all on the truth of the statement (above). Other units were not involved. I request

Anerkennung for the *I/JG* .... ' The *Kommodore* followed this with his own affirmation: 'The *Abschuss* is undoubted. The confirmation ("*Anerkennung*") for *1/JG* ... is requested. *Major* and acting *Geschwaderkommodore*.' In both the Tony Wood list and in the relevant unit history, this claim is given as one with an *Anerkennung* number and an asterisk (*), just like hundreds of others made by the same unit in that year.

Thus, claims made lacking a witness could be officially submitted and could be confirmed; in this case the printed form is numbered at the top as number '106', indicating that this *Geschwader* had made 106 such claims up till late 1943. Unwitnessed claim submissions were thus reasonably common, although not the majority of victory submissions. Of importance here is to note that the initial step in the claimed destruction of this Soviet fighter was witnessed by the relevant wingman, but not its final destruction. This was most likely an inherently necessary part of the support of such types of unwitnessed claims. Many other pilots, lacking any witnesses at all to any aspect of a claimed victory, had to be satisfied with much less, namely a victory claim adjudged '*ohne Zeuge*' (*oZ*; i.e. unwitnessed), which equated to a rejection of that claim. Also, the procedure for recognition of an unwitnessed claim was only applicable to experienced veteran pilots, as for the case above, where the claimant already had 14 witnessed *Luftsiege*. This would also have tended to favour veterans who had already scored a number of witnessed and recognised claims prior to the changes in procedure made in late July–early August 1942, on the Eastern Front. These were discussed at length above, with essentially probable-type claims (marked by * in the victory lists in some unit histories) from that time onwards, almost endemically in the East, with a few in the West also. Once the *-type claims type came in, achieving several fully recognised victories would have been much more difficult as the system no longer revolved around such types of undoubted victory claims.

Then there is one further area in the entire *Luftwaffe* claims procedure where errors could creep in if individuals were less than honest. *Oberstleutnant* Günther Scholz (*JG 54, 5*), who having progressed during the war from *Staffelkapitän* to *Kommodore* and beyond must have signed off on many victory claims, made the following comment: 'For some *Abschussmeldungen* I had the feeling that something here was not right, but according to the system "I witness your claim and you witness mine" one could not say anything about it.' He would not have made such a statement lightly. An example of this sort of problem, from an entirely different theatre, is provided by four pilots from *4/JG 27* (including the relevant *Staffelkapitän*) in the Western Desert, who appear to have made spurious claims for several weeks, each 'witnessing' the other's victory claims. They were caught out on 16 August 1942, as detailed by Christopher Shores and his co-authors in the most recent and comprehensive history of the Desert air war.[66] These authors also emphasize that the relevant facts given by them were fully supported by *JG 27 Kommodore* Eduard Neumann, as a counter to some rather misleading recent explanations which have been given for the noted behaviour of the *4/JG 27 Schwarm*.[67]

Towards a Conclusion: The German Fighter Pilots and Aces
It is also important not to over-emphasize the small number of known false or exaggerated claims made by individuals or small groups. These cannot be taken as representative of the *Luftwaffe* fighter pilots at all. In fact, such cases occurred in all air forces and in all major conflicts. While the oft-repeated mantra that the *Luftwaffe* claims submission and confirmation system was more stringent than those imposed by the Allied air forces in the Second World War does basically hold true, what is not given enough credence is the great influence on the application of the system by the *Staffelkapitän* (a relatively junior yet experienced officer).

In addition, allowing unwitnessed claims for some pilots in the Battle of Britain already, the change in late July–early August 1942 to essentially probable-type victory claims (almost endemic on the Eastern Front, much less in the West), and the formal submission of unwitnessed claims as just detailed, are all facets of the German victory claim system that have remained in the shadows. There is also potential for favouritism and nepotism in these 'loopholes' in the system. However, the most important summation that can be made on the claims system is that it was manipulated, essentially by Göring, who must have allowed the relaxations over England in 1940, the late summer 1942 imposition of probable-type claims in the East, and who insisted on radical lowering of unit scores in November 1943, never mind permitting formal submission of unwitnessed claims with an accepted form for such purposes having been provided by the *Luftwaffe*.

At the end of the day the very high scores of the German *Experten* do not reflect any large-scale dishonesty on the part of the pilots themselves; over-claiming and excessive victory scores can far rather be laid at the door of the manipulation and changes made to the claims system. In this regard personal bias, Nazi party bias and also very likely propaganda interference all played a role within a much more pliable system than is realised. In the end it was the much-vaunted claims system itself that was at fault, not the pilots, who were young, mostly ambitious and often aggressive also, and who were encouraged in every way to achieve the highest possible scores by the *Luftwaffe*'s excessive fascination with the victory numbers game.

Over-claiming has affected all air forces in all wars, and will continue to do so until the fighting pilot is no longer a part of warfare. In this regard the *Luftwaffe* erred as much as anyone else. Its fighter pilots did end up having the highest scores ever achieved, and even if it were possible to accurately correct for over-claiming for each individual ace, they would still have been way ahead of their Allied opponents' top pilots. The estimated over-claiming, for example, on the Eastern Front appears to have been about two and a quarter German victory claims for each real Russian loss (as detailed in chapter 3 in this book); this is not excessive and both sides in the Battle of Britain exceeded such proportions, and claims in many other battles and theatres did also, perhaps the 1941 Channel campaign of the RAF against *JG 2* and *JG 26* being among the worst examples with *c*. five British claims made for every *Luftwaffe* fighter actually lost.[68]

The better performance of the German fighter pilots as the top scorers of all time cannot be tied to their having been better than anyone else – the German myth of the fighting superman was a Nazi dream and propaganda theme. What is true is that the *Luftwaffe* began the war with a core of already experienced fighter pilots who had fought and been enabled to innovate over Spain. In the first few years of the war they were often faced with large numbers of inferior aircraft in the opposing forces – as in France 1940, over the Western Desert in 1941–1942 and for much of the long Malta campaign (1941–1942 also), and then of course over Russia till about the end of 1942, where very large casualties were suffered by the Soviets. From 1943 onwards, the American, British and Soviet forces began to deploy ever-increasing numbers of superior aircraft, and while the *Luftwaffe* still enjoyed almost limitless opponents, as the quality of their fighter pilots fell due to cumulative losses of the experienced men and worsening fuel shortages affecting training, so it became ever more difficult for the remaining *Experten* to keep scoring. In the East special methods enabled some pilots to continue their successes.

As increasing numbers and enhanced quality of Russian pilots and aircraft led to loss of air superiority on the Eastern Front, so the German *Jagdwaffe* adapted their tactics, which emphasised the bounce of small Soviet formations, thereby utilising the best qualities of their own aircraft, and maintaining their force's existence while inflicting high Russian fighter casualties at relatively small risk. By such means exceptionally lucky and talented individuals could build up large scores, as detailed in chapter 9 where the *Startkladde* of 7/*JG 51* provided a data base of daily operations, tactics applied and victories claimed; *Staffelkapitän* Weber was their star pilot, accumulating 136 claims between June 1941 and April 1944. This is not unreasonable at all bearing in mind all factors as discussed in this volume; other well-known aces who claimed many more victories in the East over shorter time periods may appear less convincing if the detailed operational records were still available for study.

In the end German fighter pilot casualties became prohibitive, especially in the West but also in the East, and the arm had effectively collapsed by the end of the war in the face of attrition it could not hope to resist. While formal tours of duty were not part of the *Jagdwaffe*'s philosophy, many pilots were given breaks from active frontline duty, but by no means all; longer fighting careers, generating enhanced experience and concomitantly better fighting and survival capabilities, quite simply gave higher scores to the talented few who lived long enough. The last word belongs to *Oberst* Eduard Neumann, long-time leader of *Jagdgeschwader JG 27*: 'Naturally I understand that the high victory claims of German fighter pilots have caused raised eyebrows of our enemies. However it is generally overlooked that the German fighter pilots – in comparison with those of their opponents – almost universally were sent into action much more frequently; that brings many victories but in equal proportions, also high losses.'

11

Conclusions

This volume has striven to provide an overview of the experiences and recollections of *Luftwaffe* fighter pilot veterans who served on the Eastern Front against the Russian air force (VVS). The overview has been given within a framework of factual data obtained from original records and the available published post-war accounts and research. In view of the observation that quality of training was for most of the time the major differential of the aerial conflict in the East (firstly in favour of the Germans, later in favour of their Soviet enemies as the effects of fuel shortages and front line attrition lowered German training hours), the volume also encompasses an examination of *Luftwaffe* fighter pilot training, albeit generic in character rather than just that for the Eastern Front pilots. Analogously the volume ends with a discussion on victory claims and the German system evolved to handle their confirmation, again of a generic nature albeit focussed on Eastern Front *Experten* and veterans.

And thus on 8 May 1945 the terrible struggle on the Eastern Front came to an end. It should be remembered that this was begun essentially by decision of Hitler; most of his generals were appalled by the decision to invade the Soviet Union, and Göring was utterly opposed to the move.[1] Hitler had thus voluntarily begun the two-front war that most of the professional warriors dreaded. But the conquest of Russian *Lebensraum* was part of the inner core of Hitler's vision for the 'Thousand-Year Reich' – in his view, as the Nazi super-race it was their right to the territory and resources of Soviet Russia, and those resources would include the slave labour of the Eastern *Untermenschen*, or at least that part of the population that was spared the genocide in order to serve their new masters. And a genocidal war it certainly was, the German approach evoking a similar

271

response. The murder of the Jews (and commissars, local leaders, partisans real and suspected, etc.) on a large and organised scale began here in Russia, with the *Einsatzgruppen* operational behind the frontline forces from the very beginning.[2]

For the *Luftwaffe* as well as the entire *Wehrmacht*, they had bitten off more than they could chew. Despite the terrible losses inflicted on the Russian forces, air and ground, losses that in any other political system would have crippled the country's will and ability to resist, the Russians held out, fought back, and with time learnt many painful lessons; fortunately for them, Stalin gave his professional generals just enough room and opportunity to control strategy and tactics, and turn the tide; these were concessions that Hitler never provided to his military experts in adequate amounts.

The largest weight of air power was applied by the Germans in 1941, and after that they had to scale back almost constantly on the air effort in Russia, as other theatres demanded scarce aerial resources. First it was the Mediterranean theatre that took away the *Geschwadern* and the *Gruppen* but in time, from 1943 onwards, it was mainly the Home Defence and the battle for air superiority over Germany and adjacent France, Belgium and Holland that ate up most of the available German fighter forces. And here over the centre, over the homeland, the fighter force was destroyed, not so much through loss of aircraft but through attrition of the irreplaceable experienced and very capable pilots and tactical leaders. Ever more reduced fighter forces in the East lost control of the Russian air space from about mid-1943; over the Kuban already in the first half of 1943 the Soviets established a measure of air superiority, albeit local to that area. However, at the Battle of Kursk in July–August 1943, German aerial assets wasted away very rapidly and despite a certain superiority in aircraft and crews they were only able to establish control of the air over the battlefield temporarily and locally.

On a strategic level, control of the air passed inexorably into Russian hands. For the small number of German fighters on the Eastern Front, in order to survive, they were forced to adopt specialised tactics, whereby small formations of *Luftwaffe* fighters bounced the relatively small formations of bombers, ground attack and fighter aircraft employed by the Soviets, from altitude, and then pulled up straight away again to a tactically superior height. These tactics largely avoided superior Russian aircraft manoeuvrability and better climbing performance, while playing to the strengths of the German aircraft, with their superior altitude performance, better diving and zoom-climb abilities. They also suited the temperament of many German fighter pilots, and to a large degree replicated the tried and true tactics established by that great German

Jagdflieger and role model Baron von Richthofen in the First World War. For those interested in details and for a convincing example of the success of such tactics, the reader is referred to chapter 9, based on the *Startkladde* of 7/JG 51 (13 September 1943–18 April 1944), a daily log of operations. This very rare document enables a reconstruction of the daily battles of a single *Jagdstaffel* and shows how a lucky and talented few *Experten* could build large scores given enough time and the disciplined application of the chosen tactics.

If they religiously applied such careful tactics, which required a high level of discipline and experienced leadership at tactical level by established *Experten*, then German attrition was bearable, novices could learn, survive and score a few successes with time, and the odd new pilot of superior talents could, if lucky join the ranks of the *Experten*. With long periods of service of this nature at the front (albeit not necessarily without breaks as so often claimed; transfers of *c.* six months to training establishments were more common in the *Luftwaffe* fighter arm than generally thought), the small number of really able pilots were able to build enormous scores. Certainly, while over-claiming was endemic to both sides, as on all fronts and in all aerial conflicts, it was also partly enhanced on the German side by evolving definitions of what constituted an aerial victory, never mind racial attitudes of the time and the propaganda that was such a feature of Nazi Germany.

Were the Germans thus the best fighter pilots the world has ever seen, as is implied by so many, due to the large scores racked up in the East? The answer has to be a firm 'no' – they were human like everyone else and their Russian opponents were not idiots keen to die in large numbers. Their high scores, such as they were in reality (bearing in mind the likely *c.* 2.25 over-claim factor discussed earlier in this book) rather than in pilot perception, were the result of clever tactics, persistently carried out over years. However, while the victories reflected in the scores of the *Experten* were a tactical victory indeed, it was one that did not affect the big picture; the *Luftwaffe* might win the small-scale tactical battles quite often, but they had long lost the strategic battle and control of Russian air space. The clever tactical leadership at front level (and often only for small formations, *Schwarms* or even *Rotten*) was matched by very poor leadership at the strategic level of the air force, as had also occurred in North Africa, and with similar results. They thus won local tactical successes and created aces with massive apparent scores (and in reality still high), but they lost strategic control of the air above the battle fronts, and with this being lost, inevitably so too was the ground battle.

Neglecting the enemy bombers while shredding their fighters was to cost the *Luftwaffe* air superiority and the war, over North Africa and even more so on the Eastern Front. On the latter front the real danger to the entire *Wehrmacht* was the increasing number of heavily armoured Il-2 *Sturmoviks*, whose surviving pilots rightly admitted after the war that they had much blood on their hands.[3] Strangely enough, higher *Luftwaffe* commanders in the East condoned the *Jagdfliegers'* continuing use of the 'bounce-shoot-zoom climb' tactics to support small numbers of aces with enormous scores and avoiding overdue attrition, right through to the end. In a way, this paradox of tactical excellence allied to strategic short-sightedness paralleled the war on the ground in the East. The Stalingrad debacle, with the poor-quality allied (Romanian, Italian and Hungarian) troops lining the Don flank to the German 6th Army within the Stalingrad precincts themselves,[4] when seen in hindsight (always an easy prerogative of the historian) provides a good example of this German command dichotomy. It is also an example where the oft-applied German general staff excuse that it was all Hitler's fault has no real traction.

Bibliography

Adair, Paul, *Hitler's greatest defeat* (London: Cassell, 1994)

Aders, Gebhard and Held, Werner, *Jagdgeschwader 51 'Mölders'* (Stuttgart: Motorbuch Verlag, 1985)

Axell, Albert, *Russia's Heroes 1941-1945* (London: Magpie Books, 2010)

Barbas, Bernd, *Die Geschichte der I. Gruppe des Jagdgeschwaders 52* (Überlingen: self-published, undated)

Barbas, Bernd, *Die Geschichte der II. Gruppe des Jagdgeschwaders 52* (Überlingen: self-published, undated)

Barbas, Bernd, *Die Geschichte der III. Gruppe des Jagdgeschwaders 52* (Überlingen: self-published, undated)

Beevor, Antony, *Stalingrad* (London: Penguin Books, 1999)

Bellamy, Chris, *Absolute War* (London: Pan-Macmillan, 2007)

Bergström, Christer and Mikhailov, Andrey, *Black Cross and Red Star: The Air War over the Eastern Front, Vol. 1, Operation Barbarossa, 1941* (Pacifica: Pacifica Military History, 2000)

Bergström, Christer and Mikhailov, Andrey, *Black Cross and Red Star: The Air War over the Eastern Front, Vol. 2, Resurgence, January-June 1942* (Pacifica: Pacifica Military History, 2001)

Bergström, Christer with Antipov, Vlad and Sundin, Claes, *Graf and Grislawski: A pair of aces* (Hamilton: Eagle Editions, 2003)

Bergström, Christer, Dikov, Andrey and Antipov, Vlad, *Black Cross and Red Star: The Air War over the Eastern Front, Vol. 3, Everything for Stalingrad* (Hamilton: Eagle Editions, 2006)

Blandford, Edmund, *Target England* (Shrewsbury: Airlife Publishing Ltd., 1997)

Bob, Hans Ekkehard, *Grünherzjäger im Luftkampf 1940-1945; Die Geschichte des Jagdgeschwaders 54: Kriegs-Tagebuch von Hannes Trautloft, Kommodore Jagdgeschwader 54 Grünherz* (Zweibrücken: VDM Heinz Nickel, 2006)

Boiten, Theo, *Nachtjagd War Diaries: An operational history of the German night fighter force in the West, volume 1: September 1939–March 1944* (Walton on Thames: Red Kite, 2008)

Boiten, Theo and Mackenzie, Roderick J., *Nachtjagd War Diaries: An operational history of the German night fighter force in the West, volume 2: April 1944–May 1945* (Walton on Thames: Red Kite, 2008)

Braatz, Kurt, *Gott oder ein Flugzeug. Leben und Sterben des Jagdfliegers Günther Lützow* (Moosburg: NeunundzwanzigSechs Verlag, 2005)

Buchner, Hermann, *Stormbird: flying through fire as a Luftwaffe ground attack pilot and Me 262 ace* (Aldershot: Hikoki Publications, 2000)

Burt, Kendal and Leasor, James, *The one that got away* (London: Collins, 1968)

Caldwell, Donald L., *JG 26; Top guns of the Luftwaffe* (New York: Orion Books, 1991)

Caldwell, Donald L., *JG 26 Luftwaffe Fighter Wing Diary, 1939-1942*, Vol. 1 (Mechanicsburg: Stackpole Books, 2012)

Caldwell, Donald L., *JG 26 Luftwaffe Fighter Wing Diary, 1943-1945*, Vol. 2 (Mechanicsburg: Stackpole Books, 2012)

Carell, Paul, *Hitler's war on Russia* (London: Corgi Books, 1967)

Clark, Alan, *Barbarossa: The Russian German conflict 1941–1945* (London: Cassell, 2002)

Dierich, Wolfgang, *Die Verbände der Luftwaffe 1935-1945* (Stuttgart: Motorbuch Verlag, 1976)

Ebener, Kurt, *Jägerblatt* (XXII/4, December 1972)

Erickson, John, *The road to Berlin* (London: Cassell, 1983)

Eriksson, Patrick G., *Alarmstart* (Stroud: Amberley, 2017)

Evans, Richard J., *The Third Reich at War* (London: Penguin, 2009)

Ewald, Heinz, *Esau: Heinz Ewald als Jagdflieger im erfolgreichsten Jagdgeschwader 1943-1945* (Coburg: privately published, 1980)

Fast, Niko, *Das Jagdgeschwader 52, Band 1* (Bergisch Gladbach: Bensberger Buch Verlag, 1988)

Galland, Adolf, *The first and the last* (London: Fontana/Collins, 1970)

Gilbert, Martin, *Second World War* (London: Weidenfeld and Nicolson, 1989)

Girbig, Werner, *Jagdgeschwader 5 "Eismeerjäger"* (Stuttgart: Motorbuch Verlag, 1976)

Green, William, *War planes of the Second World War: Fighters volume three* (London: Macdonald and Co., 1962)

Hardesty, Von and Grinberg, Ilya, *Red Phoenix Rising; the Soviet Air Force in World War II* (Lawrence: University Press of Kansas, 2012)

Hata, Ikuhiko, Izawa, Yasuho and Shores, Christopher, *Japanese Army Air Force fighter units and their aces 1931–1945* (London: Grub Street, 2002)

Hayward, Joel S.A., *Stopped at Stalingrad: the Luftwaffe and Hitler's defeat in the East 1942-1943* (Lawrence: University Press of Kansas, 1998)

Bibliography

Heaton, Colin D., *World War II* (1, February 2000)

Held, Werner, Trautloft, Hannes and Bob, Ekkehard, *Die Grünherzjäger: Bildchronik des Jagdgeschwaders 54* (Friedberg: Podzun-Pallas-Verlag, 1985)

Jurado, Carlos, *The Condor Legion: German troops in the Spanish Civil War* (Botley: Osprey Publishing, 2006)

Khazanov, Dmitriy B., *Air war over Kursk* (Bedford: SAM Publications, 2010)

Killen, John, *The Luftwaffe* (London: Sphere Books, 1969)

Krivosheev, Grigoriy F., *Soviet casualties and combat losses in the Twentieth Century* (London: Greenhill Books, 1997)

Kurowski, Franz, *Luftwaffe aces: German combat pilots of WWII* (Mechanicsburg: Stackpole Books, 2004)

Lepage, Jean-Denis G.G., *An illustrated dictionary of the Third Reich* (Jefferson: McFarland and Company, 2014)

Lipfert, Helmut, *Das Tagebuch des Hauptmann Lipfert* (Stuttgart: Motorbuch Verlag, 1975)

Makos, Adam with Alexander, Larry, *A Higher Call* (London: Atlantic Books, 2014)

McKee, Alexander, *Great mysteries of aviation* (New York: Stein and Day, 1986)

Ministry of Defense of the USSR, *The Soviet Air Force in World War II* (New York: Doubleday and Co., 1973; later edition of original translated by Fetzer, L., edited by Wagner, R.)

Möbius, Ingo, *Am Himmel Europas. Der Jagdflieger Günther Scholz erinnert sich* (Chemnitz: Eigenverlag, 2009)

Morgan, Hugh and Seibel, Jürgen, *Combat Kill: The drama of aerial warfare in World War 2 and the controversy surrounding victories* (Sparkford: Patrick Stephens Ltd., 1997)

Musciano, Walter, *Die berühmten Me 109 und ihre Piloten* (Stuttgart: Motorbuch Verlag, 1989)

Neitzel, Sönke and Welzer, Harald, *Soldaten: on fighting, killing and dying* (London: Simon and Schuster, 2012)

Nowarra, Heinz J., *The Messerschmitt 109 – A famous German fighter* (Letchworth: Harleyford Publications Ltd., 1966)

Oberkommando der Luftwaffe, *Bemerkungen zur feindlichen Luftrüstung Nr. 1/45 Sowjetunion – Flugzeugverluste (Fremde Luftwaffen Ost, Nr. 1485/45)* (Maxwell Air Force Base, Alabama: USAF Historical Division, Research Studies Institute, Air University, 1945)

Obermaier, Ernst, *Die Ritterkreuzträger der Luftwaffe, Band 1 Jagdflieger* (Mainz: Verlag Dieter Hoffmann, 1966)

Overy, Richard, *Russia's war* (London: Penguin Books, 1998)

Polak, Tomas with Shores, Christopher, *Stalin's falcons: The aces of the Red Star* (London, Grub Street, 1999)

Prien, Jochen, *Pik-As: Geschichte des Jagdgeschwaders 53, Teil 1* (Illertissen: Flugzeug Publikations, 1989)

Prien, Jochen, *Pik-As: Geschichte des Jagdgeschwaders 53, Teil 2* (Eutin: Struve-Druck, 1990)

Prien, Jochen, *Pik-As: Geschichte des Jagdgeschwaders 53, Teil 3* (Eutin: Struve-Druck, 1991)

Prien, Jochen, *Geschichte des Jagdgeschwaders 77, Teil 2, 1941-1942* (Eutin: Struve-Druck, 1993)

Prien, Jochen and Rodeike, Peter, *Jagdgeschwader 1 und 11. Einsatz in der Reichsverteidigung von 1939 bis 1945, Teil 1, 1939-1943* (Eutin: Struve Druck, 1993)

Prien, Jochen and Stemmer, Gerhard, *Messerschmitt Bf 109 im Einsatz bei der III./ Jagdgeschwader 3* (Eutin: Struve-Druck, 1995)

Prien, Jochen and Stemmer, Gerhard, *Messerschmitt Bf 109 im Einsatz bei der II./ Jagdgeschwader 3* (Eutin: Struve-Druck, 1996)

Prien, Jochen and Stemmer, Gerhard, *Messerschmitt Bf 109 im Einsatz bei Stab und I./Jagdgeschwader 3* (Eutin: Struve-Druck, 1997)

Prien, Jochen, *Geschichte des Jagdgeschwaders 77, Teil 4, 1944-1945* (Eutin: Struve-Druck, undated)

Prien, Jochen and Rodeike, Peter, *Jagdgeschwader 1 und 11. Einsatz in der Reichsverteidigung von 1939 bis 1945, Teil 2, 1944* (Eutin: Struve Druck, undated)

Prien, Jochen and Rodeike, Peter, *Jagdgeschwader 1 und 11. Einsatz in der Reichsverteidigung von 1939 bis 1945, Teil 3, 1944-1945* (Eutin: Struve Druck, undated)

Priller, Josef, *J.G. 26: Geschichte eines Jagdgeschwaders* (Stuttgart: Motorbuch Verlag, 1980)

Rall, Günther, *Mein Flugbuch* (Moosburg: NeunundzwanzigSechs Verlag, 2004)

Read, Anthony, *The Devil's Disciples* (London: Pimlico, Random House, 2004)

Ring, Hans and Girbig, Werner, *Jagdgeschwader 27, Die Dokumentation über den Einsatz an allen Fronten 1939-1945* (Stuttgart: Motorbuch Verlag, 1975)

Schuck, Walter, *Abschuss! Von der Me 109 zur Me 262; Erinnerungen an die Luftkämpfe beim Jagdgeschwader 5 und 7* (Aachen: Helios Verlag, 2007)

Shores, Christopher and Ring, Hans, *Fighters over the Desert* (London: Neville Spearman, 1969)

Shores, Christopher and Cull, Brian with Malizia, Nicola, *Malta: the Spitfire year 1942* (London: Grub Street, 1991)

Shores, Christopher and Massimello, Giovanni with Guest, Russell, Olynyk, Frank and Bock, Winfried, *A History of the Mediterranean Air War 1940-1945; Volume Two: North African Desert February 1942-March 1943* (London: Grub Street, 2012)

Sims, Edward H., *The Fighter Pilots* (London: Cassell, 1968)

Bibliography

Sims, Edward H., *Jagdflieger, die grossen Gegner von einst* (Stuttgart: Motorbuch Verlag, 1994)

Skawran, Paul Robert, *Ikaros; Persönlichkeit und Wesen des deutschen Jagdfliegers im Zweitem Weltkrieg* (Steinbach am Wörthsee: Luftfahrt-Verlag Walter Zuerl, 1969)

Skawran, Paul R., *Gesammelte Einzelschriften* (Pretoria: unpublished and undated manuscript)

Stargardt, Nicholas, *The German War: A nation under arms, 1939-45* (London: The Bodley Head, 2015)

Timofeeva-Egorova, Anna, *Over fields of fire* (Solihull: Helion and Company Ltd., 2015)

Toliver, Raymond F. and Constable, Trevor J., *Das waren die deutschen Jagdflieger-Asse 1939-1945* (Stuttgart: Motorbuch Verlag, 1975)

Toliver, Raymond F. and Constable, Trevor J., *Holt Hartmann vom Himmel!* (Stuttgart: Motorbuch Verlag, 1976)

United States Army Security Agency, *European Axis signal intelligence in World War II as revealed by 'TICOM' investigations and by other prisoner of war interrogations and captured material, principally German* (Washington DC: Army Security Agency, 1946)

United States Strategic Bombing Survey, *Over-all Report (European Air War)* (Washington DC: Government Printing Office, 1945)

Young, Peter (Editor), *The World Almanac Book of World War II* (New York: World Almanac Publisher, 1981)

Websites

Acred, Matthew Laird (website editor), *Jagdgeschwader 5 Abschussliste*; www.asisbiz.com/Luftwaffe.html

Antony Cribb Ltd., Arms and Armour Auctions; www.antonycribb.com

deZeng, Henry L. IV and Stankey, Douglas G., *Luftwaffe Officer Career Summaries* (2014 updated version); www.ww2.dk/lwoffz.html (hosted on Michael Holm's webpage: *The Luftwaffe, 1933-1945*; www.ww2.dk)

eMedals, Purveyors of Authentic Militaria; www.emedals.com

Hermann Historica, international auctioneers; www.hermann-historica.de

Holm, Michael, *The Luftwaffe, 1933-1945*; www.ww2.dk

Luftwaffe Archives and Records Reference Group; www.lwag.org

Ministerie van Defensie in the Netherlands, specifically the *Verliesregister* for 1944; www.defensie.nl

Romanian Armed Forces in the Second World War; www.worldwar2.ro

Rosipal, Gunther, *JG 54 loss list* (downloaded 3 July 2000); www.jps-net/wartburg/LossList.htm (homepage of *JG 54*, Bob Wartburg)

Russian aircraft losses summarised from official statistics – website PKKA*CA; http://www.dol.ru/users/hotdog/airlosses.htm – accessed 07.10.2000

Vaittinen, Juha, *The lengths of the RAF operational tours*; juhansotahistoriasivut. weebly.com

VVS RKKA, VVS Estadisticas, Estadisticas de la Aviacion Sovietica; Spanish language website (www.rkka.es) providing detailed Russian loss statistics from official sources, keyed to years, different aircraft types and different causes of combat loss; http://www.rkka.es/Estadisticas/VVS_stat/06/06_21.htm and http://www.rkka.es/Estadisticas/VVS_stat/06/06_22.htm

Wehrmacht-Awards.com militaria website; Wehrmacht-Awards.com (Part of pilot's logbook of *Feldwebel* Ernst Scotti of *8/SG 3* in Kurland, December 1944-March 1945, displayed as part of the collection of 'Olivier-F.', shown on forum on website)

Wikipedia; specifically on the Battles of Rzhev: https://en.wikipedia.org/wiki/Battles_of_Rzhev; specifically on *Gefechtsverband Kuhlmey*: https://en.wikipedia.org/wiki/Detachment_Kuhlmey; specifically on Russian invasion of Czechoslovakia: https://en.wikipedia.org/wiki/Slovakia_during_World_War_II

Wood, Tony, *Tony Wood's Combat Claims and Casualties Lists*; don-caldwell. we.bs/claims/tonywood.htm

Zapf, Andreas, *Chronicles of the Luftwaffe 1935-1945*; www.chronicles-of-the-luftwaffe.de

Archives

Militärarchiv Freiburg im Breisgau, Marine-Akten, Sektion Kriegsmarine, Reiko-See, K.M.D. Danzig; *signatur* M 519/8632 (from page 141; summary of shipping losses Libau harbour, Kurland, 1 August 1944-31 December 1944; summary made by Albrecht Licht).

Militärarchiv Freiburg im Breisgau, various *Luftwaffe* documents, specifically *Kriegstagebuch* excerpts, *Abschussmeldungen, Gefechtsberichte* and *Luftzeugenberichte* for II/JG 1, copies supplied by Otto Schmid.

Kansallisarkisto (National Archives of Finland); daily combat summary reports (*Gesamttageseinsätze*), specifically that for 11 July 1944 (Br. B. Nr. 142a/44), from *Gefechtsverband Kuhlmey*. Also the final daily report (*Tagesabschlussmeldung* 6 July 1944 20.00 *Uhr*) from *Gefechtsverband Kuhlmey*, and the intelligence report (*Feindnachrichtenblatt der Luftflotte 1* Nr. 1/43 *vom* 16–31 *Dezember* 1942) for *Luftflotte 1* for the second half of December 1942. All via Juha Vaittinen, accomplished Finnish air historian.

Notes

○

Preface

1. Eriksson, Patrick G., *Alarmstart* (Stroud: Amberley, 2017).
2. Extract from the diary of *Oberfähnrich* Hans Strelow, *5/JG 51*; Prof. P. R. Skawran who was a *Luftwaffe* psychologist spent time with various fighter units. While with *JG 51* he copied several diary entries from Strelow's private effects after his death in action. Some of these he provided to the author.
3. Heaton, Colin D., *Interview with World War II Luftwaffe eagle Johannes Steinhoff*, article in World War II magazine, issue 1, February 2000.
4. Möbius, Ingo, *Am Himmel Europas. Der Jagdflieger Günther Scholz erinnert sich* (Chemnitz: Eigenverlag, 2009).
5. Overy, Richard, *Russia's war* (London: Penguin Books, 1998).
6. *ibid.*
7. *ibid.*
8. *ibid.*
9. *ibid.*
10. Polak, Tomas with Shores, Christopher, *Stalin's falcons: The aces of the Red Star* (London, Grub Street, 1999).
11. Bergström, Christer and Mikhailov, Andrey, *Black Cross and Red Star: The Air War over the Eastern Front, Vol. 1, Operation Barbarossa, 1941* (Pacifica: Pacifica Military History, 2000).
12. Note 2, *op. cit.*
13. Jurado, Carlos, *The Condor Legion: German troops in the Spanish Civil War* (Botley: Osprey Publishing, 2006).
14. Möbius, Ingo, *op. cit.*

281

15. Jurado, Carlos, *op. cit*; Killen, John, *The Luftwaffe* (London: Sphere Books, 1969); Musciano, Walter, *Die berühmten Me 109 und ihre Piloten* (Stuttgart: Motorbuch Verlag, 1989).

16. Möbius, Ingo, *op. cit.*

17. *ibid.*

18. Polak, Tomas, *op. cit.*

19. Braatz, Kurt, *Gott oder ein Flugzeug. Leben und Sterben des Jagdfliegers Günther Lützow* (Moosburg: NeunundzwanzigSechs Verlag, 2005).

20. Möbius, Ingo, *op. cit.*

21. Jurado, Carlos, *op. cit*; Musciano, Walter, *op. cit.*

22. Möbius, Ingo, *op. cit.*

23. Polak, Tomas, *op. cit.*

24. *ibid.*

25. Hata, Ikuhiko, Izawa, Yasuho and Shores, Christopher, *Japanese Army Air Force fighter units and their aces 1931–1945* (London: Grub Street, 2002).

26. Polak, Tomas, *op. cit.*

27. Morgan, Hugh and Seibel, Jürgen, *Combat Kill: The drama of aerial warfare in World War 2 and the controversy surrounding victories* (Sparkford: Patrick Stephens Ltd., 1997).

28. Polak, Tomas, *op. cit.*

29. Morgan, Hugh, *op. cit.*

30. Full copy of *Startkladde 7/JG 51* for the period 13 September 1943 till 18 April 1944 kindly provided by *Luftwaffe* historian Andreas Zapf.

1. Training to Be a Fighter Pilot

1. Lepage, Jean-Denis G.G., *An illustrated dictionary of the Third Reich* (Jefferson: McFarland and Company, 2014).

2. Blandford, Edmund, *Target England* (Shrewsbury: Airlife Publishing Ltd., 1997).

2. Character of the Russian War

1. Hintz, Fr. Bishop Marcin, *Gdanski Protestant Yearbook, volume 5* (Sopot: Parish of the Evangelical-Augsburg Church, 2011). Accessed online: www.gre.luteranie.pl/roczniki/GRE_rocznik_2011.pdf

2. Bellamy, Chris, *Absolute War* (London: Pan-Macmillan, 2007).

3. *ibid.*

4. *ibid.*

5. *ibid.*

6. Stargardt, Nicholas, *The German War: A nation under arms, 1939-45* (London: The Bodley Head, 2015).

7. Bellamy, Chris, *op. cit.*

8. *ibid.*

9. Gilbert, Martin, *Second World War* (London: Weidenfeld and Nicolson, 1989); Neitzel, Sönke and Welzer, Harald, *Soldaten: on fighting, killing and dying* (London: Simon and Schuster, 2012).

10. Braatz, Kurt, *Gott oder ein Flugzeug* (Moosburg: NeunundzwanzigSechs Verlag, 2005). Pages 265-7 detail the incident in question.

11. Rall, Günther, *Mein Flugbuch* (Moosburg: NeunundzwanzigSechs Verlag, 2004). Page 222 details the ignorance in question.

12. Skawran, Paul R., *Gesammelte Einzelschriften* (Pretoria: unpublished and undated manuscript). Specifically, the chapter on Hans Strelow entitled *Ein ritterlicher Mensch: Die Lebensgeschichte Hans Strelows*. Copy provided to author by Professor Skawran.

13. *ibid.*

14. *ibid.*

15. *ibid.*

16. Obermaier, Ernst, *Die Ritterkreuzträger der Luftwaffe, Band 1 Jagdflieger* (Mainz: Verlag Dieter Hoffmann, 1966); Aders, Gebhard and Held, Werner, *Jagdgeschwader 51 'Mölders'* (Stuttgart: Motorbuch Verlag, 1985).

17. Skawran, Paul R., *op. cit*; Obermaier, Ernst, *op. cit.*

18. Skawran, Paul R., *op. cit.*

19. *ibid.*

20. Bellamy, Chris, *op. cit*; Gilbert, Martin, *op. cit.*

21. Axell, Albert, *Russia's Heroes 1941-1945* (London: Magpie Books, 2010).

22. Bellamy, Chris, *op. cit*; Evans, Richard J., *The Third Reich at War* (London: Penguin, 2009); Gilbert, Martin, *op. cit.*

23. Bellamy, Chris, *op. cit*; Möbius, Ingo, *Am Himmel Europas. Der Jagdflieger Günther Scholz erinnert sich* (Chemnitz: Eigenverlag, 2009); Overy, Richard, *Russia's war* (London: Penguin Books, 1998).

3. Air War on an Epic Scale; Statistics

1. Bellamy, Chris, *Absolute War* (London: Pan-Macmillan, 2007); Overy, Richard, *Russia's War* (London: Penguin Books, 1997).

2. Bellamy, Chris, *op. cit.*

3. *ibid.*

4. Neitzel, Sönke and Welzer, Harald, *Soldaten: on fighting, killing and dying* (London: Simon and Schuster, 2012).

5. Gilbert, Martin, *Second World War* (London: Weidenfeld and Nicolson, 1989).

6. Bellamy, Chris, *op. cit.*

7. *ibid.*

8. Bellamy, Chris, *op. cit*; Gilbert, Martin, *op. cit.*

9. Obermaier, Ernst, *Die Ritterkreuzträger der Luftwaffe, Band 1 Jagdflieger* (Mainz: Verlag Dieter Hoffmann, 1966).

10. Obermaier, Ernst, *op. cit.*

11. *ibid.*

12. Obermaier, Ernst, *op. cit*; Toliver, Raymond F. and Constable, Trevor J., *Das waren die deutschen Jagdflieger-Asse 1939-1945* (Stuttgart: Motorbuch Verlag, 1975); Barbas, Bernd, *Die Geschichte der I. Gruppe des Jagdgeschwaders 52* (Überlingen: self- published, undated); Barbas, Bernd, *Die Geschichte der II. Gruppe des Jagdgeschwaders 52* (Überlingen: self- published, undated); Barbas, Bernd, *Die Geschichte der III. Gruppe des Jagdgeschwaders 52* (Überlingen: self- published, undated).

13. Fast, Niko, *Das Jagdgeschwader 52, Band 1* (Bergisch Gladbach: Bensberger Buch Verlag, 1988). First volume in a seven volume series, self-published by author.

14. Von Rhoden Collection of Research Materials on the Role of the German Air Force in World War II, 1911-47. Publication Number: T-971, Air University, Maxwell-Gunter Air Force Base, Montgomery, Alabama, USA (www.au.af.mil). Specific document: *Bemerkungen zur feindlichen Luftrüstung Nr. 1/45 Sowjetunion – Flugzeugverluste (Fremde Luftwaffen Ost, Nr. 1485/45)*, dated 12.03.1945, from the *Oberkommando der Luftwaffe*.

15. *ibid.*

16. Obermaier, Ernst, *op. cit.*

17. Von Rhoden Collection, *op. cit.*

18. Krivosheev, Grigoriy F., *Soviet casualties and combat losses in the Twentieth Century* (London: Greenhill Books, 1997).

19. Russian aircraft losses summarised from official statistics – website PKKA*CA; http://www.dol.ru/users/hotdog/airlosses.htm – accessed 07.10.2000

20. Axell, Albert, *Russia's Heroes 1941-1945* (London: Magpie Books, 2010); Polak, Tomas with Shores, Christopher, *Stalin's falcons: The aces of the Red Star* (London, Grub Street, 1999).

21. VVS RKKA, VVS Estadisticas, Estadisticas de la Aviacion Sovietica; Spanish language website (www.rkka.es) providing detailed Russian loss statistics from official sources, keyed to years, different aircraft types and different causes of combat loss; http://www.rkka.es/Estadisticas/VVS_stat/06/06_21.htm and http://www.rkka.es/Estadisticas/VVS_stat/06/06_22.htm

22. Ministry of Defense of the USSR, *The Soviet Air Force in World War II* (New York: Doubleday and Co., 1973). Originally published by the Ministry of Defense of the USSR; this edition translated by L. Fetzer, edited by R. Wagner.

23. Krivosheev, Grigoriy F., *op. cit.*

24. Toliver, Raymond F. and Constable, Trevor J., *Holt Hartmann vom Himmel!* (Stuttgart: Motorbuch Verlag, 1976).

25. Obermaier, Ernst, *op. cit.*

26. Read, Anthony, *The Devil's Disciples* (London: Pimlico, Random House, 2004).

27. Bergström, Christer with Antipov, Vlad and Sundin, Claes, *Graf and Grislawski: A pair of aces* (Hamilton: Eagle Editions, 2003). The illustrations and facsimile texts on page 166 make Graf's NSFK membership clear.

28. Toliver, Raymond F., 1976, *op. cit.*

29. United States Strategic Bombing Survey, *Over-all Report* (Washington: United States Government Printing Office, 1945). In particular chart 9 on page 20 was of value. Copy obtained from University of Michigan: https://babel.hathitrust.org

30. Author's own data for fighter *Gruppen* stationed on Eastern Front; loss data from United States Strategic Bombing Survey, *Over-all Report* (Washington: United States Government Printing Office, 1945). Copy obtained from University of Michigan: https://babel.hathitrust.org

31. United States Strategic Bombing Survey, *Over-all Report* (Washington: United States Government Printing Office, 1945). In particular chart 10 on page 21 was of value. Copy obtained from University of Michigan: https://babel.hathitrust.org

32. Bellamy, Chris, *op. cit*; Dierich, Wolfgang, *Die Verbände der Luftwaffe 1935-1945* (Stuttgart: Motorbuch Verlag, 1976).

33. Aders, Gebhard and Held, Werner, *Jagdgeschwader 51 'Mölders'* (Stuttgart: Motorbuch Verlag, 1985).

34. *ibid.*

35. Dierich, Wolfgang, *op. cit.*

36. *ibid.*

37. *ibid.*

38. *ibid.*

4. Operation Barbarossa and the Russian Winter Offensive (22 June 1941–February 1942)

1. Bergström, Christer and Mikhailov, Andrey, *Black Cross and Red Star: The Air War over the Eastern Front, Vol. 1, Operation Barbarossa, 1941* (Pacifica: Pacifica Military History, 2000).

2. *ibid.*

3. Dierich, Wolfgang, *Die Verbände der Luftwaffe 1935-1945* (Stuttgart: Motorbuch Verlag, 1976).

4. Girbig, Werner, *Jagdgeschwader 5 "Eismeerjäger"* (Stuttgart: Motorbuch Verlag, 1976).

5. Dierich, Wolfgang, *op. cit.*

6. Bergström, Christer, *op. cit.*

7. *ibid.*

8. Prien, Jochen, *Geschichte des Jagdgeschwaders 77, Teil 2, 1941-1942* (Eutin: Struve-Druck, 1993).

9. Bergström, Christer, *op. cit.*
10. Prien, Jochen, *Pik-As: Geschichte des Jagdgeschwaders 53, Teil 1* (Illertissen: Flugzeug Publikations, 1989).
11. Josef Kronschnabel here uses the nickname 'Rata' for the I-15 Russian biplane fighter, which is strictly speaking incorrect, Rata applying rather to the I-16 monoplane fighter.
12. Bellamy, Chris, *Absolute War* (London: Pan-Macmillan, 2007).
13. Bellamy, Chris, *op. cit*; Overy, Richard, *Russia's war* (London: Penguin Books, 1998); Bergström, Christer, *op. cit.*
14. Bellamy, Chris, *op. cit.*
15. Overy, Richard, *op. cit.*
16. Gunther Rosipal (and co-workers), JG 54 Home Page, *JG 54 Loss List.* Website: www.jps.net/wartburg/LossList.htm, accessed on 07.03.2000.
17. Obermaier, Ernst, *Die Ritterkreuzträger der Luftwaffe, Band 1 Jagdflieger* (Mainz: Verlag Dieter Hoffmann, 1966).
18. Bellamy, Chris, *op. cit.*
19. *ibid.*
20. Aders, Gebhard and Held, Werner, *Jagdgeschwader 51 'Mölders'* (Stuttgart: Motorbuch Verlag, 1985).
21. *ibid.*
22. Extract from the diary of *Oberfähnrich* Hans Strelow, *5/JG 51*; Prof. P. R. Skawran who was a *Luftwaffe* psychologist spent time with various fighter units. While with *JG 51* he copied several diary entries from Strelow's private effects after his death in action. Some of these he provided to the author.
23. *ibid.*
24. Prien, Jochen and Stemmer, Gerhard, *Messerschmitt Bf 109 im Einsatz bei der II./Jagdgeschwader 3, 1940-1945* (Eutin: Struve-Druck, 1996).
25. Prien, Jochen, 1989, *op. cit.*
26. Holm, Michael, webpage, *The Luftwaffe, 1933-1945*; www.ww2.dk
27. *ibid.*
28. Note 22, *op. cit.*
29. Obermaier, Ernst, *op. cit*; Prien, Jochen, 1989, *op. cit.*
30. Note 22, *op. cit.*
31. This victory of Major Trübenbach claimed on 13 July 1941 has been related to a raid on the Ploiesti oilfields in volume two of the unit history of *JG 77*, on page 687: Prien, Jochen, 1993, *op. cit.*
32. Bellamy, Chris, *op. cit.*
33. Overy, Richard, *op. cit.*
34. Holm, Michael, *op. cit.*
35. Note 22, *op. cit.*
36. Günther Schack kept a hand-written diary during most of his time on the Eastern Front (which time lasted for this entire campaign, June 1941-May

1945) which eventually filled four volumes. He summarised and typed these up into a single volume, and kindly made some excerpts (from 1941-1944) of the latter version available to the author.

37. Gilbert, Martin, *Second World War* (London: Weidenfeld and Nicolson, 1989); Overy, Richard, *op. cit.*

38. Barbas, Bernd, *Die Geschichte der II. Gruppe des Jagdgeschwaders 52* (Überlingen: self- published, undated).

39. Barbas, Bernd, *op. cit*; Bergström, Christer, *op. cit.*

40. Barbas, Bernd, *op. cit*; Bergström, Christer, *op. cit*; Holm, Michael, *op. cit.*

41. Holm, Michael, *op. cit*; Bergström, Christer, *op. cit.*

42. Bergström, Christer, *op. cit.*

43. Bellamy, Chris, *op. cit*; Bergström, Christer, *op. cit.*

44. Aders, Gebhard, *op. cit.*

5. 1942: New Offensives by the Wehrmacht; Stalingrad

1. Bellamy, Chris, *Absolute War* (London: Pan-Macmillan, 2007); Gilbert, Martin, *Second World War* (London: Weidenfeld and Nicolson, 1989); Overy, Richard, *Russia's war* (London: Penguin Books, 1998).

2. *ibid.*

3. Girbig, Werner, *Jagdgeschwader 5 "Eismeerjäger"* (Stuttgart: Motorbuch Verlag, 1976).

4. *ibid.*

5. *ibid.*

6. Möbius, Ingo, *Am Himmel Europas. Der Jagdflieger Günther Scholz erinnert sich* (Chemnitz: Eigenverlag, 2009).

7. Schuck, Walter, *Abschuss! Von der Me 109 zur Me 262; Erinnerungen an die Luftkämpfe beim Jagdgeschwader 5 und 7* (Aachen: Helios Verlag, 2007).

8. *ibid.*

9. Obermaier, Ernst, *Die Ritterkreuzträger der Luftwaffe, Band 1 Jagdflieger* (Mainz: Verlag Dieter Hoffmann, 1966).

10. Holm, Michael, webpage, *The Luftwaffe, 1933-1945*; www.ww2.dk; Held, Werner, Trautloft, Hannes and Bob, Ekkehard, *Die Grünherzjäger: Bildchronik des Jagdgeschwaders 54* (Friedberg: Podzun-Pallas-Verlag, 1985).

11. Aders, Gebhard and Held, Werner, *Jagdgeschwader 51 'Mölders'* (Stuttgart: Motorbuch Verlag, 1985); Holm, Michael, *op. cit.*

12. Prien, Jochen and Stemmer, Gerhard, *Messerschmitt Bf 109 im Einsatz bei der III./Jagdgeschwader 3* (Eutin: Struve-Druck, 1995).

13. Held, Werner, *op. cit*; Bob, Hans Ekkehard, *Grünherzjäger im Luftkampf 1940-1945; Die Geschichte des Jagdgeschwaders 54: Kriegs-Tagebuch von Hannes Trautloft, Kommodore Jagdgeschwader 54 Grünherz* (Zweibrücken: VDM Heinz Nickel, 2006). (*Aufzeichnungen aus dem Tagebuch des*

Kommodore des JG 54 Hannes Trautloft bearbeitet von Hans Ekkehard Bob als Herausgeber).

14. Holm, Michael, *op. cit*; Held, Werner, *op. cit.*

15. Bellamy, Chris, *op. cit.*

16. Bob, Hans Ekkehard, *op. cit*; Held, Werner, *op. cit.*

17. Bellamy, Chris, *op. cit.*

18. Bob, Hans Ekkehard, *op. cit.*

19. Held, Werner, *op. cit.*

20. Bergström, Christer and Mikhailov, Andrey, *Black Cross and Red Star: The Air War over the Eastern Front, Vol. 2, Resurgence, January-June 1942* (Pacifica: Pacifica Military History, 2001); Bob, Hans Ekkehard, *op. cit.*

21. Carell, Paul, *Hitler's war on Russia* (London: Corgi Books, 1967).

22. *ibid.*

23. *ibid.*

24. Bergström, Christer, *op. cit.*

25. Carell, Paul, *op. cit*; Bergström, Christer, *op. cit.*

26. Bergström, Christer, *op. cit*; Prien, Jochen and Stemmer, Gerhard, *Messerschmitt Bf 109 im Einsatz bei der II./Jagdgeschwader 3, 1940-1945* (Eutin: Struve-Druck, 1996).

27. Prien, Jochen, *Geschichte des Jagdgeschwaders 77, Teil 2, 1941-1942* (Eutin: Struve-Druck, 1993).

28. Bob, Hans Ekkehard, *op. cit.*

29. Part of page from pilot's logbook of *Oberleutnant* Hans Beisswenger, 6/JG 54 showing eighteen missions flown between 14 and 26 September 1942 displayed on www.antonycribb.com where the logbook was offered for sale by Antony Cribb Ltd., Arms and Armour Auctions.

30. Prien, Jochen, 1996, *op. cit.*

31. *ibid.*

32. *ibid.*

33. Bergström, Christer, *op. cit.*

34. Bob, Hans Ekkehard, *op. cit*; Prien, Jochen, 1995, *op. cit*; Bergström, Christer, *op. cit.*

35. Obermaier, Ernst, *op. cit.*

36. Held, Werner, *op. cit.*

37. Bob, Hans Ekkehard, *op. cit.*

38. Skawran, Paul Robert, *Ikaros; Persönlichkeit und Wesen des deutschen Jagdfliegers im Zweitem Weltkrieg* (Steinbach am Wörthsee: Luftfahrt-Verlag Walter Zuerl, 1969).

39. *ibid.*

40. Bellamy, Chris, *op. cit.*

41. *ibid.*

42. Prien, Jochen, 1993, *op. cit.*

43. Bellamy, Chris, *op. cit.*

44. Bellamy, Chris, *op. cit*; Bergström, Christer, *op. cit.*

45. Bergström, Christer, 2001, *op. cit*; Bergström, Christer, Dikov, Andrey and Antipov, Vlad, *Black Cross and Red Star: The Air War over the Eastern Front, Vol. 3, Everything for Stalingrad* (Hamilton: Eagle Editions, 2006).

46. Bergström, Christer, 2006, *op. cit*; https://en.wikipedia.org/wiki/Battles_of_Rzhev

47. Barbas, Bernd, *Die Geschichte der I. Gruppe des Jagdgeschwaders 52* (Überlingen: self-published, undated) (official edition of the *Traditionsgemeinschaft JG 52*); Prien, Jochen, 1996, *op. cit*; Bob, Hans Ekkehard, *op. cit.*

48. Holm, Michael, *op. cit.*

49. *ibid.*

50. *ibid.*

51. *ibid.*

52. *ibid.*

53. Günther Schack kept a hand-written diary during most of his time on the Eastern Front (which time lasted for this entire campaign, June 1941-May 1945) which eventually filled four volumes. He summarised and typed these up into a single volume, and kindly made some excerpts (from 1941-1944) of the latter version available to the author.

54. Aders, Gebhard, *op. cit.*

55. Bellamy, Chris, *op. cit.*

56. Prien, Jochen and Stemmer, Gerhard, *Messerschmitt Bf 109 im Einsatz bei Stab und I./Jagdgeschwader 3* (Eutin: Struve-Druck, 1997); Prien, Jochen, 1996, *op. cit*; Prien, Jochen, 1995, *op. cit*; Barbas, Bernd, *I Gruppe*, *op. cit*; Barbas, Bernd, *Die Geschichte der II. Gruppe des Jagdgeschwaders 52* (Überlingen: self-published, undated) (official edition of the *Traditionsgemeinschaft JG 52*); Prien, Jochen, 1993, *op. cit.*

57. Barbas, Bernd, *Die Geschichte der III. Gruppe des Jagdgeschwaders 52* (Überlingen: self-published, undated) (official edition of the *Traditionsgemeinschaft JG 52*); Prien, Jochen, 1993, *op. cit.*

58. The expression in German – *Geburtstag feiern* (celebrating a birthday) – amongst the *Luftwaffe* pilots it referred to having a narrow escape from a dangerous or life-threatening experience.

59. Bellamy, Chris, *op. cit.*

60. *ibid.*

61. *ibid.*

62. Barbas, Bernd, *II Gruppe*, *op. cit*; Barbas, Bernd, *III Gruppe*, *op. cit*; Prien, Jochen, 1997, *op. cit.*

63. Bergström, Christer, 2001, *op. cit.*

64. Bergström, Christer with Antipov, Vlad and Sundin, Claes, *Graf and Grislawski: A pair of aces* (Hamilton: Eagle Editions, 2003).
65. Bellamy, Chris, *op. cit.*
66. *ibid.*
67. Barbas, Bernd, *I Gruppe*, *op. cit*; Barbas, Bernd, *II Gruppe*, *op. cit*; Barbas, Bernd, *III Gruppe*, *op. cit*; Prien, Jochen, 1997, *op. cit*; Prien, Jochen, 1996, *op. cit*; Prien, Jochen, 1995, *op. cit*; Prien, Jochen, 1993, *op. cit.*
68. Bergström, Christer, 2001, *op. cit.*
69. *ibid.*
70. Prien, Jochen, 1993, *op. cit*; Prien, Jochen, 1995, *op. cit.*
71. Bellamy, Chris, *op. cit.*
72. *ibid.*
73. Bellamy, Chris, *op. cit*; Gilbert, Martin, *op. cit.*
74. Prien, Jochen, 1997, *op. cit*; Prien, Jochen, 1996, *op. cit*; Prien, Jochen, 1995, *op. cit*; Prien, Jochen, 1993, *op. cit*; Barbas, Bernd, *I Gruppe*, *op. cit*; Barbas, Bernd, *II Gruppe*, *op. cit*; Barbas, Bernd, *III Gruppe*, *op. cit*; Prien, Jochen, *Pik-As: Geschichte des Jagdgeschwaders 53, Teil 1* (Illertissen: Flugzeug Publikations, 1989).
75. Prien, Jochen, 1993, *op. cit.*
76. Prien, Jochen, 1997, *op. cit*; Prien, Jochen, 1996, *op. cit*; Prien, Jochen, 1995, *op. cit*; Barbas, Bernd, *I Gruppe*, *op. cit*; Barbas, Bernd, *II Gruppe*, *op. cit*; Barbas, Bernd, *III Gruppe*, *op. cit*; Prien, Jochen, 1989, *op. cit.*
77. Webpage; *Romanian Armed Forces in the Second World War*; www.worldwar2.ro.
78. Bellamy, Chris, *op. cit.*
79. *ibid.*
80. *ibid.*
81. Prien, Jochen, 1997, *op. cit*; Prien, Jochen, 1996, *op. cit*; Prien, Jochen, 1995, *op. cit*; Barbas, Bernd, *II Gruppe*, *op. cit*; Prien, Jochen, 1989, *op. cit.*
82. Prien, Jochen, 1997, *op. cit*; Prien, Jochen, 1995, *op. cit*; Prien, Jochen, 1989, *op. cit.*
83. Bellamy, Chris, *op. cit*; Gilbert, Martin, *op. cit.*
84. Beevor, Antony, *Stalingrad* (London: Penguin Books, 1999).
85. Bellamy, Chris, *op. cit.*
86. *ibid.*
87. Hayward, Joel S.A., *Stopped at Stalingrad: the Luftwaffe and Hitler's defeat in the East 1942-1943* (Lawrence: University Press of Kansas, 1998).
88. *ibid.*
89. Prien, Jochen, 1997, *op. cit*; Prien, Jochen, 1995, *op. cit.*
90. Prien, Jochen, 1997, *op. cit.*
91. Ebener, Kurt, *Platzschutzstaffel Pitomnik*. Short article in *Jägerblatt*, December 1972 issue, Nr. 4/XXII, pages 6-7.

92. Prien, Jochen, 1997, *op. cit.*

93. Ebener, Kurt, *op. cit.*

94. *ibid.*

95. Prien, Jochen, 1997, *op. cit.*

96. Ebener, Kurt, *op. cit.*

97. Obermaier, Ernst, *op. cit*; Ebener, Kurt, *op. cit.*

98. Hayward, Joel, *op. cit.*

99. *ibid.*

100. Bellamy, Chris, *op. cit.*

101. Barbas, Bernd, *II Gruppe, op. cit.*

102. Barbas, Bernd, *I Gruppe, op. cit.*

103. Barbas, Bernd, *III Gruppe, op. cit.*

104. *ibid.*

105. *ibid.*

106. Obermaier, Ernst, *op. cit.*

6. 1943: Year of Decision, the Tide Turns; Kuban and Kursk

1. *Jagdgeschwader 5 Abschussliste* (list of claimed victories), from www.asisbiz.com/Luftwaffe.html (website editor: Matthew Laird Acred).

2. Holm, Michael, webpage, *The Luftwaffe, 1933-1945*; www.ww2.dk

3. Erickson, John, *The road to Berlin* (London: Cassell, 1983).

4. *ibid.*

5. *ibid.*

6. Caldwell, Donald L., *JG 26; Top guns of the Luftwaffe* (New York: Orion Books, 1991); Priller, Josef, *J.G. 26: Geschichte eines Jagdgeschwaders* (Stuttgart: Motorbuch Verlag, 1980).

7. Holm, Michael, *op. cit*; Caldwell, Donald L., *op. cit*; Priller, Josef, *op. cit.*

8. Caldwell, Donald L., *op. cit.*

9. Holm, Michael, *op. cit*; Held, Werner, Trautloft, Hannes and Bob, Ekkehard, *Die Grünherzjäger: Bildchronik des Jagdgeschwaders 54* (Friedberg: Podzun-Pallas-Verlag, 1985); Caldwell, Donald L., *op. cit.*

10. Bob, Hans Ekkehard, *Grünherzjäger im Luftkampf 1940-1945; Die Geschichte des Jagdgeschwaders 54: Kriegs-Tagebuch von Hannes Trautloft, Kommodore Jagdgeschwader 54 Grünherz* (Zweibrücken: VDM Heinz Nickel, 2006) (*Aufzeichnungen aus dem Tagebuch des Kommodore des JG 54 Hannes Trautloft bearbeitet von Hans Ekkehard Bob als Herausgeber*); Held, Werner, *op. cit.*

11. Holm, Michael, *op. cit.*

12. One page from handwritten, shortened copy of *Leistungsbuch* (detailed military record of achievement) of *Leutnant* Wolfgang Kretschmer, 6/JG 54, for the period 4 to 21 March 1943; from eMedals web page advertising militaria for sale: www.emedals.com

13. *ibid.*
14. deZeng, Henry L. IV and Stankey, Douglas G., *Luftwaffe Officer Career Summaries* (2014 updated version); www.ww2.dk/lwoffz.html (hosted on Michael Holm's webpage: *The Luftwaffe, 1933-1945*; www.ww2.dk)
15. Holm, Michael, *op. cit.*
16. *ibid.*
17. *ibid.*
18. *ibid.*
19. *ibid.*
20. *ibid.*
21. *ibid.*
22. Erickson, John, *op. cit.*
23. Erickson, John, *op. cit*; Young, Peter (Editor), *The World Almanac Book of World War II* (New York: World Almanac Publisher, 1981).
24. Young, Peter, *op. cit*; Hardesty, Von and Grinberg, Ilya, *Red Phoenix Rising; the Soviet Air Force in World War II* (Lawrence: University Press of Kansas, 2012).
25. Erickson, John, *op. cit*; Young, Peter, *op. cit.*
26. Barbas, Bernd, *Die Geschichte der I. Gruppe des Jagdgeschwaders 52* (Überlingen: self-published, undated) (official edition of the *Traditionsgemeinschaft JG 52*); Barbas, Bernd, *Die Geschichte der II. Gruppe des Jagdgeschwaders 52* (Überlingen: self-published, undated) (official edition of the *Traditionsgemeinschaft JG 52*); Barbas, Bernd, *Die Geschichte der III. Gruppe des Jagdgeschwaders 52* (Überlingen: self-published, undated) (official edition of the *Traditionsgemeinschaft JG 52*).
27. Barbas, Bernd, *II Gruppe*, *op. cit*; Barbas, Bernd, *III Gruppe*, *op. cit.*
28. Barbas, Bernd, *I Gruppe*, *op. cit.*
29. Holm, Michael, *op. cit.*
30. Barbas, Bernd, *III Gruppe*, *op. cit.*
31. *ibid.*
32. Prien, Jochen and Stemmer, Gerhard, *Messerschmitt Bf 109 im Einsatz bei Stab und I./Jagdgeschwader 3* (Eutin: Struve-Druck, 1997).
33. Prien, Jochen and Stemmer, Gerhard, *Messerschmitt Bf 109 im Einsatz bei der II./Jagdgeschwader 3, 1940-1945* (Eutin: Struve-Druck, 1996).
34. *ibid.*
35. Prien, Jochen and Stemmer, Gerhard, *Messerschmitt Bf 109 im Einsatz bei der III./Jagdgeschwader 3* (Eutin: Struve-Druck, 1995).
36. Holm, Michael, *op. cit*; Prien, Jochen, 1996, *op. cit.*
37. Holm, Michael, *op. cit.*
38. A few pages of the flying logbook (and data from some other documents) of *Unteroffizier* Wilhelm Hauswirth, 8/JG 52 (dated from 24 April-30 May

1943), from web page advertising militaria for sale: Hermann Historica, international auctioneers, www.hermann-historica.de

39. Barbas, Bernd, *III Gruppe, op. cit.*
40. *ibid.*
41. Barbas, Bernd, *III Gruppe, op. cit*; note 38, *op. cit.*
42. Barbas, Bernd, *III Gruppe, op. cit.*
43. *ibid.*
44. Note 38, *op. cit.*
45. Hardesty, Von, *op. cit.*
46. *ibid.*
47. Note 38, *op. cit.*
48. Obermaier, Ernst, *Die Ritterkreuzträger der Luftwaffe, Band 1 Jagdflieger* (Mainz: Verlag Dieter Hoffmann, 1966).
49. deZeng, Henry, *op. cit.*
50. Holm, Michael, *op. cit.*
51. Barbas, Bernd, *I Gruppe, op. cit*; Barbas, Bernd, *III Gruppe, op. cit.*
52. Barbas, Bernd, *III Gruppe, op. cit.*
53. Barbas, Bernd, *I Gruppe, op. cit.*
54. Barbas, Bernd, *III Gruppe, op. cit.*
55. Note 38, *op. cit.*
56. *ibid.*
57. Barbas, Bernd, *III Gruppe, op. cit.*
58. Note 38, *op. cit.*
59. Prien, Jochen, 1996, *op. cit.*
60. Prien, Jochen, 1995, *op. cit.*
61. Prien, Jochen, 1996, *op. cit.*
62. *ibid.*
63. *ibid.*
64. *ibid.*
65. *ibid.*
66. *ibid.*
67. *ibid.*
68. Prien, Jochen, 1995, *op. cit.*
69. Holm, Michael, *op. cit.*
70. *ibid.*
71. deZeng, Henry, *op. cit.*
72. Holm, Michael, *op. cit.*
73. *ibid.*
74. deZeng, Henry, *op. cit.*
75. Handwritten, shortened copy of *Leistungsbuch* (detailed military record of achievement) of *Unteroffizier* Ulrich Wernitz, 3/JG 54; several pages giving data for four periods: 17 June– 15 July 1943; 31 July–25 September 1943;

9-17 October 1943; 13 March 1944-2 June 1944, from eMedals web page advertising militaria for sale: www.emedals.com

76. *ibid.*
77. *ibid.*
78. *ibid.*
79. *ibid.*
80. *ibid.*
81. Barbas, Bernd, *III Gruppe, op. cit.*
82. *ibid.*
83. *ibid.*
84. Barbas, Bernd, *II Gruppe, op. cit.*
85. Barbas, Bernd, *I Gruppe, op. cit.*
86. Holm, Michael, *op. cit.*
87. *ibid.*
88. Toliver, Raymond F. and Constable, Trevor J., *Das waren die deutschen Jagdflieger-Asse 1939-1945* (Stuttgart: Motorbuch Verlag, 1975).
89. Note 75, *op. cit.*
90. *ibid.*
91. *ibid.*
92. *ibid.*
93. Holm, Michael, *op. cit.*
94. *ibid.*
95. *ibid.*
96. *ibid.*
97. *ibid.*
98. *ibid.*
99. Aders, Gebhard and Held, Werner, *Jagdgeschwader 51 'Mölders'* (Stuttgart: Motorbuch Verlag, 1985); Holm, Michael, *op. cit.*
100. Aders, Gebhard, *op. cit.*
101. Dierich, Wolfgang, *Die Verbände der Luftwaffe 1935-1945* (Stuttgart: Motorbuch Verlag, 1976).
102. Holm, Michael, *op. cit*; Buchner, Hermann, *Stormbird: flying through fire as a Luftwaffe ground attack pilot and Me 262 ace* (Aldershot: Hikoki Publications, 2000).
103. Buchner, Hermann, *op. cit.*
104. Khazanov, Dmitriy B., *Air war over Kursk* (Bedford: SAM Publications, 2010).

7. *Endless Retreats; The Bagration Debacle (January–August 1944)*

1. Obermaier, Ernst, *Die Ritterkreuzträger der Luftwaffe, Band 1 Jagdflieger* (Mainz: Verlag Dieter Hoffmann, 1966).
2. Girbig, Werner, *Jagdgeschwader 5 "Eismeerjäger"* (Stuttgart: Motorbuch Verlag, 1976); Holm, Michael, webpage, *The Luftwaffe, 1933-1945*, www.

ww2.dk; *Jagdgeschwader 5 Abschussliste* (list of claimed victories), from www.asisbiz.com/Luftwaffe.html (website editor: Matthew Laird Acred).

3. *ibid.*
4. Holm, Michael, *op. cit.*
5. *ibid.*
6. Holm, Michael, *op. cit*; *Jagdgeschwader 5 Abschussliste, op. cit.*
7. Holm, Michael, *op. cit.*
8. Young, Peter (Editor), *The World Almanac Book of World War II* (New York: World Almanac Publisher, 1981); *Gefechtsverband Kuhlmey* (a *Luftwaffe* combat detachment, temporarily created in Finland and commanded by *Oberstleutnant* Kuhlmey), history summarised on: https://en.wikipedia.org/wiki/Detachment_Kuhlmey
9. *Gefechtsverband Kuhlmey, op. cit.*
10. Copies of the reports from *Gefechtsverband Kuhlmey* were provided to the Finns during the war and these are preserved in the Finnish military archives. Records translated, with minor editing, by author. Via Finnish aviation historian Juha Vaittinen, from Finnish military archives.
11. Möbius, Ingo, *Am Himmel Europas. Der Jagdflieger Günther Scholz erinnert sich* (Chemnitz: Eigenverlag, 2009); Young, Peter, *op. cit.*
12. Paragraph based on: Bellamy, Chris, *Absolute War* (London: Pan-Macmillan, 2007); Gilbert, Martin, *Second World War* (London: Weidenfeld and Nicolson, 1989); Overy, Richard, *Russia's war* (London: Penguin Books, 1998); Erickson, John, *The road to Berlin* (London: Cassell, 1983); Young, Peter, *op. cit.*
13. Holm, Michael, *op. cit.*
14. *ibid.*
15. *ibid.*
16. Held, Werner, Trautloft, Hannes and Bob, Ekkehard, *Die Grünherzjäger: Bildchronik des Jagdgeschwaders 54* (Friedberg: Podzun-Pallas-Verlag, 1985).
17. Holm, Michael, *op. cit.*
18. Erickson, John, *op. cit.*
19. Bellamy, Chris, *op. cit.*
20. Holm, Michael, *op. cit.*
21. Handwritten, shortened copy of *Leistungsbuch* (detailed military record of achievement) of *Unteroffizier* Ulrich Wernitz, 3/JG 54; several pages giving data for four periods: 17 June– 15 July 1943; 31 July–25 September 1943; 9-17 October 1943; 13 March 1944-2 June 1944, from eMedals web page advertising militaria for sale: www.emedals.com
22. *ibid.*
23. Holm, Michael, *op. cit.*
24. *ibid.*

25. *ibid.*

26. Barbas, Bernd, *Die Geschichte der III. Gruppe des Jagdgeschwaders 52* (Überlingen: self-published, undated) (official edition of the *Traditionsgemeinschaft JG 52*).

27. Holm, Michael, *op. cit.*

28. *ibid.*

29. *ibid.*

30. Barbas, Bernd, *op. cit*; Holm, Michael, *op. cit.*

31. Barbas, Bernd, *op. cit.*

32. Barbas, Bernd, *Die Geschichte der II. Gruppe des Jagdgeschwaders 52* (Überlingen: self-published, undated) (official edition of the *Traditionsgemeinschaft JG 52*).

33. Barbas, Bernd, *II Gruppe, op. cit*; Ewald, Heinz, *Esau: Heinz Ewald als Jagdflieger im erfolgreichsten Jagdgeschwader 1943-1945* (Coburg: privately published, 1980).

34. *ibid.*

35. Barbas, Bernd, *II Gruppe, op. cit*; Barbas, Bernd, *III Gruppe, op. cit.*

36. Krivosheev, Grigoriy F., *Soviet casualties and combat losses in the Twentieth Century* (London: Greenhill Books, 1997).

37. Barbas, Bernd, *Die Geschichte der I. Gruppe des Jagdgeschwaders 52* (Überlingen: self-published, undated) (official edition of the *Traditionsgemeinschaft JG 52*).

38. Adair, Paul, *Hitler's greatest defeat* (London: Cassell, 1994).

39. Holm, Michael, *op. cit.*

40. *ibid.*

41. *ibid.*

42. *ibid.*

43. Prien, Jochen and Rodeike, Peter, *Jagdgeschwader 1 und 11. Einsatz in der Reichsverteidigung von 1939 bis 1945, Teil 3, 1944-1945* (Eutin: Struve Druck, undated).

44. *ibid.*

45. *ibid.*

46. Barbas, Bernd, *III Gruppe, op. cit.*

47. Erickson, John, *op. cit.*

48. *ibid.*

49. *ibid.*

50. *ibid.*

51. *ibid.*

52. *ibid.*

53. *ibid.*

54. Holm, Michael, *op. cit.*

55. *ibid.*
56. Data for confirmed victory claims mostly from the lists first published on the web by Tony Wood: *Tony Wood's Combat Claims and Casualties Lists;* accessed via Don Caldwell's website: don-caldwell.we.bs/claims/tonywood.htm (with many succeeding repeats and relatively minor edits by fellow historians). These claims lists are not complete and contain gaps, some large also, especially for certain Me 110 units in 1940; however, they do reflect accredited victory claims and not just submitted and unverified claims.
57. Barbas, Bernd, *III Gruppe, op. cit.*
58. Erickson, John, *op. cit.*
59. Holm, Michael, *op. cit.*
60. *ibid.*
61. Obermaier, Ernst, *op. cit.*
62. Holm, Michael, *op. cit.*
63. *ibid.*
64. Erickson, John, *op. cit.*
65. Barbas, Bernd, *I Gruppe, op. cit*; Barbas, Bernd, *II Gruppe, op. cit*; Barbas, Bernd, *III Gruppe, op. cit*; Holm, Michael, *op. cit.*
66. Barbas, Bernd, *I Gruppe, op. cit*; Barbas, Bernd, *II Gruppe, op. cit*; Barbas, Bernd, *III Gruppe, op. cit.*
67. Barbas, Bernd, *I Gruppe, op. cit.*
68. Prien, Jochen, *Geschichte des Jagdgeschwaders 77, Teil 4, 1944-1945* (Eutin: Struve-Druck, undated); Prien, Jochen, *Pik-As: Geschichte des Jagdgeschwaders 53, Teil 3* (Eutin: Struve-Druck, 1991).
69. Prien, Jochen, *Jagdgeschwader 77, Teil 4, op. cit.*
70. *ibid.*
71. *ibid.*
72. Barbas, Bernd, *II Gruppe, op. cit.*

8. Late 1944–1945: The End of the Campaign in the East

1. Paragraph based on: Bellamy, Chris, *Absolute War* (London: Pan-Macmillan, 2007); Gilbert, Martin, *Second World War* (London: Weidenfeld and Nicolson, 1989); Overy, Richard, *Russia's war* (London: Penguin Books, 1998); Erickson, John, *The road to Berlin* (London: Cassell, 1983); Young, Peter (Editor), *The World Almanac Book of World War II* (New York: World Almanac Publisher, 1981).
2. Erickson, John, *op. cit.*
3. *ibid.*
4. *ibid.*
5. *ibid.*

6. *ibid.*
7. *ibid.*
8. Holm, Michael, webpage, *The Luftwaffe, 1933-1945*, www.ww2.dk
9. Barbas, Bernd, *Die Geschichte der I. Gruppe des Jagdgeschwaders 52* (Überlingen: self-published, undated) (official edition of the *Traditionsgemeinschaft JG 52*); Barbas, Bernd, *Die Geschichte der III. Gruppe des Jagdgeschwaders 52* (Überlingen: self-published, undated) (official edition of the *Traditionsgemeinschaft JG 52*).
10. Holm, Michael, *op. cit.*
11. Aders, Gebhard and Held, Werner, *Jagdgeschwader 51 'Mölders'* (Stuttgart: Motorbuch Verlag, 1985).
12. In the *Luftwaffe*, as in all air forces, it was possible to move from the enlisted ranks to officer status, without attending a war college, based on good performance in action. A rank term such as *Fahnenjunker-Feldwebel* illustrates this concept, the first part (*Fahnenjunker*) referring to an officer cadet chosen from the ranks and *Feldwebel* to the rank held by the NCO. Others might analogously be called *Fahnenjunker-Oberfeldwebel* or *Fahnenjunker-Unteroffizier* etc. They would maintain such interim ranks during the transition to these wartime officer appointments. Officers stemming from the regular, war college route, would also spend quite some time as cadets before finally being commissioned, and they were known as *Fähnrich* and then *Oberfähnrich* before becoming a *Leutnant*. The time taken for these various promotion stages to final officer's commission would depend on both performance in action as well as disciplinary record.
13. Aders, Gebhard, *op. cit.*
14. Erickson, John, *op. cit.*
15. *ibid.*
16. *ibid.*
17. *ibid.*
18. Holm, Michael, *op. cit.*
19. *ibid.*
20. *ibid.*
21. Sims, Edward H., *Jagdflieger, die grossen Gegner von einst* (Stuttgart: Motorbuch Verlag, 1994).
22. Held, Werner, Trautloft, Hannes and Bob, Ekkehard, *Die Grünherzjäger: Bildchronik des Jagdgeschwaders 54* (Friedberg: Podzun-Pallas-Verlag, 1985).
23. *ibid.*
24. Sims, Edward H., *op. cit.*
25. Summary of shipping losses Libau harbour, Kurland, 1 August 1944-31 December 1944, source of data: *Marine-Akten, Militärarchiv Freiburg im*

Breisgau, Sektion Kriegsmarine, Reiko-See, K.M.D. Danzig; *signatur M 519/8632*, from page 141. Summary made by Albrecht Licht.

26. Obermaier, Ernst, *Die Ritterkreuzträger der Luftwaffe, Band 1 Jagdflieger* (Mainz: Verlag Dieter Hoffmann, 1966).

27. deZeng, Henry L. IV and Stankey, Douglas G., *Luftwaffe Officer Career Summaries* (2014 updated version); www.ww2.dk/lwoffz.html (hosted on Michael Holm's webpage: *The Luftwaffe, 1933-1945*; www.ww2.dk)

28. Part of pilot's logbook of *Feldwebel* Ernst Scotti of *8/SG 3* in Kurland, December 1944-March 1945, displayed as part of the collection of 'Olivier-F.', shown on forum on website Wehrmacht Awards.com

29. Erickson, John, *op. cit.*

30. Erickson, John, *op. cit*; https://en.wikipedia.org/wiki/Slovakia_during_World_War_II

31. Barbas, Bernd, *I Gruppe*, *op. cit.*

32. Erickson, John, *op. cit.*

33. *ibid.*

34. *ibid.*

35. Barbas, Bernd, *Die Geschichte der II. Gruppe des Jagdgeschwaders 52* (Überlingen: self-published, undated) (official edition of the *Traditionsgemeinschaft JG 52*); Prien, Jochen, *Geschichte des Jagdgeschwaders 77, Teil 4, 1944-1945* (Eutin: Struve-Druck, undated); Prien, Jochen, *Pik-As: Geschichte des Jagdgeschwaders 53, Teil 3* (Eutin: Struve-Druck, 1991).

36. Barbas, Bernd, *II Gruppe*, *op. cit*; Prien, Jochen, 1991, *op. cit.*

37. Ewald, Heinz, *Esau: Heinz Ewald als Jagdflieger im erfolgreichsten Jagdgeschwader 1943-1945* (Coburg: privately published, 1980).

38. Prien, Jochen, 1991, *op. cit.*

39. Prien, Jochen, *Pik-As: Geschichte des Jagdgeschwaders 53, Teil 2* (Eutin: Struve-Druck, 1990); Prien, Jochen, 1991, *op. cit.*

40. Prien, Jochen, 1991, *op. cit.*

41. Erickson, John, *op. cit.*

42. *ibid.*

43. *ibid.*

44. Dierich, Wolfgang, *Die Verbände der Luftwaffe 1935-1945* (Stuttgart: Motorbuch Verlag, 1976).

45. Erickson, John, *op. cit.*

46. Prien, Jochen and Stemmer, Gerhard, *Messerschmitt Bf 109 im Einsatz bei Stab und I./Jagdgeschwader 3* (Eutin: Struve-Druck, 1997).

47. *ibid.*

48. *ibid.*

49. Green, William, *War planes of the Second World War: Fighters volume three* (London: Macdonald and Co., 1962).

9. The Startkladde of 7/JG 51: Understanding German Fighter Tactics and High Claims in the East

1. Zapf, Andreas, *Chronicles of the Luftwaffe 1935-1945*; www.chronicles-of-the-luftwaffe.de
2. deZeng, Henry L. IV and Stankey, Douglas G., *Luftwaffe Officer Career Summaries* (2014 updated version); www.ww2.dk/lwoffz.html (hosted on Michael Holm's webpage: *The Luftwaffe, 1933-1945*; www.ww2.dk); Wood, Tony, *Tony Wood's Combat Claims and Casualties Lists*; accessed via Don Caldwell's website: don-caldwell.we.bs/claims/tonywood.htm (with many succeeding repeats and relatively minor edits by fellow historians) (These very extensive lists, first published on the web by Tony Wood, contain data for confirmed victory claims; while these claims lists are not complete and contain gaps, some large also, especially for certain Me 110 units in 1940, they do however reflect accredited victory claims and not just submitted and unverified claims.)
3. Obermaier, Ernst, *Die Ritterkreuzträger der Luftwaffe, Band 1 Jagdflieger* (Mainz: Verlag Dieter Hoffmann, 1966).
4. *ibid.*
5. Obermaier, Ernst, *op. cit*; deZeng, Henry, *op. cit.*
6. deZeng, Henry, *op. cit.*
7. Wood, Tony, *op. cit.*
8. *ibid.*
9. *ibid.*
10. Wood, Tony, *op. cit*; Aders, Gebhard and Held, Werner, *Jagdgeschwader 51 'Mölders'* (Stuttgart: Motorbuch Verlag, 1985).
11. Wood, Tony, *op. cit.*
12. Aders, Gebhard, *op. cit.*
13. Wood, Tony, *op. cit.*
14. *ibid.*
15. *ibid.*
16. *ibid.*
17. Aders, Gebhard, *op. cit.*
18. *ibid.*
19. *ibid.*
20. Prien, Jochen and Rodeike, Peter, *Jagdgeschwader 1 und 11. Einsatz in der Reichsverteidigung von 1939 bis 1945, Teil 3, 1944-1945* (Eutin: Struve Druck, undated).
21. Wood, Tony, *op. cit.*
22. Aders, Gebhard, *op. cit.*
23. *ibid.*
24. *ibid.*
25. *ibid.*

26. *ibid.*

27. Vaittinen, Juha, *The lengths of the RAF operational tours;* juhansotahistoriasivut.weebly.com (includes also discussion on definitions of terms *Einsatz, Frontflug/Feindflug*).

28. Prien, Jochen and Rodeike, Peter, *Jagdgeschwader 1 und 11. Einsatz in der Reichsverteidigung von 1939 bis 1945, Teil 2, 1944* (Eutin: Struve Druck, undated).

29. Wood, Tony, *op. cit.*

30. *ibid.*

31. *ibid.*

32. *ibid.*

33. United States Army Security Agency, *European Axis signal intelligence in World War II as revealed by 'TICOM' investigations and by other prisoner of war interrogations and captured material, principally German* (Washington DC: Army Security Agency, 1946) (available from the National Security Agency-Central Security Service: www.nsa.gov/public_ info/declass/european_axis_sigint.shtml).

34. *ibid.*

35. Wood, Tony, *op. cit.*

36. Prien, Jochen, *Jagdgeschwader 1 und 11, Teil 2, op. cit.*

37. *ibid.*

38. *ibid.*

39. *ibid.*

40. *ibid.*

41. *ibid.*

42. *ibid.*

43. *ibid.*

44. Prien, Jochen, *Jagdgeschwader 1 und 11, Teil 2, op. cit*; Prien, Jochen, *Jagdgeschwader 1 und 11, Teil 3, op. cit.*

45. Prien, Jochen, *Jagdgeschwader 1 und 11, Teil 3, op. cit.*

46. *ibid.*

47. Aders, Gebhard, *op. cit.*

48. Aders, Gebhard, *op. cit*; Ring, Hans and Girbig, Werner, *Jagdgeschwader 27, Die Dokumentation über den Einsatz an allen Fronten 1939-1945* (Stuttgart: Motorbuch Verlag, 1975).

49. Aders, Gebhard, *op. cit.*

50. Aders, Gebhard, *op. cit*; Ring, Hans, *op. cit.*

51. Prien, Jochen, *Jagdgeschwader 1 und 11, Teil 3, op. cit.*

52. Aders, Gebhard, *op. cit.*

53. Obermaier, Ernst, *op. cit.*

54. Günther Schack kept a hand-written diary during most of his time on the Eastern Front (which time lasted for this entire campaign, June 1941-May

1945) which eventually filled four volumes. He summarised and typed these up into a single volume, and kindly made some excerpts (from 1941-1944) of the latter version available to the author.

10. *The Victory Claims Debate*

1. Lipfert, Helmut, *Das Tagebuch des Hauptmann Lipfert* (Stuttgart: Motorbuch Verlag, 1975).

2. The documents shown in illustrations 46, 47 and 48 are copies of originals held by the *Bundesarchiv-Militärarchiv* in Freiburg, Germany, and were kindly provided by ex-*Feldwebel* in *II/JG 1* Otto Schmid.

3. Prien, Jochen and Rodeike, Peter, *Jagdgeschwader 1 und 11. Einsatz in der Reichsverteidigung von 1939 bis 1945, Teil 1, 1939-1943* (Eutin: Struve Druck, 1993).

4. *ibid.*

5. *ibid.*

6. Wood, Tony, *Tony Wood's Combat Claims and Casualties Lists*; accessed via Don Caldwell's website: don-caldwell.we.bs/claims/tonywood.htm (with many succeeding repeats and relatively minor edits by fellow historians). These very extensive lists, first published on the web by Tony Wood, contain data for confirmed victory claims. While these claims lists are not complete and contain gaps, some large also, especially for certain Me 110 units in 1940 and for Eastern Front claims in the first half of 1942, they do however reflect accredited victory claims and not just submitted and unverified claims.

7. Prien, Jochen, 1993, *op. cit.*

8. Obermaier, Ernst, *Die Ritterkreuzträger der Luftwaffe, Band 1 Jagdflieger* (Mainz: Verlag Dieter Hoffmann, 1966).

9. McKee, Alexander, *Great mysteries of aviation* (New York: Stein and Day, 1986). The page from *JG 2's Abschussliste* is among the illustrations in this book.

10. Möbius, Ingo, *Am Himmel Europas. Der Jagdflieger Günther Scholz erinnert sich* (Chemnitz: Eigenverlag, 2009).

11. Kurowski, Franz, *Luftwaffe aces: German combat pilots of WWII* (Mechanicsburg: Stackpole Books, 2004).

12. Eriksson, Patrick G., *Alarmstart South to North*; planned third volume in the *Alarmstart* series with focus on the Mediterannean air war, currently being revised.

13. Wood, Tony, *op. cit.*

14. To obtain a better understanding of the Tony Wood German fighter victory claims lists, the reader is referred to the website of the *Luftwaffe* Archives and Records Reference Group (www.lwag.org) and particularly

to the relevant discussion board. This gives the history and background information, as well as critical comments to improve any interested person's understanding of these records.

15. Caldwell, Donald L., *JG 26 Luftwaffe Fighter Wing Diary, 1939-1942,* Vol. 1 (Mechanicsburg: Stackpole Books, 2012); Caldwell, Donald L., *JG 26 Luftwaffe Fighter Wing Diary, 1943-1945,* Vol. 2 (Mechanicsburg: Stackpole Books, 2012); Wood, Tony, *op. cit.*

16. The website of the *Ministerie van Defensie* in the Netherlands, specifically the *Verliesregister* for 1944, showing all aircraft known to have fallen over Holland in that year; www.defensie.nl

17. *ibid.*

18. This particular document is one of the daily combat summary reports (*Gesamttageseinsätze*), specifically that for 11 July 1944 (Br. B. Nr. 142a/44), from *Gefechtsverband Kuhlmey*, an informal short-lived unit operating in support of Finland in June and July 1944. Juha Vaittinen, accomplished Finnish air historian, kindly supplied copies of certain original documents relating to the *Luftwaffe* from the National Archives of Finland.

19. *ibid.*

20. *ibid.*

21. Morgan, Hugh and Seibel, Jürgen, *Combat Kill: The drama of aerial warfare in World War 2 and the controversy surrounding victories* (Sparkford: Patrick Stephens Ltd., 1997). The relevant translation of Galland's order is shown on page 180.

22. *ibid.*

23. Galland, Adolf, *The first and the last* (London: Fontana/Collins, 1970). English translation of original German text. The relevant footnote detailing Galland's comments on German claims is on page 272 in this edition of a much published book.

24. Prien, Jochen, *Pik-As: Geschichte des Jagdgeschwaders 53, Teil 3* (Eutin: Struve-Druck, 1991).

25. *ibid.*

26. Shores, Christopher and Cull, Brian with Malizia, Nicola, *Malta: the Spitfire year 1942* (London: Grub Street, 1991). The 288th victory of I/JG 53 is recorded on page 180.

27. Prien, Jochen, 1991, *op. cit.*

28. Prien, Jochen and Stemmer, Gerhard, *Messerschmitt Bf 109 im Einsatz bei der III./Jagdgeschwader 3* (Eutin: Struve-Druck, 1995).

29. *ibid.*

30. Prien, Jochen, *Geschichte des Jagdgeschwaders 77, Teil 4, 1944-1945* (Eutin: Struve-Druck, undated).

31. *ibid.*

32. Barbas, Bernd, *Die Geschichte der I. Gruppe des Jagdgeschwaders 52* (Überlingen: self-published, undated) (official edition of the *Traditionsgemeinschaft JG 52*); Barbas, Bernd, *Die Geschichte der III. Gruppe des Jagdgeschwaders 52* (Überlingen: self-published, undated) (official edition of the *Traditionsgemeinschaft JG 52*).

33. Barbas, Bernd, *Die Geschichte der II. Gruppe des Jagdgeschwaders 52* (Überlingen: self-published, undated) (official edition of the *Traditionsgemeinschaft JG 52*).

34. Barbas, Bernd, *III Gruppe, op. cit.*

35. *ibid.*

36. *ibid.*

37. Barbas, Bernd, *I Gruppe, op. cit*; Barbas, Bernd, *III Gruppe, op. cit.*

38. Barbas, Bernd, *III Gruppe, op. cit.*

39. *ibid.*

40. Shores, Christopher, *op. cit.*

41. Prien, Jochen, 1991, *op. cit.*

42. Barbas, Bernd, *III Gruppe, op. cit.*

43. *ibid.*

44. *ibid.*

45. Prien, Jochen, 1991, *op. cit.*

46. Prien, Jochen, 1995, *op. cit.*

47. Wood, Tony, *op. cit.*

48. Prien, Jochen, 1991, *op. cit.*

49. Boiten, Theo, *Nachtjagd War Diaries: An operational history of the German night fighter force in the West, volume 1: September 1939 – March 1944* (Walton on Thames: Red Kite, 2008); Boiten, Theo and Mackenzie, Roderick J., *Nachtjagd War Diaries: An operational history of the German night fighter force in the West, volume 2: April 1944–May 1945* (Walton on Thames: Red Kite, 2008).

50. *ibid.*

51. *ibid.*

52. Wood, Tony, *op. cit*; Barbas, Bernd, *I Gruppe, op. cit*; Barbas, Bernd, *II Gruppe, op. cit*; Barbas, Bernd, *III Gruppe, op. cit.*

53. Wood, Tony, *op. cit.*

54. Barbas, Bernd, *III Gruppe, op. cit.*

55. Morgan, Hugh, *op. cit.*

56. Galland, Adolf, *op. cit.*

57. Barbas, Bernd, *III Gruppe, op. cit.*

58. Shores, Christopher and Ring, Hans, *Fighters over the Desert* (London: Neville Spearman, 1969).

59. Prien, Jochen and Stemmer, Gerhard, *Messerschmitt Bf 109 im Einsatz bei Stab und I./Jagdgeschwader 3* (Eutin: Struve-Druck, 1997).

60. Caldwell, Donald L., Vol. 1, *op. cit.*

61. Burt, Kendal and Leasor, James, *The one that got away* (London: Collins, 1968).

62. Wood, Tony, *op. cit.*

63. Burt, Kendal, *op. cit.*

64. Prien, Jochen and Stemmer, Gerhard, *Messerschmitt Bf 109 im Einsatz bei der II./Jagdgeschwader 3, 1940-1945* (Eutin: Struve-Druck, 1996).

65. The correct abbreviated nomenclature of the Messerschmitt 109 often encompasses some confusion: is 'Bf 109' or 'Me 109' correct? Willy Messerschmitt, the principal designer of the '109' had been the technical director of *Bayerische Flugzeugwerke A.G.* in Augsburg, which became the *Messerschmitt-Flugzeug-Werke A.G.* in 1938 [details in: Nowarra, Heinz J., *The Messerschmitt 109 – A famous German fighter* (Letchworth: Harleyford Publications Ltd., 1966) – see page twelve therein]. Despite all subsequent aircraft models being given the 'Me' prefix (e.g. Me 410, Me 262) those already extant in their early versions and including the '109' and '110' retained their initial official designation of 'Bf 109' and 'Bf 110', although unofficially often known as Me 109 and Me 110. Strictly speaking thus, using Bf 109 and Bf 110 would be correct, but this volume is grounded in the reminiscences of German fighter pilots, who from the recollections inherent in this volume, referred to their aircraft affectionately, most often as 'Me' or 'Messer', and specific models had additional nicknames: Bf 109 E – 'Emil'; Bf 109 F – 'Friedrich'; Bf 109 G – 'Gustav' or often 'Beule' (a word meaning 'bump', used due to the bulges on both sides of the engine cowling resulting from enlarged breechblocks of larger caliber nose-mounted cannons fitted in many G-models). In *Luftwaffe* documents and original German sources, both 'Bf 109' and 'Me 109' can be found – see illustration 46 for an example of the former usage; captions provided by individual veterans to illustrations 4 and 27 refer to the 'Me 109'. For these reasons, the author has chosen to use the 'Me 109' nomenclature throughout this volume (the only exceptions being direct quotes from *Luftwaffe* documents). Just to complicate the scenario a bit more, there was an independent factory in Regensburg building the '109' amongst other machines, known from 1938 as *Bayerische-Flugzeug-Werke G.m.b.H.*, and with its own director (Nowarra, Heinz, J., *op cit.*).

66. Shores, Christopher and Massimello, Giovanni with Guest, Russell, Olynyk, Frank and Bock, Winfried, *A History of the Mediterranean Air War 1940-1945; Volume Two: North African Desert February 1942-March 1943* (London: Grub Street, 2012). The incident in question when these four pilots of 4/JG 27 were caught out faking victory claims is detailed on pages 306-307 in this book.

67. Makos, Adam with Alexander, Larry, *A Higher Call* (London: Atlantic Books, 2014).
68. Sims, Edward H., *The Fighter Pilots* (London: Cassell, 1968).

11. Conclusions

1. Bellamy, Chris, *Absolute War* (London: Pan-Macmillan, 2007); Gilbert, Martin, *Second World War* (London: Weidenfeld and Nicolson, 1989); Overy, Richard, *Russia's war* (London: Penguin Books, 1998); Clark, Alan, *Barbarossa: The Russian German conflict 1941–1945* (London: Cassell, 2002).
2. Gilbert, Martin, *op cit*; Neitzel, Sönke and Welzer, Harald, *Soldaten: on fighting, killing and dying* (London: Simon and Schuster, 2012).
3. Timofeeva-Egorova, Anna, *Over fields of fire* (Solihull: Helion and Company Ltd., 2015).
4. Gilbert, Martin, *op cit*; Clark, Alan, *op cit*; Overy, Richard, *op cit*.

Acknowledgements

This book is centred around the recollections of veterans of the *Luftwaffe* on the Eastern Front in the Second World War. As such it was totally dependent on their support and goodwill. The support and responses I received from these pilots and rear-gunner/radio-operators was extremely generous and, for some of the veterans, continued for years. They supplied me with direct testimony of their wartime experiences, supplied copies of original documents, portions of diaries, their flying log books as well as photographs. Although I am extremely grateful to all of them, a few merit special mention.

Oberst Hanns Trübenbach, who was *Kommodore JG 52* as well as *Jagdfliegerführer* of the German *Luftwaffe* Mission in Romania, with the prime duty of protecting the vital oil fields of Ploiesti, still managed to see quite a bit of combat against the Russians in the general Odessa region of the southernmost part of the Eastern Front. He not only supplied voluminous material but spoke at all times with great authority, integrity and from significant experience in senior positions. His comments also on German victory claims and the system for their evaluation were critical.

Another totally honest and greatly supportive witness was *Hauptmann* Günther Schack, who basically experienced the entire Eastern war from its onset in June 1941 through to the end, and with the same *Geschwader*, *JG 51*, flying for a long time in *III Gruppe* and rising from a junior rank to *Hauptmann* and *Gruppenkommandeur I/JG 51*. He had kept a diary through this entire period, which he typed up and summarised after the war, and very kindly provided the author with extensive excerpts therefrom and answered many questions. He was a very serious person, and disapproved strongly of any sort of hero-worship of highly successful *Luftwaffe* aces.

Oberstleutnant Günther Scholz, despite losing his parents to an Allied air raid in the war, and spending much of his post-war life trapped behind the 'iron curtain', held no bitterness and was of considerable help. His last years were in a united and free Germany, where he lived to the ripe old age of 102. Having served in *III/JG 54*, commanded *III/JG 5*, and later the entire *Jagdgeschwader 5* on the far north of the Eastern Front (and Norway), and having been *Jagdfliegerführer* Norway, his recollections were of great value as well.

Oberleutnant Walter Bohatsch, *I* and *II/JG 3* and his great friend *Oberleutnant* Hans Grünberg, *II/JG 3* were towers of strength in providing material on the *Udet Geschwader*. Hans Grünberg's description of the fall of Pitomnik airfield in the Stalingrad pocket almost beggars belief, as does his own miraculous escape from this terrible situation. *Oberleutnant* Gerd Schindler served with the famous *III/JG 52* in Russia and provided a wealth of recollections; he served with some of the leading German aces in the famous *Karaya Staffel, 9/JG 52*, including their top scorer, Erich Hartmann. *Unteroffizier* Albrecht Licht joined *I/JG 54* in late 1943 at a time when the German campaign in the East was already unravelling and had a most unsettling introduction to the realities of frontline service. He went on to serve with *II/JG 54*, also throughout the existence of the *Kurland* pocket where much of Army Group North had been trapped, described numerous adventures there and gave most generously of his time and memories. He managed to escape from the pocket on the day the war ended. Finally, *Leutnant* Peter Düttmann, a humorous and famous raconteur, and leader of festivities at many a post-war get-together of the *II/JG 52* veterans, provided the most amazing account of his first few days of frontline experience in such detail that the reader almost feels like they were there too.

I was very fortunate to have got to know these grand old warriors and to have enjoyed their friendship and support, without which this book would never have seen the light of day.

The *Luftwaffe* veterans went out of their way to help me, answering endless queries on subject matter often somewhat controversial; they always gave honest and forthright answers. Recollecting painful experiences long buried in their memories was no easy thing to do and I am very grateful to all those listed below. Most of those acknowledged here detailed their memories of flying on the Eastern Front, and some described the training of German fighter pilots for all fronts, and others dealt in depth, and generically also, with the vexed question of victory claims, their inherent inaccuracies and the system used for their evaluation. I am in debt to them all; those not already mentioned above are listed here: *Unteroffizier* Kurt Beecken, *II /JG 54*; *Major* Hans-Ekkehard Bob, *III/JG 54, IV/JG 51*; *Major* Erhard Braune, *III/JG 27*; *Waffenmeister* Ernst Brunns, *I/JG 54*; *Oberfeldwebel* Hermann Buchner, *III/SG 1, II/SG 2*; *Fahnenjunker-Feldwebel* Lothar Busse, *Stab* and *Stabstaffel/JG 51*; *Leutnant* Dr. Max Clerico, *III/JG 54*; *Oberfeldwebel* Josef Ederer, *I/JG 53*; *Oberleutnant* Fritz Engau, *I/JG 11*; *Hauptmann* Rudolf Engleder, *I/JG 1*; *Unteroffizier* Karl-Heinz Erler, *IV/JG 5*; *Leutnant* Heinz Ewald, *II/JG 52*; *Leutnant* Georg Füreder, *I/JG 26, IV/JG 54, II/JG 11*; *Major* Horst Geyer, *Stab* and *II/JG 51*; *Hauptmann* Rudolf Glöckner, *II/JG 5*; *Oberleutnant* Adolf Glunz, *II/JG 52*; *Feldwebel* Günther Granzow, *Stabstaffel/JG 51*; *Hauptmann* Alfred Grislawski, *III/JG 52*; *Unteroffizier* Gerd Hauter, *II/ JG 52*; *Oberleutnant* Alfred Heckmann, *II/JG 3, I/JG 26*; *Leutnant* Bodo Helms, *III/JG 5*; *Oberfeldwebel* Rudolf Hener, *I/JG 3*; *Gefreiter* Karl Heinz Hirsch, *III/JG 27*; *Unteroffizier* Heinz Hommes, *I/JG 53*; *Unteroffizier* Werner Killer, *III/JG 77*; *Obergefreiter* Pay Kleber, *EJG 1*; *Oberfeldwebel* Josef Kronschnabel, *III/JG 53*; *Major* Dr. Heinz Lange, *I* and *III/JG 54, I, IV* and *Stab/JG 51*; *Oberleutnant* Erwin Leykauf, *III/JG 54, III/JG 26, IV/JG 54*; *Leutnant* Friedrich Lüdecke, *II/JG 5*; *Unteroffizier* Heinz Ludwig, *I/ZG 1*; *Gefreiter* Rudolf Miese, *II/JG 2*; *Oberleutnant* Victor Mölders, *I/ZG 1, I/JG 51*; *Leutnant* Josef Neuhaus, *II/ZG 26*; *Oberst* Eduard Neumann, *Stab* and *I/JG 27*; *Oberfeldwebel* Helmut Notemann, *II/JG 3*; *Oberfeldwebel* Georg Pavenzinger, *I/JG 51*; *Feldwebel* Horst Petzschler, *Stabstaffel and I/JG 51*; *Hauptmann* Werner Pichon-Kalau vom Hofe, *Stab* and *III/JG 54*; *Feldwebel* Erich Rahner, *III/JG 51*; *Major* Günther Rall, *III/JG 52*; *Leutnant* Alfred Rauch, *II, IV* and *Stabstaffel/ JG 51*; *Oberfeldwebel* Richard Raupach, *I* and *IV/JG 54*; *Oberfeldwebel* Ernst Richter, *I/JG 54*; *Oberst* Gustav Rödel, *Stab* and *II/JG 27*; *Oberfeldwebel* Heinrich Rosenberg, *III/JG 27*; *Major* Erich Rudorffer, *IV* and *II/JG 54*; *Leutnant* Dr. Felix Sauer, *II/JG 53, 10/JG 53*; *Hauptmann* Günther Schack, *I and III/JG 51*; *Oberleutnant* Ernst Scheufele, *II/JG 5*; *Hauptmann* Karl-Friedrich Schlossstein, *Zerstörerstaffel JG 77* and *JG 5, II/JG 76*; *Feldwebel* Otto Schmid, *II/JG 1*; *Major* Gerhard Schöpfel, *III* and *Stab/JG 26, Stab/JG 4*; *Unteroffizier* Ernst Schröder, *II/JG 300*; *Leutnant* Jochen Schröder, *II/ZG 1, III/ZG 76*; *Hauptmann* Günther Schwanecke, *III/JG 77, II* and *III/JG 5*; *Oberleutnant* Alfred Seidl, *III/JG 53, I/JG 3*; *Major* Rudolf Sinner, *IV/JG 54*; *Leutnant* Erich Sommavilla, *III/JG 77, I/JG 53*; *Major* Wolfgang Späte, *II* and *IV/JG 54*; *Oberleuntant* Otto Stammberger, *II* and *III/JG 26*; *Leutnant* Hermann Wolf, *III/JG 52*.

My special thanks go to Juha Vaittinen, a Finnish air historian who supplied documents from Finnish archives for both Finnish and German air forces, and Professor Paul Robert Skawran, psychologist in the

Luftwaffe. Having spent much of the war with various *Jagdgruppen* on different fronts, he got to know many individuals very well, and also gave me free rein in his considerable documentary archive.

Shaun Barrington of Amberley Publishing was always most encouraging and supportive and I thank him and his colleagues most sincerely, especially Alex Bennett for his excellent editing. My wife, Mariánne, a talented writer and illustrator of children's books in her own right, provided much-needed inspiration and support, as always. I thank my brother, Dr Andrew Eriksson, who addressed my digital ignorance, stored back-ups, and kindly read several chapters. A final word of thanks goes to my parents, who paid for flying lessons from age 13, alas a waste of money; I was a rotten pilot.

Index